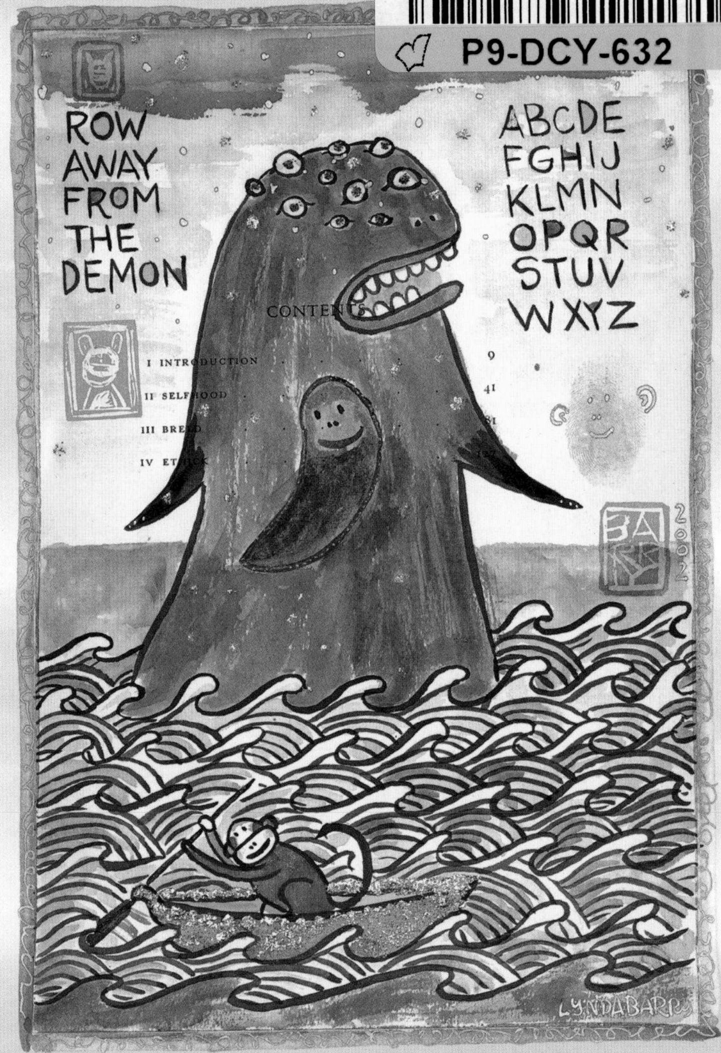
ROW AWAY FROM THE DEMON
ABCDE
FGHIJ
KLMN
OPQR
STUV
WXYZ
CONTENTS
I INTRODUCTION 9
II SELFHOOD 41
LYNDABARRY

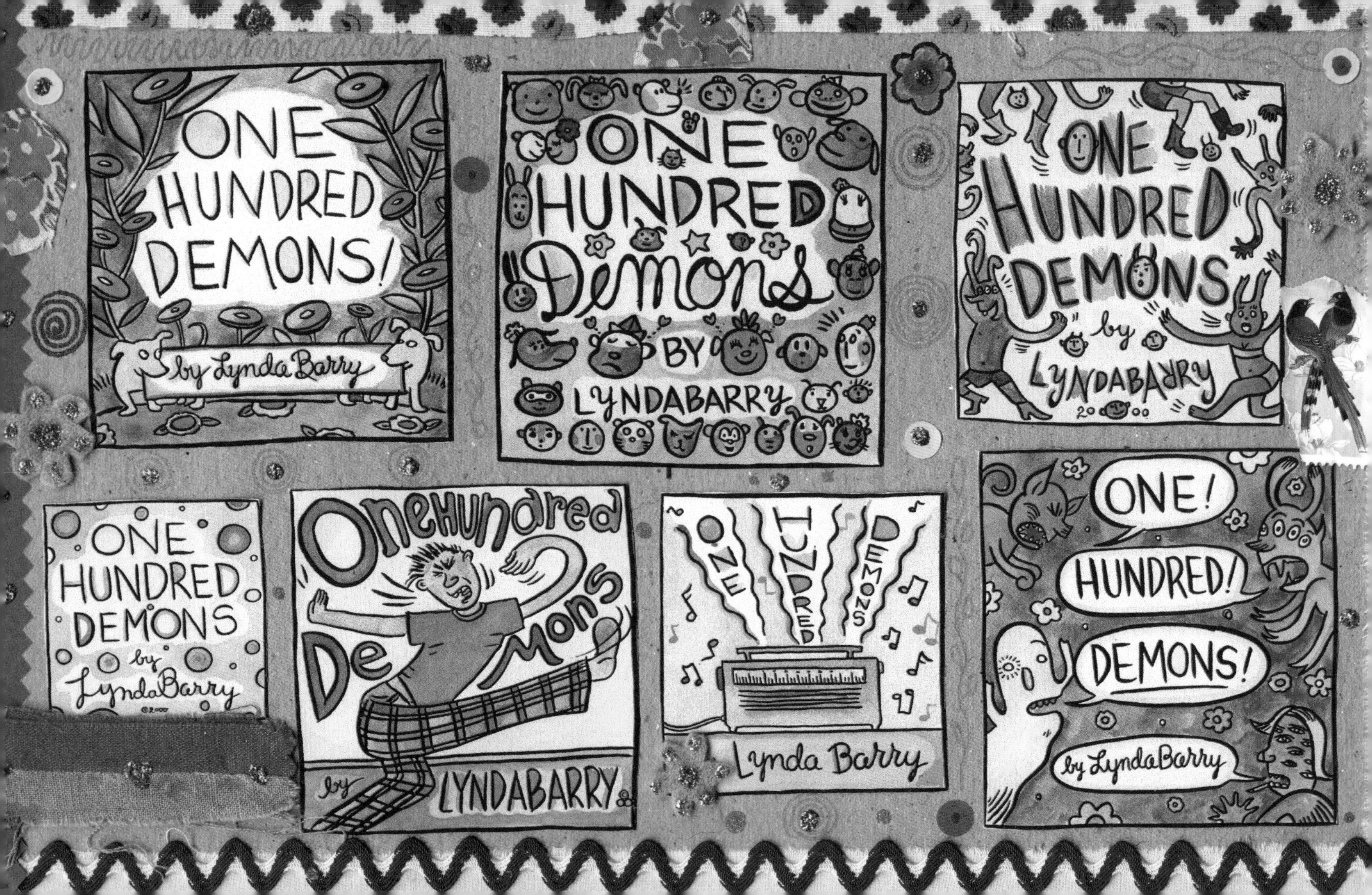
ONE HUNDRED DEMONS!
by Lynda Barry
ONE HUNDRED Demons
BY LYNDABARRY
ONE HUNDRED DEMONS
by LYNDABARRY
ONE HUNDRED DEMONS
by LyndaBarry
OneHundred DeMons
by LYNDABARRY
ONE HUNDRED DEMONS
Lynda Barry
ONE!
HUNDRED!
DEMONS!
by LyndaBarry

One Hundred Demons

by Lynda Barry

SASQUATCH BOOKS
SEATTLE

For Jennifer Sweeney

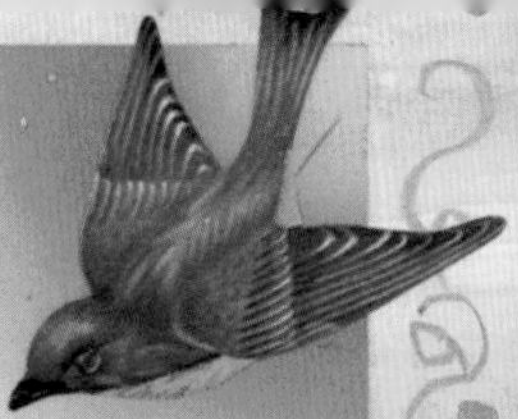

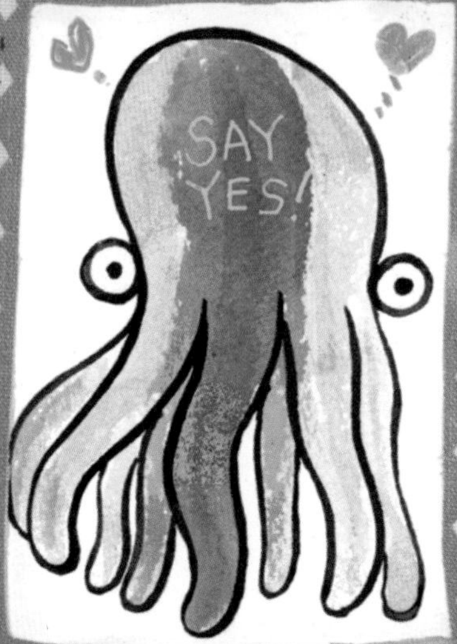

SAY YES!

Special Thanks
L.C. Kevin Kawula, Liz Darhansoff, Jennifer Sweeney & Staff @ Salon.com, Gary Luke & Staff @ Sasquatch Books, Ying Xing Wang @ Acornplanet.com, Tom Thumb Hobbies and Crafts, Evanston, Ill, and especially to Amie Z Gleed and Tom Greensfelder who worked so hard on this dang book. P.S. Matt Gisse ill Funk Lord of USA

Also thank you Daniel at marlysmagazine.com

Please NoTE: THIS IS A WORK OF AUTOBIFICTIONALOGRAPHY

Book Design Team:
- Amie Z. Gleed
- Lynda Barry
- Tom Greensfelder

watercolor help and contributing demon illustration: Kevin Kawula

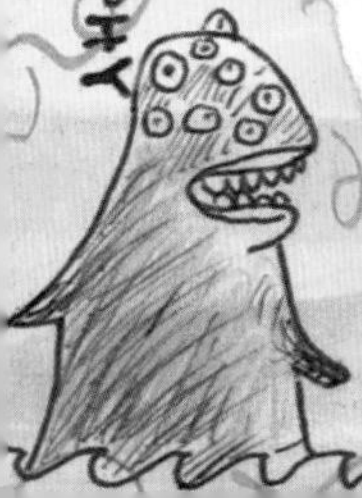

these comic strips first appeared on Salon.com!

Sasquatch Books
119 South Main Street, suite 400
Seattle, WA 98104
(206) 467-4300
www.SasquatchBooks.com
books@SasquatchBooks.com

Published by Sasquatch Books
Distributed by ~~publisher's Group wes~~ Publishers Group West

Library of Congress Cataloging in Publication Data
Barry, Lynda, 1956–
One hundred demons / Lynda Barry.
p. cm.
ISBN 1-57061-459-8
I. Title: 100 demons. II. Title.
PN6727.B36 O54 2002
741.5'973—dc21 2002021657
Printed in China

14 13 12 11 10 09 7 6 5 4

Table of Contents

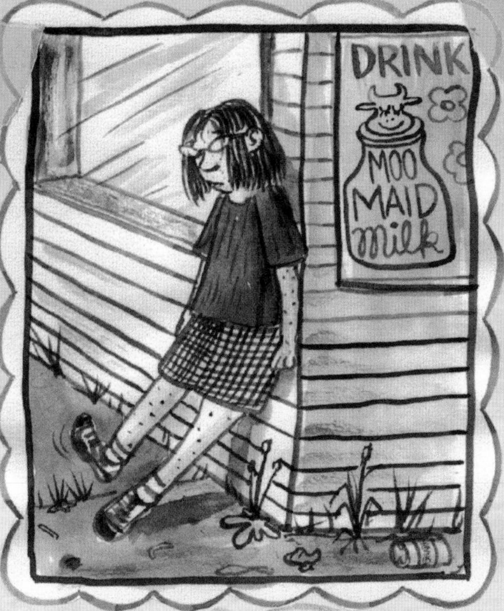
DRINK
MOO MAID milk

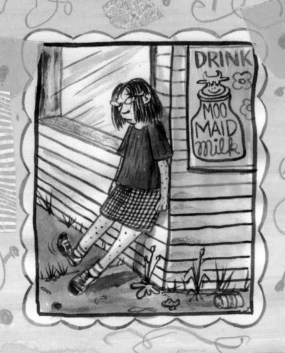

autobifictionalography

are these stories ☑ true OR ☑ FALSE?

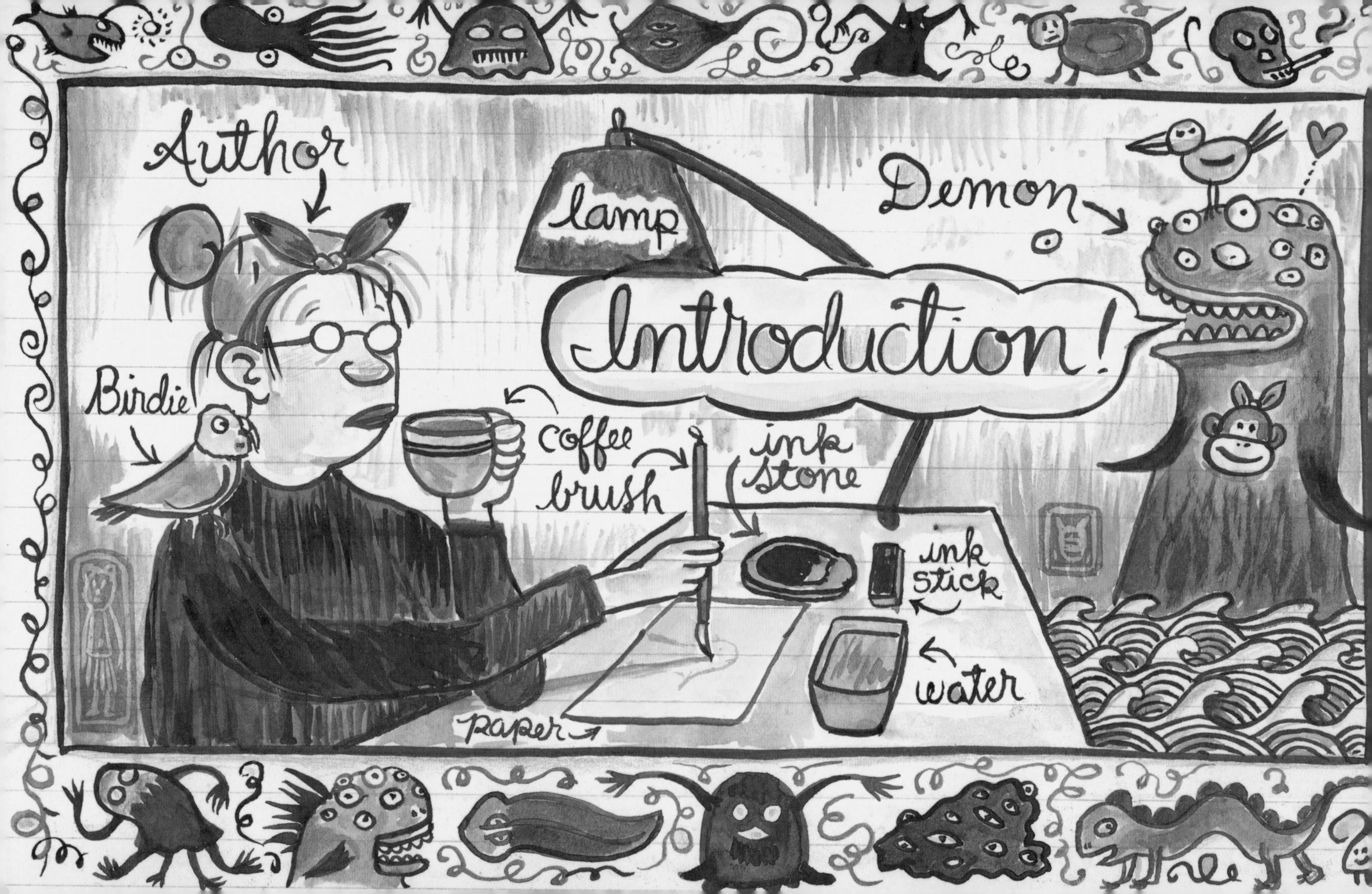
Author
lamp
Demon
Introduction!
Birdie
coffee
brush
ink stone
ink stick
water
paper

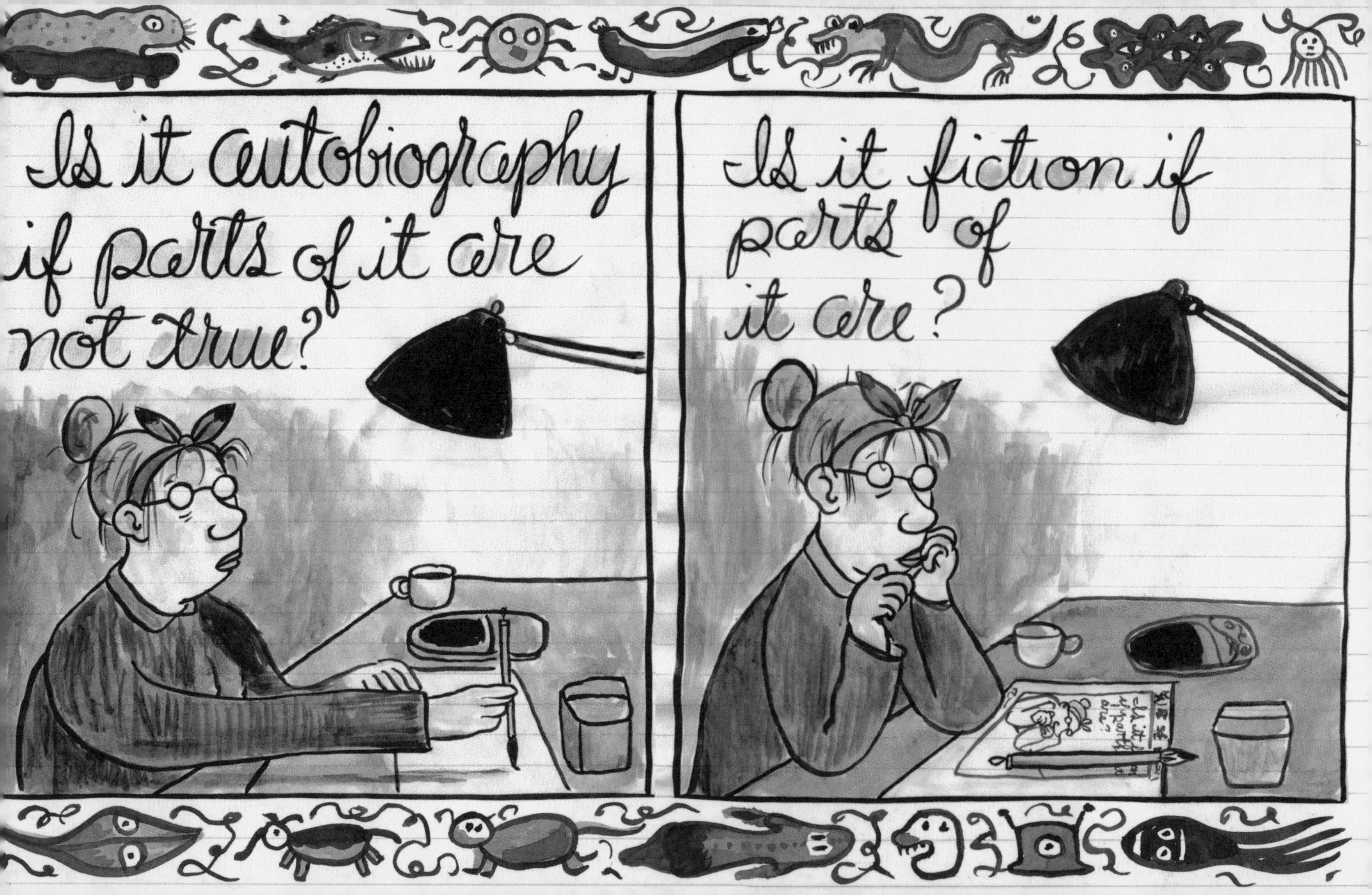
Is it autobiography if parts of it are not true?
Is it fiction if parts of it are?

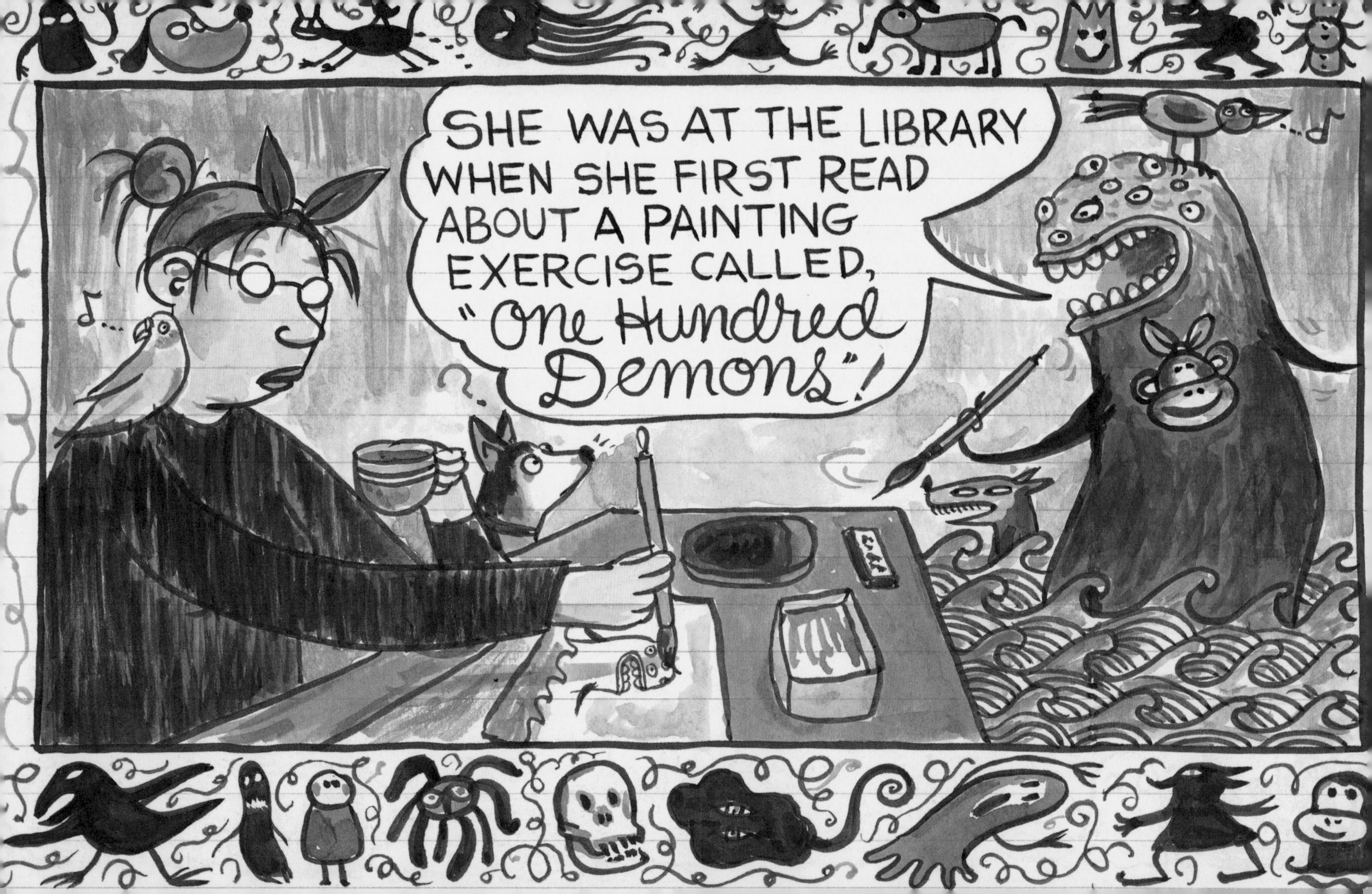
SHE WAS AT THE LIBRARY WHEN SHE FIRST READ ABOUT A PAINTING EXERCISE CALLED, "One Hundred Demons"!

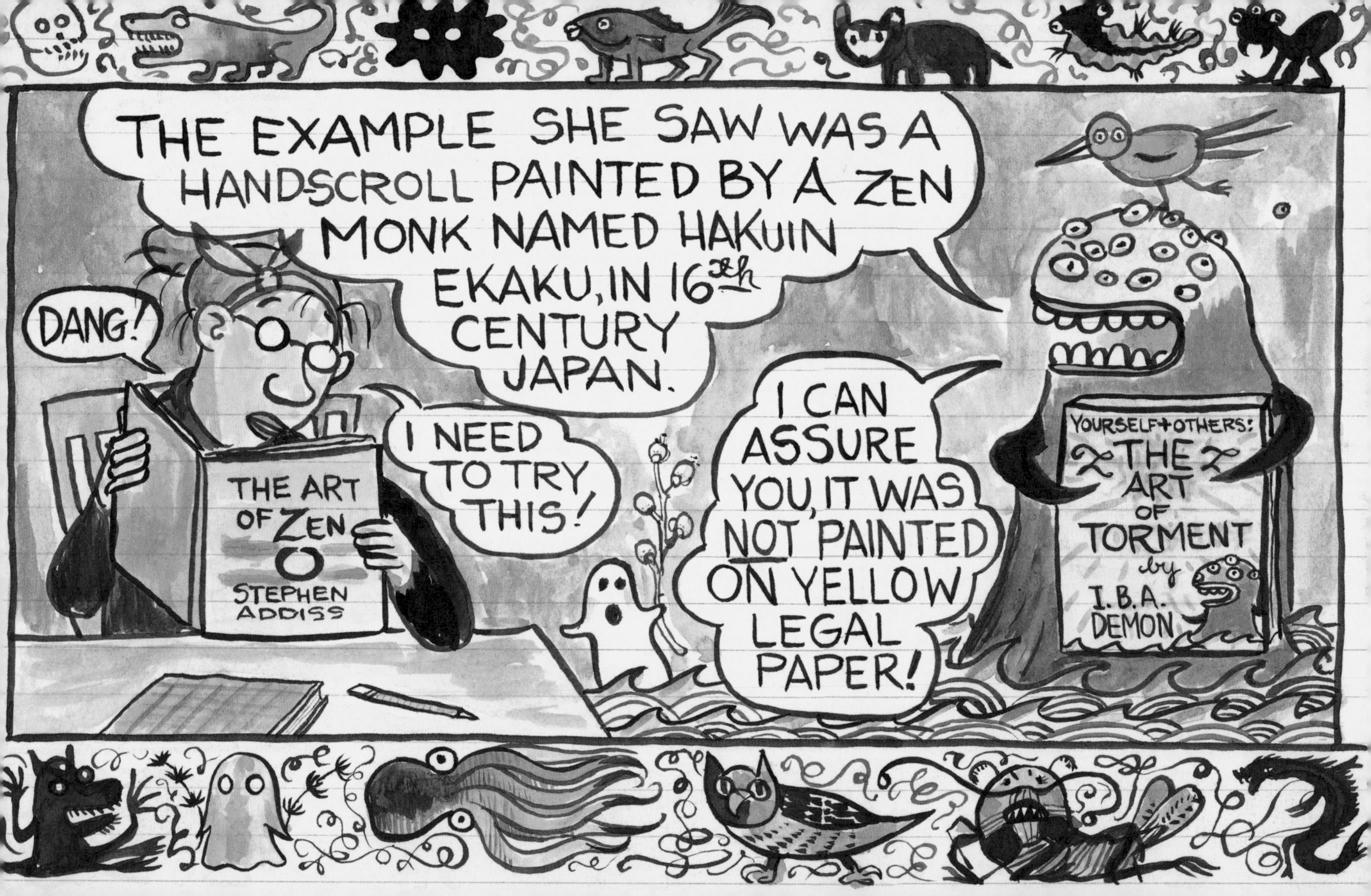
THE EXAMPLE SHE SAW WAS A HANDSCROLL PAINTED BY A ZEN MONK NAMED HAKUIN EKAKU, IN 16th CENTURY JAPAN.
DANG!
I NEED TO TRY THIS!
THE ART OF ZEN
STEPHEN ADDISS
I CAN ASSURE YOU, IT WAS NOT PAINTED ON YELLOW LEGAL PAPER!
YOURSELF + OTHERS: THE ART OF TORMENT by I.B.A. DEMON

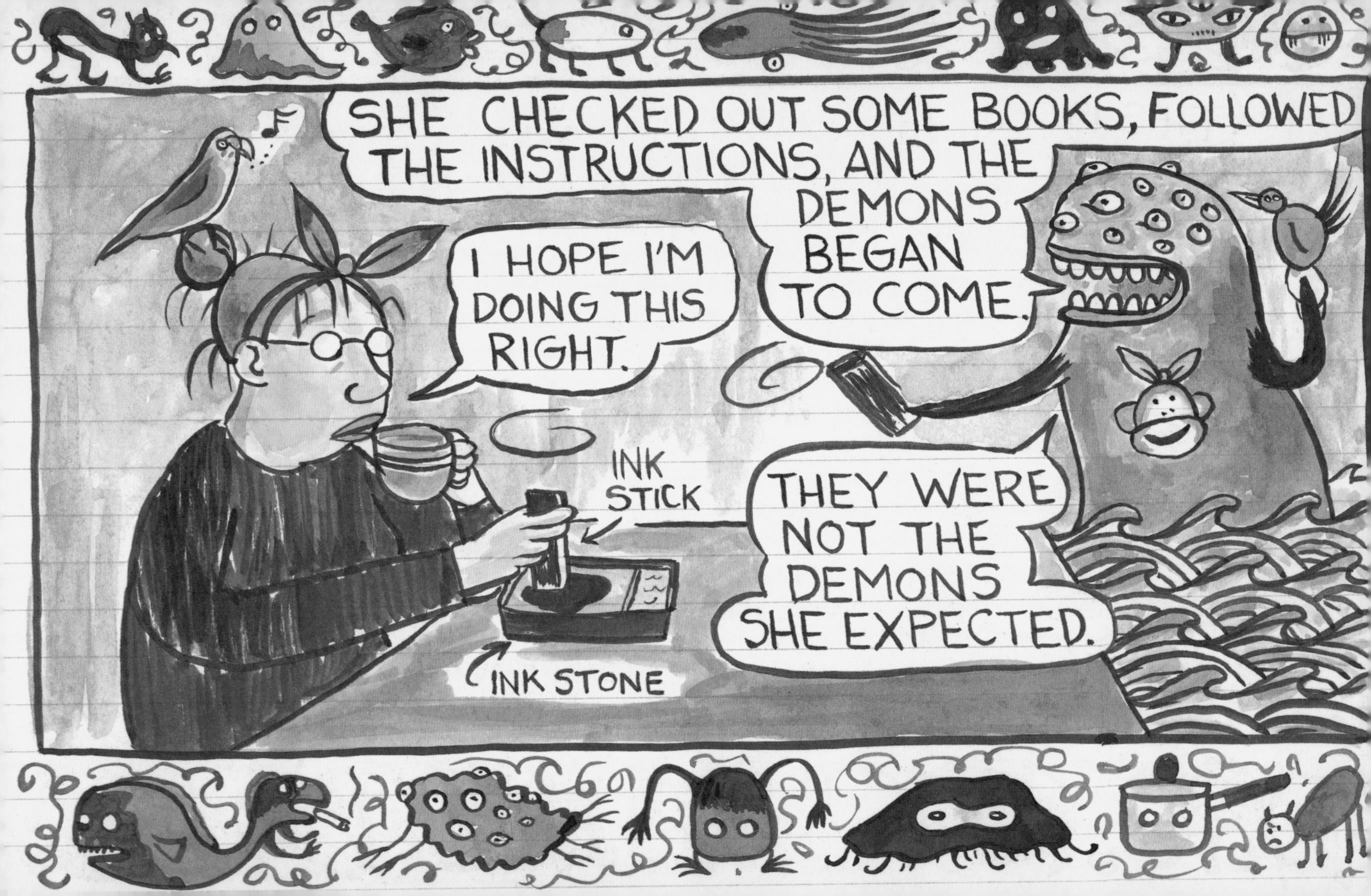
SHE CHECKED OUT SOME BOOKS, FOLLOWED THE INSTRUCTIONS, AND THE DEMONS BEGAN TO COME.
I HOPE I'M DOING THIS RIGHT.
INK STICK
INK STONE
THEY WERE NOT THE DEMONS SHE EXPECTED.

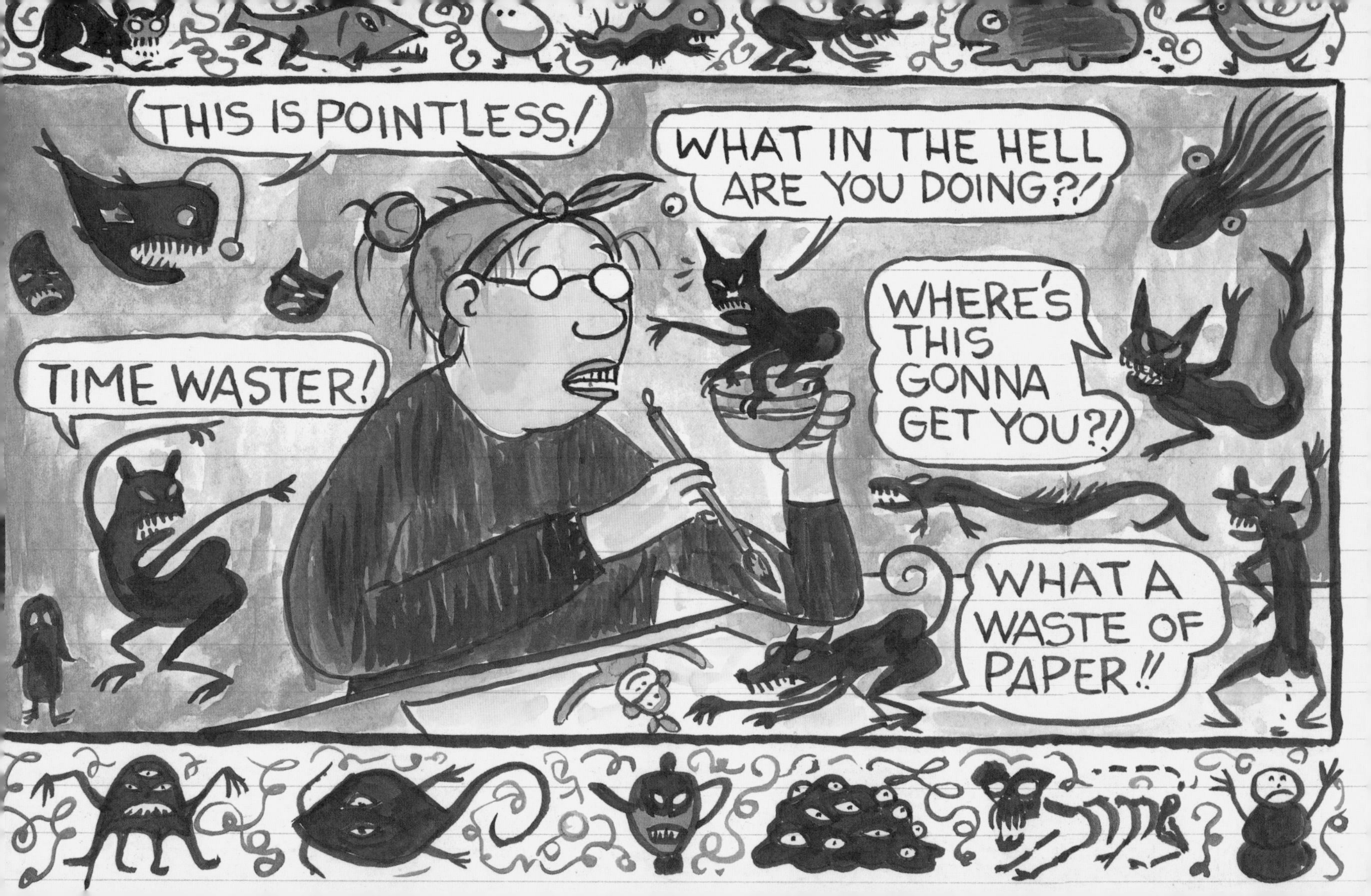
THIS IS POINTLESS!
WHAT IN THE HELL ARE YOU DOING?!
TIME WASTER!
WHERE'S THIS GONNA GET YOU?!
WHAT A WASTE OF PAPER!!

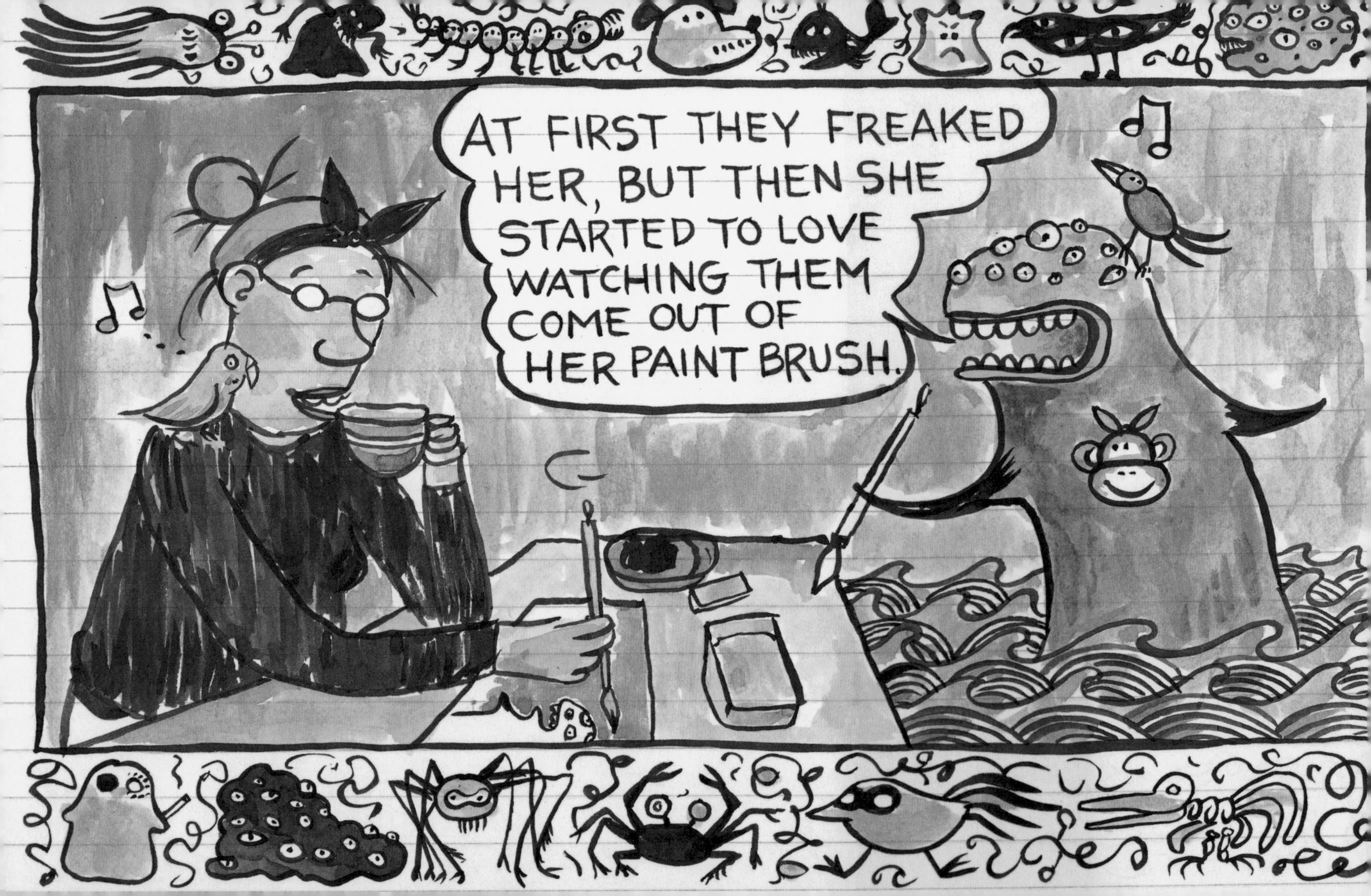
AT FIRST THEY FREAKED HER, BUT THEN SHE STARTED TO LOVE WATCHING THEM COME OUT OF HER PAINT BRUSH.

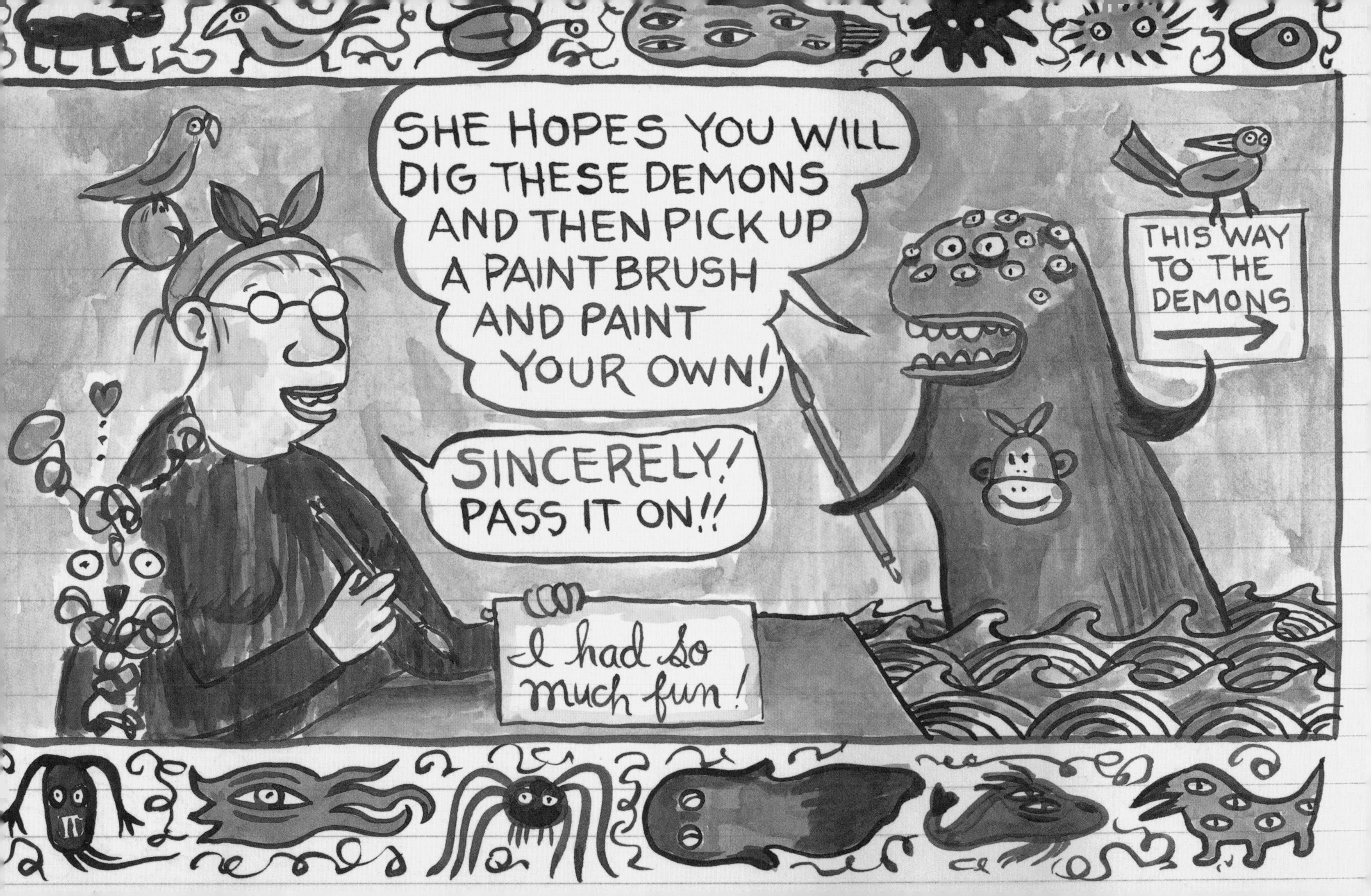
SHE HOPES YOU WILL DIG THESE DEMONS AND THEN PICK UP A PAINTBRUSH AND PAINT YOUR OWN!
SINCERELY! PASS IT ON!!
THIS WAY TO THE DEMONS
I had so much fun!

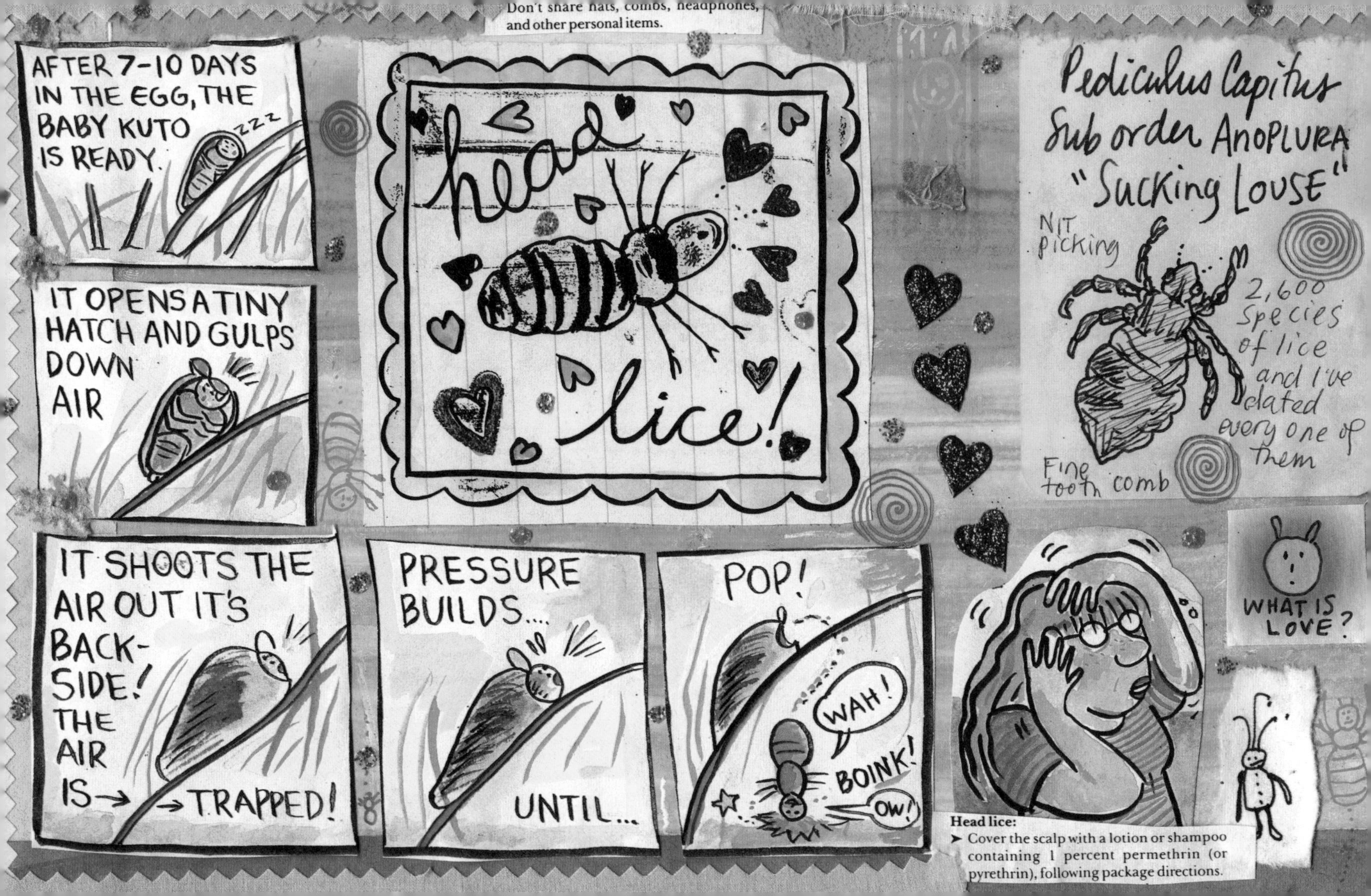
Don't share hats, combs, headphones, and other personal items.
AFTER 7-10 DAYS IN THE EGG, THE BABY KUTO IS READY.
ZZZ
IT OPENS A TINY HATCH AND GULPS DOWN AIR
head lice!
Pediculus Capitus
Sub order ANOPLURA
"Sucking Louse"
NIT picking
2,600 Species of lice and I've dated every one of them
Fine tooth comb
IT SHOOTS THE AIR OUT IT'S BACK-SIDE! THE AIR IS → → TRAPPED!
PRESSURE BUILDS....
UNTIL...
POP!
WAH!
BOINK!
OW!
WHAT IS LOVE?
Head lice:
➤ Cover the scalp with a lotion or shampoo containing 1 percent permethrin (or pyrethrin), following package directions.

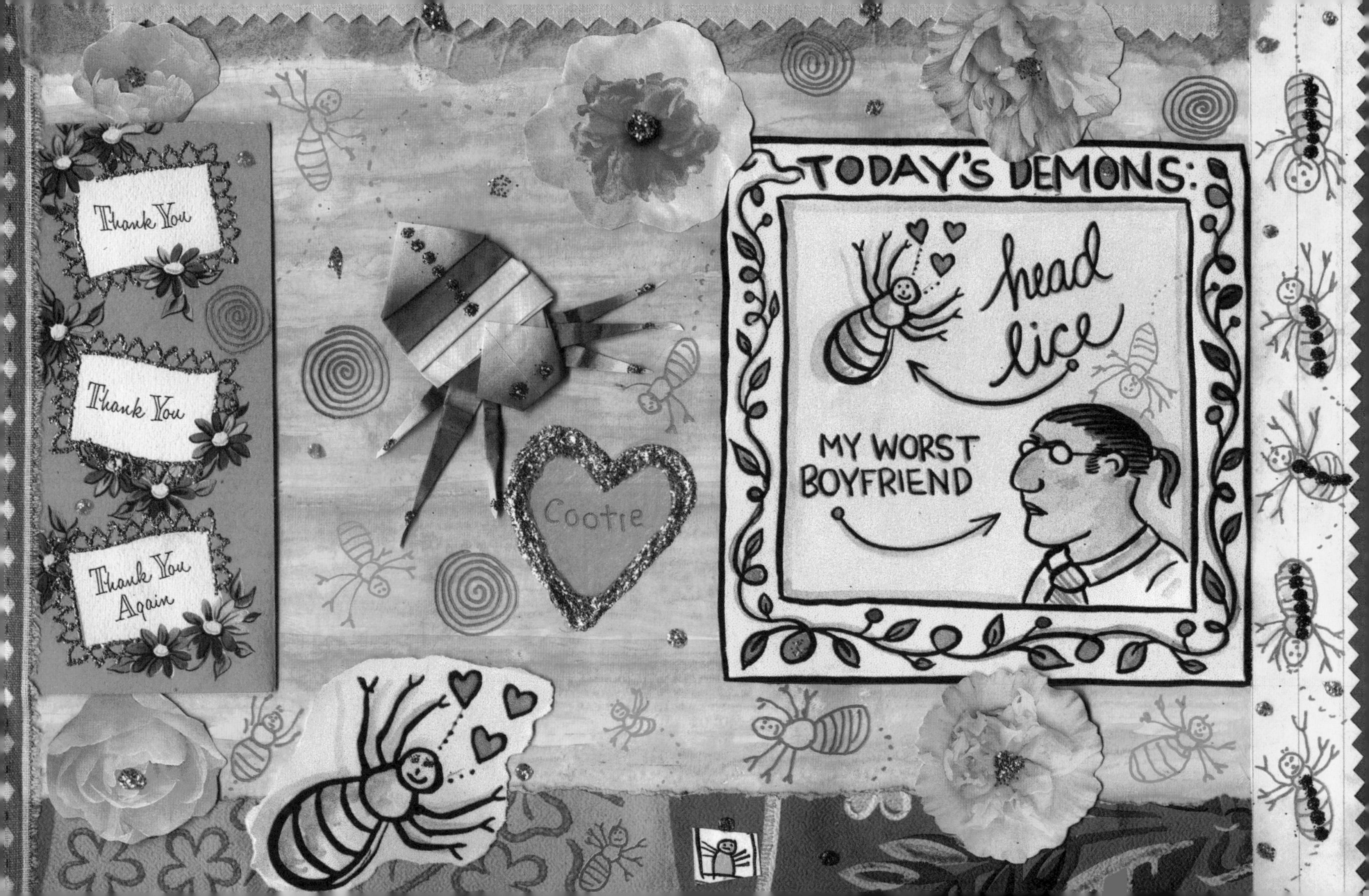
Thank You
Thank You
Thank You Again
Cootie
TODAY'S DEMONS:
head lice
MY WORST BOYFRIEND

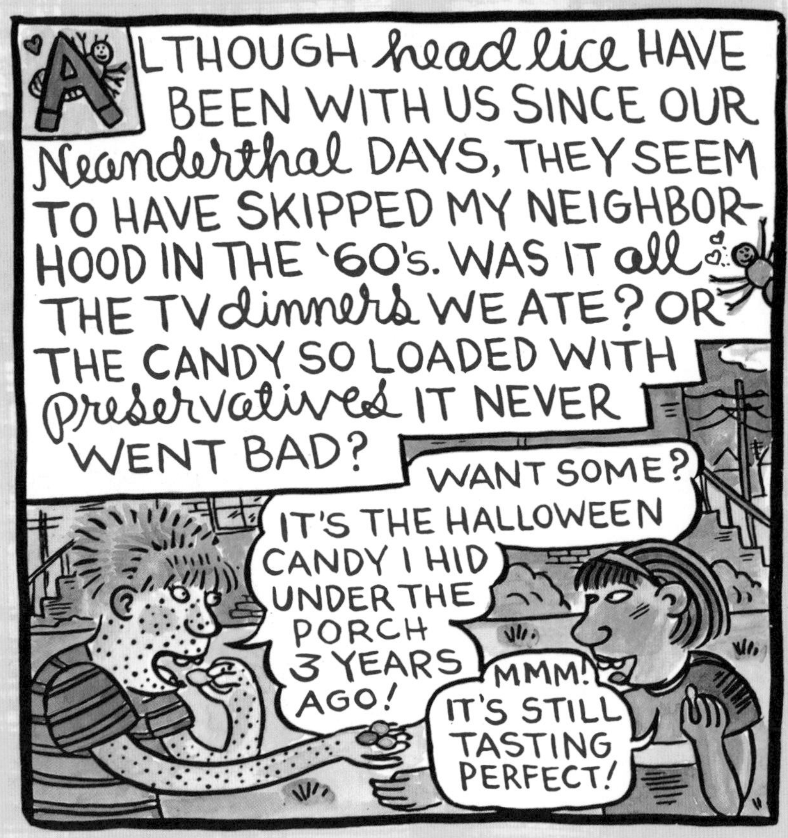
ALTHOUGH headlice HAVE BEEN WITH US SINCE OUR Neanderthal DAYS, THEY SEEM TO HAVE SKIPPED MY NEIGHBORHOOD IN THE '60's. WAS IT all THE TV dinners WE ATE? OR THE CANDY SO LOADED WITH preservatives IT NEVER WENT BAD?
WANT SOME?
IT'S THE HALLOWEEN CANDY I HID UNDER THE PORCH 3 YEARS AGO!
MMM! IT'S STILL TASTING PERFECT!

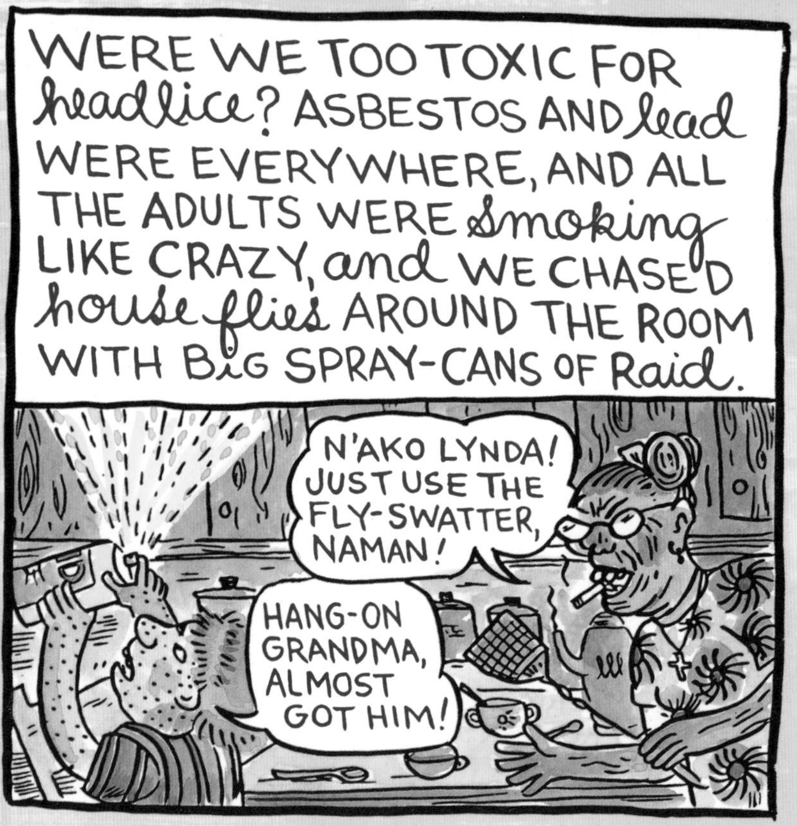
WERE WE TOO TOXIC FOR headlice? ASBESTOS AND lead WERE EVERYWHERE, AND ALL THE ADULTS WERE smoking LIKE CRAZY, and WE CHASED house flies AROUND THE ROOM WITH BIG SPRAY-CANS OF Raid.
N'AKO LYNDA! JUST USE THE FLY-SWATTER, NAMAN!
HANG-ON GRANDMA, ALMOST GOT HIM!

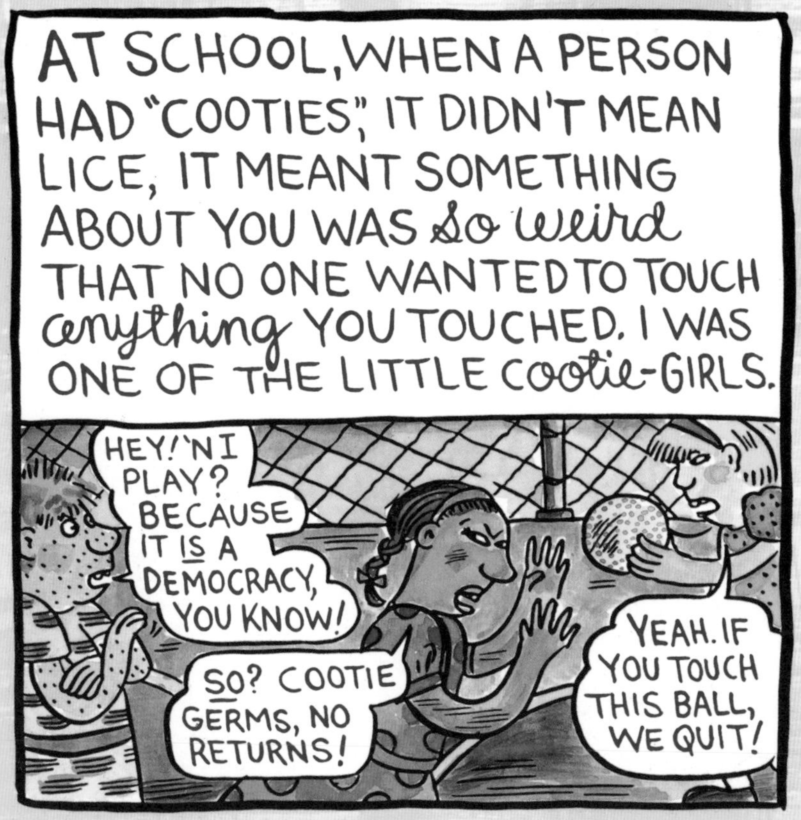
AT SCHOOL, WHEN A PERSON HAD "COOTIES," IT DIDN'T MEAN LICE, IT MEANT SOMETHING ABOUT YOU WAS so weird THAT NO ONE WANTED TO TOUCH anything YOU TOUCHED. I WAS ONE OF THE LITTLE cootie-GIRLS.
HEY! 'N I PLAY? BECAUSE IT IS A DEMOCRACY, YOU KNOW!
SO? COOTIE GERMS, NO RETURNS!
YEAH. IF YOU TOUCH THIS BALL, WE QUIT!

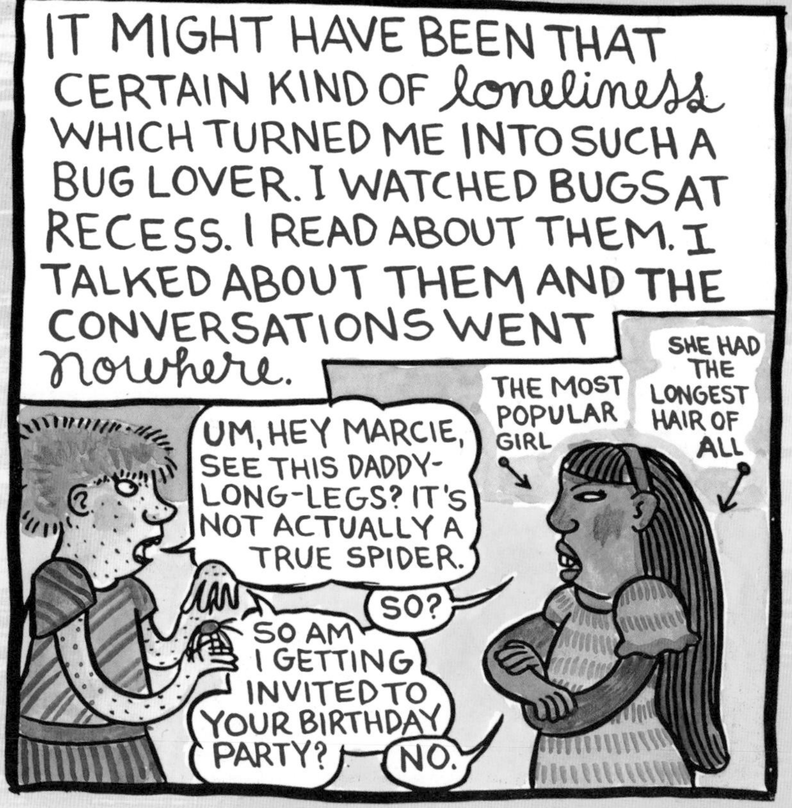
IT MIGHT HAVE BEEN THAT CERTAIN KIND OF loneliness WHICH TURNED ME INTO SUCH A BUG LOVER. I WATCHED BUGS AT RECESS. I READ ABOUT THEM. I TALKED ABOUT THEM AND THE CONVERSATIONS WENT nowhere.
THE MOST POPULAR GIRL
SHE HAD THE LONGEST HAIR OF ALL
UM, HEY MARCIE, SEE THIS DADDY-LONG-LEGS? IT'S NOT ACTUALLY A TRUE SPIDER.
SO?
SO AM I GETTING INVITED TO YOUR BIRTHDAY PARTY?
NO.

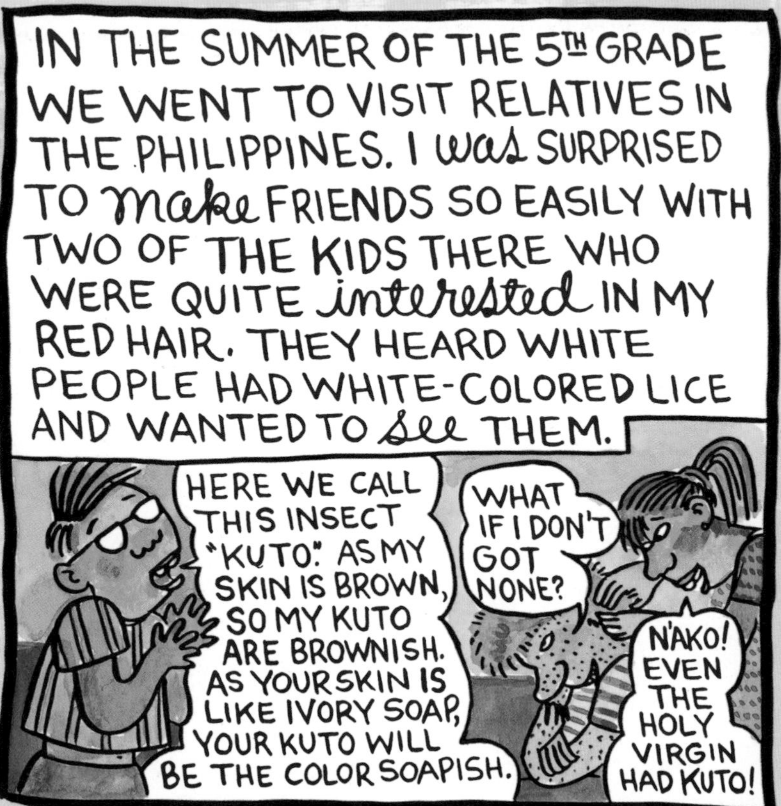

IN THE SUMMER OF THE 5TH GRADE WE WENT TO VISIT RELATIVES IN THE PHILIPPINES. I was SURPRISED TO make FRIENDS SO EASILY WITH TWO OF THE KIDS THERE WHO WERE QUITE interested IN MY RED HAIR. THEY HEARD WHITE PEOPLE HAD WHITE-COLORED LICE AND WANTED TO see THEM.
HERE WE CALL THIS INSECT "KUTO." AS MY SKIN IS BROWN, SO MY KUTO ARE BROWNISH. AS YOUR SKIN IS LIKE IVORY SOAP, YOUR KUTO WILL BE THE COLOR SOAPISH.
WHAT IF I DON'T GOT NONE?
N'AKO! EVEN THE HOLY VIRGIN HAD KUTO!

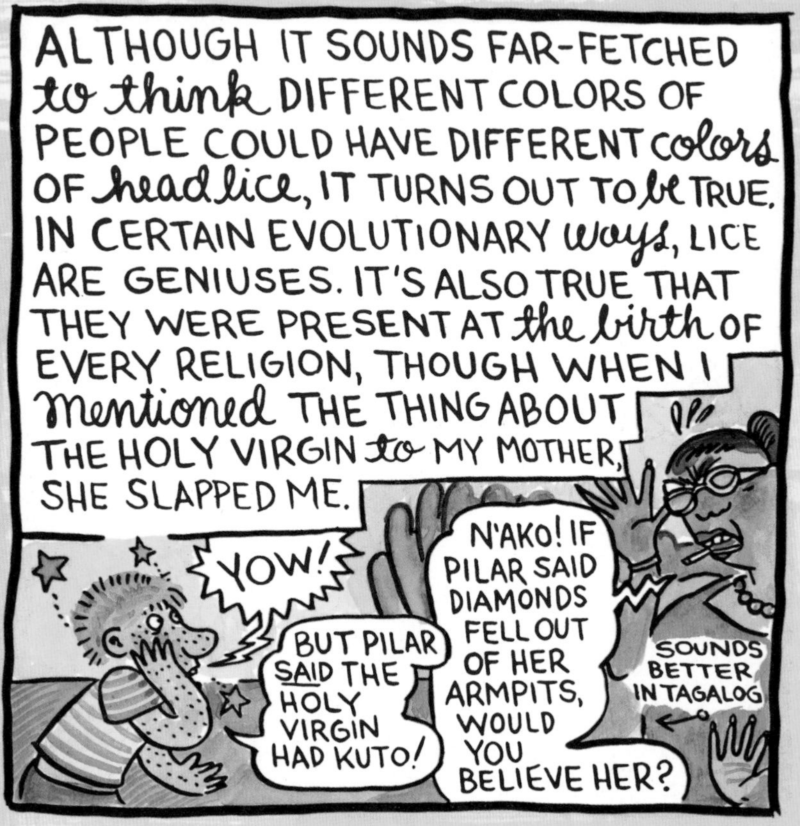

ALTHOUGH IT SOUNDS FAR-FETCHED to think DIFFERENT COLORS OF PEOPLE COULD HAVE DIFFERENT colors OF head lice, IT TURNS OUT TO be TRUE. IN CERTAIN EVOLUTIONARY ways, LICE ARE GENIUSES. IT'S ALSO TRUE THAT THEY WERE PRESENT AT the birth OF EVERY RELIGION, THOUGH WHEN I mentioned THE THING ABOUT THE HOLY VIRGIN to MY MOTHER, SHE SLAPPED ME.
YOW!
BUT PILAR SAID THE HOLY VIRGIN HAD KUTO!
N'AKO! IF PILAR SAID DIAMONDS FELL OUT OF HER ARMPITS, WOULD YOU BELIEVE HER?
SOUNDS BETTER IN TAGALOG

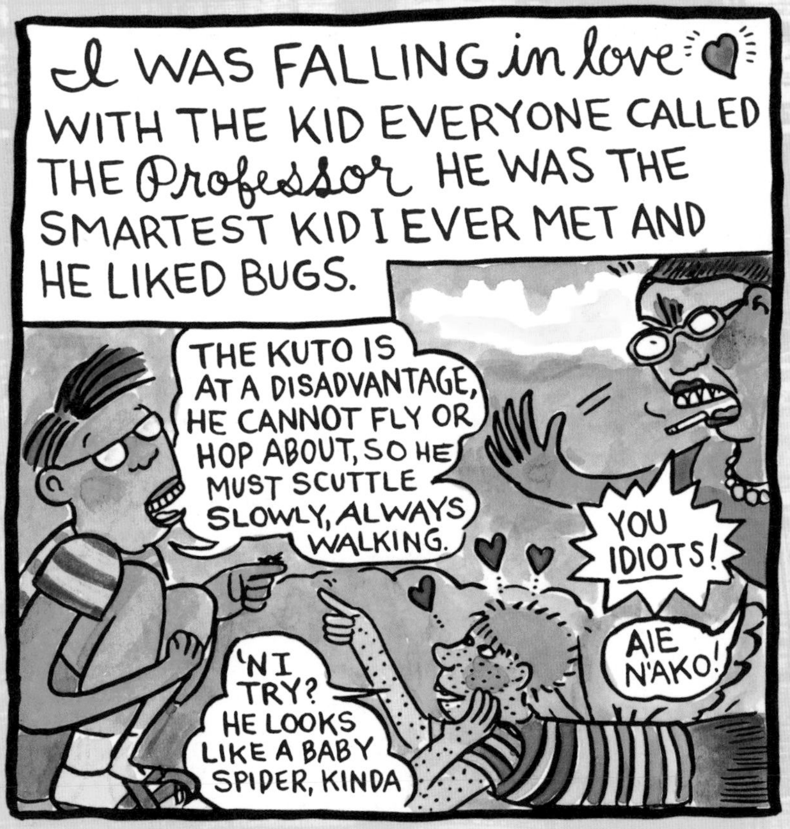
I WAS FALLING in love WITH THE KID EVERYONE CALLED THE Professor HE WAS THE SMARTEST KID I EVER MET AND HE LIKED BUGS.
THE KUTO IS AT A DISADVANTAGE, HE CANNOT FLY OR HOP ABOUT, SO HE MUST SCUTTLE SLOWLY, ALWAYS WALKING.
YOU IDIOTS!
'N I TRY? HE LOOKS LIKE A BABY SPIDER, KINDA
AIE N'AKO!

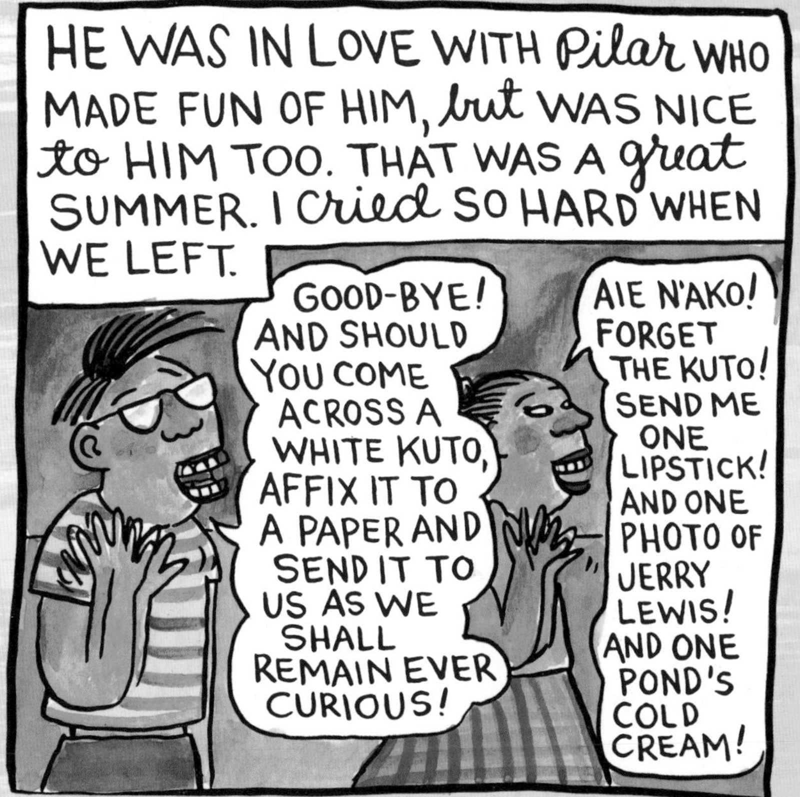
HE WAS IN LOVE WITH Pilar WHO MADE FUN OF HIM, but WAS NICE to HIM TOO. THAT WAS A great SUMMER. I Cried SO HARD WHEN WE LEFT.
GOOD-BYE! AND SHOULD YOU COME ACROSS A WHITE KUTO, AFFIX IT TO A PAPER AND SEND IT TO US AS WE SHALL REMAIN EVER CURIOUS!
AIE N'AKO! FORGET THE KUTO! SEND ME ONE LIPSTICK! AND ONE PHOTO OF JERRY LEWIS! AND ONE POND'S COLD CREAM!

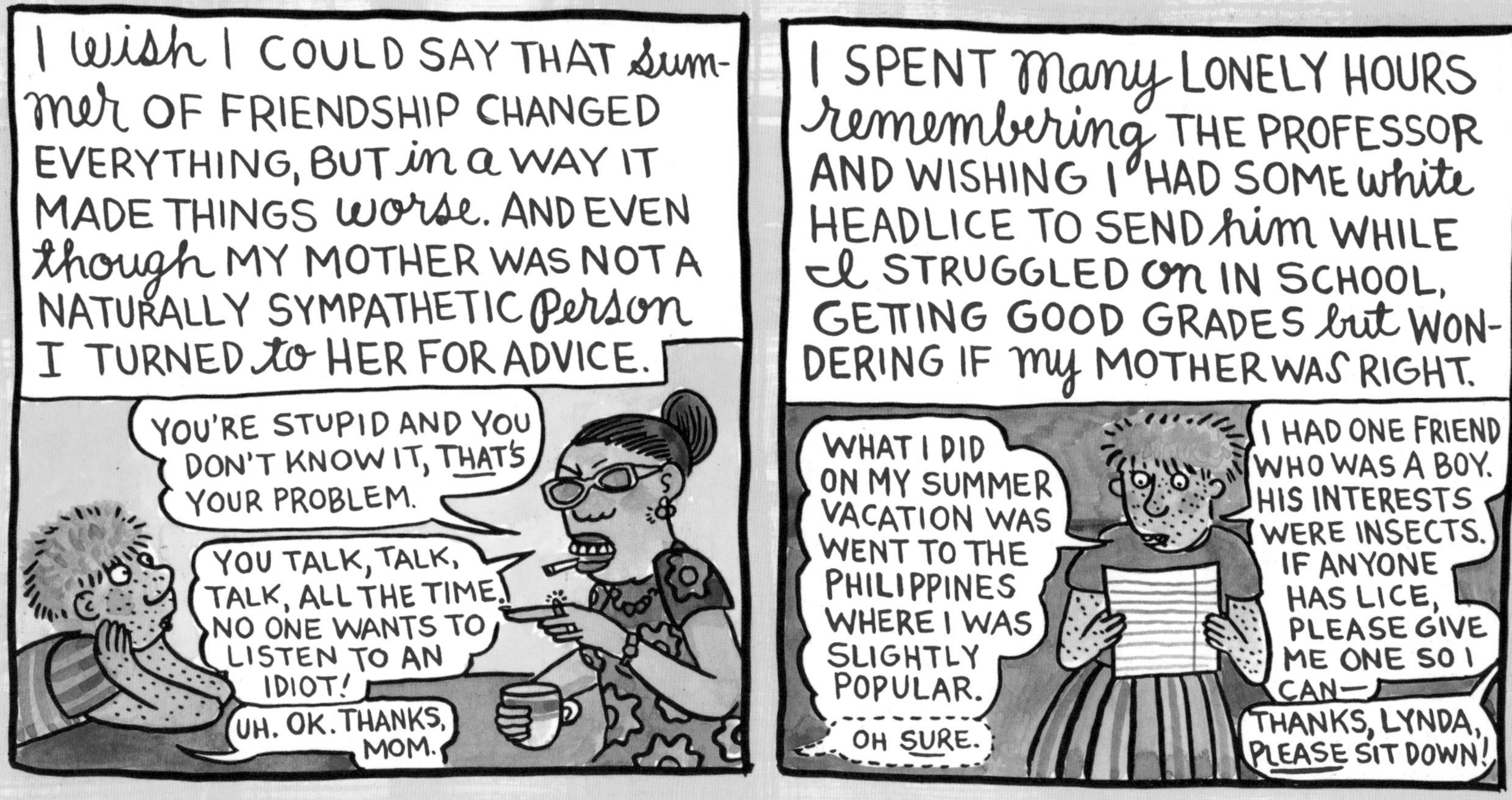
I wish I COULD SAY THAT summer OF FRIENDSHIP CHANGED EVERYTHING, BUT in a WAY IT MADE THINGS worse. AND EVEN though MY MOTHER WAS NOT A NATURALLY SYMPATHETIC person I TURNED to HER FOR ADVICE.
YOU'RE STUPID AND YOU DON'T KNOW IT, THAT'S YOUR PROBLEM.
YOU TALK, TALK, TALK, ALL THE TIME. NO ONE WANTS TO LISTEN TO AN IDIOT!
UH. OK. THANKS, MOM.
I SPENT many LONELY HOURS remembering THE PROFESSOR AND WISHING I HAD SOME white HEADLICE TO SEND him WHILE I STRUGGLED on IN SCHOOL, GETTING GOOD GRADES but WONDERING IF my MOTHER WAS RIGHT.
WHAT I DID ON MY SUMMER VACATION WAS WENT TO THE PHILIPPINES WHERE I WAS SLIGHTLY POPULAR.
I HAD ONE FRIEND WHO WAS A BOY. HIS INTERESTS WERE INSECTS. IF ANYONE HAS LICE, PLEASE GIVE ME ONE SO I CAN—
OH SURE.
THANKS, LYNDA, PLEASE SIT DOWN!

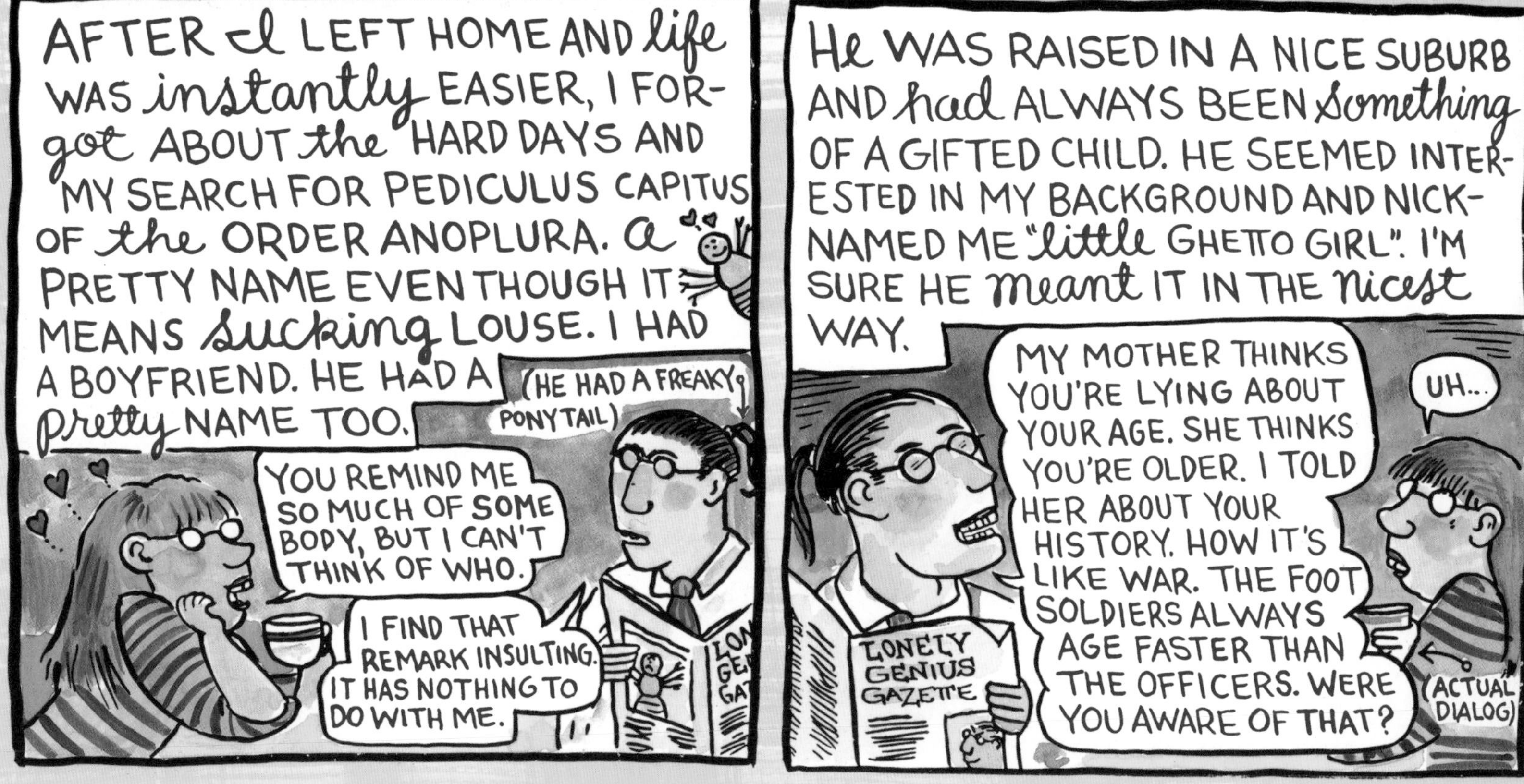
AFTER I LEFT HOME AND life WAS instantly EASIER, I FORgot ABOUT the HARD DAYS AND MY SEARCH FOR PEDICULUS CAPITUS OF the ORDER ANOPLURA. a PRETTY NAME EVEN THOUGH IT MEANS Sucking LOUSE. I HAD A BOYFRIEND. HE HAD A pretty NAME TOO.
(HE HAD A FREAKY PONYTAIL)
YOU REMIND ME SO MUCH OF SOME BODY, BUT I CAN'T THINK OF WHO.
I FIND THAT REMARK INSULTING. IT HAS NOTHING TO DO WITH ME.
He WAS RAISED IN A NICE SUBURB AND had ALWAYS BEEN Something OF A GIFTED CHILD. HE SEEMED INTERESTED IN MY BACKGROUND AND NICKNAMED ME "little GHETTO GIRL". I'M SURE HE meant IT IN THE nicest WAY.
MY MOTHER THINKS YOU'RE LYING ABOUT YOUR AGE. SHE THINKS YOU'RE OLDER. I TOLD HER ABOUT YOUR HISTORY. HOW IT'S LIKE WAR. THE FOOT SOLDIERS ALWAYS AGE FASTER THAN THE OFFICERS. WERE YOU AWARE OF THAT?
UH...
LONELY GENIUS GAZETTE
(ACTUAL DIALOG)

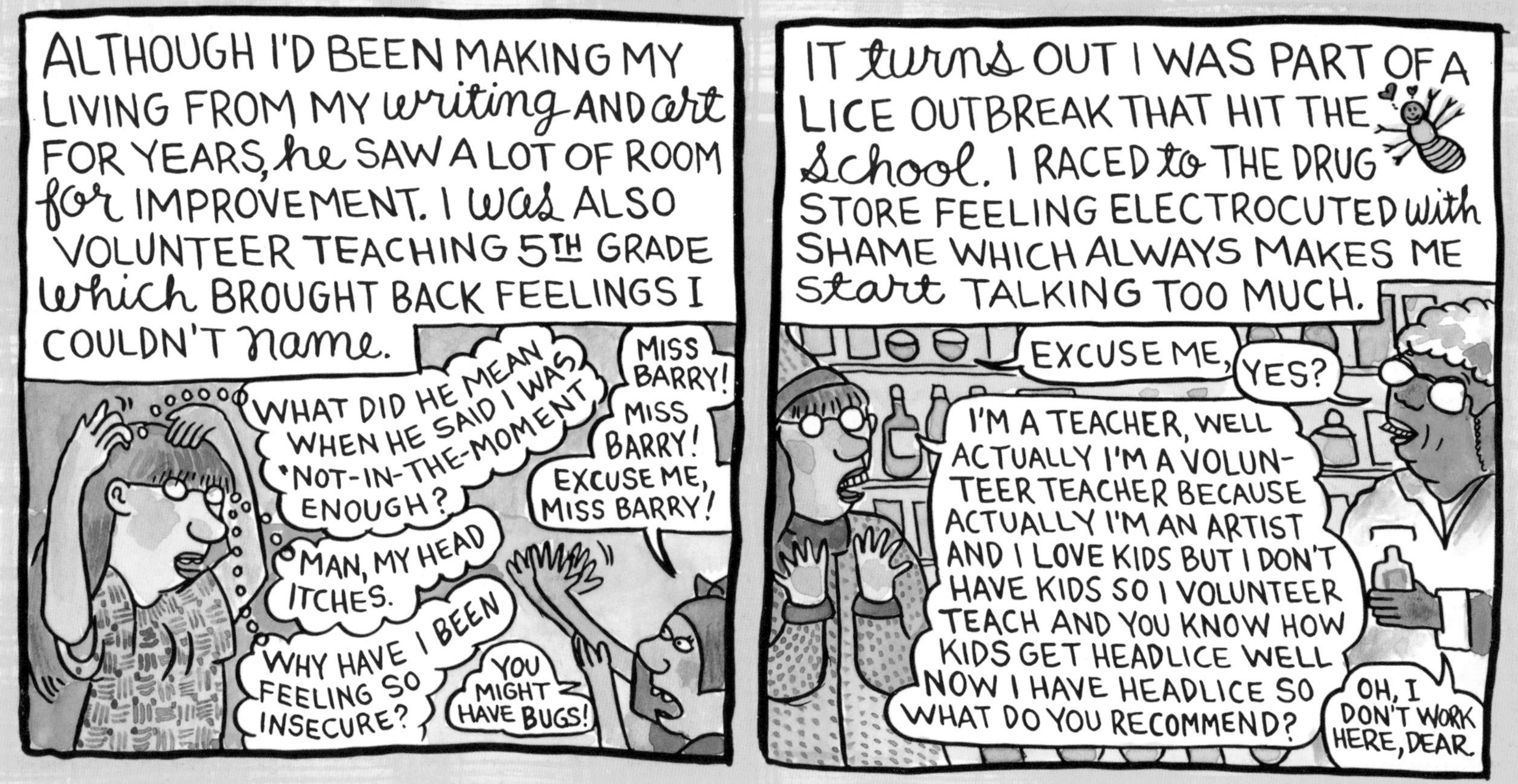
ALTHOUGH I'D BEEN MAKING MY LIVING FROM MY writing AND art FOR YEARS, he SAW A LOT OF ROOM for IMPROVEMENT. I was ALSO VOLUNTEER TEACHING 5TH GRADE which BROUGHT BACK FEELINGS I COULDN'T name.
WHAT DID HE MEAN WHEN HE SAID I WAS 'NOT-IN-THE-MOMENT ENOUGH?
MISS BARRY!
MISS BARRY!
EXCUSE ME, MISS BARRY!
MAN, MY HEAD ITCHES.
WHY HAVE I BEEN FEELING SO INSECURE?
YOU MIGHT HAVE BUGS!
IT turns OUT I WAS PART OF A LICE OUTBREAK THAT HIT THE school. I RACED to THE DRUG STORE FEELING ELECTROCUTED with SHAME WHICH ALWAYS MAKES ME start TALKING TOO MUCH.
EXCUSE ME,
YES?
I'M A TEACHER, WELL ACTUALLY I'M A VOLUNTEER TEACHER BECAUSE ACTUALLY I'M AN ARTIST AND I LOVE KIDS BUT I DON'T HAVE KIDS SO I VOLUNTEER TEACH AND YOU KNOW HOW KIDS GET HEADLICE WELL NOW I HAVE HEADLICE SO WHAT DO YOU RECOMMEND?
OH, I DON'T WORK HERE, DEAR.

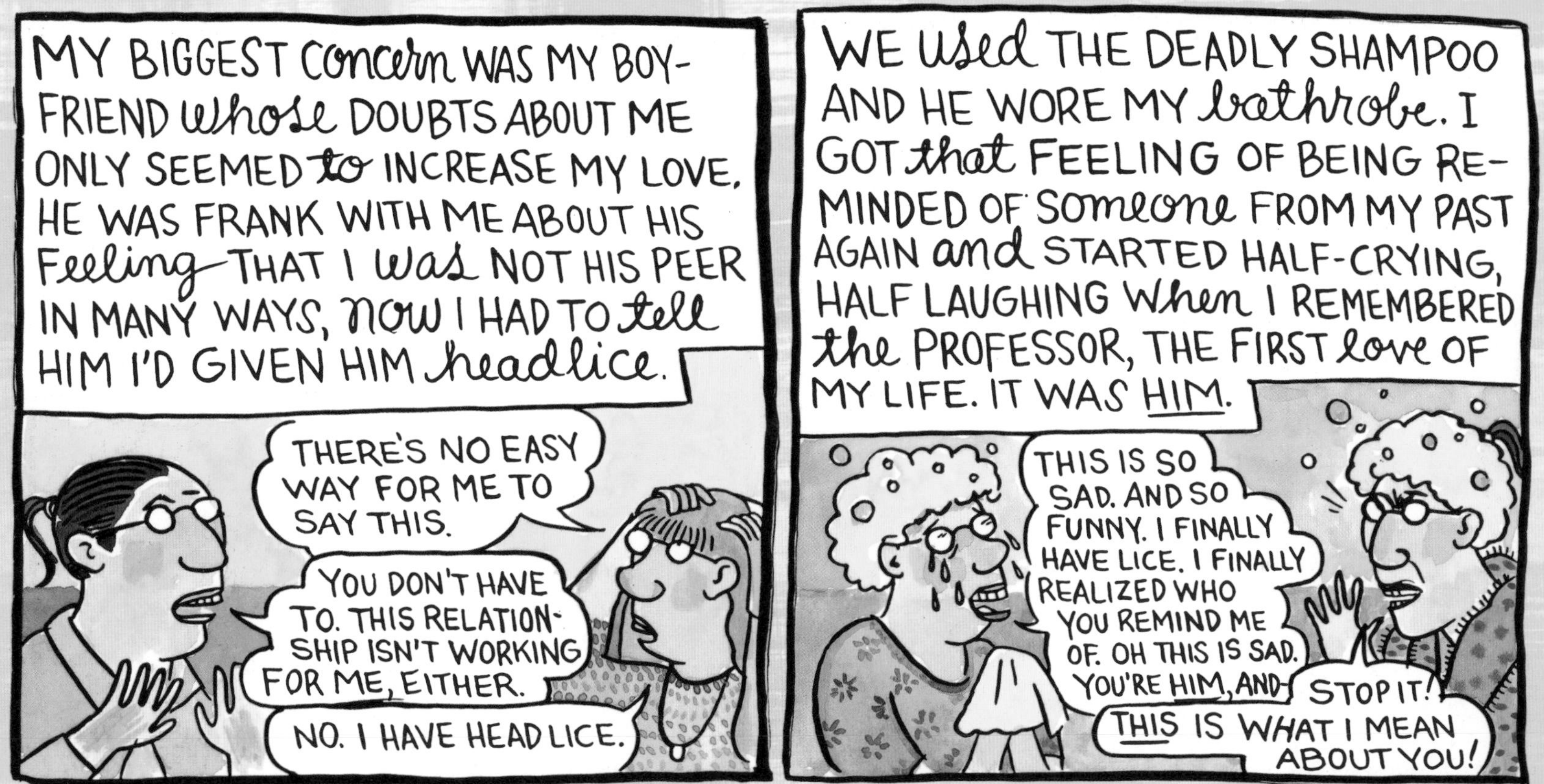
MY BIGGEST concern WAS MY BOYFRIEND whose DOUBTS ABOUT ME ONLY SEEMED to INCREASE MY LOVE. HE WAS FRANK WITH ME ABOUT HIS Feeling THAT I was NOT HIS PEER IN MANY WAYS, now I HAD TO tell HIM I'D GIVEN HIM headlice.
THERE'S NO EASY WAY FOR ME TO SAY THIS.
YOU DON'T HAVE TO. THIS RELATIONSHIP ISN'T WORKING FOR ME, EITHER.
NO. I HAVE HEAD LICE.
WE used THE DEADLY SHAMPOO AND HE WORE MY bathrobe. I GOT that FEELING OF BEING REMINDED OF Someone FROM MY PAST AGAIN and STARTED HALF-CRYING, HALF LAUGHING When I REMEMBERED the PROFESSOR, THE FIRST love OF MY LIFE. IT WAS HIM.
THIS IS SO SAD. AND SO FUNNY. I FINALLY HAVE LICE. I FINALLY REALIZED WHO YOU REMIND ME OF. OH THIS IS SAD. YOU'RE HIM, AND-
STOP IT! THIS IS WHAT I MEAN ABOUT YOU!

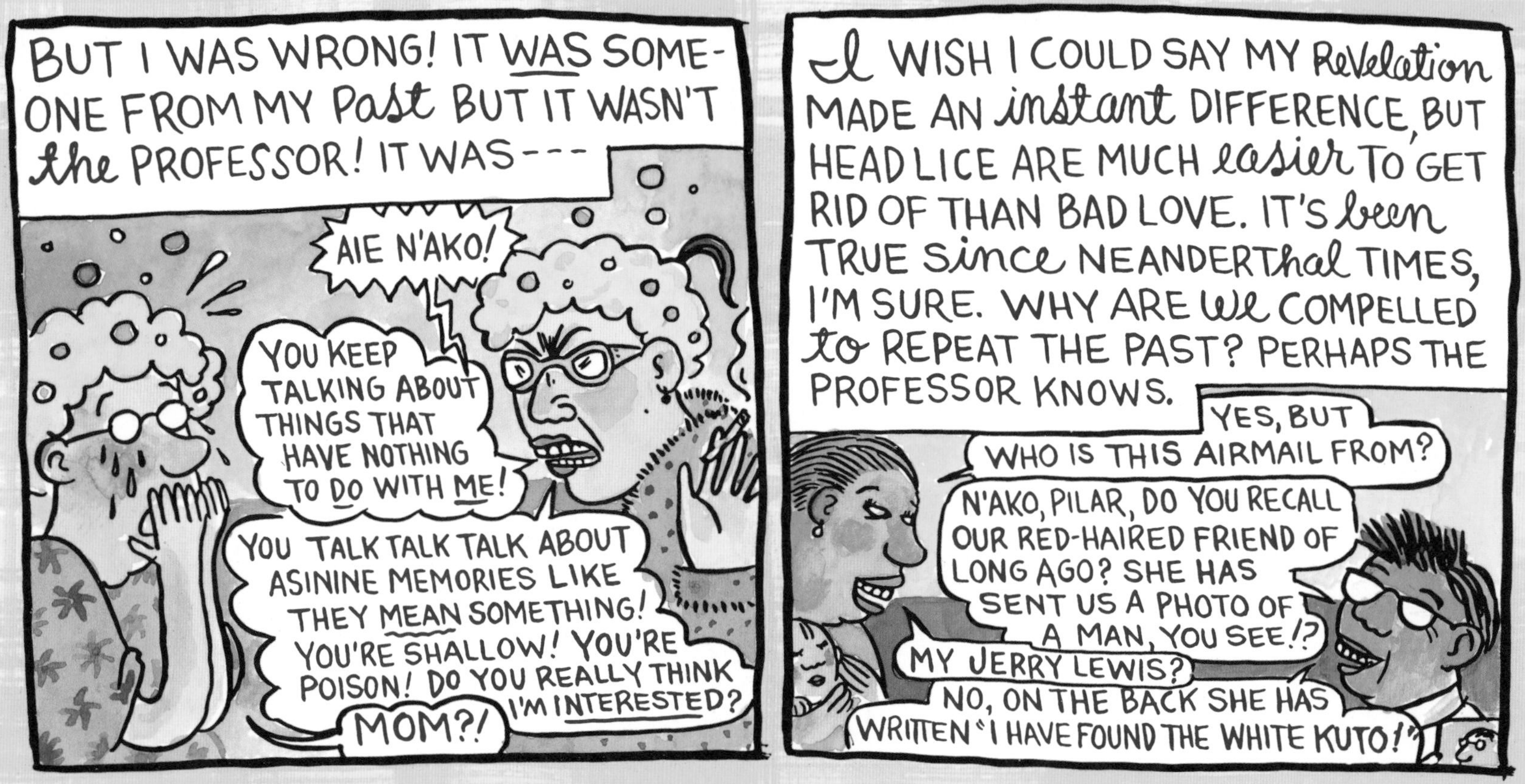
BUT I WAS WRONG! IT WAS SOME-ONE FROM MY PAST BUT IT WASN'T THE PROFESSOR! IT WAS---
AIE N'AKO!
YOU KEEP TALKING ABOUT THINGS THAT HAVE NOTHING TO DO WITH ME!
YOU TALK TALK TALK ABOUT ASININE MEMORIES LIKE THEY MEAN SOMETHING! YOU'RE SHALLOW! YOU'RE POISON! DO YOU REALLY THINK I'M INTERESTED?
MOM?!
I WISH I COULD SAY MY REVELATION MADE AN INSTANT DIFFERENCE, BUT HEAD LICE ARE MUCH EASIER TO GET RID OF THAN BAD LOVE. IT'S BEEN TRUE SINCE NEANDERTHAL TIMES, I'M SURE. WHY ARE WE COMPELLED TO REPEAT THE PAST? PERHAPS THE PROFESSOR KNOWS.
YES, BUT WHO IS THIS AIRMAIL FROM?
N'AKO, PILAR, DO YOU RECALL OUR RED-HAIRED FRIEND OF LONG AGO? SHE HAS SENT US A PHOTO OF A MAN, YOU SEE!?
MY JERRY LEWIS?
NO, ON THE BACK SHE HAS WRITTEN "I HAVE FOUND THE WHITE KUTO!"

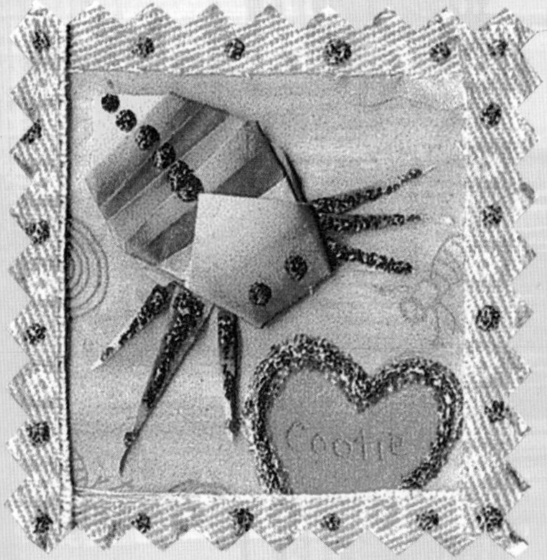
Cootie

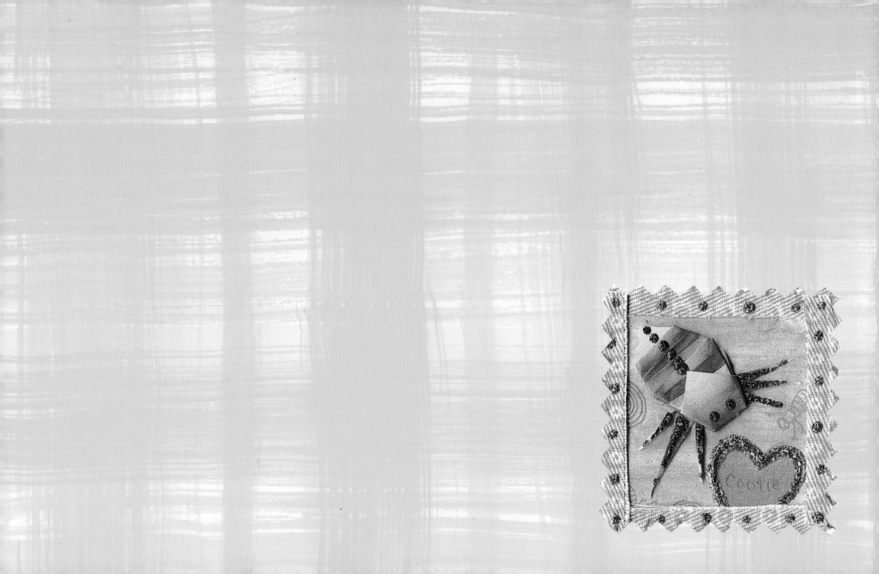

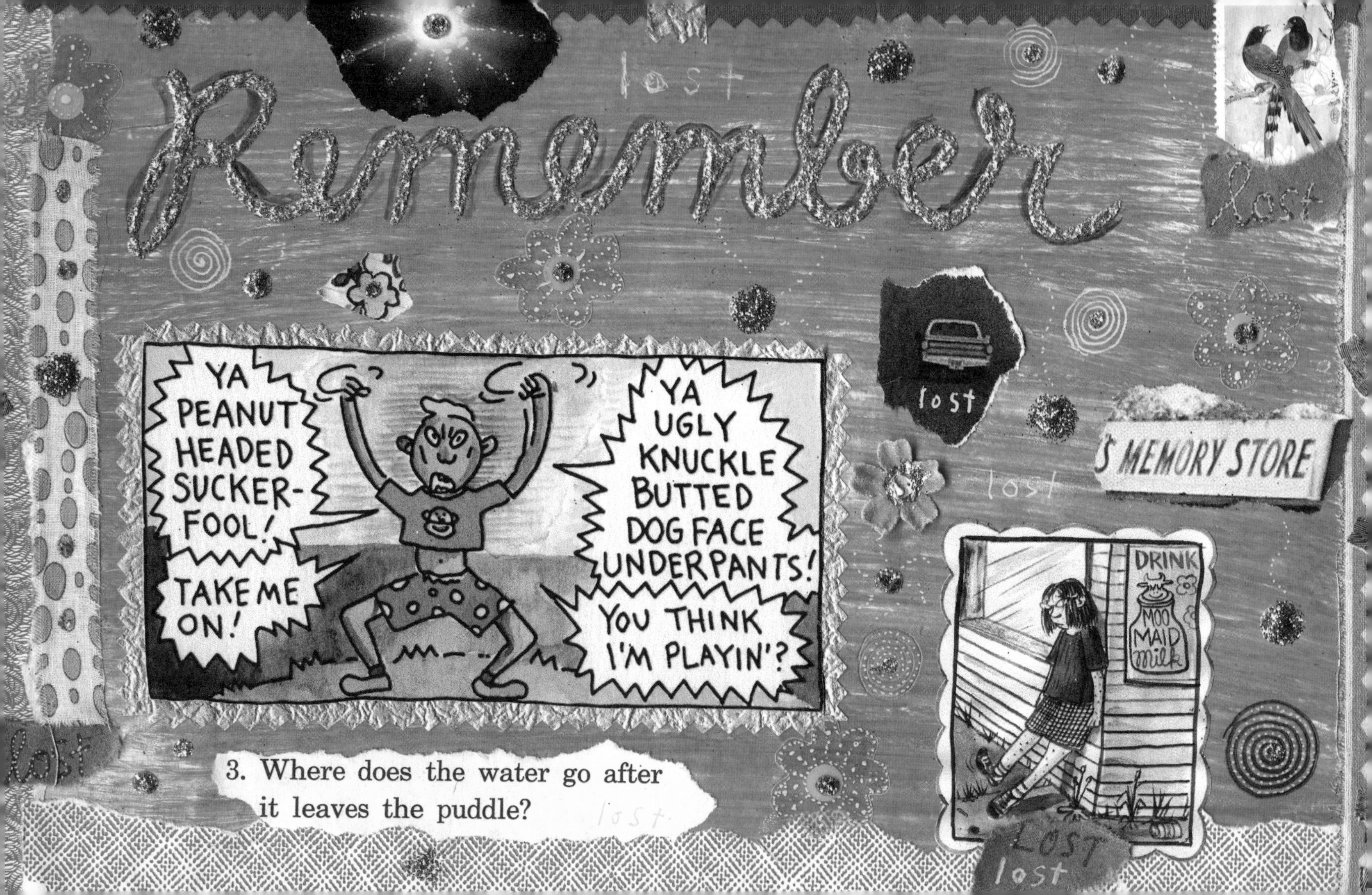
Remember
lost
lost
YA PEANUT HEADED SUCKER-FOOL!
TAKE ME ON!
YA UGLY KNUCKLE BUTTED DOG FACE UNDERPANTS!
YOU THINK I'M PLAYIN'?
lost
'S MEMORY STORE
lost
DRINK MOO MAID milk
lost
3. Where does the water go after it leaves the puddle?
lost
LOST
lost

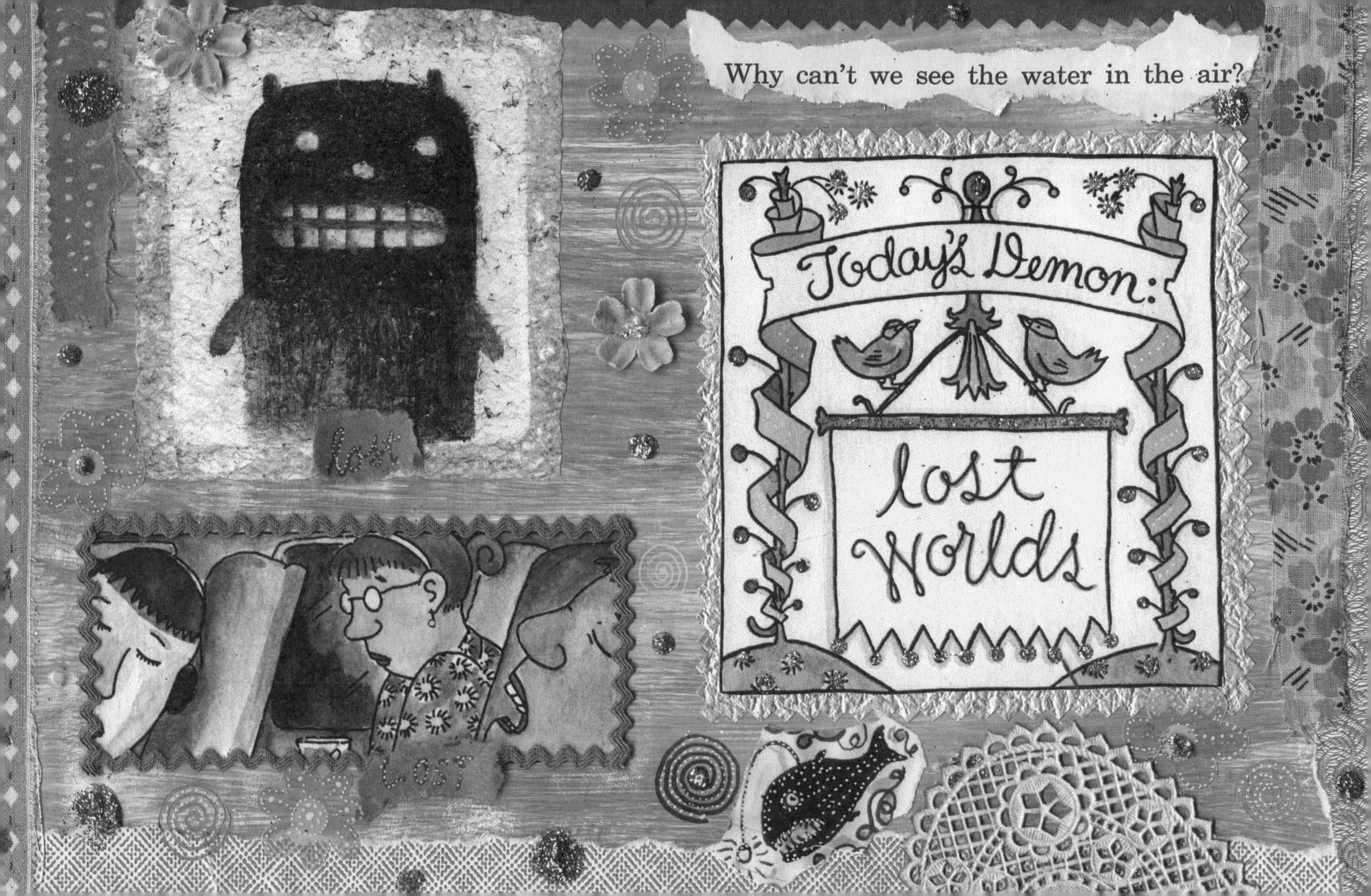
Why can't we see the water in the air?
lost
Today's Demon:
lost worlds
LOST

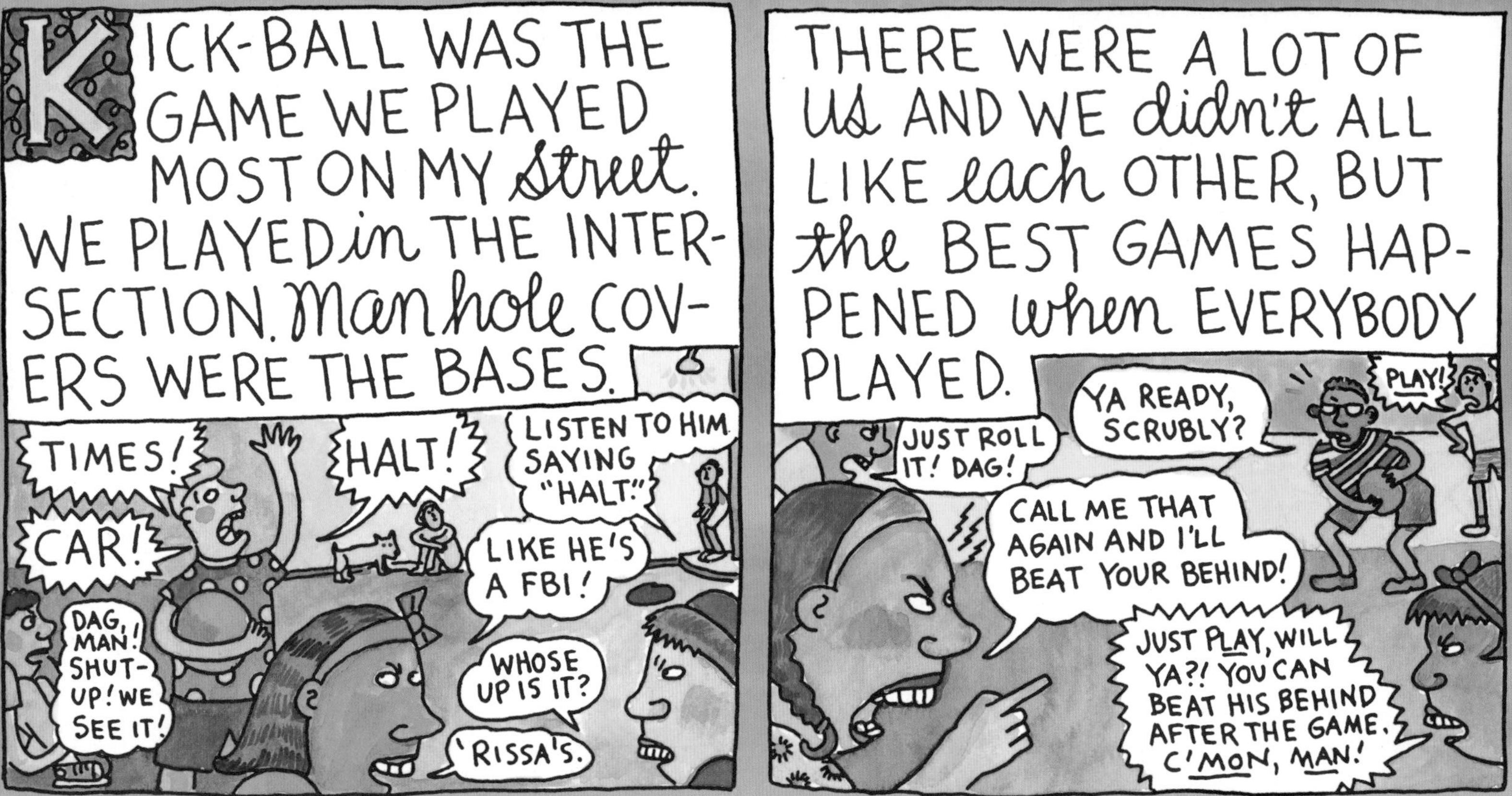
KICK-BALL WAS THE GAME WE PLAYED MOST ON MY STREET. WE PLAYED IN THE INTER-SECTION. MANHOLE COV-ERS WERE THE BASES.
TIMES!
CAR!
DAG, MAN! SHUT-UP! WE SEE IT!
HALT!
LISTEN TO HIM SAYING "HALT!"
LIKE HE'S A FBI!
WHOSE UP IS IT?
'RISSA'S.
THERE WERE A LOT OF US AND WE DIDN'T ALL LIKE EACH OTHER, BUT THE BEST GAMES HAP-PENED WHEN EVERYBODY PLAYED.
JUST ROLL IT! DAG!
YA READY, SCRUBLY?
PLAY!
CALL ME THAT AGAIN AND I'LL BEAT YOUR BEHIND!
JUST PLAY, WILL YA?! YOU CAN BEAT HIS BEHIND AFTER THE GAME. C'MON, MAN!

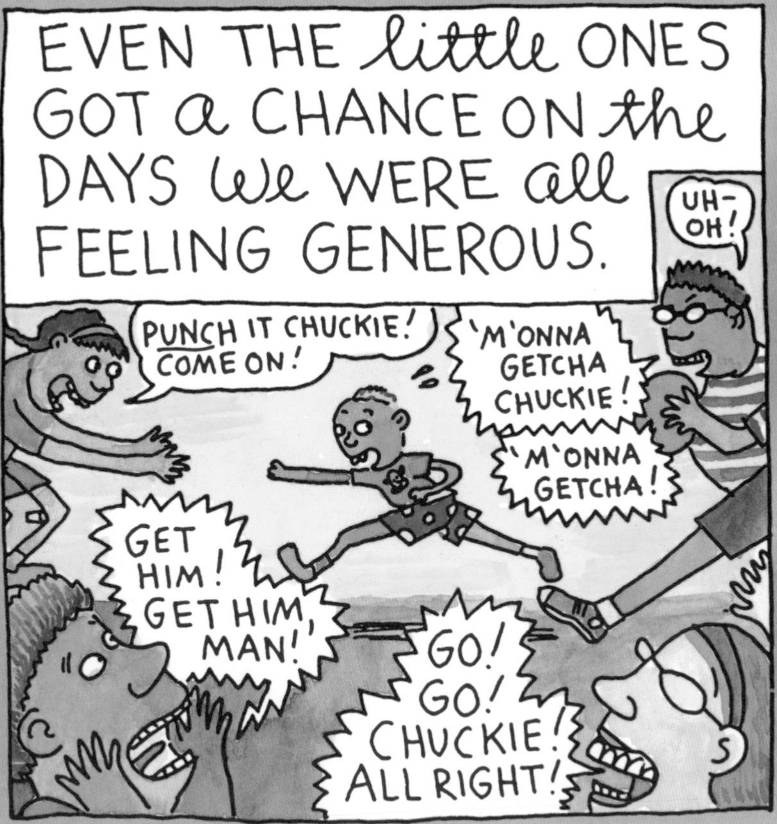
EVEN THE little ONES GOT a CHANCE ON the DAYS we WERE all FEELING GENEROUS.
UH-OH!
PUNCH IT CHUCKIE! COME ON!
'M'ONNA GETCHA CHUCKIE!
'M'ONNA GETCHA!
GET HIM! GET HIM, MAN!
GO! GO! CHUCKIE! ALL RIGHT!

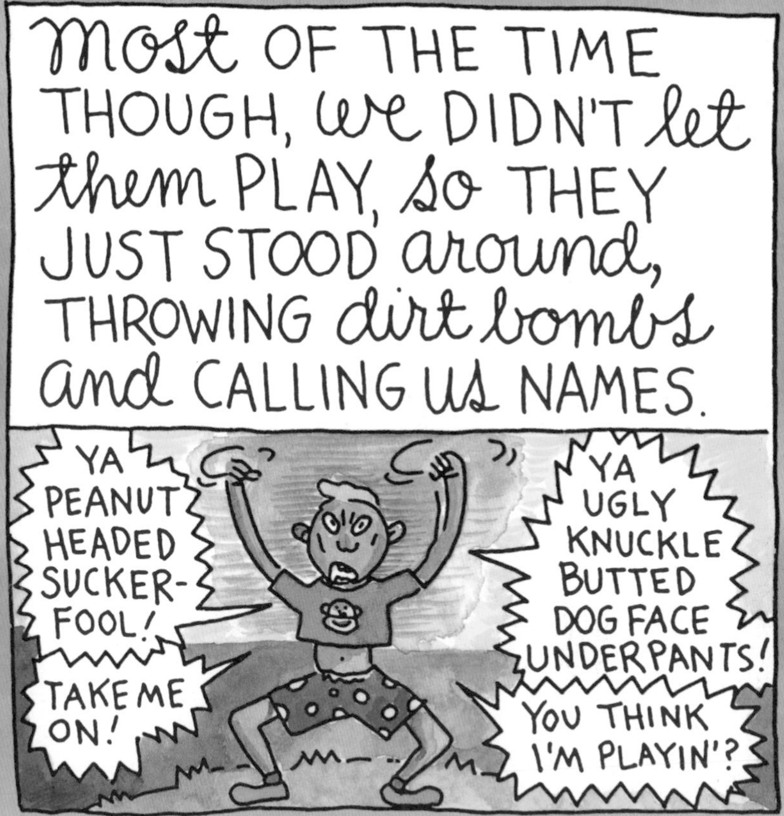
most OF THE TIME THOUGH, we DIDN'T let them PLAY, so THEY JUST STOOD around, THROWING dirt bombs and CALLING us NAMES.
YA PEANUT HEADED SUCKER-FOOL!
TAKE ME ON!
YA UGLY KNUCKLE BUTTED DOG FACE UNDERPANTS!
YOU THINK I'M PLAYIN'?

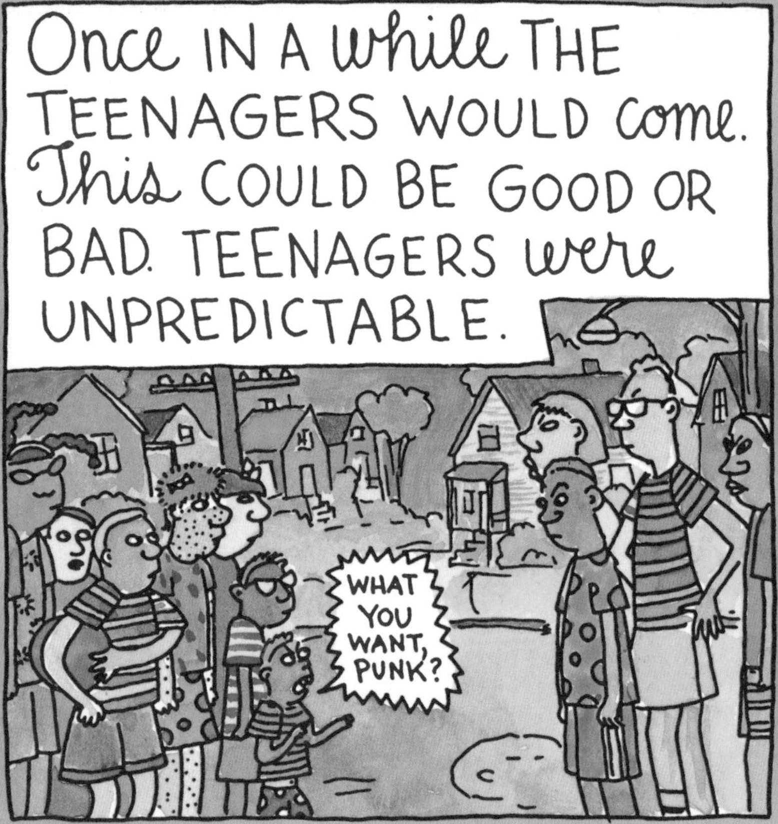
Once IN A while THE TEENAGERS WOULD come. This COULD BE GOOD OR BAD. TEENAGERS were UNPREDICTABLE.
WHAT YOU WANT, PUNK?

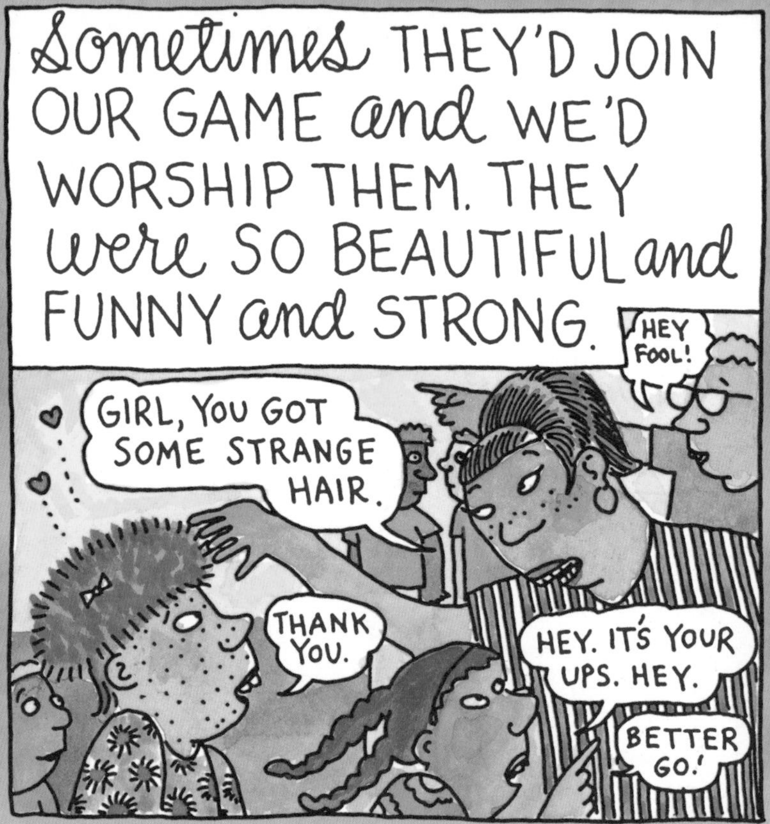
Sometimes THEY'D JOIN OUR GAME and WE'D WORSHIP THEM. THEY were SO BEAUTIFUL and FUNNY and STRONG.
HEY FOOL!
GIRL, YOU GOT SOME STRANGE HAIR.
THANK YOU.
HEY. IT'S YOUR UPS. HEY.
BETTER GO!

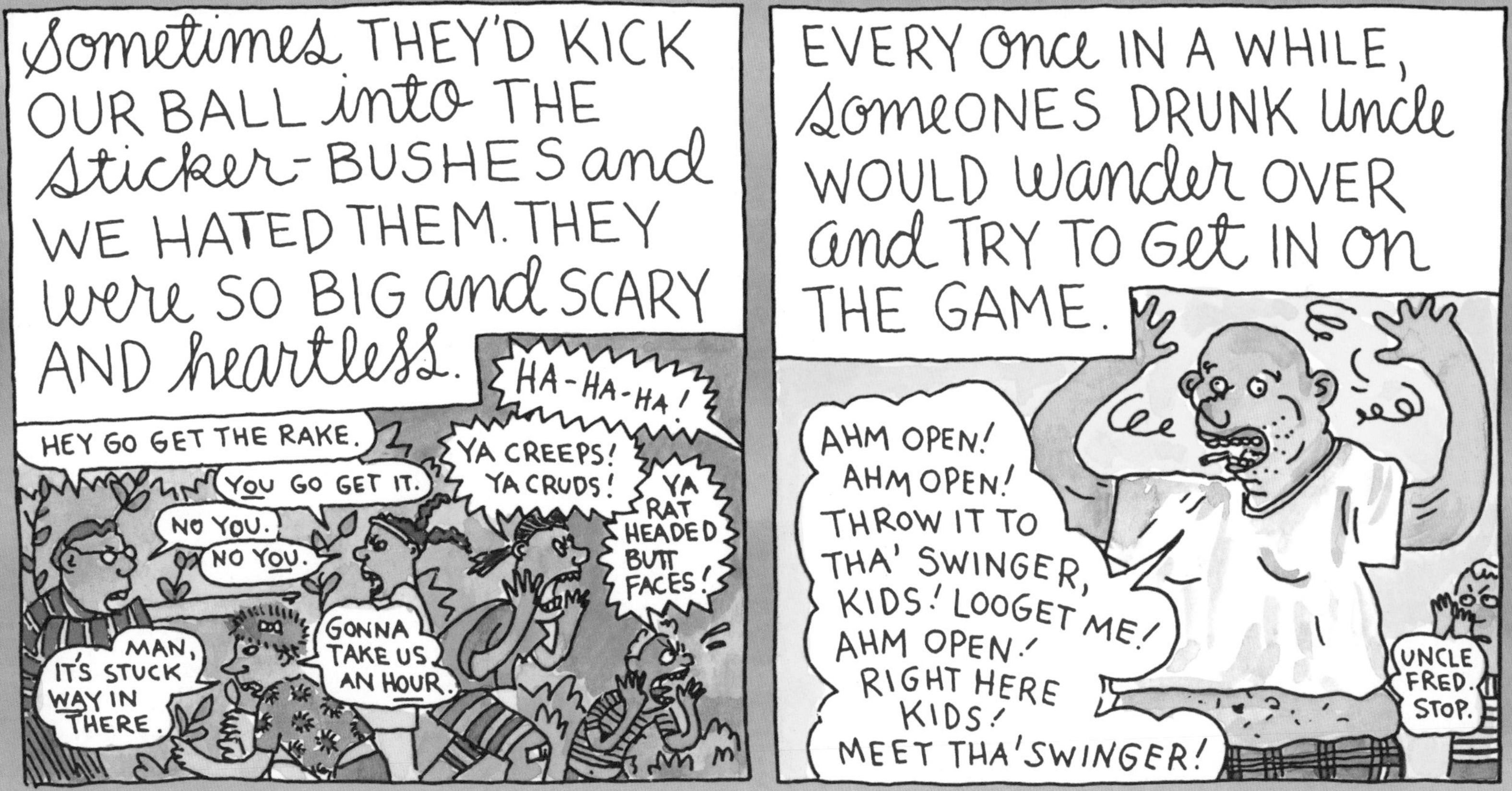
Sometimes THEY'D KICK OUR BALL into THE sticker-BUSHES and WE HATED THEM. THEY were SO BIG and SCARY AND heartless.
HA-HA-HA!
HEY GO GET THE RAKE.
YOU GO GET IT.
YA CREEPS! YA CRUDS!
YA RAT HEADED BUTT FACES!
NO YOU.
NO YOU.
MAN, IT'S STUCK WAY IN THERE.
GONNA TAKE US AN HOUR.
EVERY Once IN A WHILE, SomeONES DRUNK Uncle WOULD Wander OVER and TRY TO Get IN On THE GAME.
AHM OPEN! AHM OPEN! THROW IT TO THA' SWINGER, KIDS! LOOGET ME! AHM OPEN! RIGHT HERE KIDS! MEET THA' SWINGER!
UNCLE FRED. STOP.

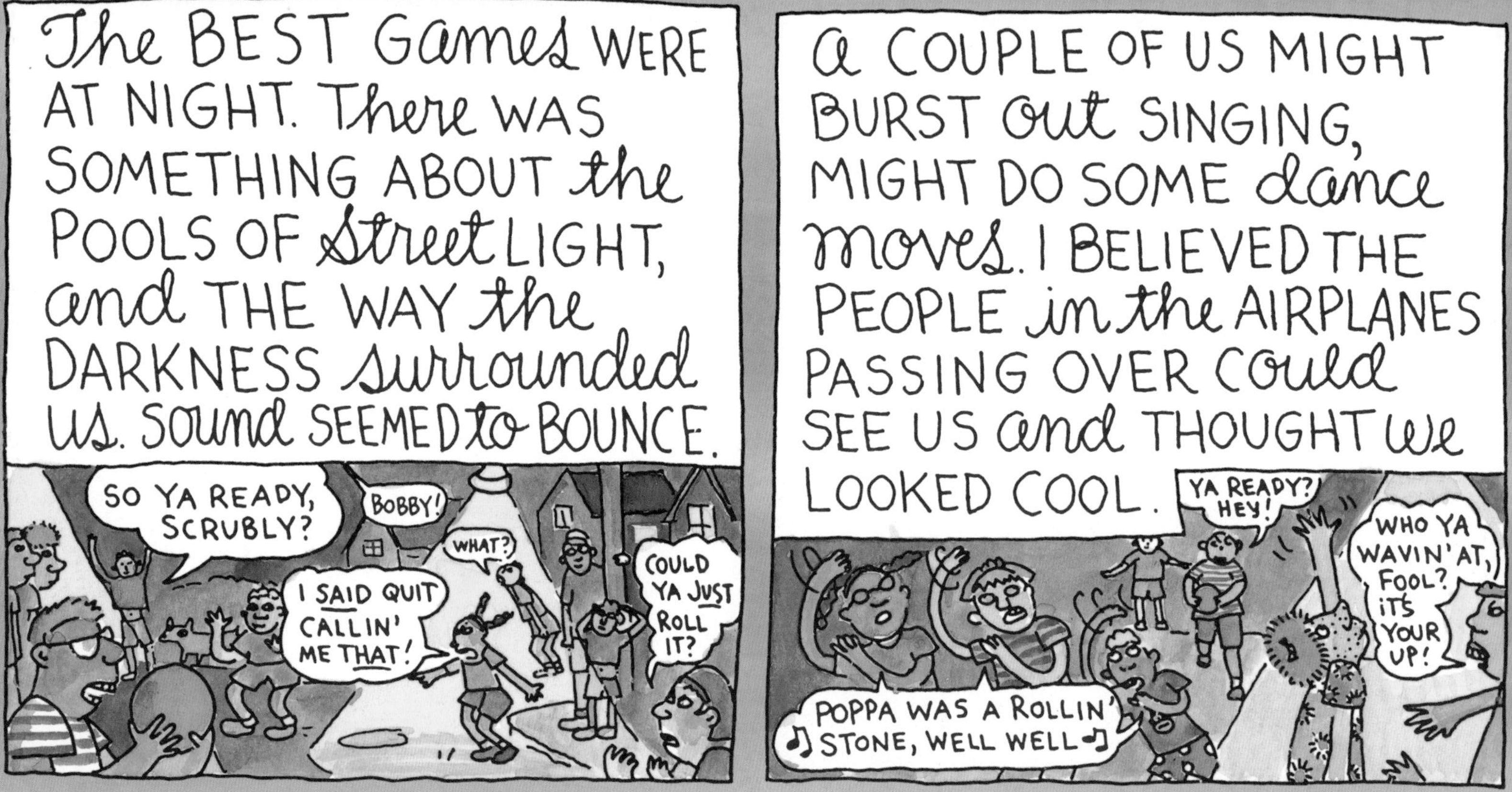
The BEST Games WERE AT NIGHT. There WAS SOMETHING ABOUT the POOLS OF Street LIGHT, and THE WAY the DARKNESS surrounded us. Sound SEEMED to BOUNCE.
SO YA READY, SCRUBLY?
BOBBY!
WHAT?
I SAID QUIT CALLIN' ME THAT!
COULD YA JUST ROLL IT?
a COUPLE OF US MIGHT BURST out SINGING, MIGHT DO SOME dance moves. I BELIEVED THE PEOPLE in the AIRPLANES PASSING OVER could SEE US and THOUGHT we LOOKED COOL.
YA READY? HEY!
WHO YA WAVIN' AT, FOOL? IT'S YOUR UP!
POPPA WAS A ROLLIN' STONE, WELL WELL

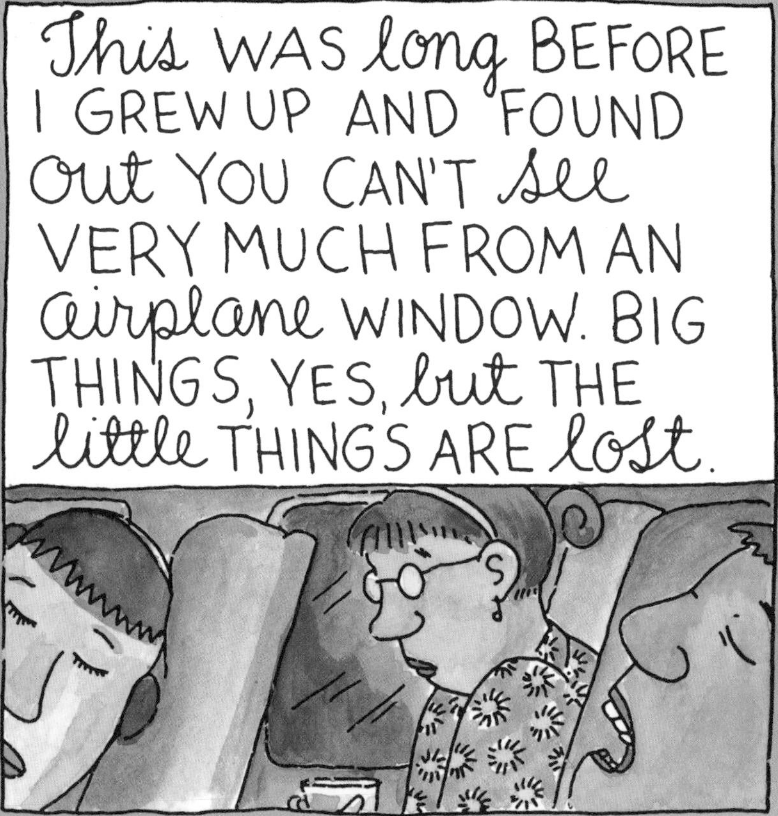
This WAS long BEFORE I GREW UP AND FOUND out YOU CAN'T see VERY MUCH FROM AN airplane WINDOW. BIG THINGS, YES, but THE little THINGS ARE lost.

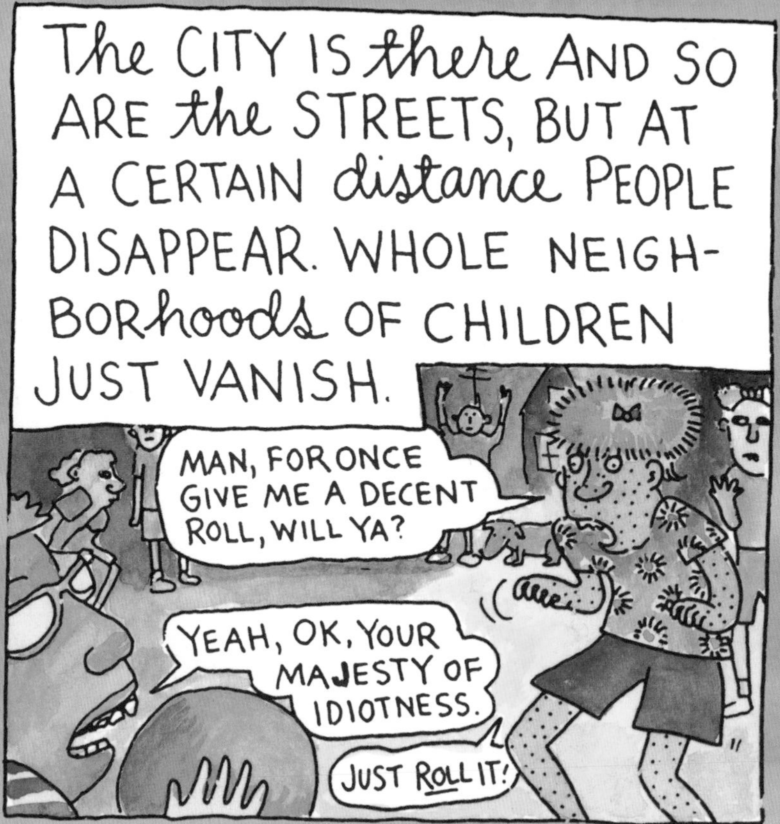
The CITY IS there AND SO ARE the STREETS, BUT AT A CERTAIN distance PEOPLE DISAPPEAR. WHOLE NEIGH-BORhoods OF CHILDREN JUST VANISH.
MAN, FOR ONCE GIVE ME A DECENT ROLL, WILL YA?
YEAH, OK, YOUR MAJESTY OF IDIOTNESS.
JUST ROLL IT!

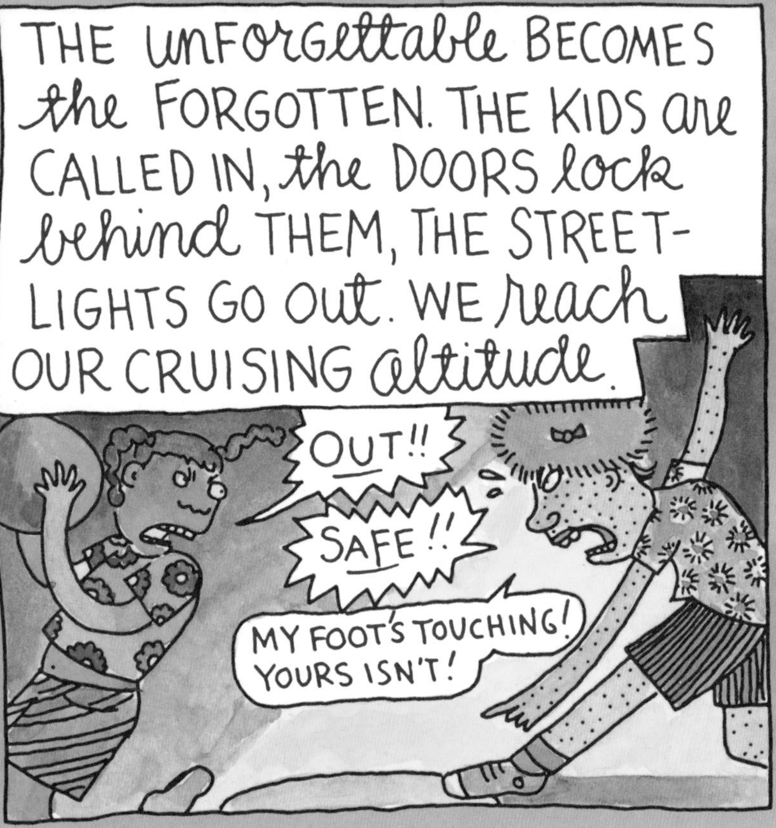
THE unforgettable BECOMES the FORGOTTEN. THE KIDS are CALLED IN, the DOORS lock behind THEM, THE STREET-LIGHTS GO out. WE reach OUR CRUISING altitude.
OUT!!
SAFE!!
MY FOOT'S TOUCHING! YOURS ISN'T!

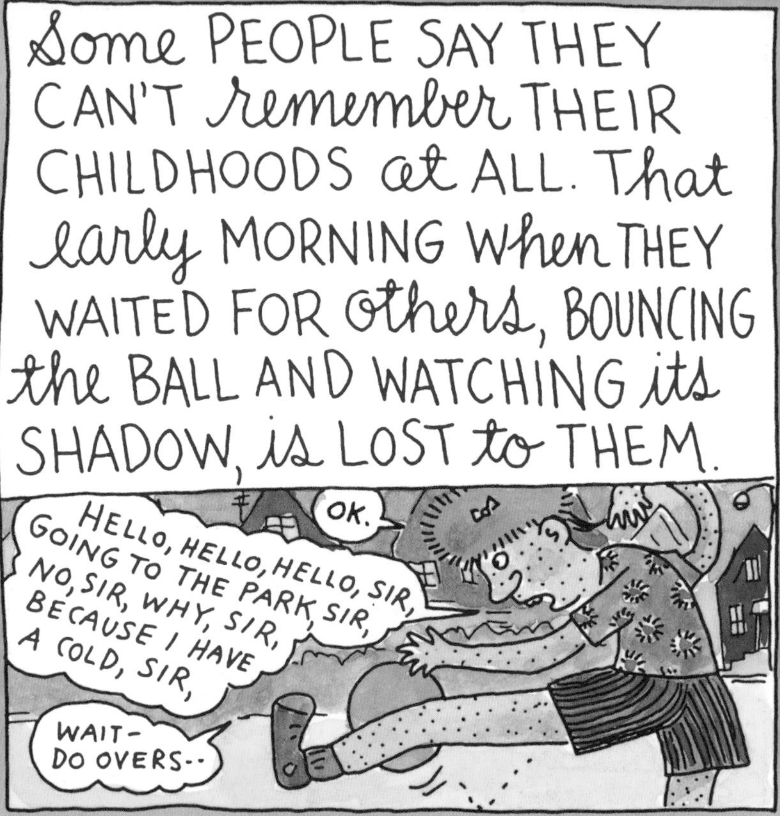
Some PEOPLE SAY THEY CAN'T remember THEIR CHILDHOODS at ALL. That early MORNING when THEY WAITED FOR others, BOUNCING the BALL AND WATCHING its SHADOW, is LOST to THEM.
HELLO, HELLO, HELLO, SIR, GOING TO THE PARK, SIR, NO, SIR, WHY, SIR, BECAUSE I HAVE A COLD, SIR,
OK.
WAIT- DO OVERS--

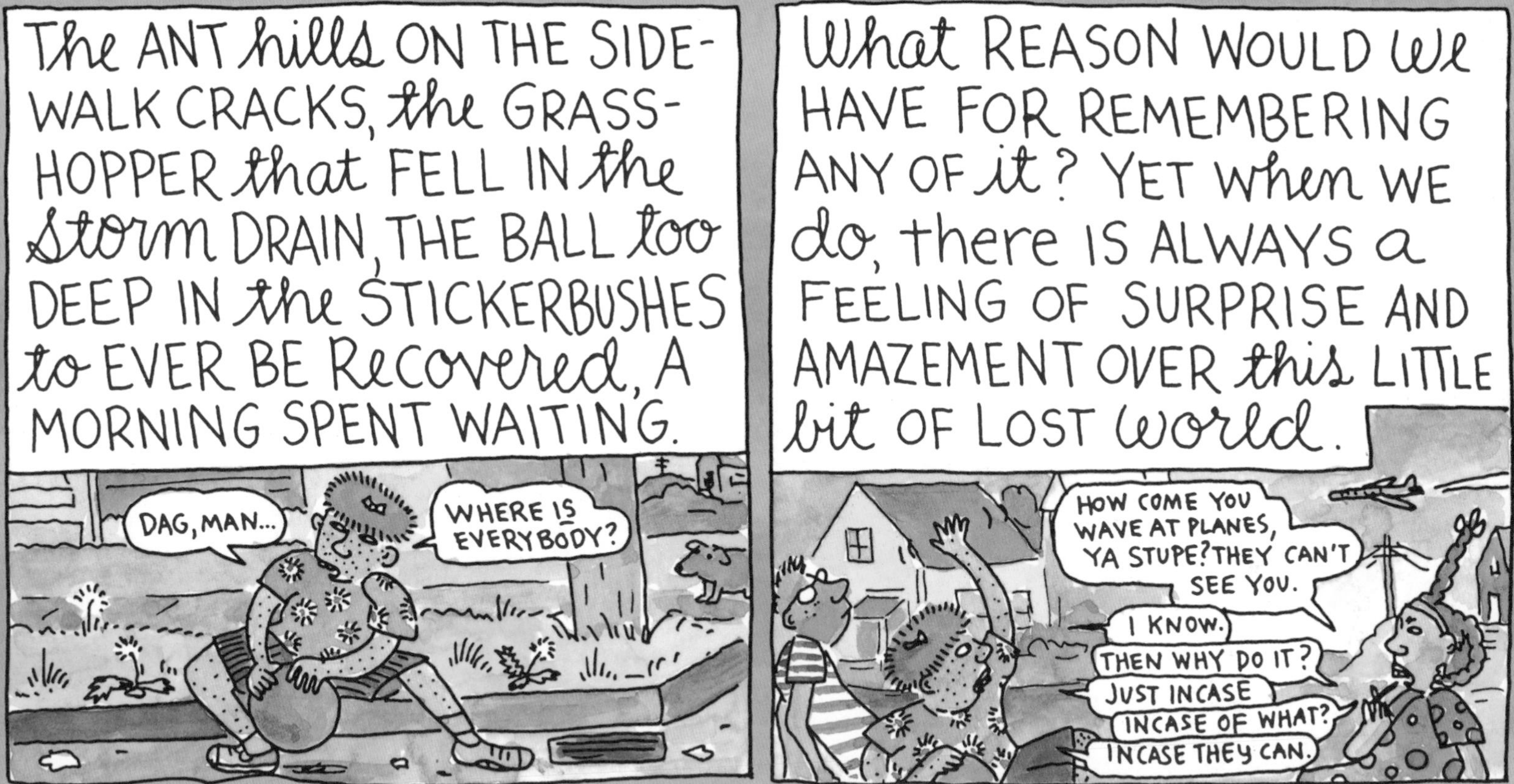
The ANT hills ON THE SIDE-WALK CRACKS, the GRASS-HOPPER that FELL IN the storm DRAIN, THE BALL too DEEP IN the STICKERBUSHES to EVER BE Recovered, A MORNING SPENT WAITING.
DAG, MAN...
WHERE IS EVERYBODY?
What REASON WOULD we HAVE FOR REMEMBERING ANY OF it? YET when WE do, there IS ALWAYS a FEELING OF SURPRISE AND AMAZEMENT OVER this LITTLE bit OF LOST world.
HOW COME YOU WAVE AT PLANES, YA STUPE? THEY CAN'T SEE YOU.
I KNOW.
THEN WHY DO IT?
JUST INCASE
INCASE OF WHAT?
INCASE THEY CAN.

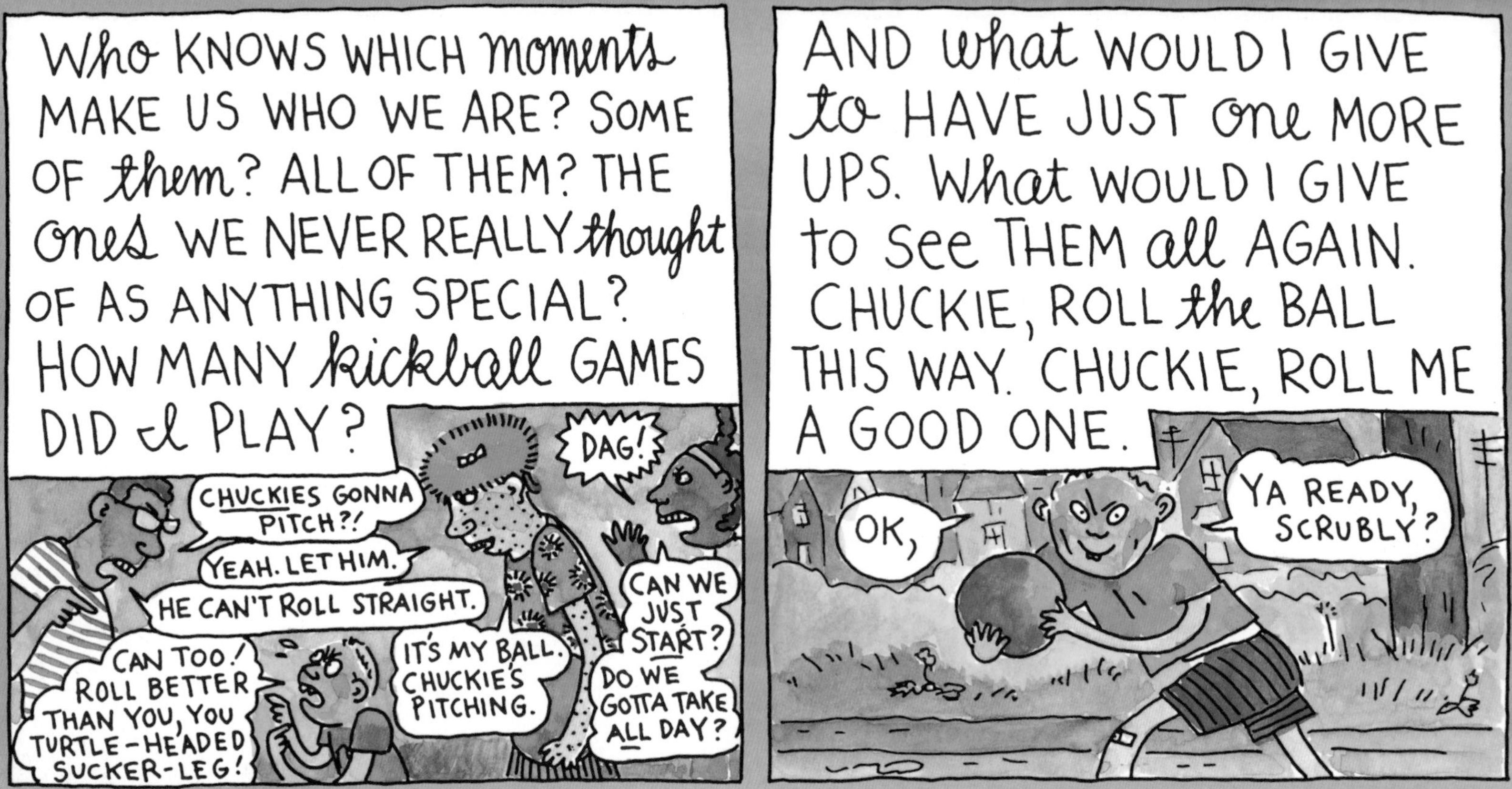
WHO KNOWS WHICH MOMENTS MAKE US WHO WE ARE? SOME OF THEM? ALL OF THEM? THE ONES WE NEVER REALLY THOUGHT OF AS ANYTHING SPECIAL? HOW MANY KICKBALL GAMES DID I PLAY?
CHUCKIES GONNA PITCH?!
DAG!
YEAH. LET HIM.
HE CAN'T ROLL STRAIGHT.
CAN WE JUST START?
CAN TOO! ROLL BETTER THAN YOU, YOU TURTLE-HEADED SUCKER-LEG!
IT'S MY BALL. CHUCKIE'S PITCHING.
DO WE GOTTA TAKE ALL DAY?
AND WHAT WOULD I GIVE TO HAVE JUST ONE MORE UPS. WHAT WOULD I GIVE TO SEE THEM ALL AGAIN. CHUCKIE, ROLL THE BALL THIS WAY. CHUCKIE, ROLL ME A GOOD ONE.
OK,
YA READY, SCRUBLY?

3. Where does the water go after it leaves the puddle?

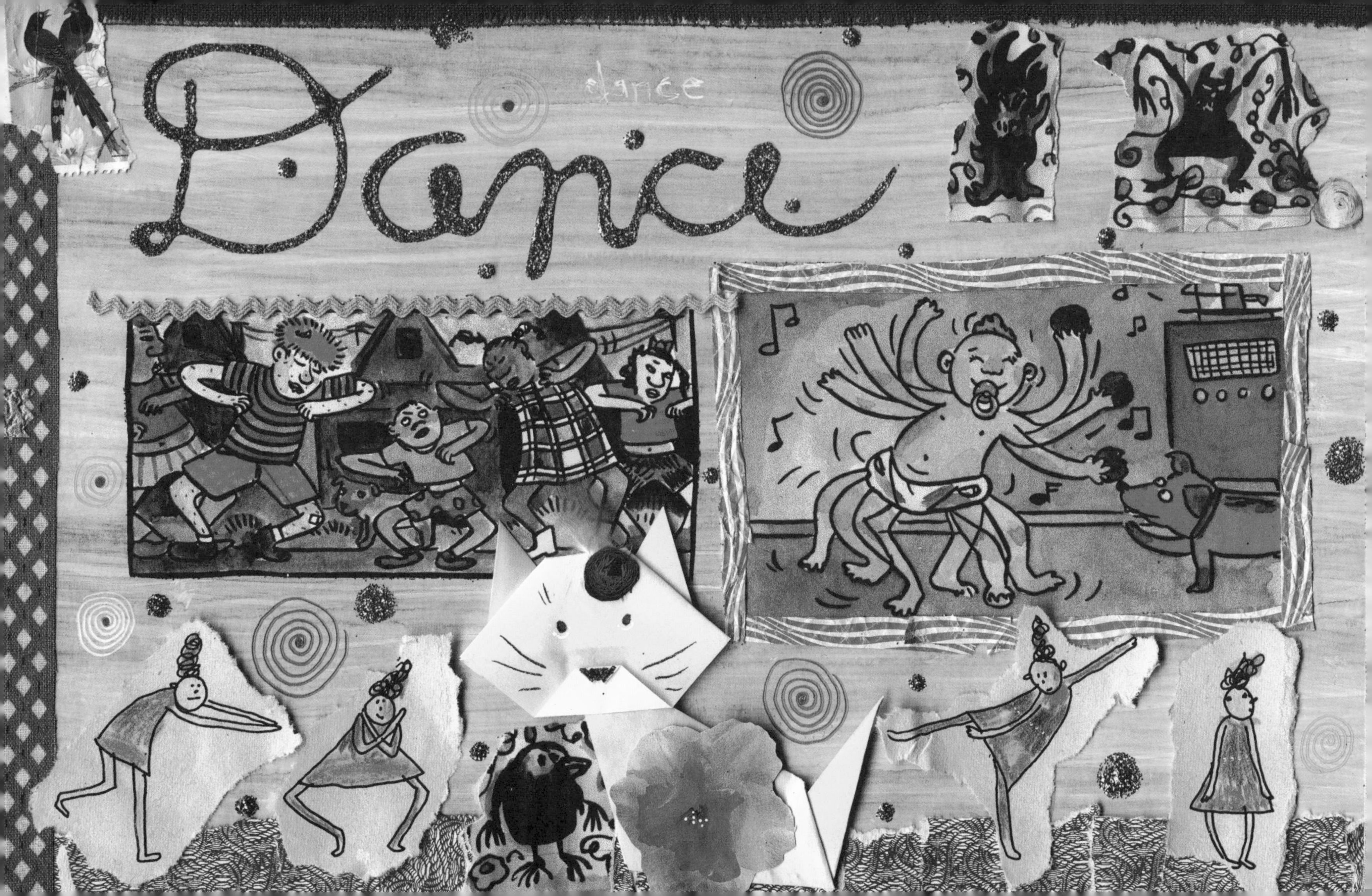
dance
Dance

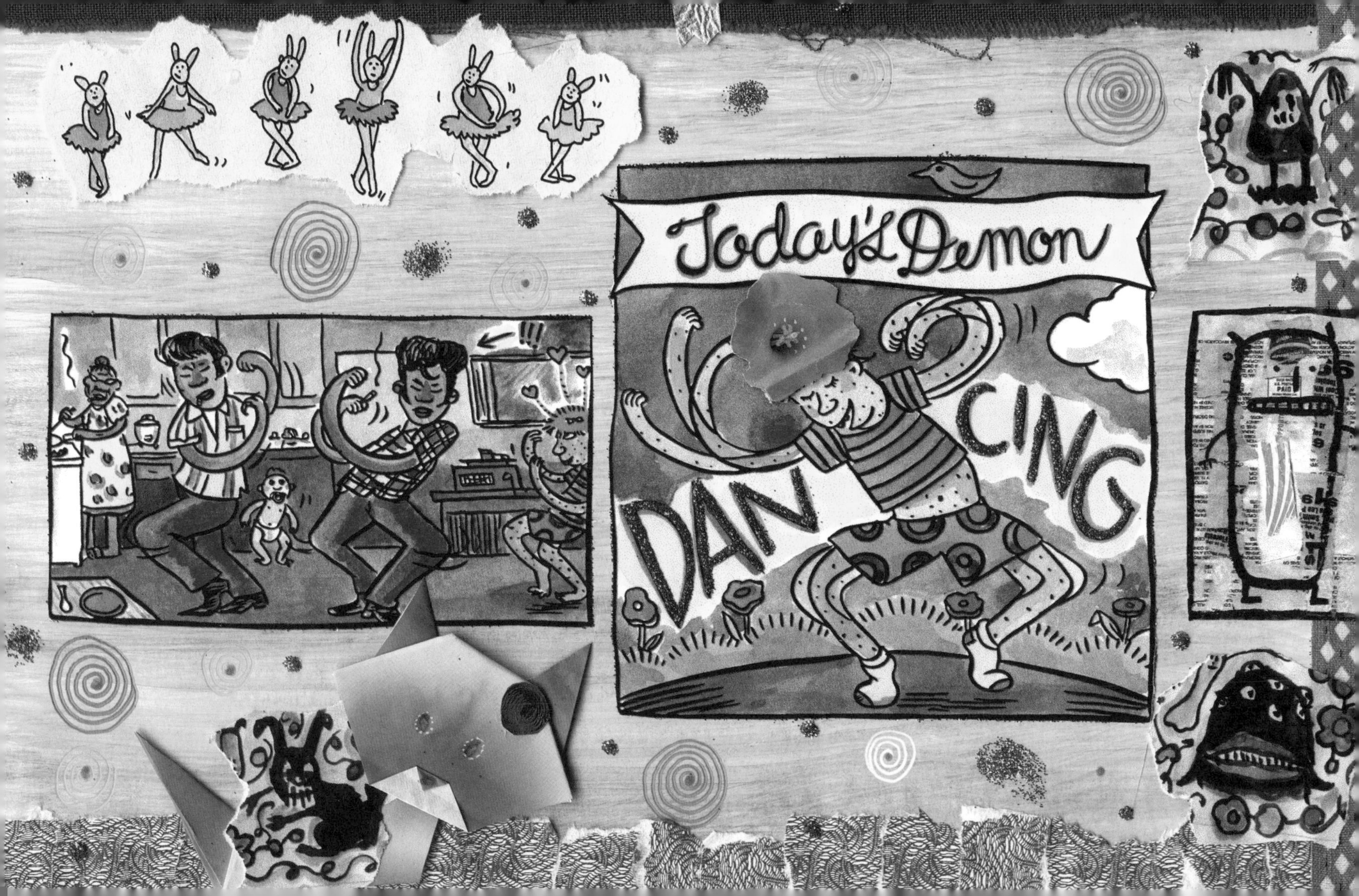
Today's Demon
DAN
CING

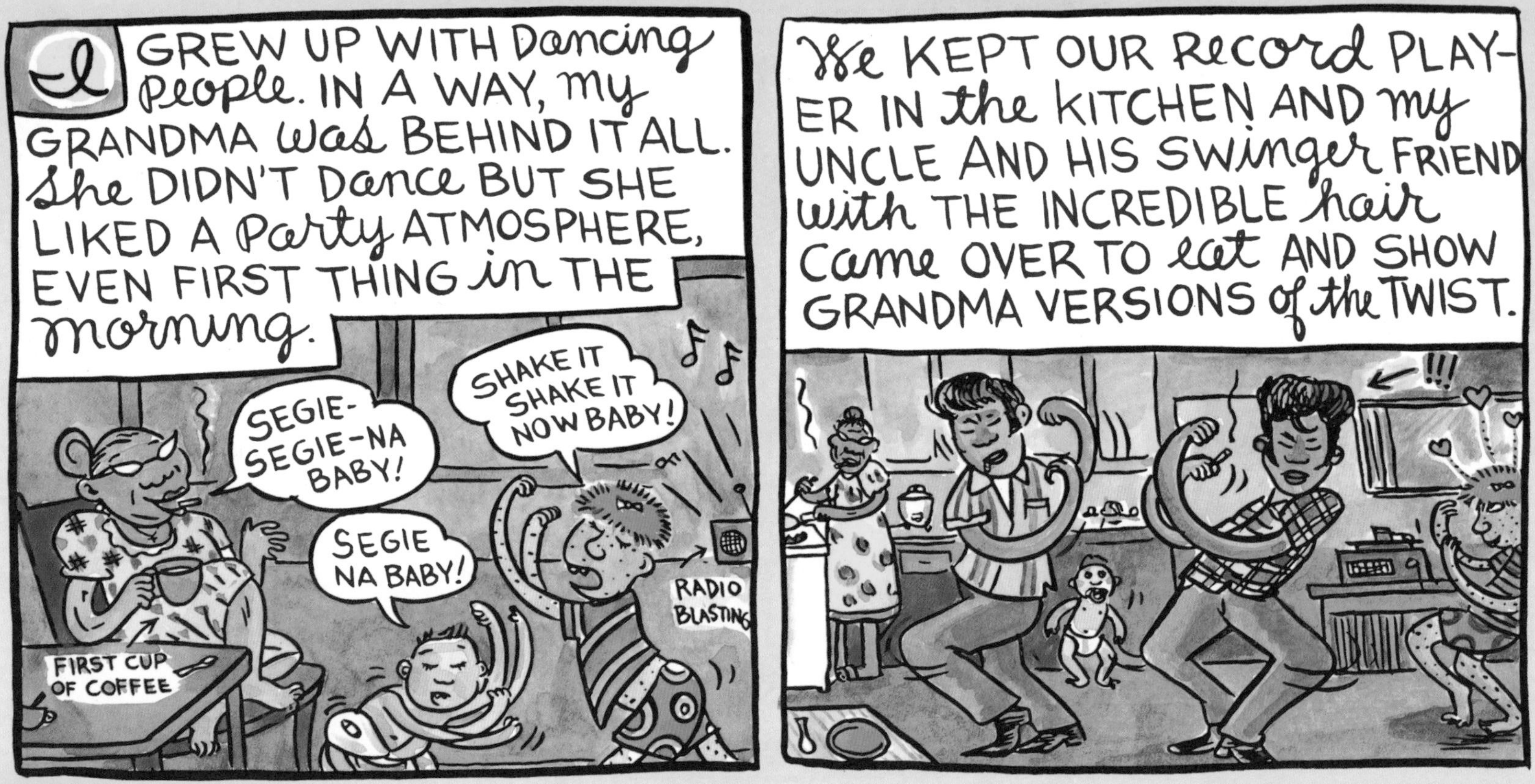
I GREW UP WITH Dancing People. IN A WAY, my GRANDMA was BEHIND IT ALL. She DIDN'T Dance BUT SHE LIKED A Party ATMOSPHERE, EVEN FIRST THING in THE morning.
SEGIE-SEGIE-NA BABY!
SHAKE IT SHAKE IT NOW BABY!
SEGIE NA BABY!
RADIO BLASTING
FIRST CUP OF COFFEE
We KEPT OUR Record PLAY-ER IN the KITCHEN AND my UNCLE AND HIS Swinger FRIEND with THE INCREDIBLE hair Came OVER TO eat AND SHOW GRANDMA VERSIONS of the TWIST.
!!!

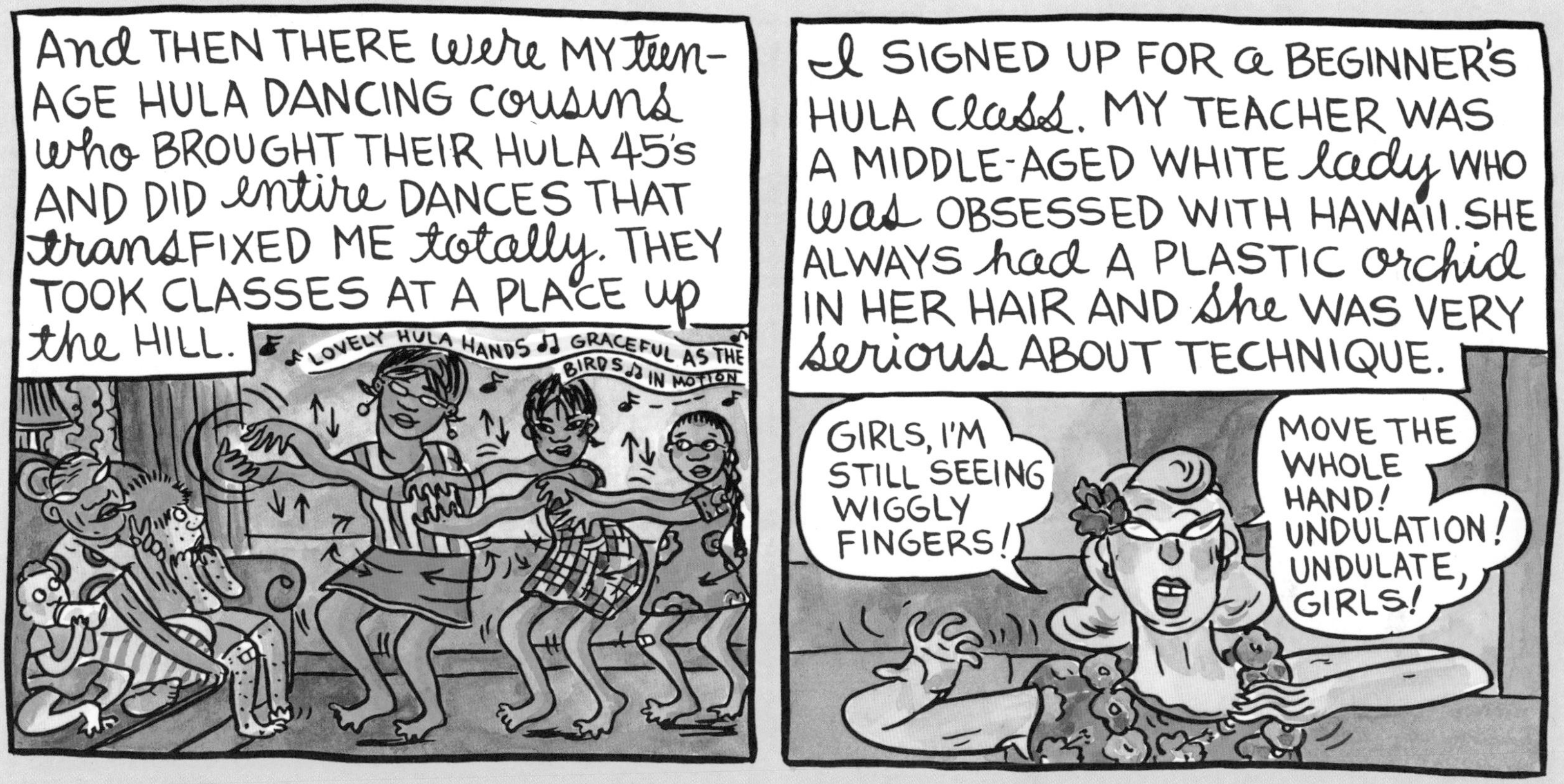
And THEN THERE were MY teen-AGE HULA DANCING cousins who BROUGHT THEIR HULA 45's AND DID entire DANCES THAT transFIXED ME totally. THEY TOOK CLASSES AT A PLACE up the HILL.
LOVELY HULA HANDS GRACEFUL AS THE BIRDS IN MOTION
I SIGNED UP FOR a BEGINNER'S HULA class. MY TEACHER WAS A MIDDLE-AGED WHITE lady WHO was OBSESSED WITH HAWAII. SHE ALWAYS had A PLASTIC orchid IN HER HAIR AND she WAS VERY serious ABOUT TECHNIQUE.
GIRLS, I'M STILL SEEING WIGGLY FINGERS!
MOVE THE WHOLE HAND! UNDULATION! UNDULATE, GIRLS!

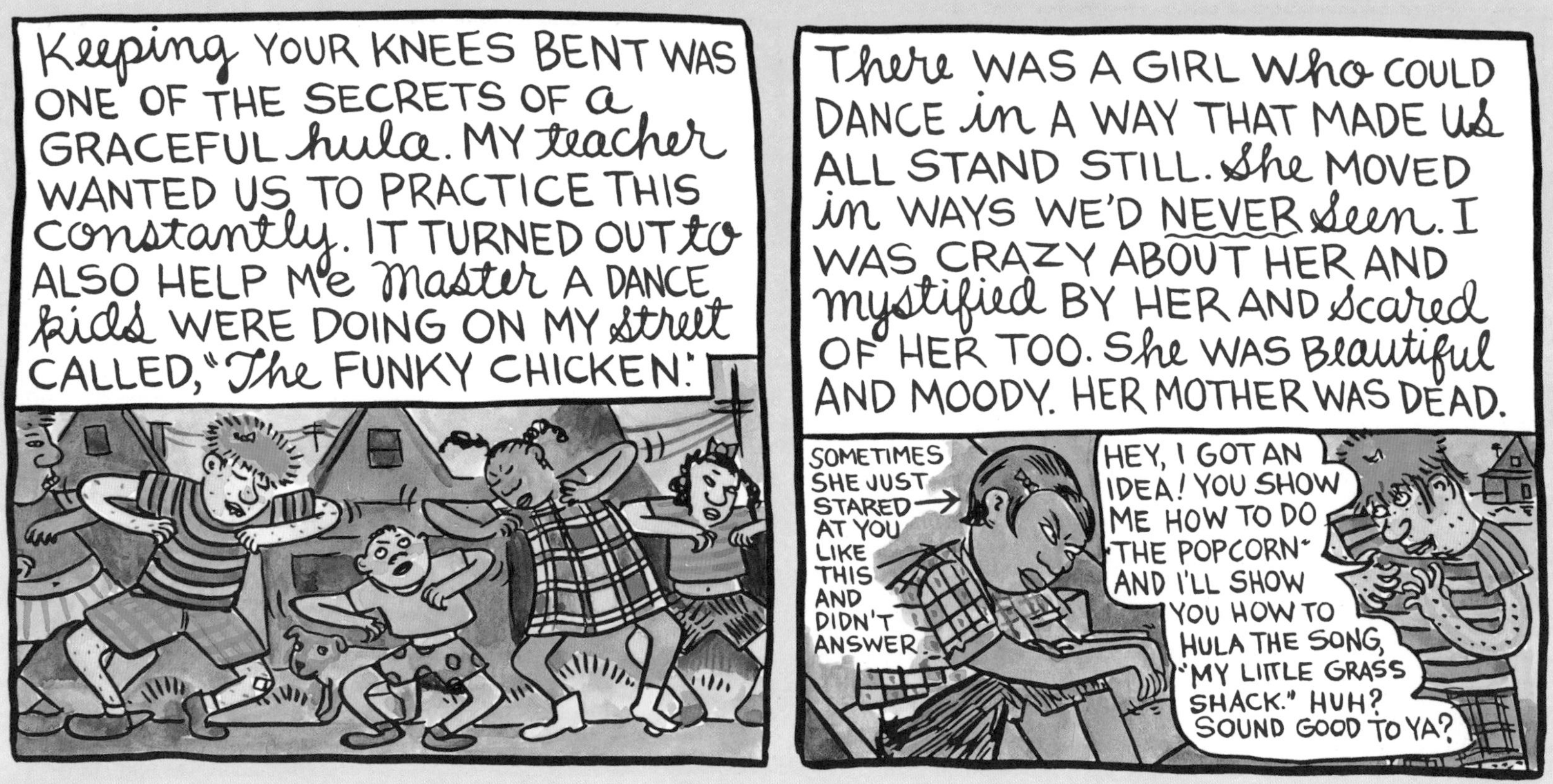
Keeping YOUR KNEES BENT WAS ONE OF THE SECRETS OF a GRACEFUL hula. MY teacher WANTED US TO PRACTICE THIS constantly. IT TURNED OUT to ALSO HELP Me master A DANCE kids WERE DOING ON MY street CALLED, "The FUNKY CHICKEN."
There WAS A GIRL Who COULD DANCE in A WAY THAT MADE us ALL STAND STILL. She MOVED in WAYS WE'D NEVER Seen. I WAS CRAZY ABOUT HER AND mystified BY HER AND Scared OF HER TOO. She WAS Beautiful AND MOODY. HER MOTHER WAS DEAD.
SOMETIMES SHE JUST STARED AT YOU LIKE THIS AND DIDN'T ANSWER
HEY, I GOT AN IDEA! YOU SHOW ME HOW TO DO "THE POPCORN" AND I'LL SHOW YOU HOW TO HULA THE SONG, "MY LITTLE GRASS SHACK." HUH? SOUND GOOD TO YA?

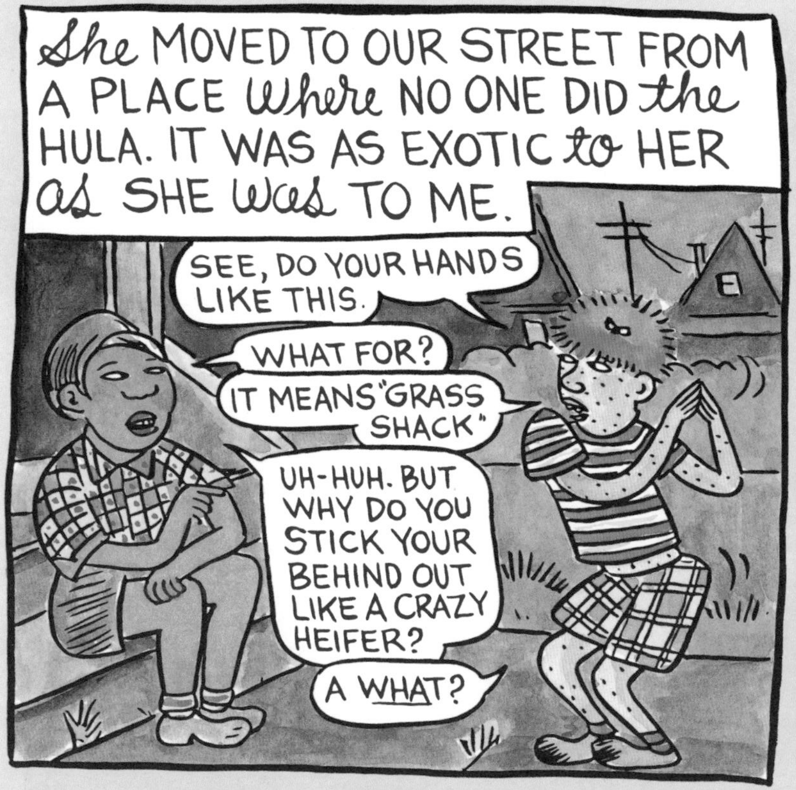
She MOVED TO OUR STREET FROM A PLACE Where NO ONE DID the HULA. IT WAS AS EXOTIC to HER as SHE was TO ME.
SEE, DO YOUR HANDS LIKE THIS.
WHAT FOR?
IT MEANS "GRASS SHACK"
UH-HUH. BUT WHY DO YOU STICK YOUR BEHIND OUT LIKE A CRAZY HEIFER?
A WHAT?

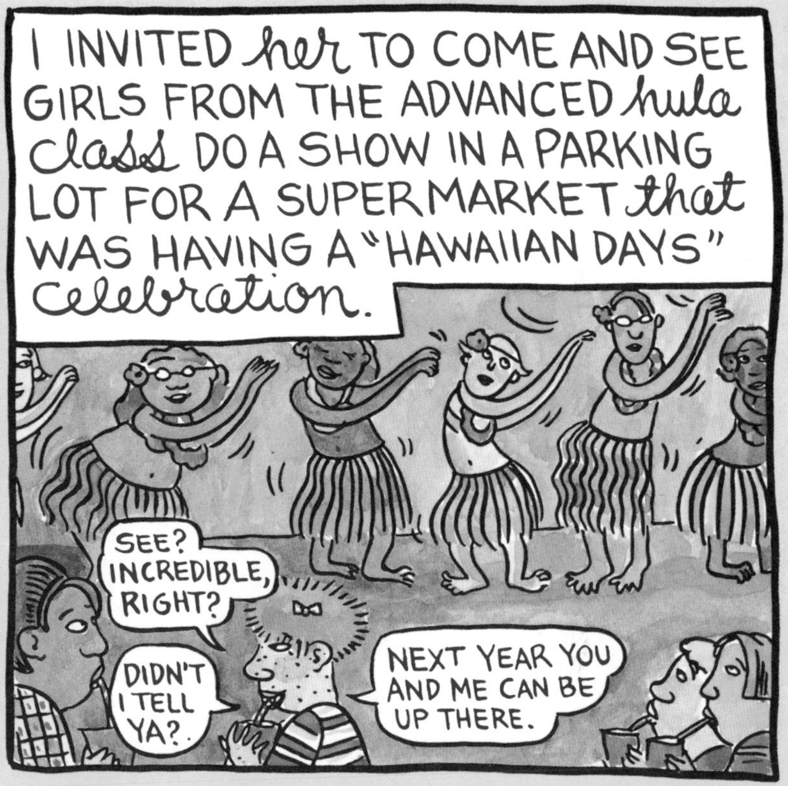
I INVITED her TO COME AND SEE GIRLS FROM THE ADVANCED hula class DO A SHOW IN A PARKING LOT FOR A SUPERMARKET that WAS HAVING A "HAWAIIAN DAYS" Celebration.
SEE? INCREDIBLE, RIGHT?
DIDN'T I TELL YA?
NEXT YEAR YOU AND ME CAN BE UP THERE.

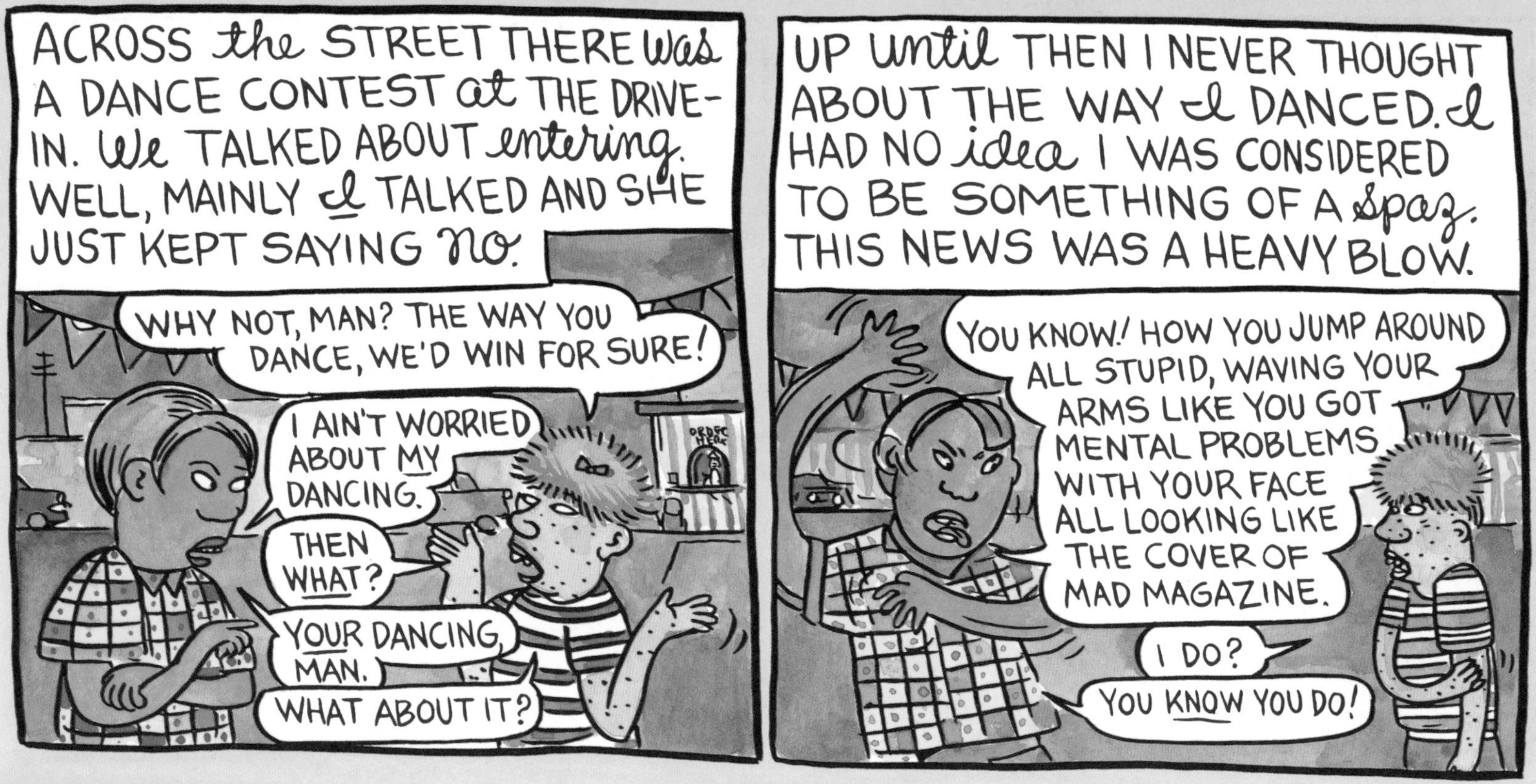
ACROSS the STREET THERE was A DANCE CONTEST at THE DRIVE-IN. We TALKED ABOUT entering. WELL, MAINLY I TALKED AND SHE JUST KEPT SAYING no.
WHY NOT, MAN? THE WAY YOU DANCE, WE'D WIN FOR SURE!
I AIN'T WORRIED ABOUT MY DANCING.
THEN WHAT?
YOUR DANCING, MAN.
WHAT ABOUT IT?
UP until THEN I NEVER THOUGHT ABOUT THE WAY I DANCED. I HAD NO idea I WAS CONSIDERED TO BE SOMETHING OF A Spaz. THIS NEWS WAS A HEAVY BLOW.
YOU KNOW! HOW YOU JUMP AROUND ALL STUPID, WAVING YOUR ARMS LIKE YOU GOT MENTAL PROBLEMS WITH YOUR FACE ALL LOOKING LIKE THE COVER OF MAD MAGAZINE.
I DO?
YOU KNOW YOU DO!

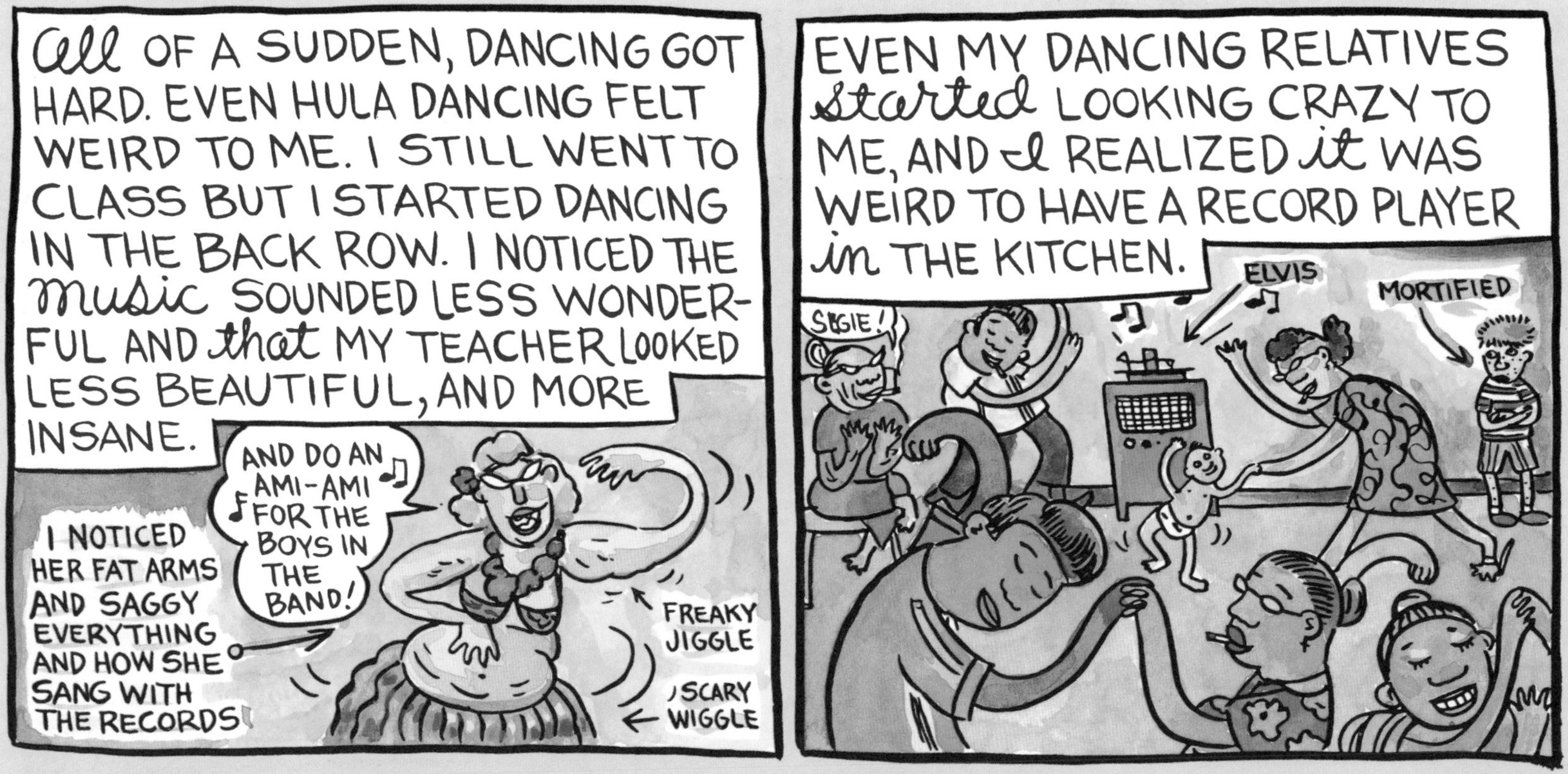
ALL OF A SUDDEN, DANCING GOT HARD. EVEN HULA DANCING FELT WEIRD TO ME. I STILL WENT TO CLASS BUT I STARTED DANCING IN THE BACK ROW. I NOTICED THE MUSIC SOUNDED LESS WONDERFUL AND THAT MY TEACHER LOOKED LESS BEAUTIFUL, AND MORE INSANE.
AND DO AN AMI-AMI FOR THE BOYS IN THE BAND!
I NOTICED HER FAT ARMS AND SAGGY EVERYTHING AND HOW SHE SANG WITH THE RECORDS!
FREAKY JIGGLE
SCARY WIGGLE
EVEN MY DANCING RELATIVES STARTED LOOKING CRAZY TO ME, AND I REALIZED IT WAS WEIRD TO HAVE A RECORD PLAYER IN THE KITCHEN.
SEGIE!
ELVIS
MORTIFIED

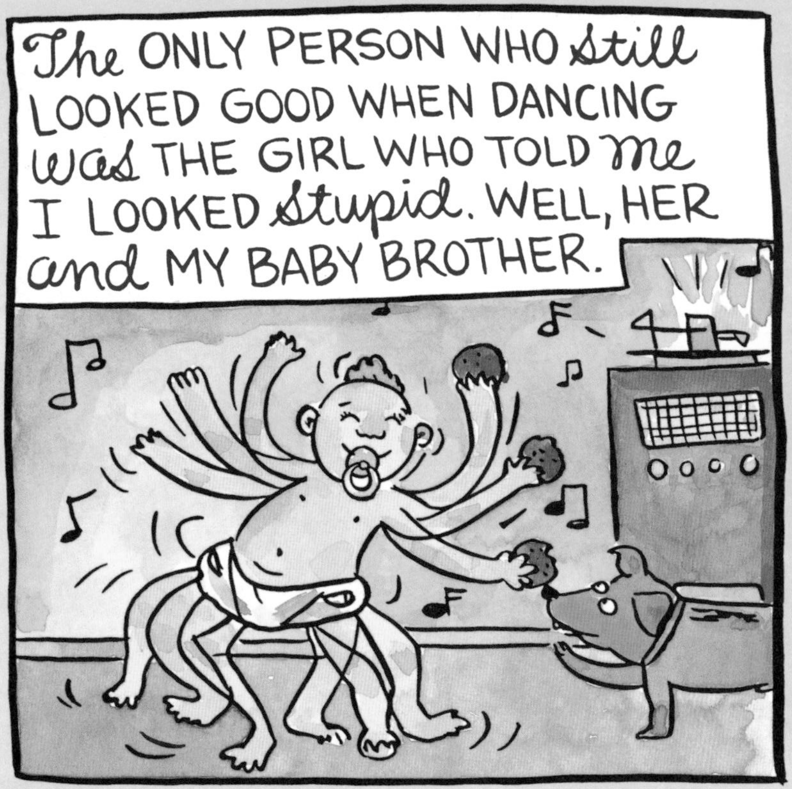
The ONLY PERSON WHO still LOOKED GOOD WHEN DANCING was THE GIRL WHO TOLD me I LOOKED stupid. WELL, HER and MY BABY BROTHER.

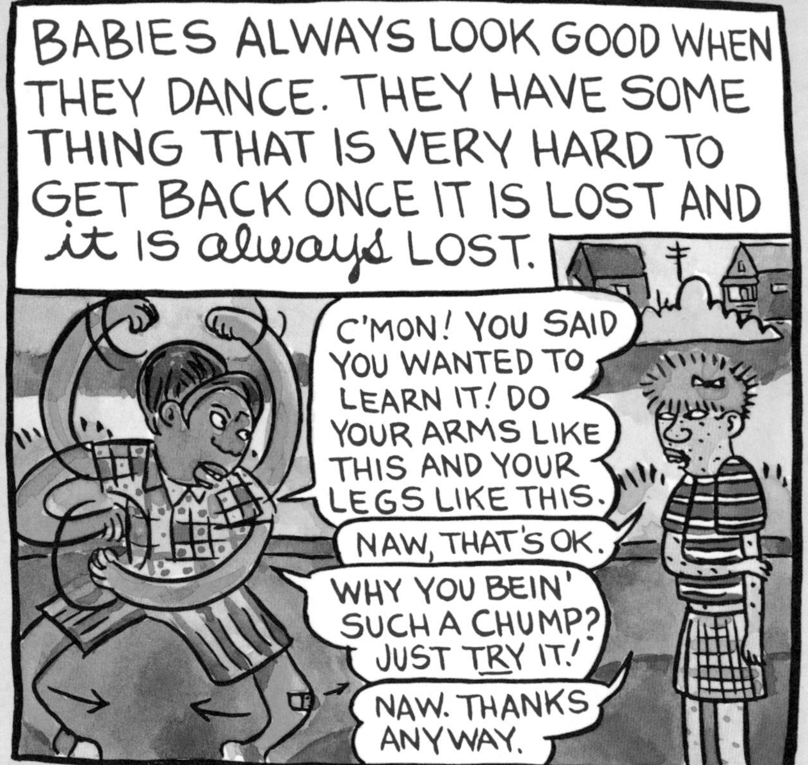
BABIES ALWAYS LOOK GOOD WHEN THEY DANCE. THEY HAVE SOME THING THAT IS VERY HARD TO GET BACK ONCE IT IS LOST AND it IS always LOST.
C'MON! YOU SAID YOU WANTED TO LEARN IT! DO YOUR ARMS LIKE THIS AND YOUR LEGS LIKE THIS.
NAW, THAT'S OK.
WHY YOU BEIN' SUCH A CHUMP? JUST TRY IT!
NAW. THANKS ANYWAY.

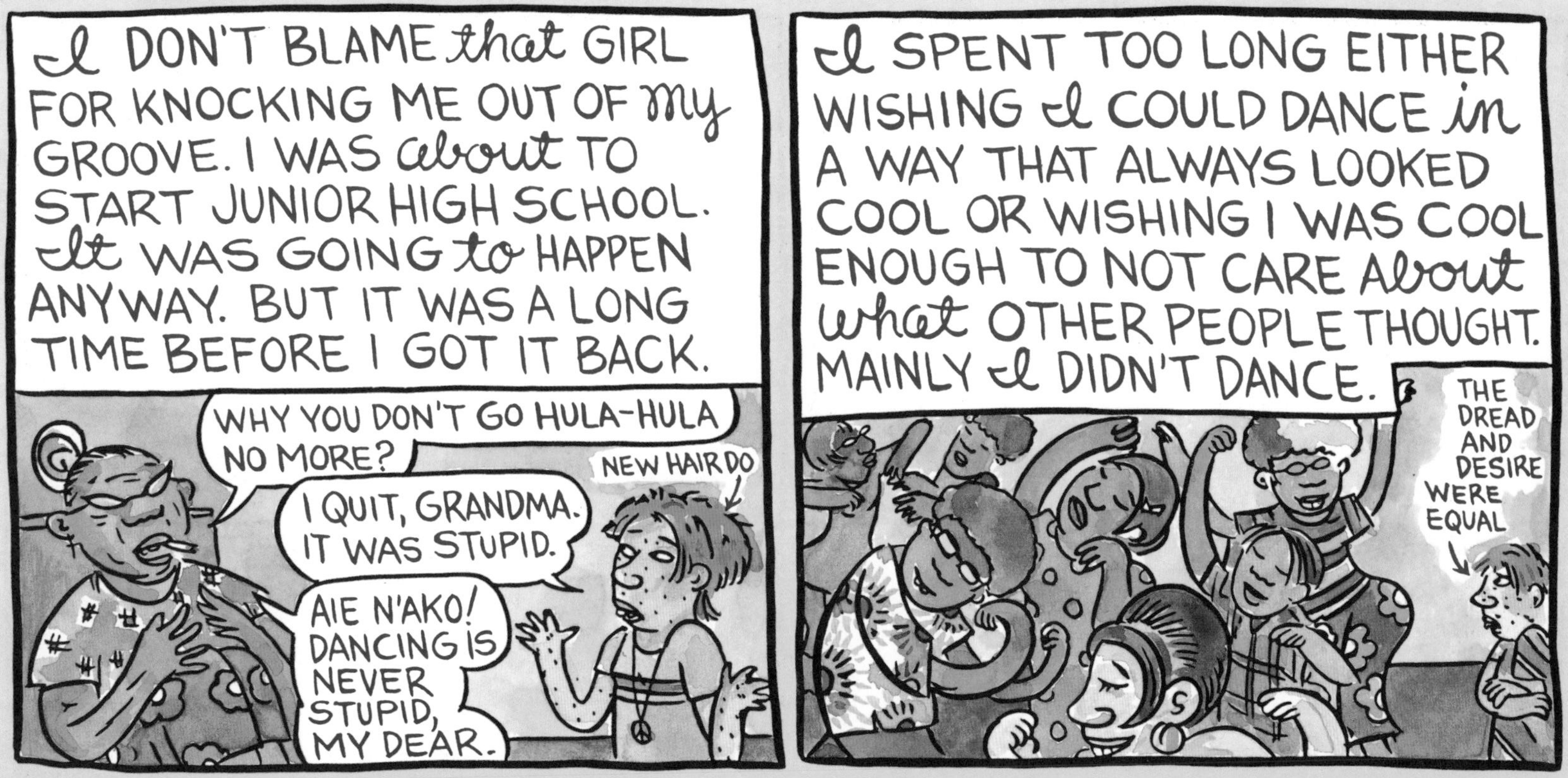
I DON'T BLAME that GIRL FOR KNOCKING ME OUT OF my GROOVE. I WAS about TO START JUNIOR HIGH SCHOOL. It WAS GOING to HAPPEN ANYWAY. BUT IT WAS A LONG TIME BEFORE I GOT IT BACK.
WHY YOU DON'T GO HULA-HULA NO MORE?
I QUIT, GRANDMA. IT WAS STUPID.
NEW HAIRDO
AIE N'AKO! DANCING IS NEVER STUPID, MY DEAR.
I SPENT TOO LONG EITHER WISHING I COULD DANCE in A WAY THAT ALWAYS LOOKED COOL OR WISHING I WAS COOL ENOUGH TO NOT CARE About what OTHER PEOPLE THOUGHT. MAINLY I DIDN'T DANCE.
THE DREAD AND DESIRE WERE EQUAL

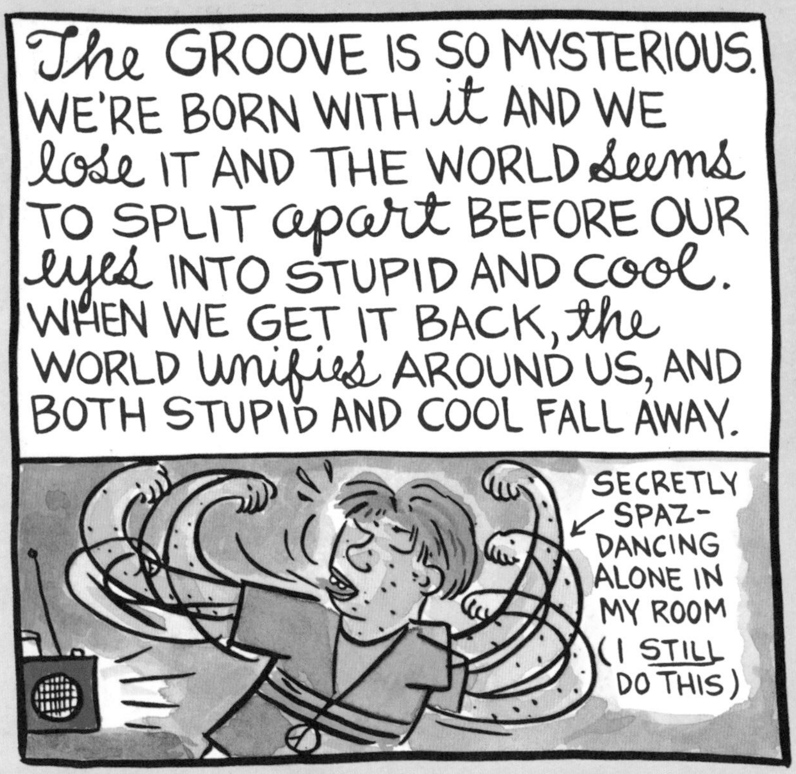
The GROOVE IS SO MYSTERIOUS. WE'RE BORN WITH it AND WE lose IT AND THE WORLD seems TO SPLIT apart BEFORE OUR eyes INTO STUPID AND cool. WHEN WE GET IT BACK, the WORLD unifies AROUND US, AND BOTH STUPID AND COOL FALL AWAY.
SECRETLY SPAZ-DANCING ALONE IN MY ROOM (I STILL DO THIS)

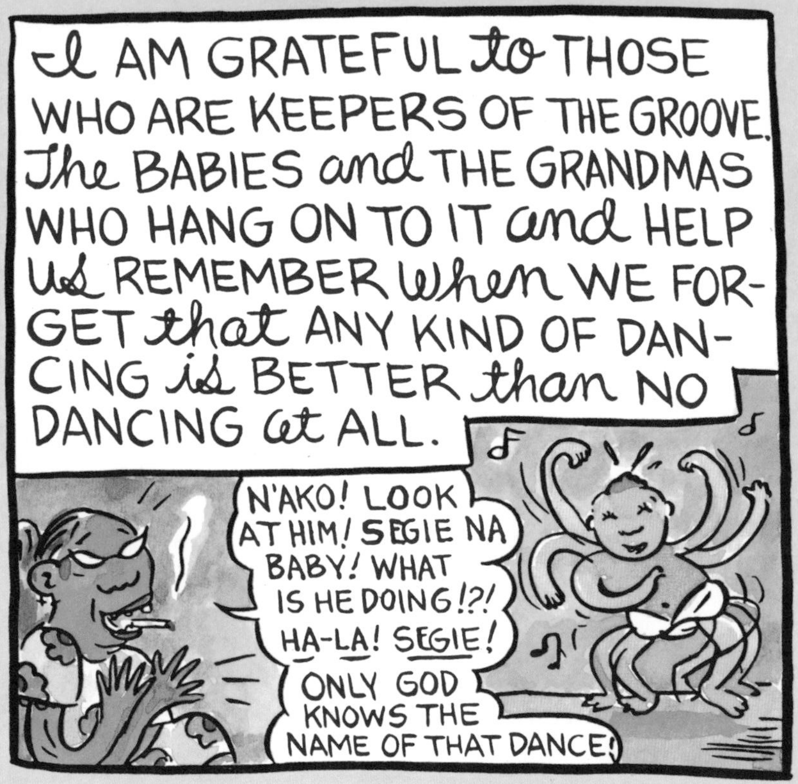
I AM GRATEFUL to THOSE WHO ARE KEEPERS OF THE GROOVE. The BABIES and THE GRANDMAS WHO HANG ON TO IT and HELP us REMEMBER when WE FORGET that ANY KIND OF DANCING is BETTER than NO DANCING at ALL.
N'AKO! LOOK AT HIM! SEGIE NA BABY! WHAT IS HE DOING!?! HA-LA! SEGIE! ONLY GOD KNOWS THE NAME OF THAT DANCE!

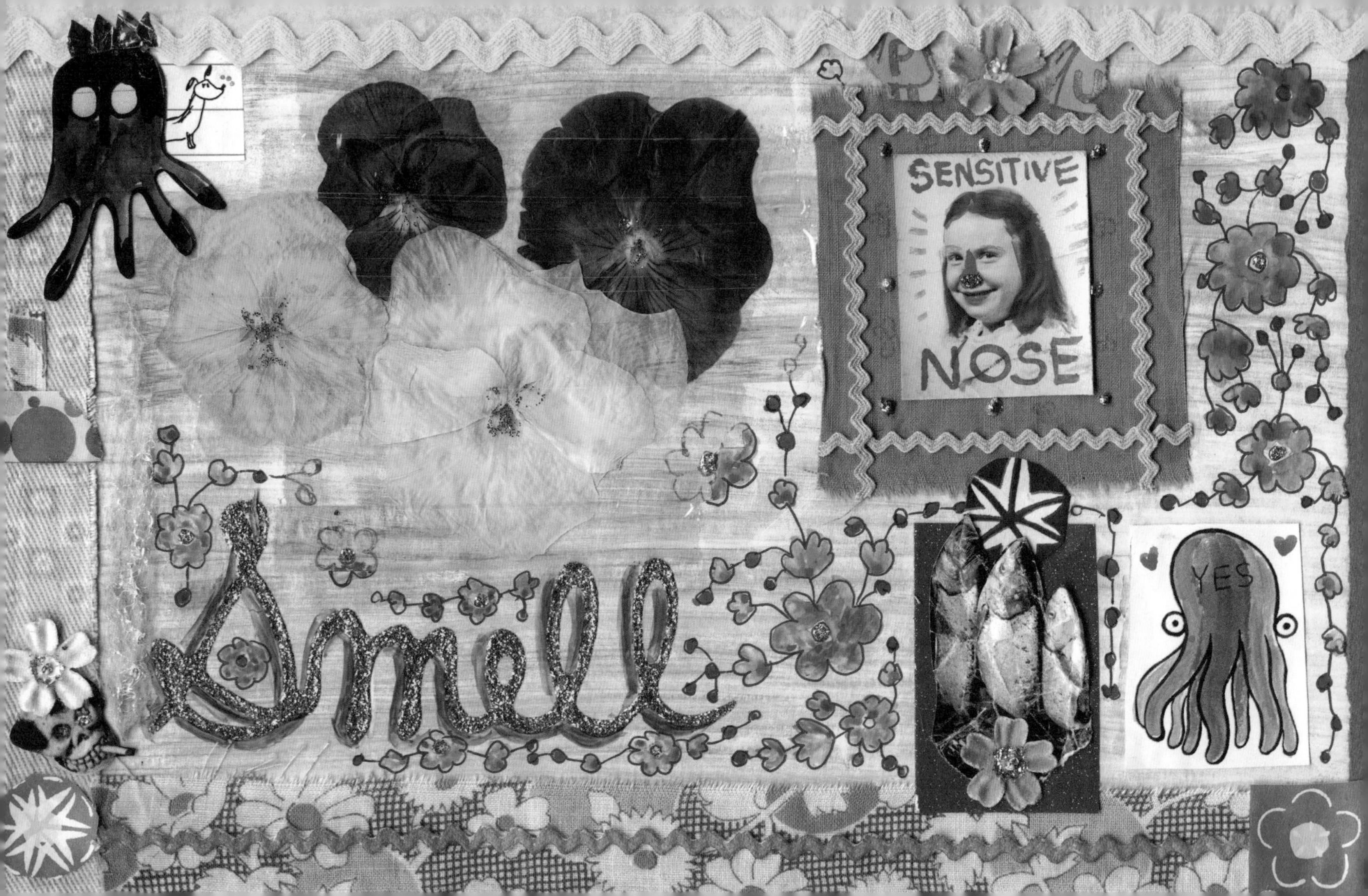
SENSITIVE
NOSE
Smell
YES

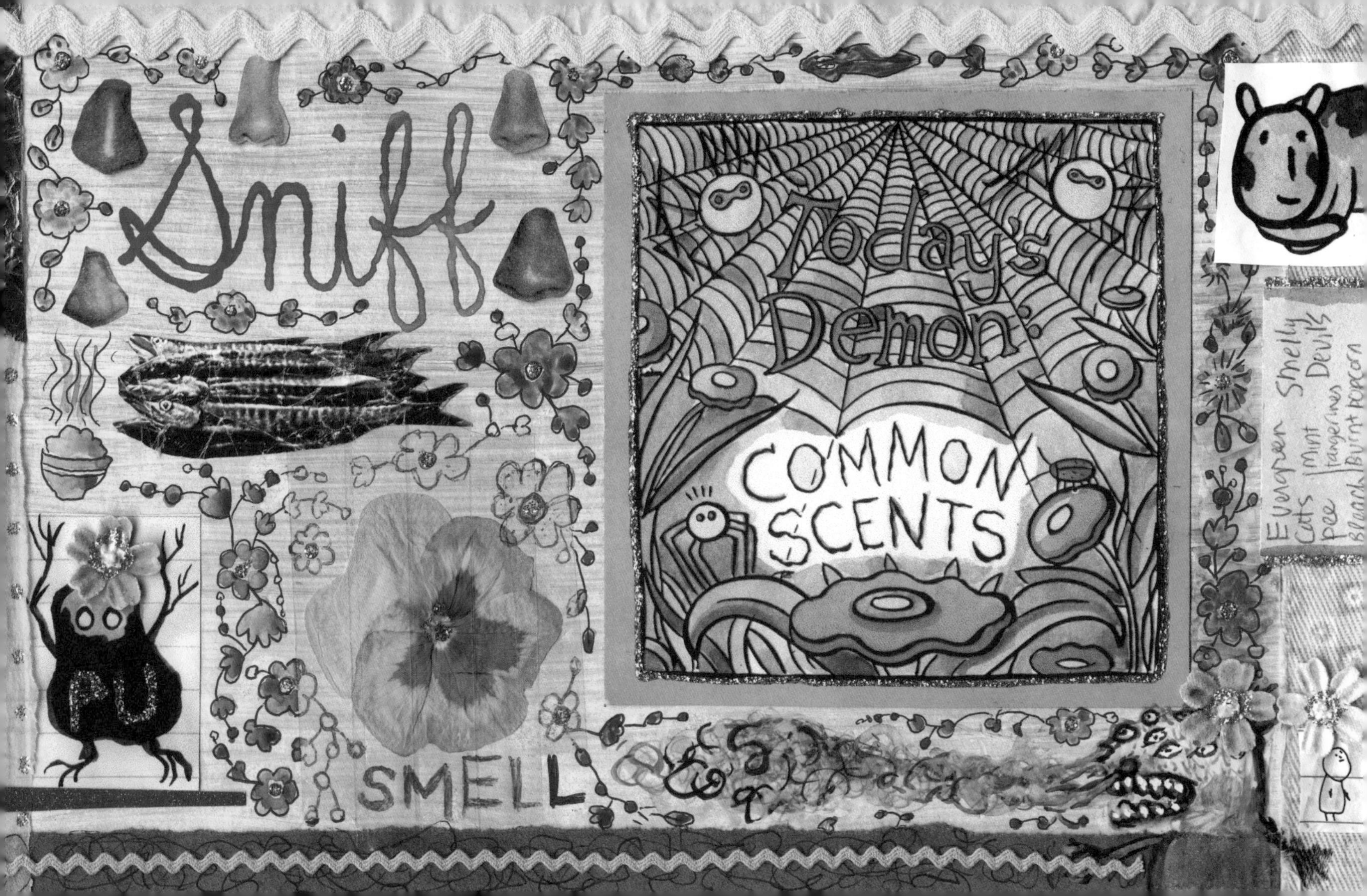
Sniff
Today's Demon:
COMMON SCENTS
Evergreen
Cats pee
Bleach
Smelly
Mint
tangerines
Burnt popcorn
Devils
PU
SMELL

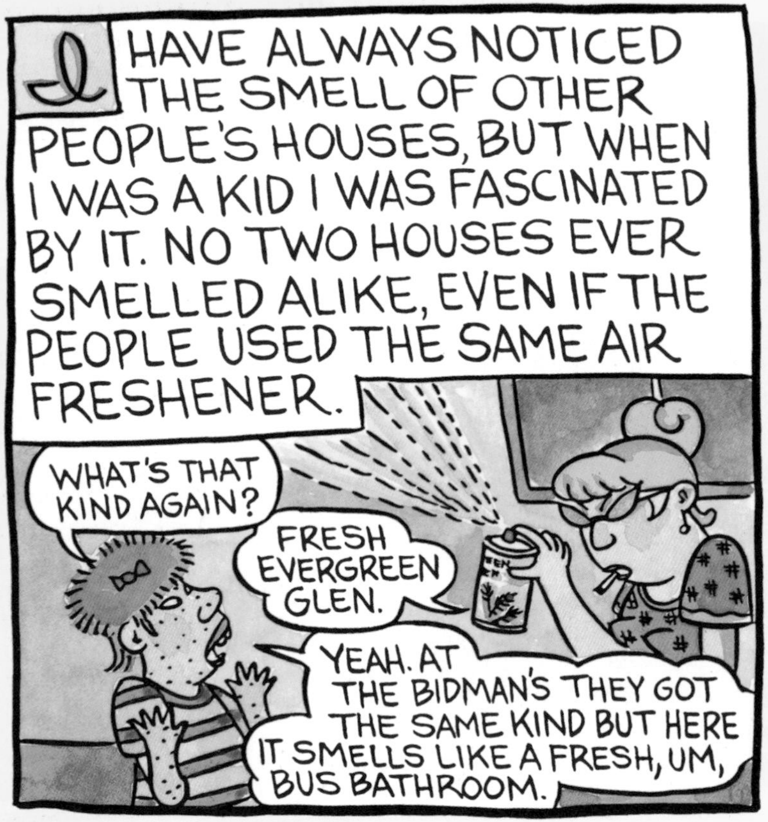
I HAVE ALWAYS NOTICED THE SMELL OF OTHER PEOPLE'S HOUSES, BUT WHEN I WAS A KID I WAS FASCINATED BY IT. NO TWO HOUSES EVER SMELLED ALIKE, EVEN IF THE PEOPLE USED THE SAME AIR FRESHENER.
WHAT'S THAT KIND AGAIN?
FRESH EVERGREEN GLEN.
YEAH. AT THE BIDMAN'S THEY GOT THE SAME KIND BUT HERE IT SMELLS LIKE A FRESH, UM, BUS BATHROOM.

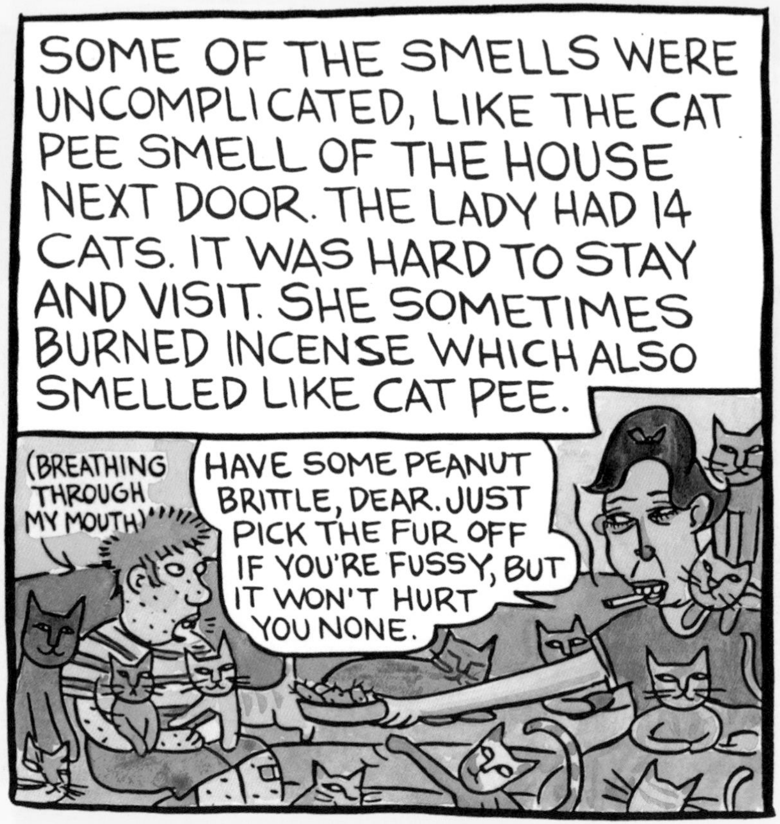
SOME OF THE SMELLS WERE UNCOMPLICATED, LIKE THE CAT PEE SMELL OF THE HOUSE NEXT DOOR. THE LADY HAD 14 CATS. IT WAS HARD TO STAY AND VISIT. SHE SOMETIMES BURNED INCENSE WHICH ALSO SMELLED LIKE CAT PEE.
(BREATHING THROUGH MY MOUTH)
HAVE SOME PEANUT BRITTLE, DEAR. JUST PICK THE FUR OFF IF YOU'RE FUSSY, BUT IT WON'T HURT YOU NONE.

BUT THERE WERE BAD MYSTERIES TOO, LIKE THE MYSTERY OF THE BLEACH PEOPLE WHOSE HOUSE GAVE OFF FUMES YOU COULD SMELL FROM THE STREET. WE KEPT WAITING FOR THAT HOUSE TO EXPLODE. THE BUGS DIDN'T EVEN GO IN THEIR YARD.

ALSO GIVING OFF BLEACH FUMES

HEYA, JANINA.

HEYA.

'N I ASK YOU A PERSONAL THING?

POSSIBLY.

HOW COME YOUR HOUSE SMELLS LIKE THAT?

SMELLS LIKE WHAT?

SOME SMELLS WERE MYSTERIOUSLY WONDERFUL LIKE AT THE PALINKI'S WHERE IT WAS A COMBINATION OF MINT, TANGERINES, AND LIBRARY BOOKS. BUT HOW? I NEVER SAW ANY OF THOSE THINGS THERE.

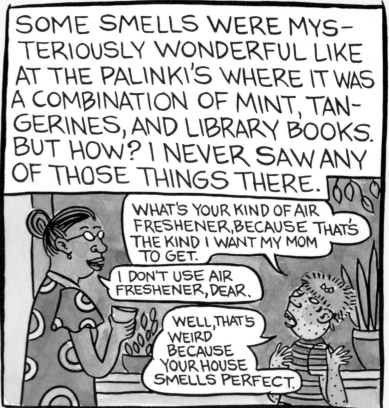

WHAT'S YOUR KIND OF AIR FRESHENER, BECAUSE THAT'S THE KIND I WANT MY MOM TO GET.

I DON'T USE AIR FRESHENER, DEAR.

WELL, THAT'S WEIRD BECAUSE YOUR HOUSE SMELLS PERFECT.

53

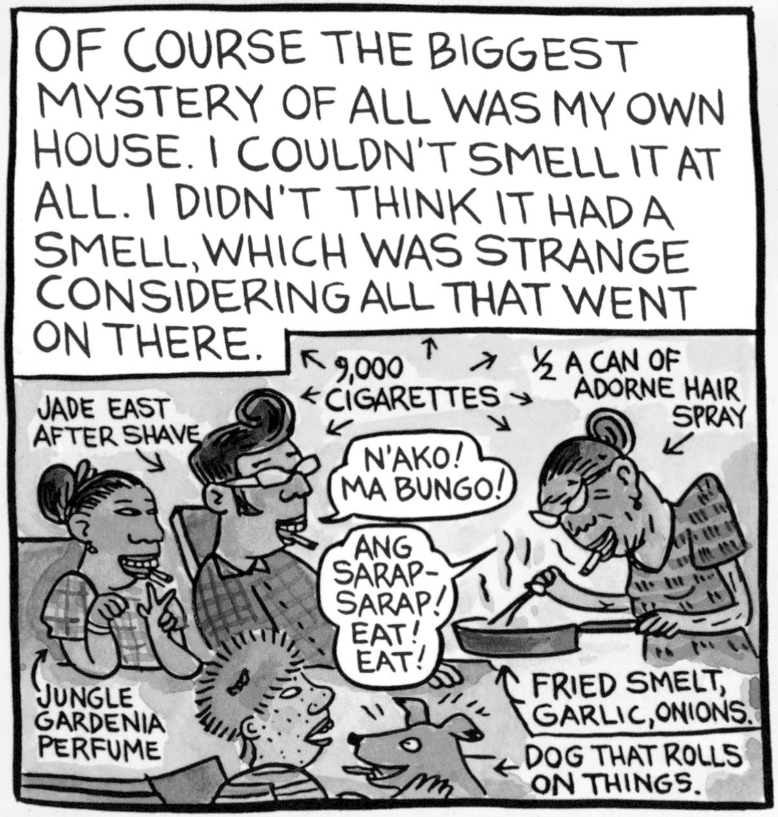
OF COURSE THE BIGGEST MYSTERY OF ALL WAS MY OWN HOUSE. I COULDN'T SMELL IT AT ALL. I DIDN'T THINK IT HAD A SMELL, WHICH WAS STRANGE CONSIDERING ALL THAT WENT ON THERE.
9,000 CIGARETTES
1/2 A CAN OF ADORNE HAIR SPRAY
JADE EAST AFTER SHAVE
N'AKO! MA BUNGO!
ANG SARAP-SARAP! EAT! EAT!
JUNGLE GARDENIA PERFUME
FRIED SMELT, GARLIC, ONIONS.
DOG THAT ROLLS ON THINGS.

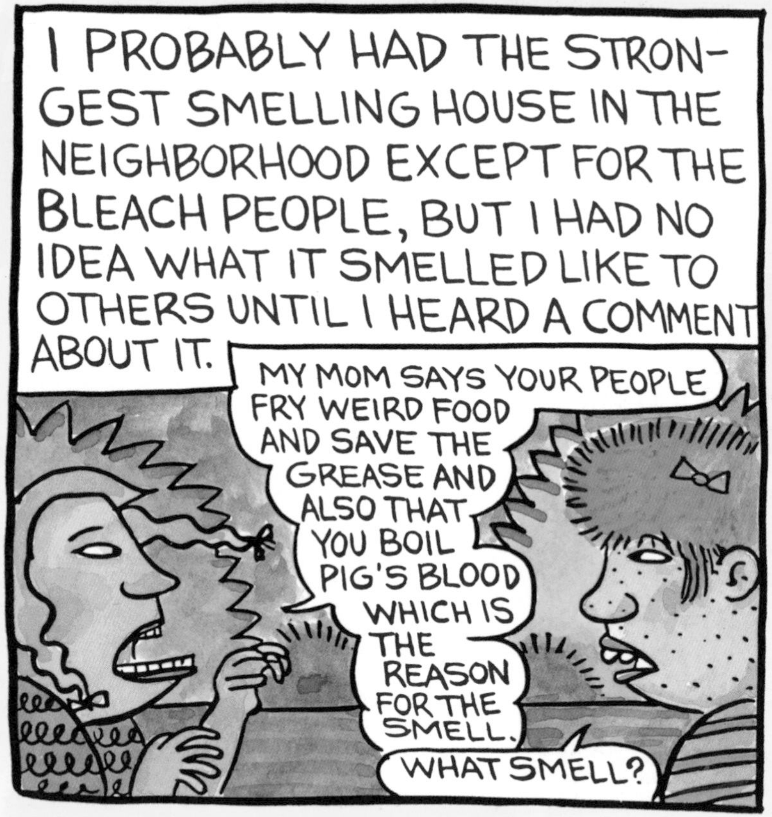
I PROBABLY HAD THE STRONGEST SMELLING HOUSE IN THE NEIGHBORHOOD EXCEPT FOR THE BLEACH PEOPLE, BUT I HAD NO IDEA WHAT IT SMELLED LIKE TO OTHERS UNTIL I HEARD A COMMENT ABOUT IT.
MY MOM SAYS YOUR PEOPLE FRY WEIRD FOOD AND SAVE THE GREASE AND ALSO THAT YOU BOIL PIG'S BLOOD WHICH IS THE REASON FOR THE SMELL.
WHAT SMELL?

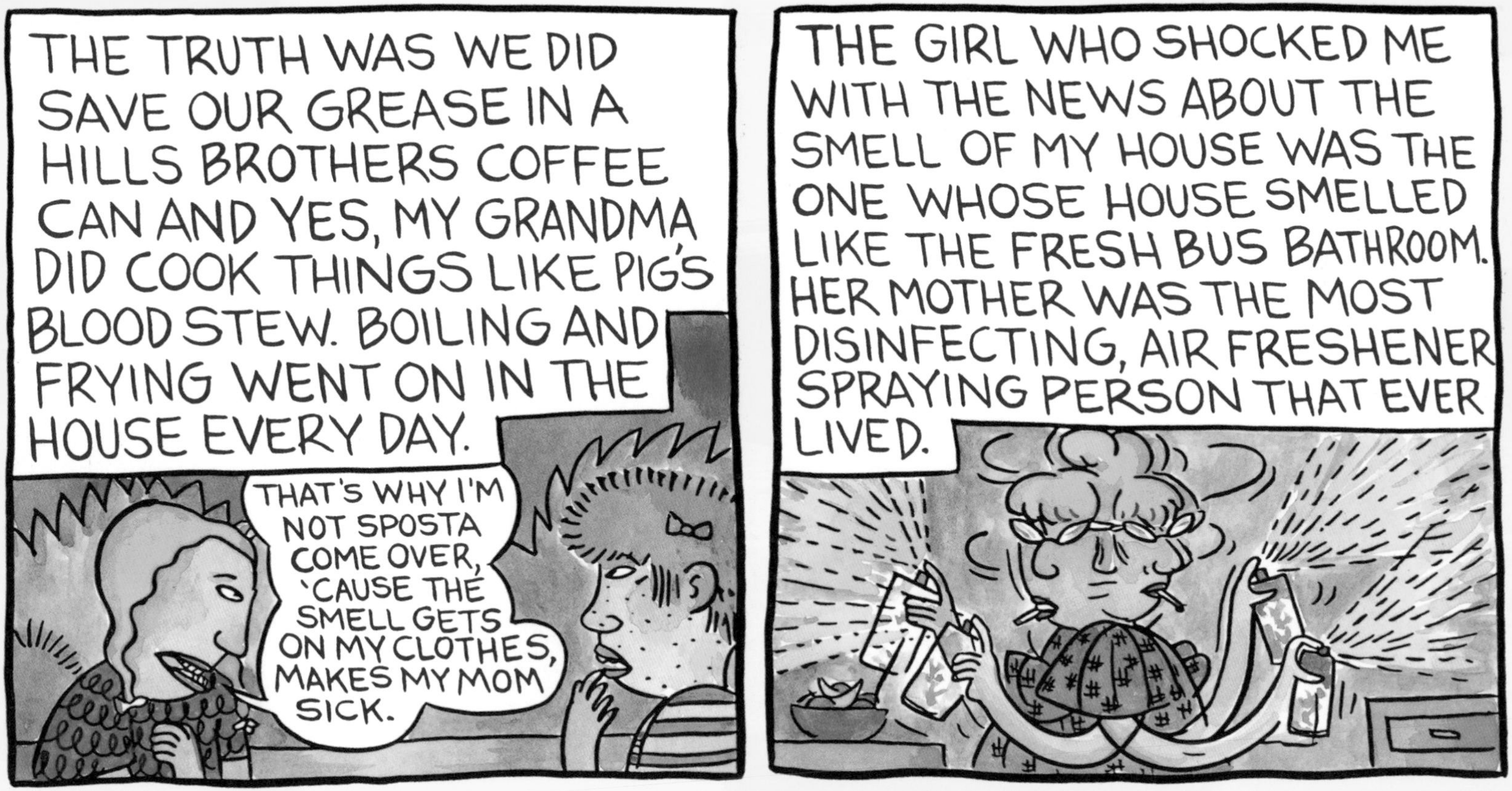

THE TRUTH WAS WE DID SAVE OUR GREASE IN A HILLS BROTHERS COFFEE CAN AND YES, MY GRANDMA DID COOK THINGS LIKE PIG'S BLOOD STEW. BOILING AND FRYING WENT ON IN THE HOUSE EVERY DAY.
THAT'S WHY I'M NOT SPOSTA COME OVER, 'CAUSE THE SMELL GETS ON MY CLOTHES, MAKES MY MOM SICK.
THE GIRL WHO SHOCKED ME WITH THE NEWS ABOUT THE SMELL OF MY HOUSE WAS THE ONE WHOSE HOUSE SMELLED LIKE THE FRESH BUS BATHROOM. HER MOTHER WAS THE MOST DISINFECTING, AIR FRESHENER SPRAYING PERSON THAT EVER LIVED.

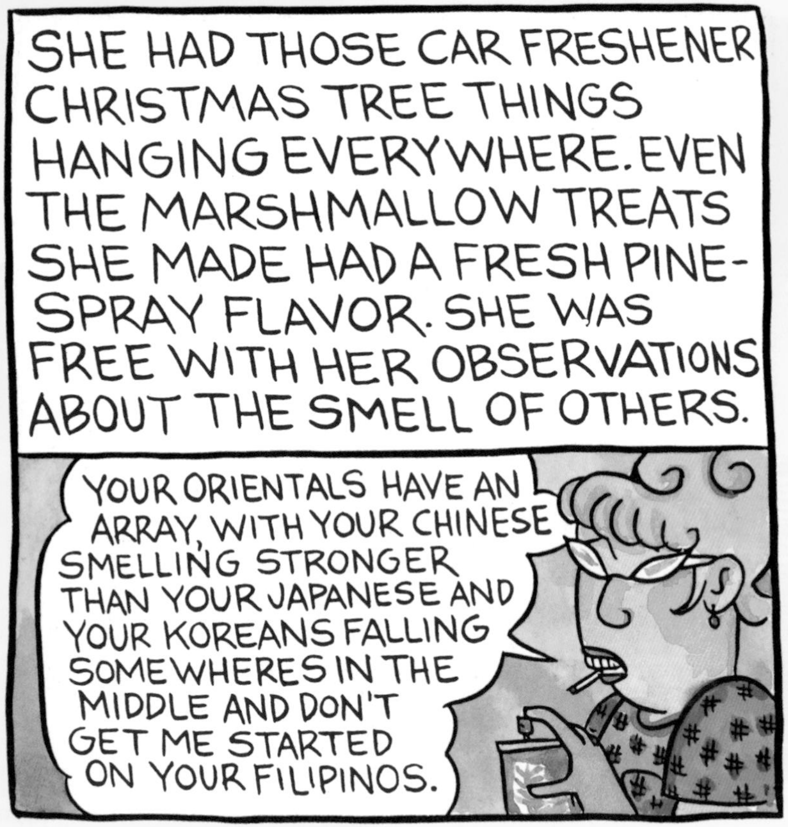
SHE HAD THOSE CAR FRESHENER CHRISTMAS TREE THINGS HANGING EVERYWHERE. EVEN THE MARSHMALLOW TREATS SHE MADE HAD A FRESH PINE-SPRAY FLAVOR. SHE WAS FREE WITH HER OBSERVATIONS ABOUT THE SMELL OF OTHERS.
YOUR ORIENTALS HAVE AN ARRAY, WITH YOUR CHINESE SMELLING STRONGER THAN YOUR JAPANESE AND YOUR KOREANS FALLING SOMEWHERES IN THE MIDDLE AND DON'T GET ME STARTED ON YOUR FILIPINOS.

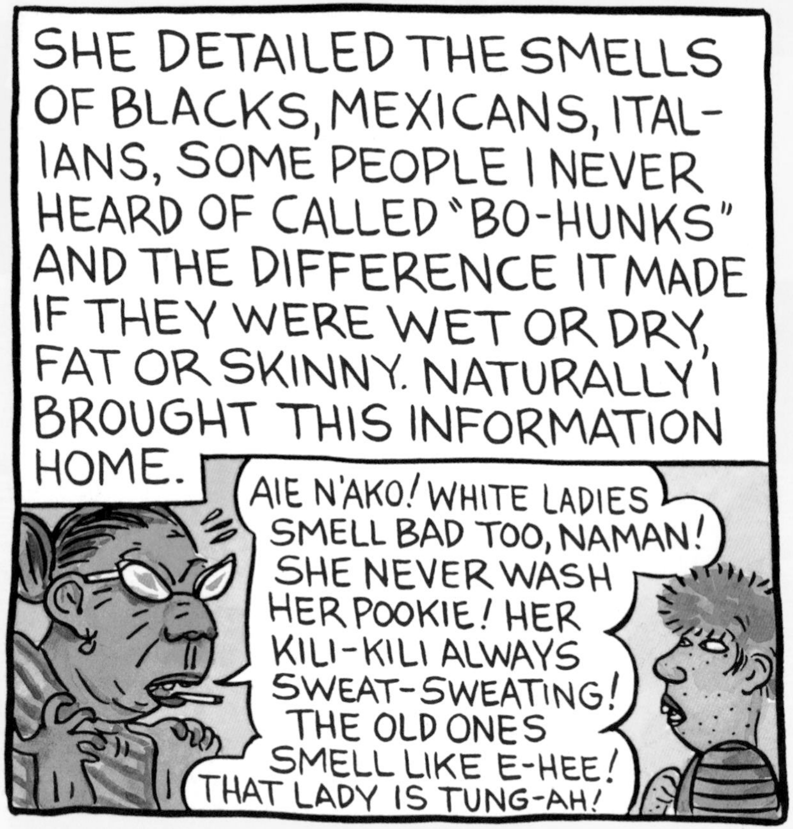
SHE DETAILED THE SMELLS OF BLACKS, MEXICANS, ITALIANS, SOME PEOPLE I NEVER HEARD OF CALLED "BO-HUNKS" AND THE DIFFERENCE IT MADE IF THEY WERE WET OR DRY, FAT OR SKINNY. NATURALLY I BROUGHT THIS INFORMATION HOME.
AIE N'AKO! WHITE LADIES SMELL BAD TOO, NAMAN! SHE NEVER WASH HER POOKIE! HER KILI-KILI ALWAYS SWEAT-SWEATING! THE OLD ONES SMELL LIKE E-HEE! THAT LADY IS TUNG-AH!

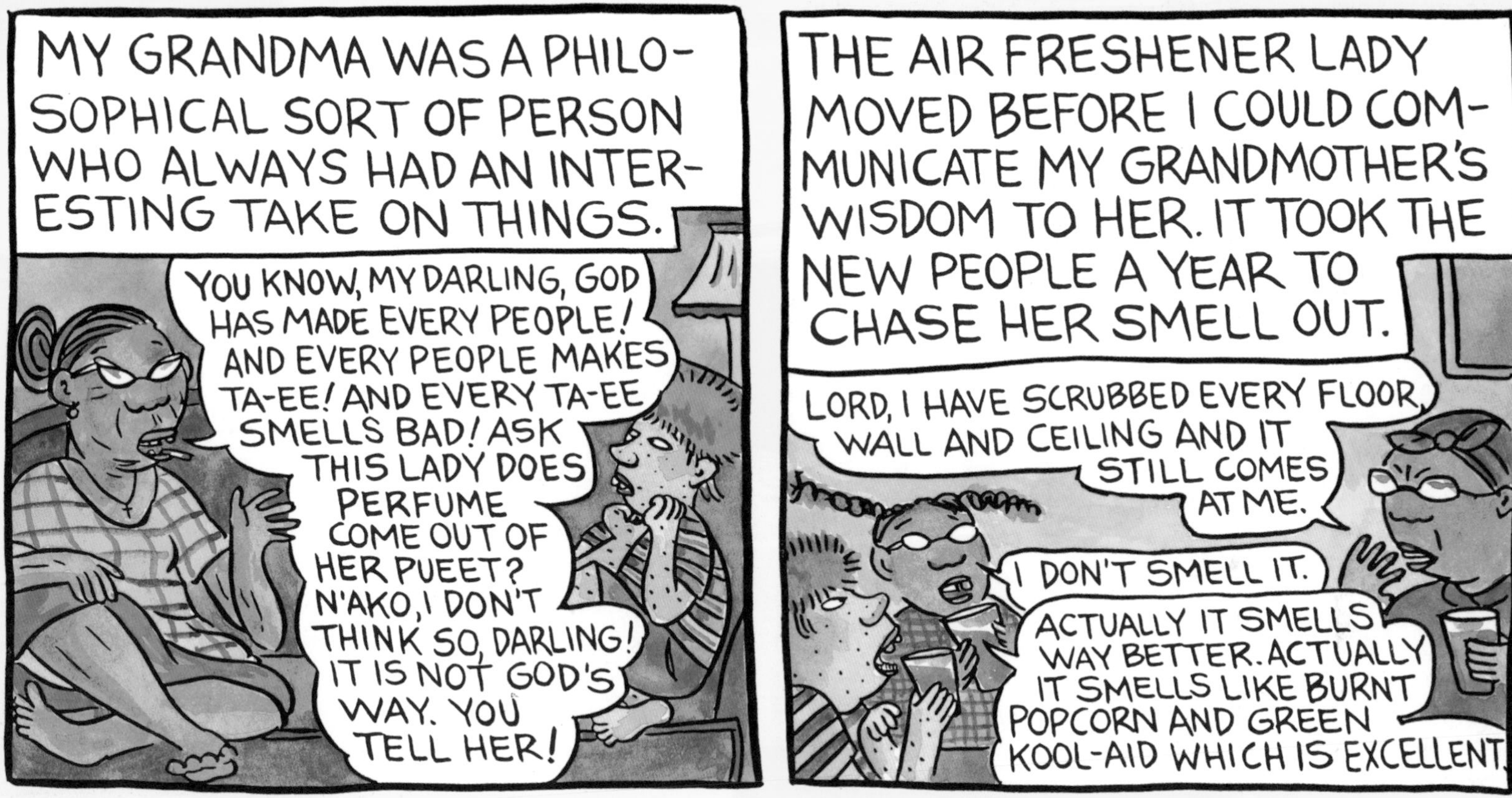
MY GRANDMA WAS A PHILOSOPHICAL SORT OF PERSON WHO ALWAYS HAD AN INTERESTING TAKE ON THINGS.
YOU KNOW, MY DARLING, GOD HAS MADE EVERY PEOPLE! AND EVERY PEOPLE MAKES TA-EE! AND EVERY TA-EE SMELLS BAD! ASK THIS LADY DOES PERFUME COME OUT OF HER PUEET? N'AKO, I DON'T THINK SO, DARLING! IT IS NOT GOD'S WAY. YOU TELL HER!
THE AIR FRESHENER LADY MOVED BEFORE I COULD COMMUNICATE MY GRANDMOTHER'S WISDOM TO HER. IT TOOK THE NEW PEOPLE A YEAR TO CHASE HER SMELL OUT.
LORD, I HAVE SCRUBBED EVERY FLOOR, WALL AND CEILING AND IT STILL COMES AT ME.
I DON'T SMELL IT.
ACTUALLY IT SMELLS WAY BETTER. ACTUALLY IT SMELLS LIKE BURNT POPCORN AND GREEN KOOL-AID WHICH IS EXCELLENT.

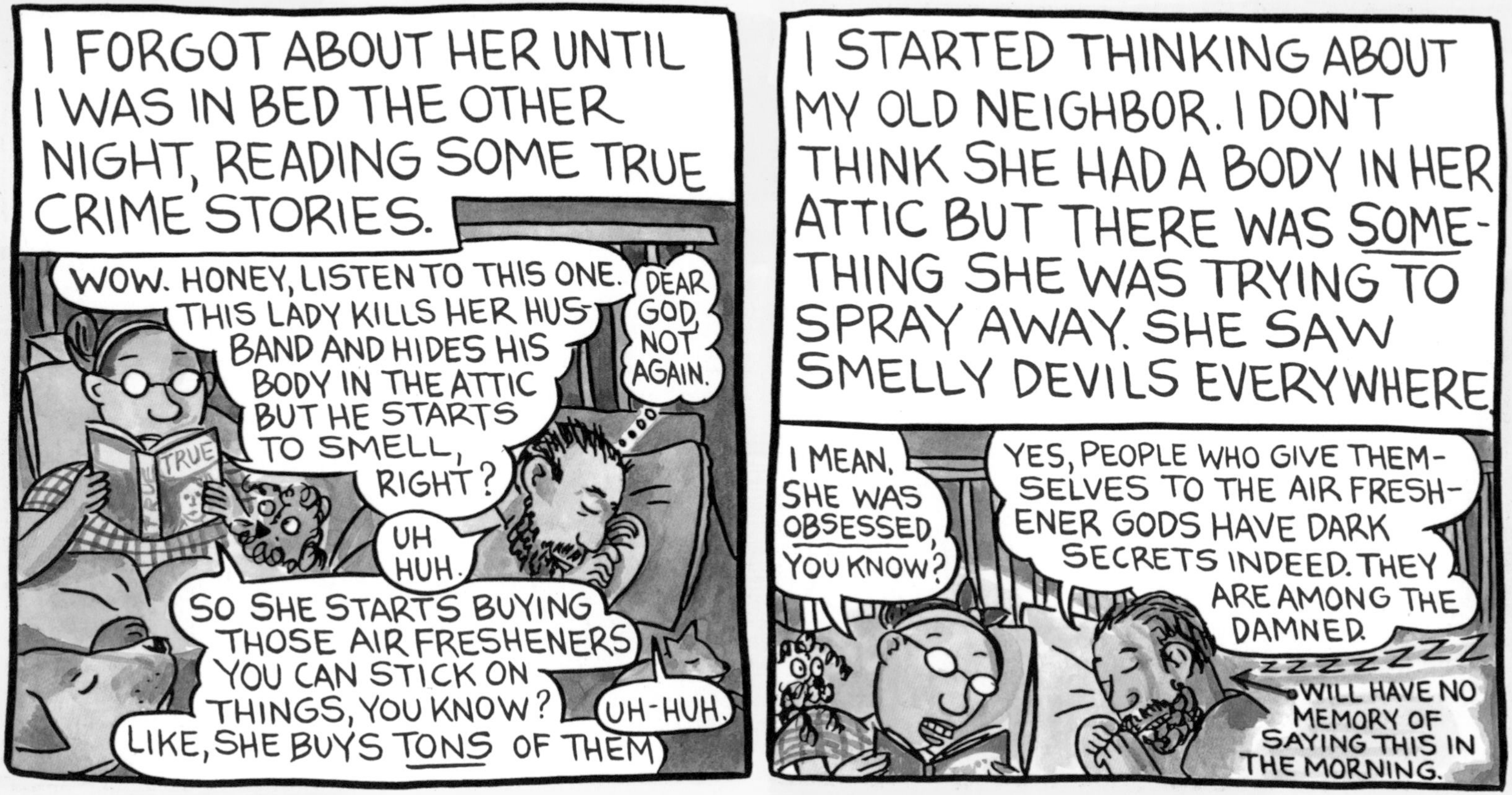
I FORGOT ABOUT HER UNTIL I WAS IN BED THE OTHER NIGHT, READING SOME TRUE CRIME STORIES.
WOW. HONEY, LISTEN TO THIS ONE. THIS LADY KILLS HER HUSBAND AND HIDES HIS BODY IN THE ATTIC BUT HE STARTS TO SMELL, RIGHT?
DEAR GOD, NOT AGAIN.
TRUE
UH HUH.
SO SHE STARTS BUYING THOSE AIR FRESHENERS YOU CAN STICK ON THINGS, YOU KNOW?
UH-HUH.
LIKE, SHE BUYS TONS OF THEM
I STARTED THINKING ABOUT MY OLD NEIGHBOR. I DON'T THINK SHE HAD A BODY IN HER ATTIC BUT THERE WAS SOMETHING SHE WAS TRYING TO SPRAY AWAY. SHE SAW SMELLY DEVILS EVERYWHERE.
I MEAN, SHE WAS OBSESSED, YOU KNOW?
YES, PEOPLE WHO GIVE THEMSELVES TO THE AIR FRESHENER GODS HAVE DARK SECRETS INDEED. THEY ARE AMONG THE DAMNED.
ZZZZZZZZ
WILL HAVE NO MEMORY OF SAYING THIS IN THE MORNING.

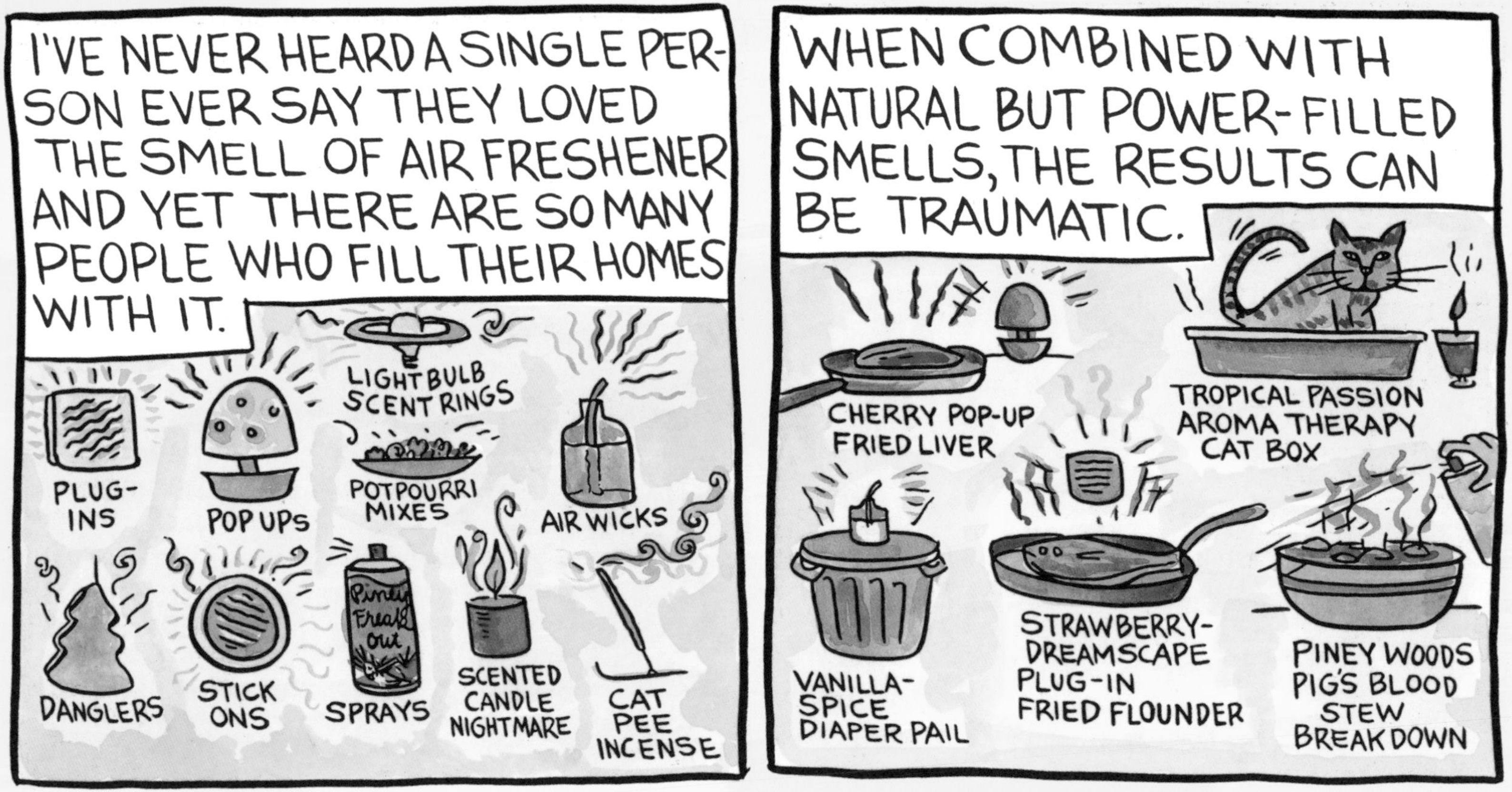
I'VE NEVER HEARD A SINGLE PERSON EVER SAY THEY LOVED THE SMELL OF AIR FRESHENER AND YET THERE ARE SO MANY PEOPLE WHO FILL THEIR HOMES WITH IT.
PLUG-INS
POP UPS
LIGHT BULB SCENT RINGS
POTPOURRI MIXES
AIR WICKS
DANGLERS
STICK ONS
Piney Freak out
SPRAYS
SCENTED CANDLE NIGHTMARE
CAT PEE INCENSE
WHEN COMBINED WITH NATURAL BUT POWER-FILLED SMELLS, THE RESULTS CAN BE TRAUMATIC.
CHERRY POP-UP FRIED LIVER
TROPICAL PASSION AROMA THERAPY CAT BOX
VANILLA-SPICE DIAPER PAIL
STRAWBERRY-DREAMSCAPE PLUG-IN FRIED FLOUNDER
PINEY WOODS PIG'S BLOOD STEW BREAKDOWN

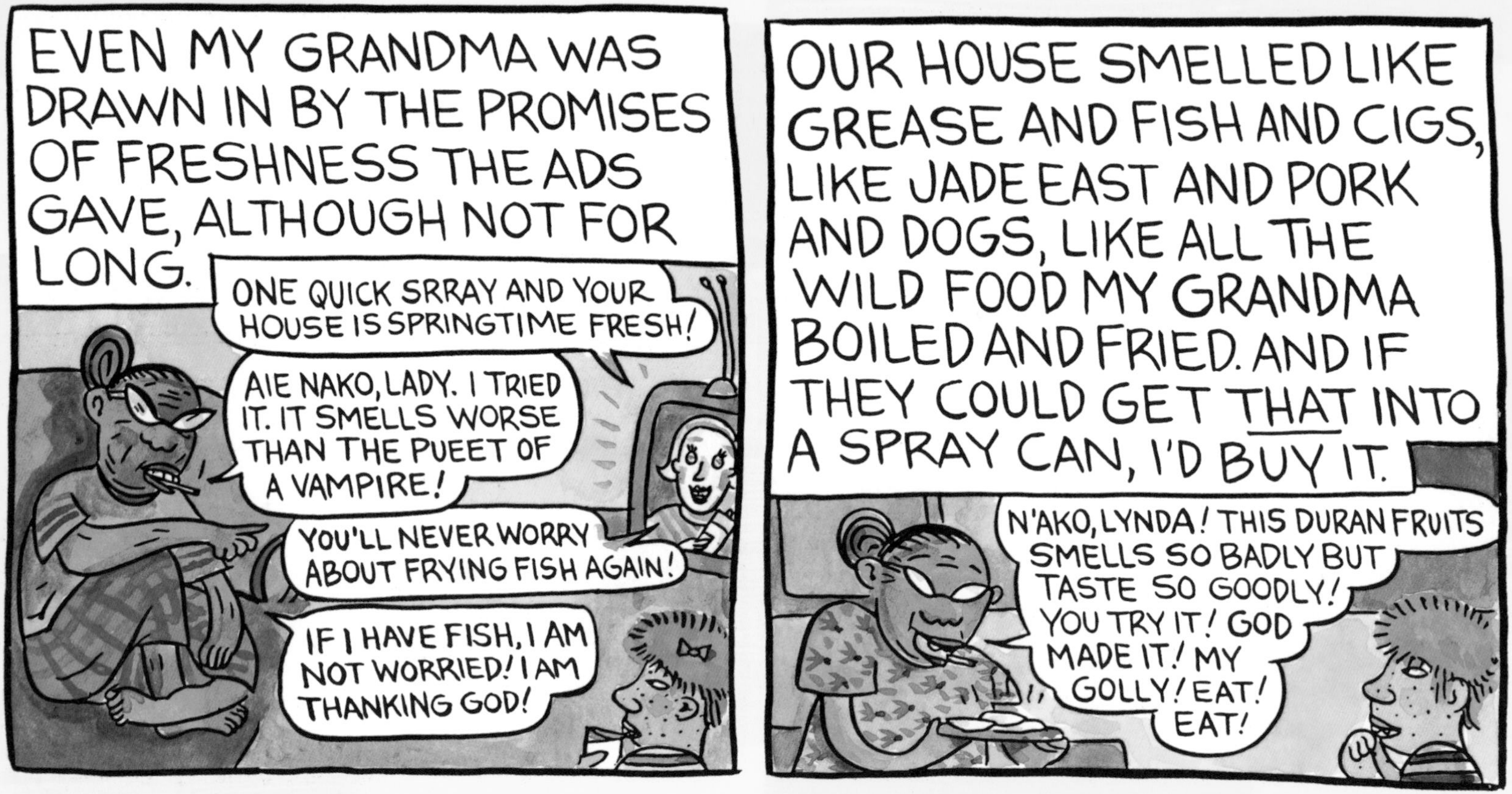
EVEN MY GRANDMA WAS DRAWN IN BY THE PROMISES OF FRESHNESS THE ADS GAVE, ALTHOUGH NOT FOR LONG.
ONE QUICK SRRAY AND YOUR HOUSE IS SPRINGTIME FRESH!
AIE NAKO, LADY. I TRIED IT. IT SMELLS WORSE THAN THE PUEET OF A VAMPIRE!
YOU'LL NEVER WORRY ABOUT FRYING FISH AGAIN!
IF I HAVE FISH, I AM NOT WORRIED! I AM THANKING GOD!
OUR HOUSE SMELLED LIKE GREASE AND FISH AND CIGS, LIKE JADE EAST AND PORK AND DOGS, LIKE ALL THE WILD FOOD MY GRANDMA BOILED AND FRIED. AND IF THEY COULD GET THAT INTO A SPRAY CAN, I'D BUY IT.
N'AKO, LYNDA! THIS DURAN FRUITS SMELLS SO BADLY BUT TASTE SO GOODLY! YOU TRY IT! GOD MADE IT! MY GOLLY! EAT! EAT!

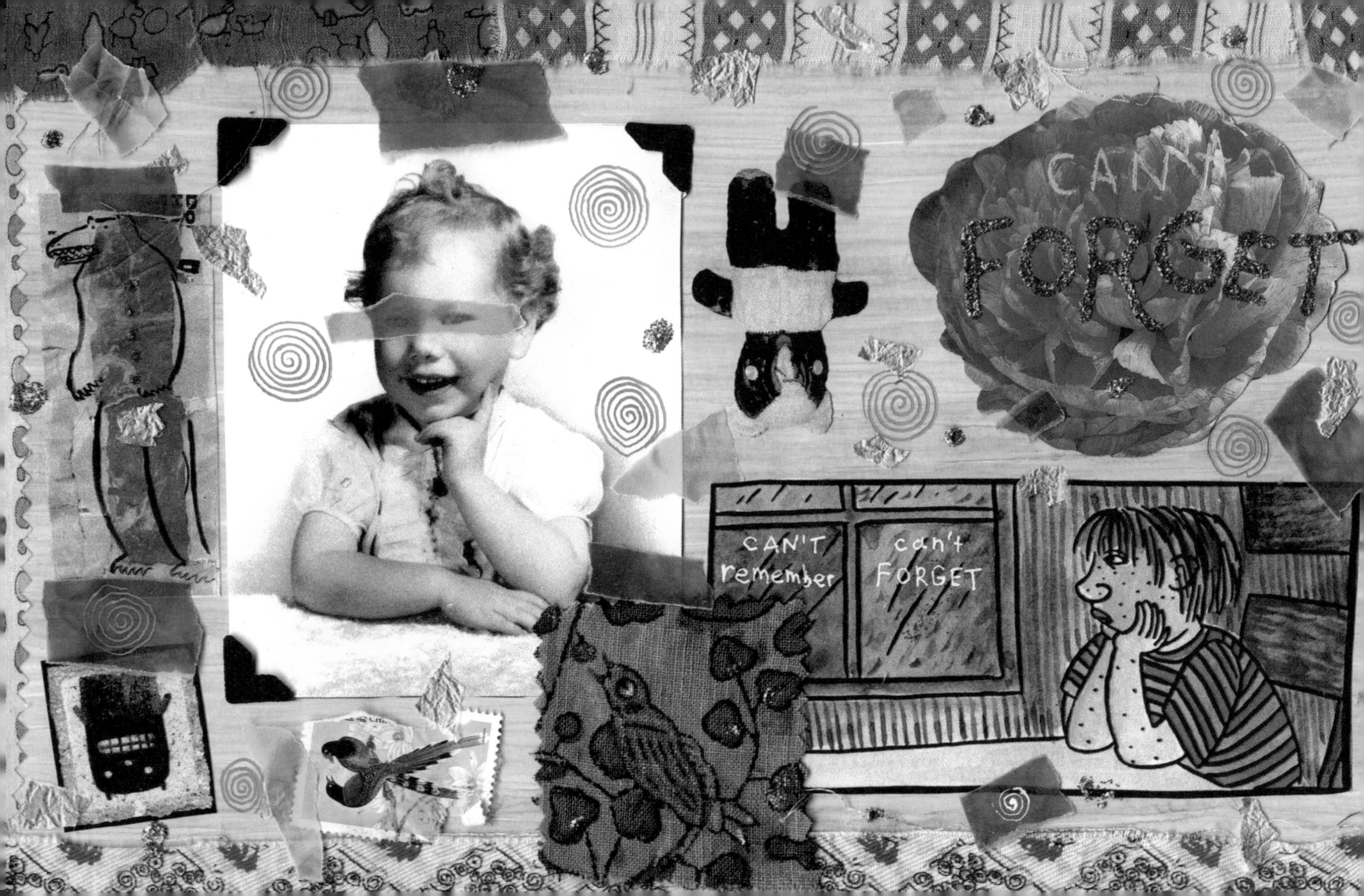
CAN'T
FORGET
CAN'T
remember
can't
FORGET

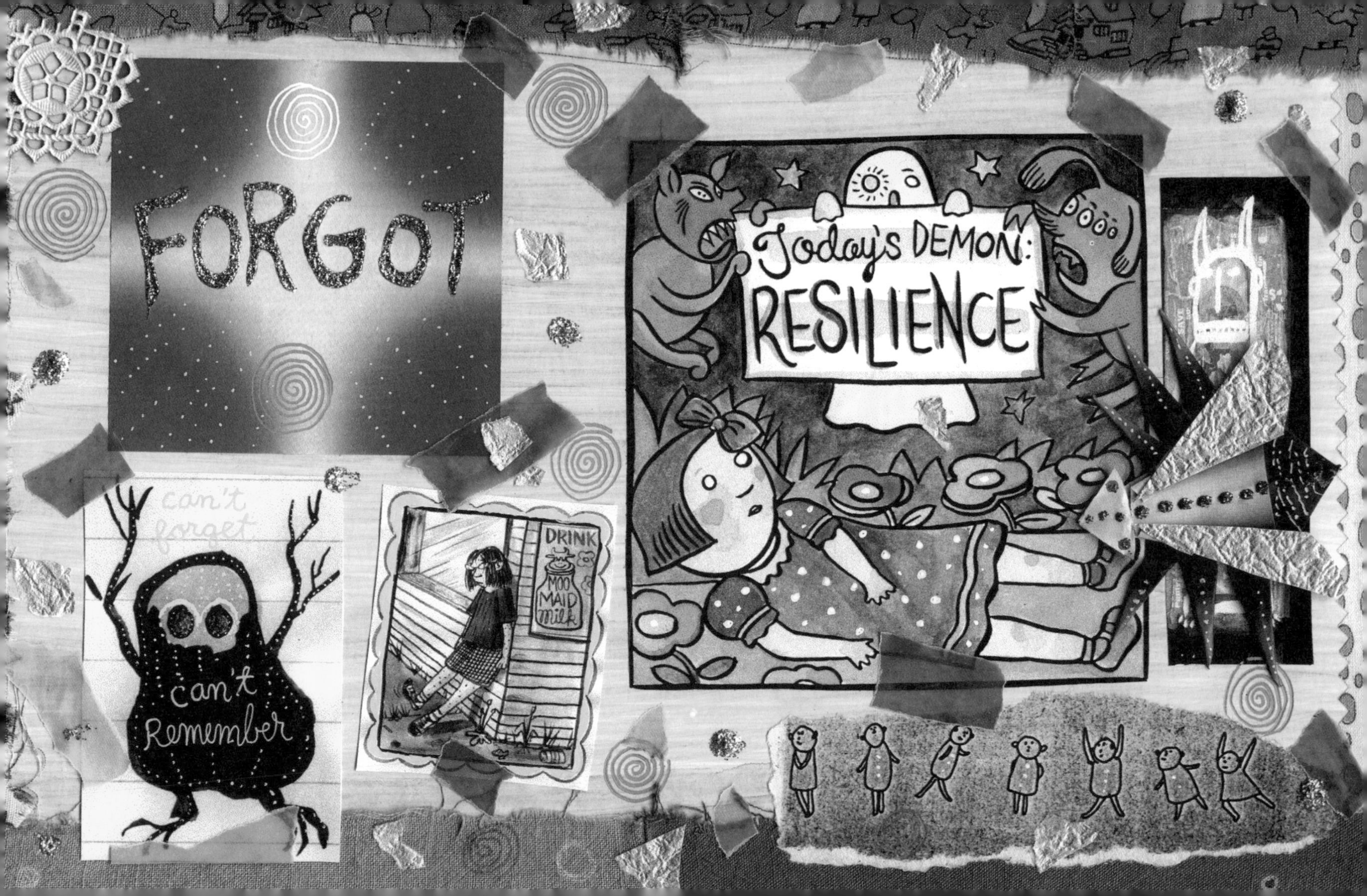
FORGOT
can't forget
can't Remember
DRINK
MOO MAID milk
Today's DEMON:
RESILIENCE

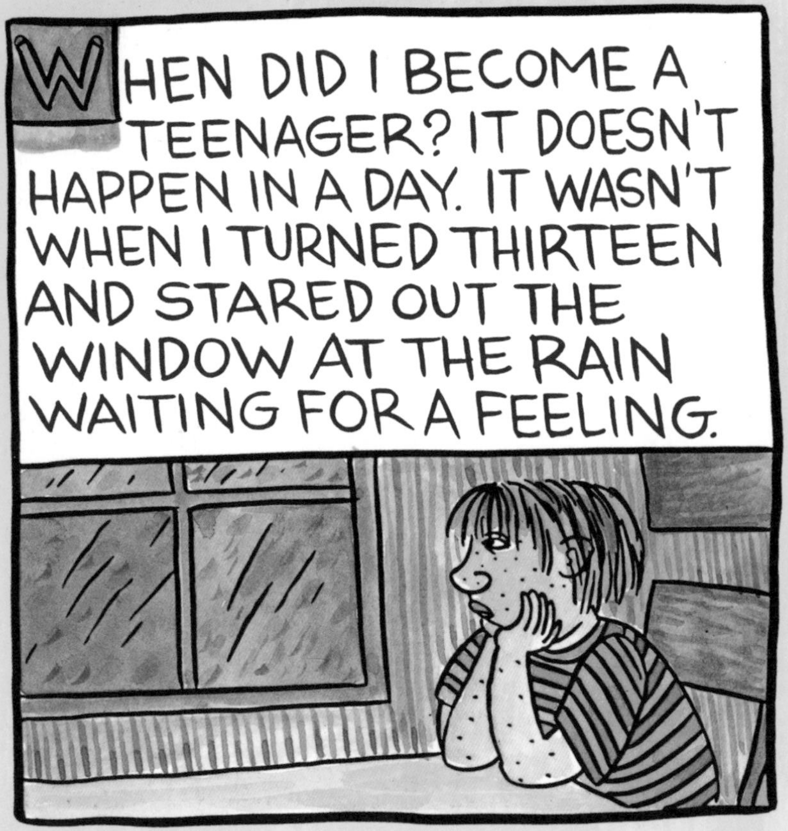
WHEN DID I BECOME A TEENAGER? IT DOESN'T HAPPEN IN A DAY. IT WASN'T WHEN I TURNED THIRTEEN AND STARED OUT THE WINDOW AT THE RAIN WAITING FOR A FEELING.

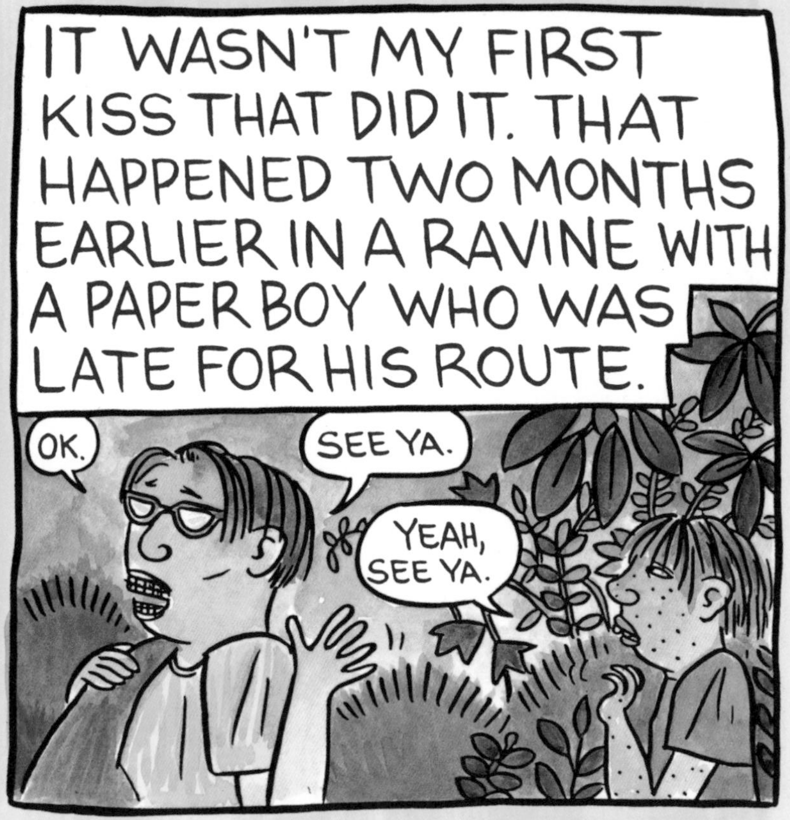
IT WASN'T MY FIRST KISS THAT DID IT. THAT HAPPENED TWO MONTHS EARLIER IN A RAVINE WITH A PAPER BOY WHO WAS LATE FOR HIS ROUTE.
OK.
SEE YA.
YEAH, SEE YA.

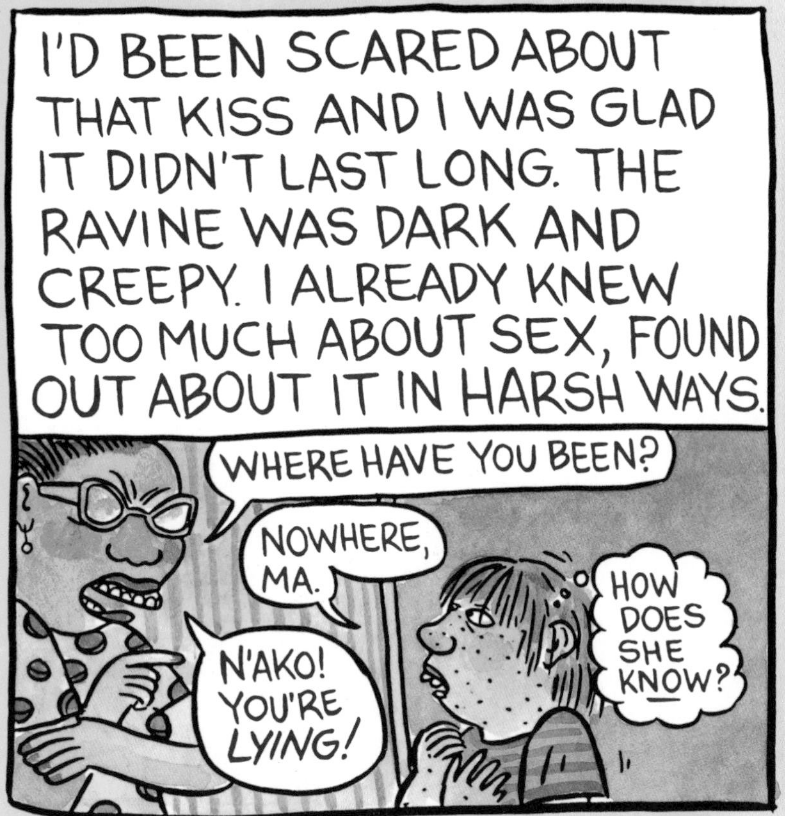
I'D BEEN SCARED ABOUT THAT KISS AND I WAS GLAD IT DIDN'T LAST LONG. THE RAVINE WAS DARK AND CREEPY. I ALREADY KNEW TOO MUCH ABOUT SEX, FOUND OUT ABOUT IT IN HARSH WAYS.
WHERE HAVE YOU BEEN?
NOWHERE, MA.
N'AKO! YOU'RE LYING!
HOW DOES SHE KNOW?

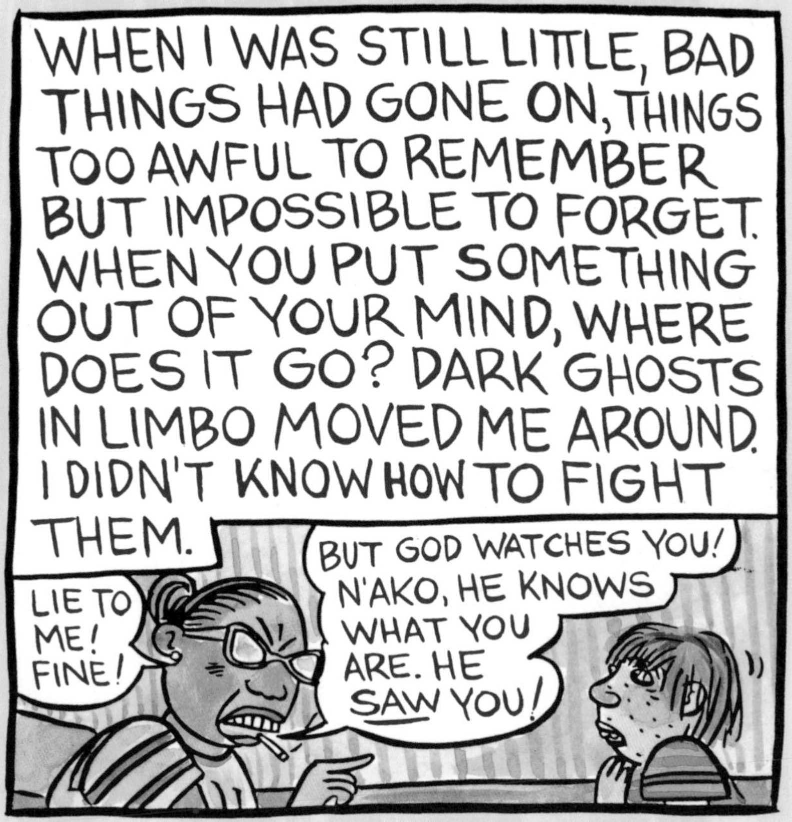
WHEN I WAS STILL LITTLE, BAD THINGS HAD GONE ON, THINGS TOO AWFUL TO REMEMBER BUT IMPOSSIBLE TO FORGET. WHEN YOU PUT SOMETHING OUT OF YOUR MIND, WHERE DOES IT GO? DARK GHOSTS IN LIMBO MOVED ME AROUND. I DIDN'T KNOW HOW TO FIGHT THEM.
LIE TO ME! FINE!
BUT GOD WATCHES YOU! N'AKO, HE KNOWS WHAT YOU ARE. HE SAW YOU!

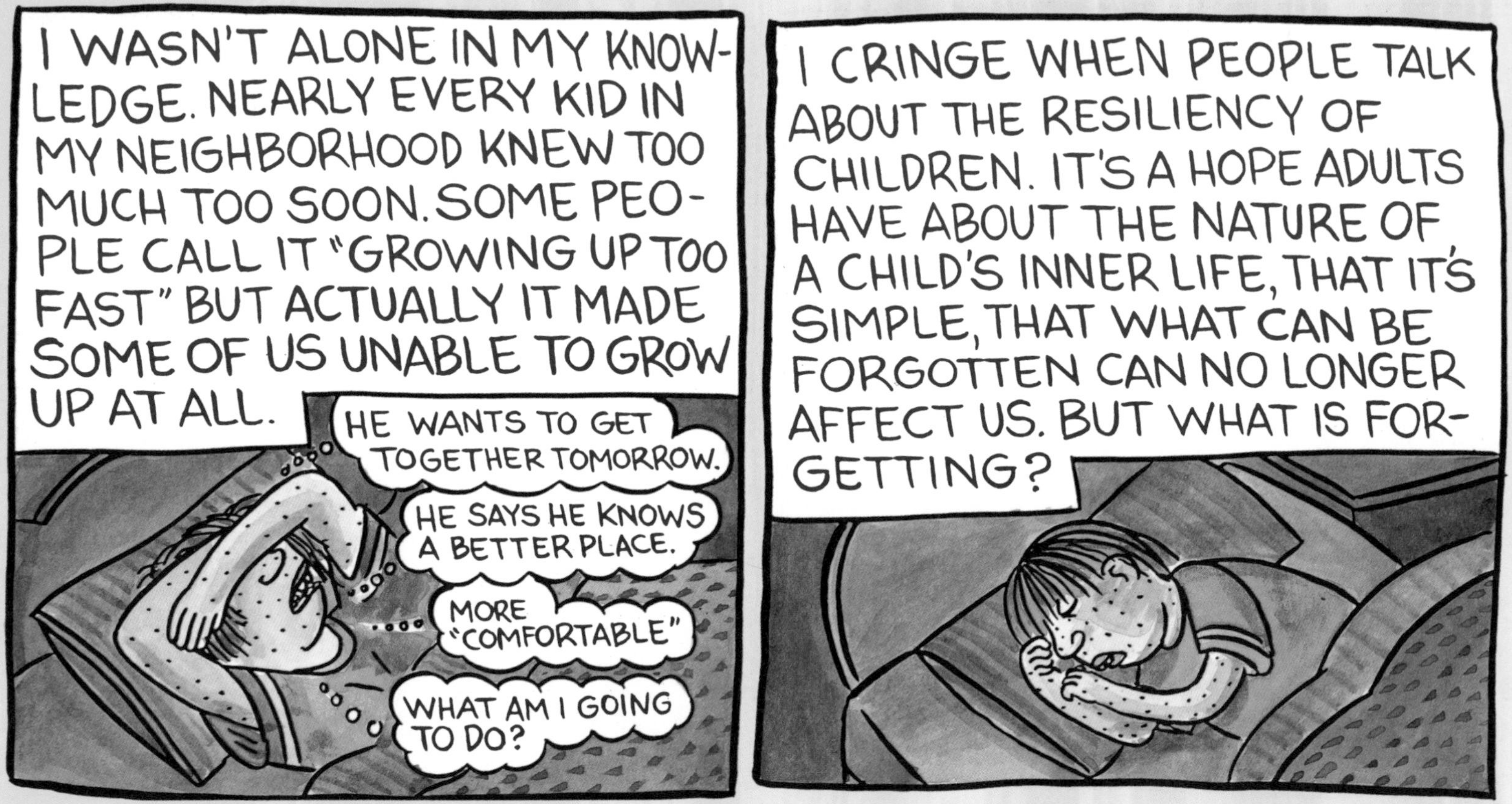
I WASN'T ALONE IN MY KNOWLEDGE. NEARLY EVERY KID IN MY NEIGHBORHOOD KNEW TOO MUCH TOO SOON. SOME PEOPLE CALL IT "GROWING UP TOO FAST" BUT ACTUALLY IT MADE SOME OF US UNABLE TO GROW UP AT ALL.
HE WANTS TO GET TOGETHER TOMORROW.
HE SAYS HE KNOWS A BETTER PLACE.
MORE "COMFORTABLE"
WHAT AM I GOING TO DO?
I CRINGE WHEN PEOPLE TALK ABOUT THE RESILIENCY OF CHILDREN. IT'S A HOPE ADULTS HAVE ABOUT THE NATURE OF A CHILD'S INNER LIFE, THAT IT'S SIMPLE, THAT WHAT CAN BE FORGOTTEN CAN NO LONGER AFFECT US. BUT WHAT IS FORGETTING?

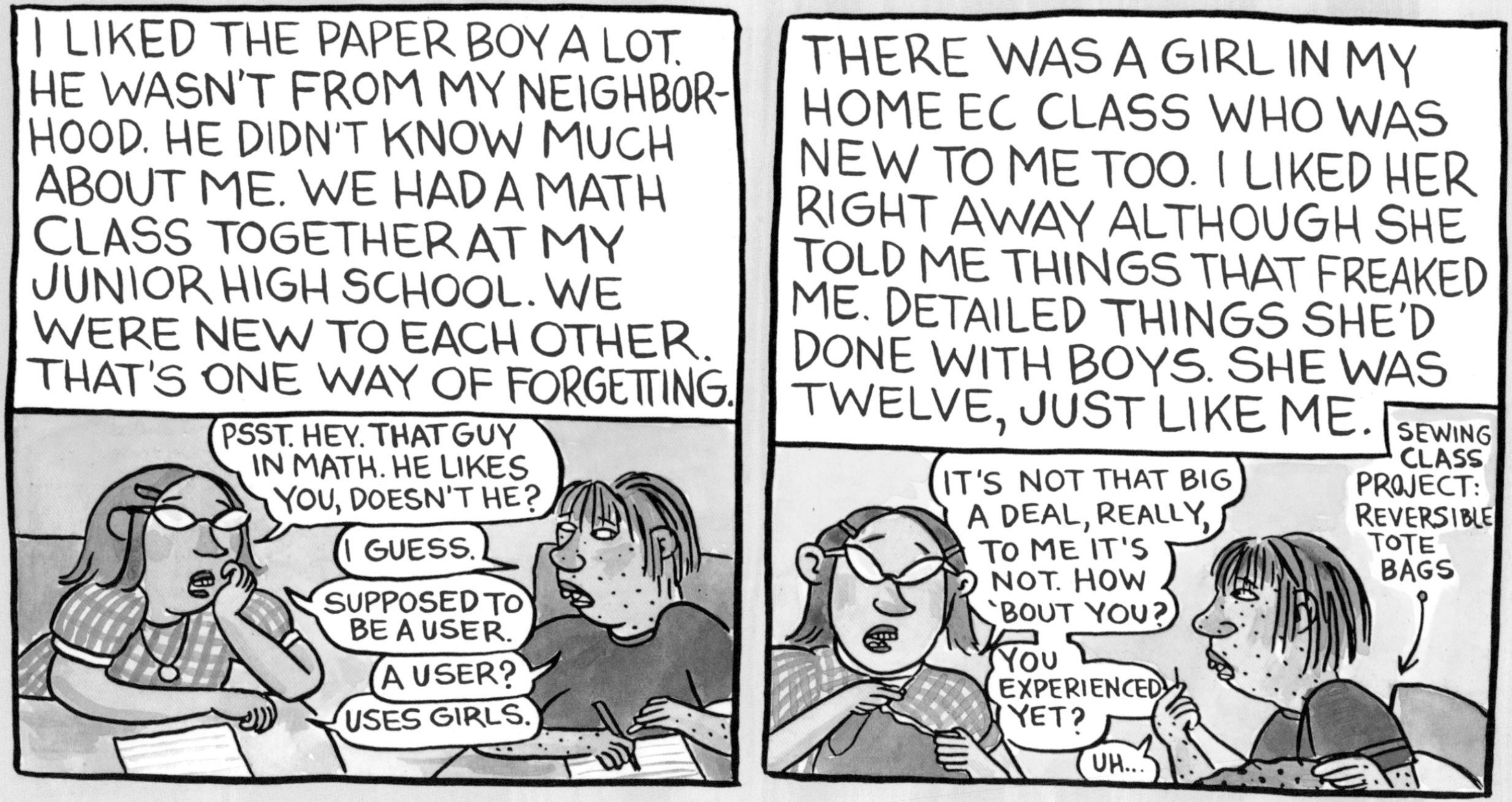
I LIKED THE PAPER BOY A LOT. HE WASN'T FROM MY NEIGHBORHOOD. HE DIDN'T KNOW MUCH ABOUT ME. WE HAD A MATH CLASS TOGETHER AT MY JUNIOR HIGH SCHOOL. WE WERE NEW TO EACH OTHER. THAT'S ONE WAY OF FORGETTING.
PSST. HEY. THAT GUY IN MATH. HE LIKES YOU, DOESN'T HE?
I GUESS.
SUPPOSED TO BE A USER.
A USER?
USES GIRLS.
THERE WAS A GIRL IN MY HOME EC CLASS WHO WAS NEW TO ME TOO. I LIKED HER RIGHT AWAY ALTHOUGH SHE TOLD ME THINGS THAT FREAKED ME. DETAILED THINGS SHE'D DONE WITH BOYS. SHE WAS TWELVE, JUST LIKE ME.
SEWING CLASS PROJECT: REVERSIBLE TOTE BAGS
IT'S NOT THAT BIG A DEAL, REALLY, TO ME IT'S NOT. HOW `BOUT YOU?
YOU EXPERIENCED YET?
UH...

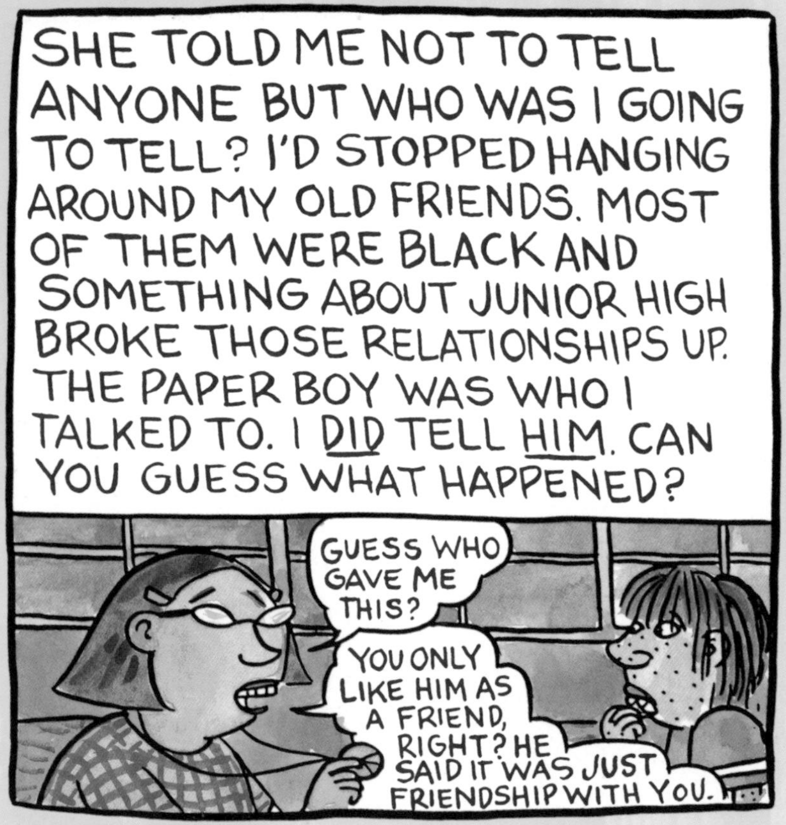
SHE TOLD ME NOT TO TELL ANYONE BUT WHO WAS I GOING TO TELL? I'D STOPPED HANGING AROUND MY OLD FRIENDS. MOST OF THEM WERE BLACK AND SOMETHING ABOUT JUNIOR HIGH BROKE THOSE RELATIONSHIPS UP. THE PAPER BOY WAS WHO I TALKED TO. I DID TELL HIM. CAN YOU GUESS WHAT HAPPENED?
GUESS WHO GAVE ME THIS?
YOU ONLY LIKE HIM AS A FRIEND, RIGHT? HE SAID IT WAS JUST FRIENDSHIP WITH YOU.

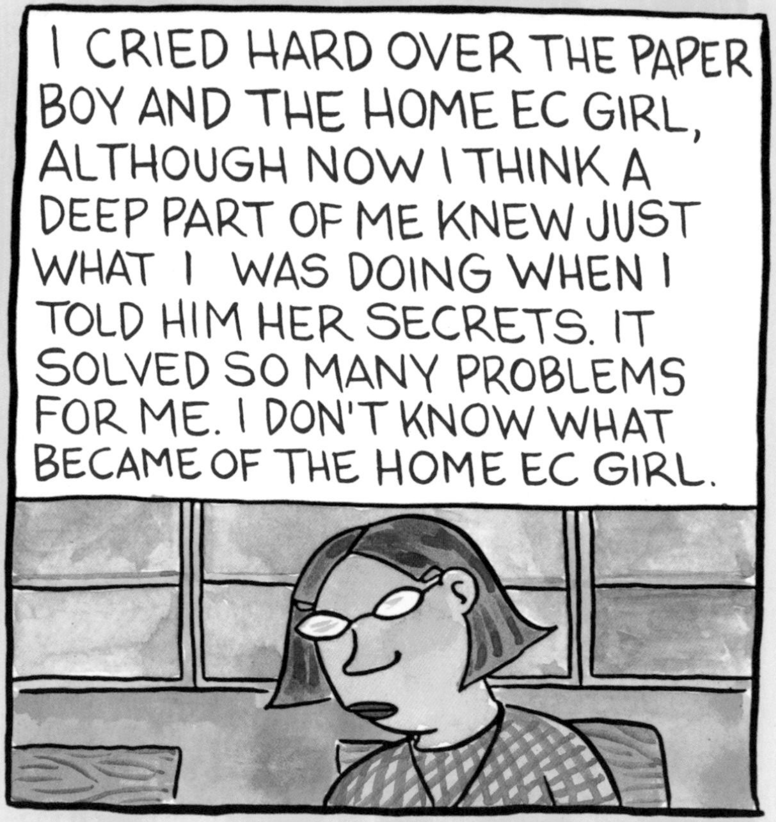
I CRIED HARD OVER THE PAPER BOY AND THE HOME EC GIRL, ALTHOUGH NOW I THINK A DEEP PART OF ME KNEW JUST WHAT I WAS DOING WHEN I TOLD HIM HER SECRETS. IT SOLVED SO MANY PROBLEMS FOR ME. I DON'T KNOW WHAT BECAME OF THE HOME EC GIRL.

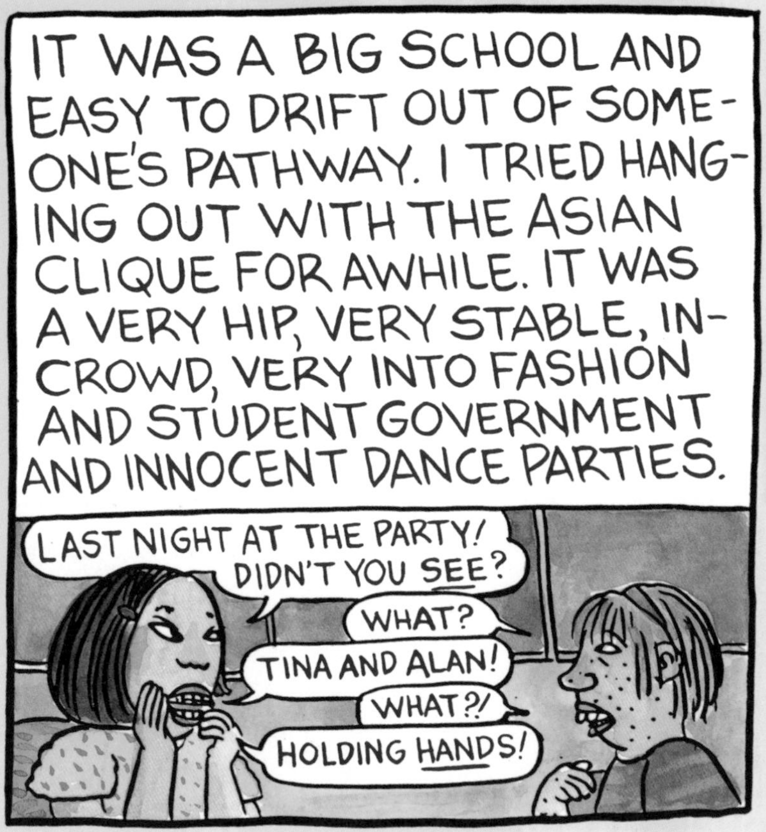
IT WAS A BIG SCHOOL AND EASY TO DRIFT OUT OF SOMEONE'S PATHWAY. I TRIED HANGING OUT WITH THE ASIAN CLIQUE FOR AWHILE. IT WAS A VERY HIP, VERY STABLE, IN-CROWD, VERY INTO FASHION AND STUDENT GOVERNMENT AND INNOCENT DANCE PARTIES.
LAST NIGHT AT THE PARTY! DIDN'T YOU SEE?
WHAT?
TINA AND ALAN!
WHAT?!
HOLDING HANDS!

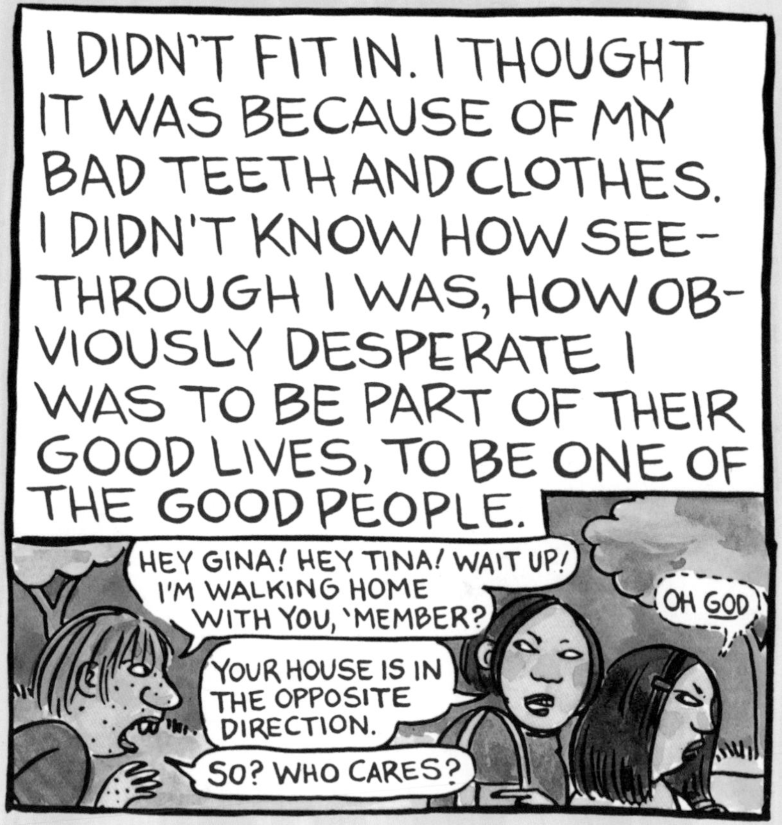
I DIDN'T FIT IN. I THOUGHT IT WAS BECAUSE OF MY BAD TEETH AND CLOTHES. I DIDN'T KNOW HOW SEE-THROUGH I WAS, HOW OBVIOUSLY DESPERATE I WAS TO BE PART OF THEIR GOOD LIVES, TO BE ONE OF THE GOOD PEOPLE.
HEY GINA! HEY TINA! WAIT UP! I'M WALKING HOME WITH YOU, 'MEMBER?
OH GOD!
YOUR HOUSE IS IN THE OPPOSITE DIRECTION.
SO? WHO CARES?

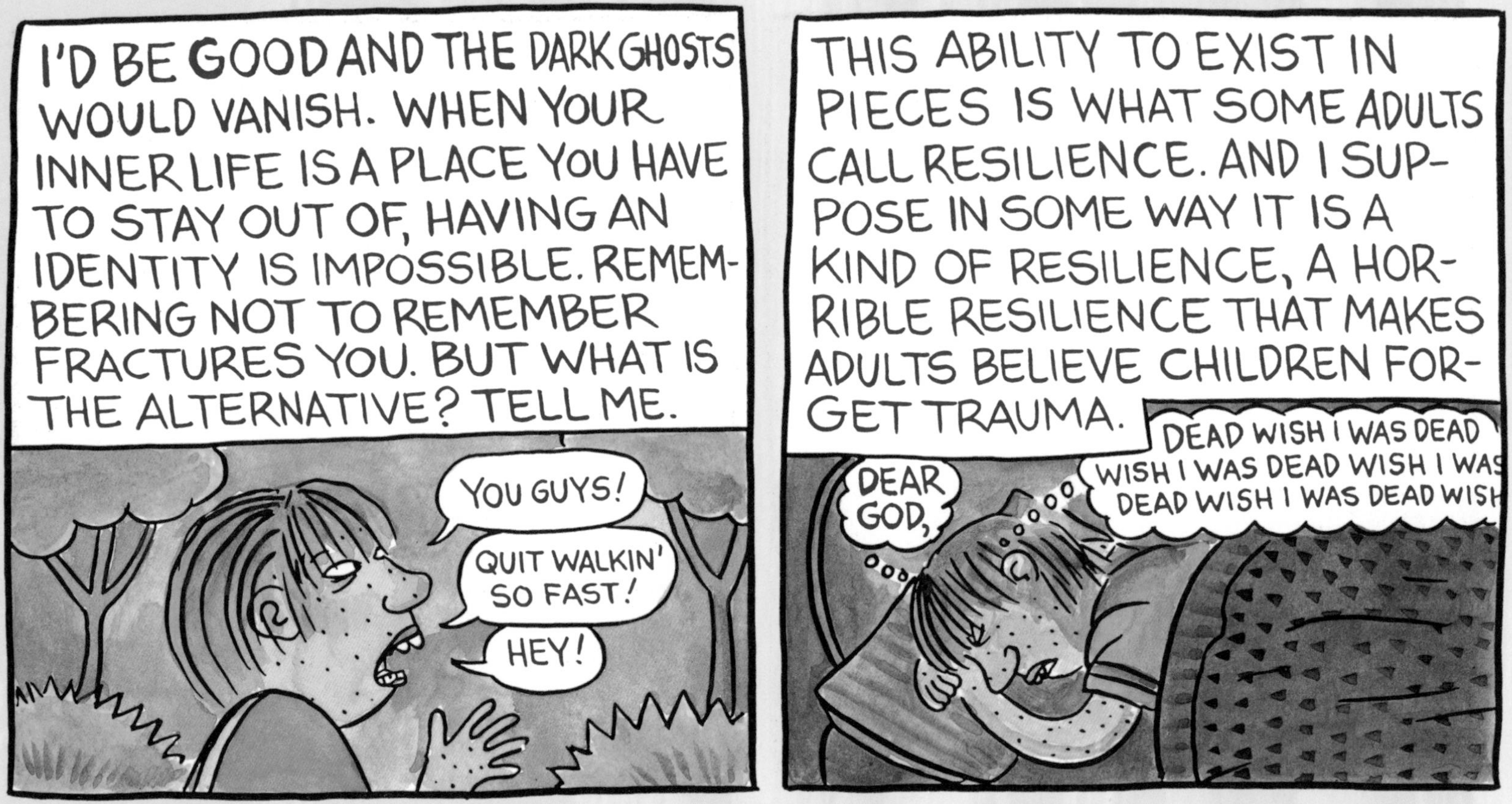
I'D BE GOOD AND THE DARK GHOSTS WOULD VANISH. WHEN YOUR INNER LIFE IS A PLACE YOU HAVE TO STAY OUT OF, HAVING AN IDENTITY IS IMPOSSIBLE. REMEMBERING NOT TO REMEMBER FRACTURES YOU. BUT WHAT IS THE ALTERNATIVE? TELL ME.
YOU GUYS!
QUIT WALKIN' SO FAST!
HEY!
THIS ABILITY TO EXIST IN PIECES IS WHAT SOME ADULTS CALL RESILIENCE. AND I SUPPOSE IN SOME WAY IT IS A KIND OF RESILIENCE, A HORRIBLE RESILIENCE THAT MAKES ADULTS BELIEVE CHILDREN FORGET TRAUMA.
DEAR GOD,
DEAD WISH I WAS DEAD
WISH I WAS DEAD WISH I WAS
DEAD WISH I WAS DEAD WISH

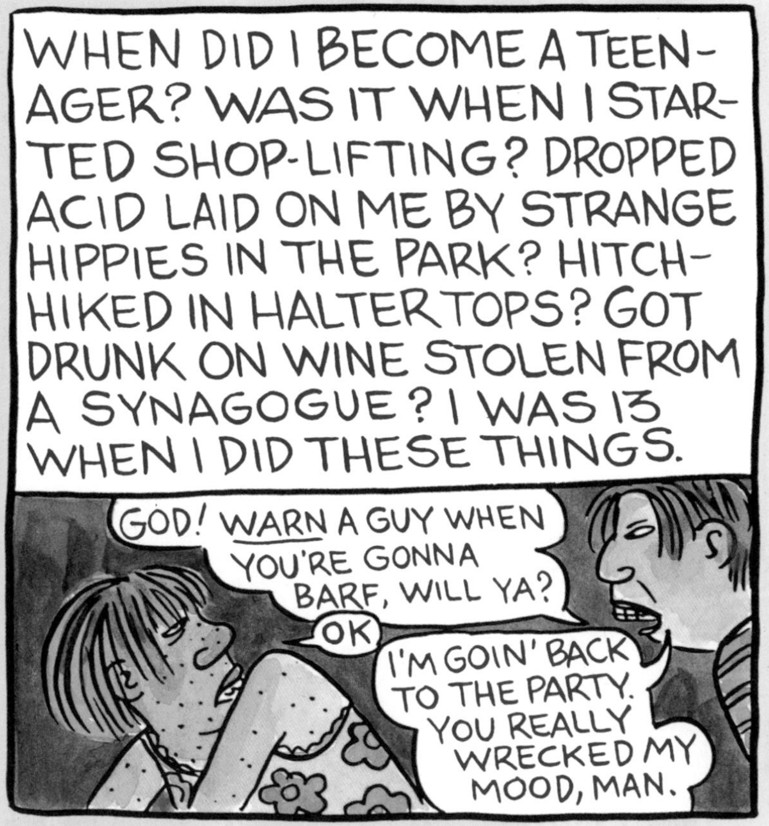
WHEN DID I BECOME A TEEN-AGER? WAS IT WHEN I STARTED SHOP-LIFTING? DROPPED ACID LAID ON ME BY STRANGE HIPPIES IN THE PARK? HITCH-HIKED IN HALTER TOPS? GOT DRUNK ON WINE STOLEN FROM A SYNAGOGUE? I WAS 13 WHEN I DID THESE THINGS.
GOD! WARN A GUY WHEN YOU'RE GONNA BARF, WILL YA?
OK
I'M GOIN' BACK TO THE PARTY. YOU REALLY WRECKED MY MOOD, MAN.

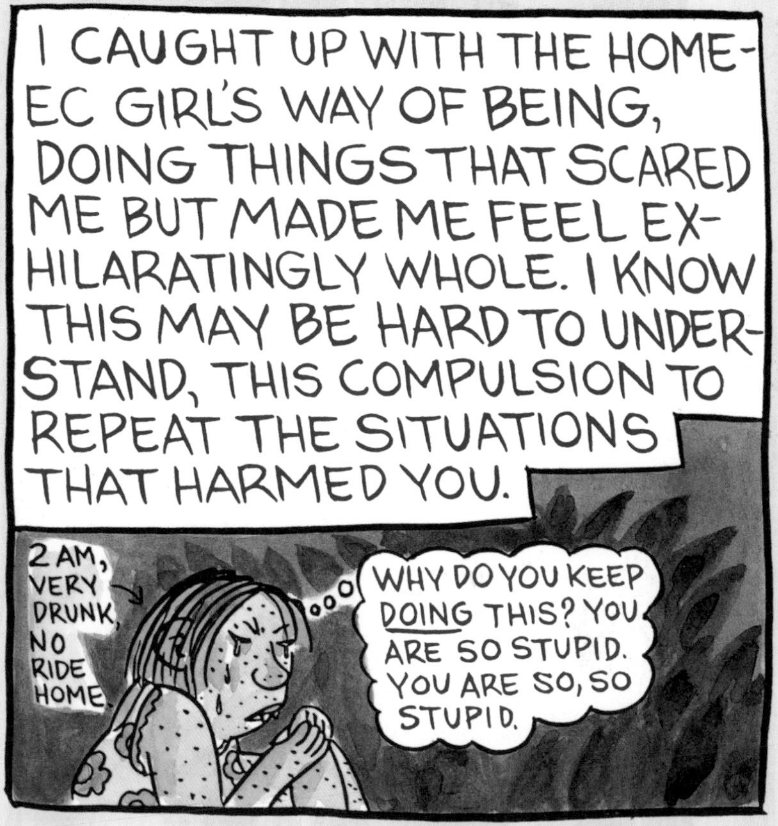
I CAUGHT UP WITH THE HOME-EC GIRL'S WAY OF BEING, DOING THINGS THAT SCARED ME BUT MADE ME FEEL EX-HILARATINGLY WHOLE. I KNOW THIS MAY BE HARD TO UNDERSTAND, THIS COMPULSION TO REPEAT THE SITUATIONS THAT HARMED YOU.
2 AM, VERY DRUNK, NO RIDE HOME
WHY DO YOU KEEP DOING THIS? YOU ARE SO STUPID. YOU ARE SO, SO STUPID.

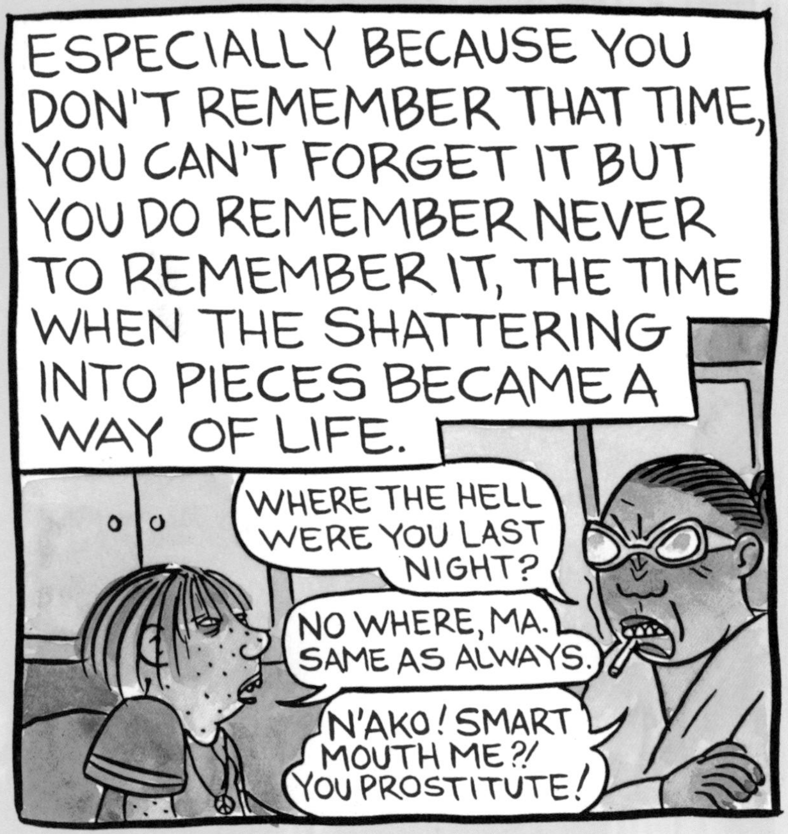
ESPECIALLY BECAUSE YOU DON'T REMEMBER THAT TIME, YOU CAN'T FORGET IT BUT YOU DO REMEMBER NEVER TO REMEMBER IT, THE TIME WHEN THE SHATTERING INTO PIECES BECAME A WAY OF LIFE.
WHERE THE HELL WERE YOU LAST NIGHT?
NO WHERE, MA. SAME AS ALWAYS.
N'AKO! SMART MOUTH ME?! YOU PROSTITUTE!

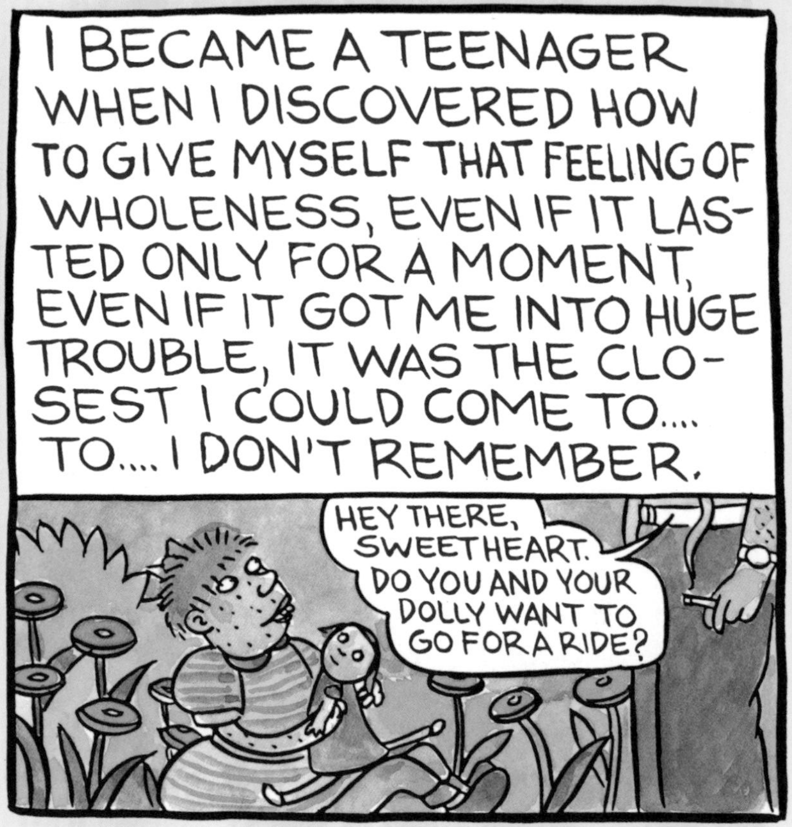
I BECAME A TEENAGER WHEN I DISCOVERED HOW TO GIVE MYSELF THAT FEELING OF WHOLENESS, EVEN IF IT LASTED ONLY FOR A MOMENT, EVEN IF IT GOT ME INTO HUGE TROUBLE, IT WAS THE CLOSEST I COULD COME TO.... TO.... I DON'T REMEMBER.
HEY THERE, SWEETHEART. DO YOU AND YOUR DOLLY WANT TO GO FOR A RIDE?

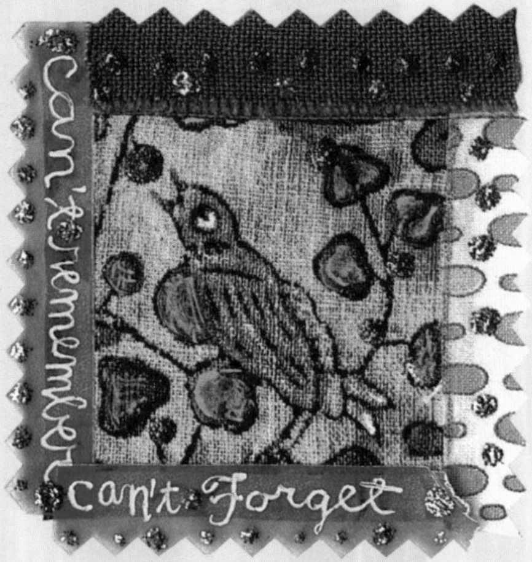
can't remember
can't forget

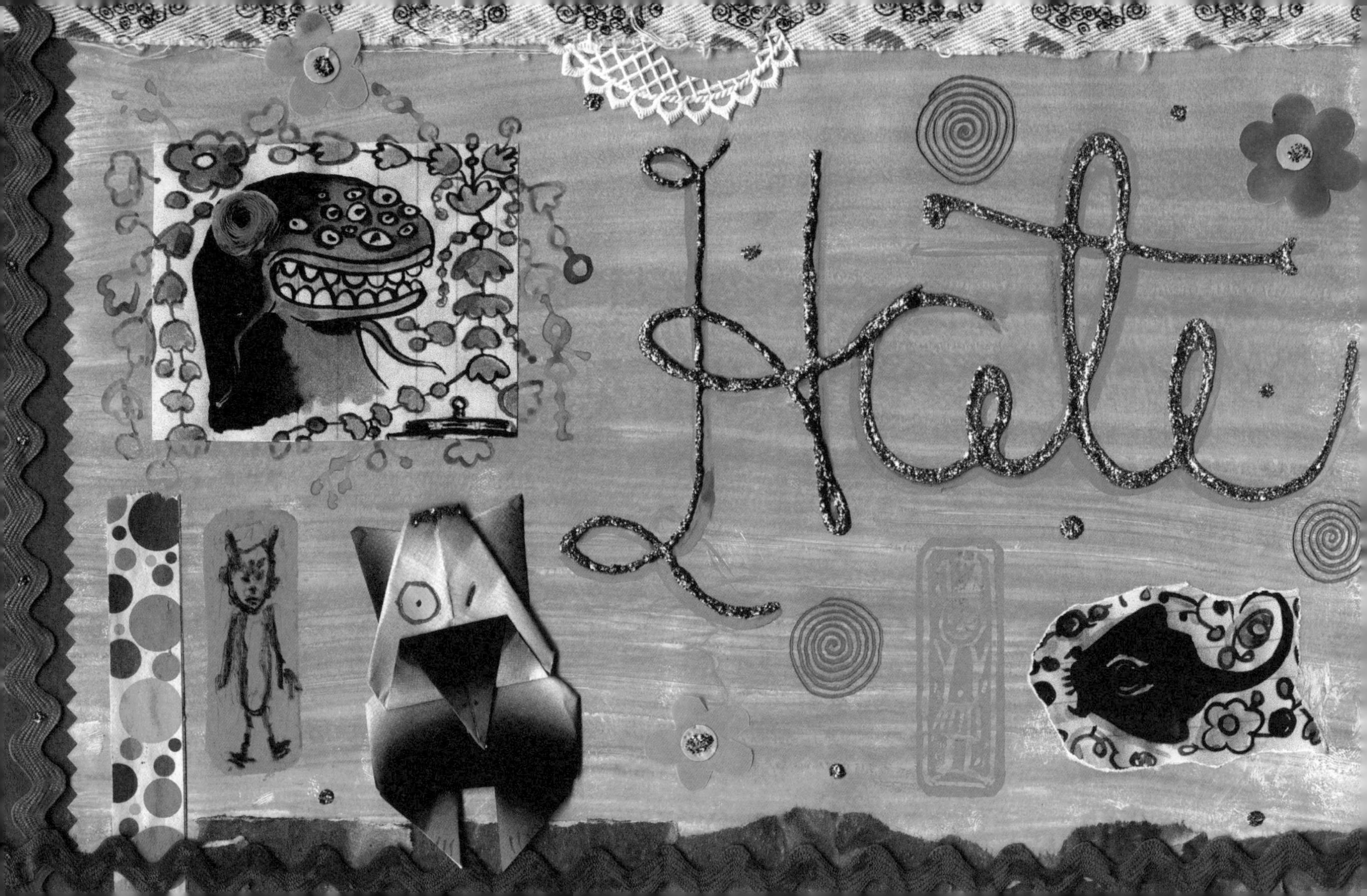
Hate

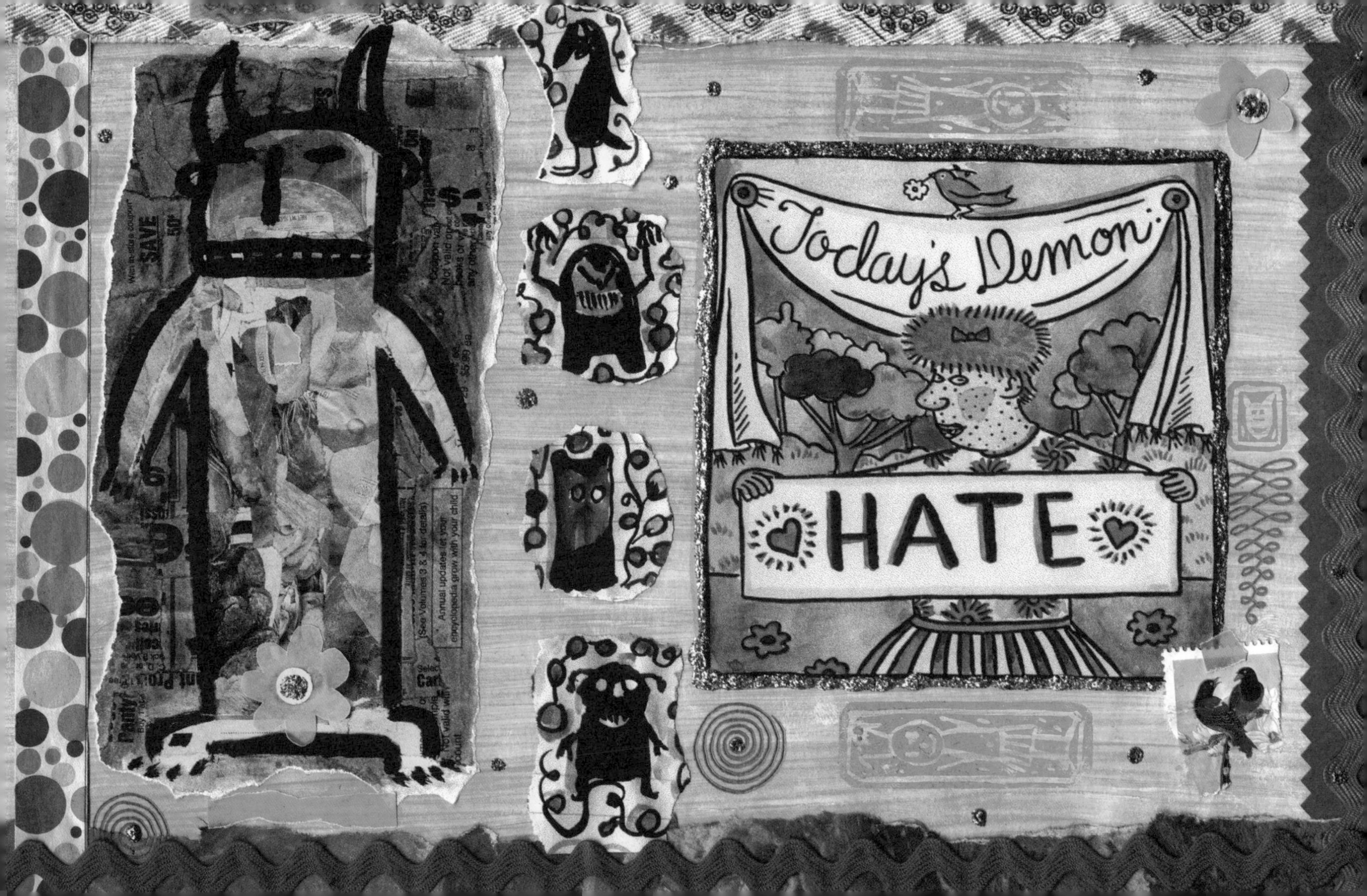
Today's Demon:
HATE

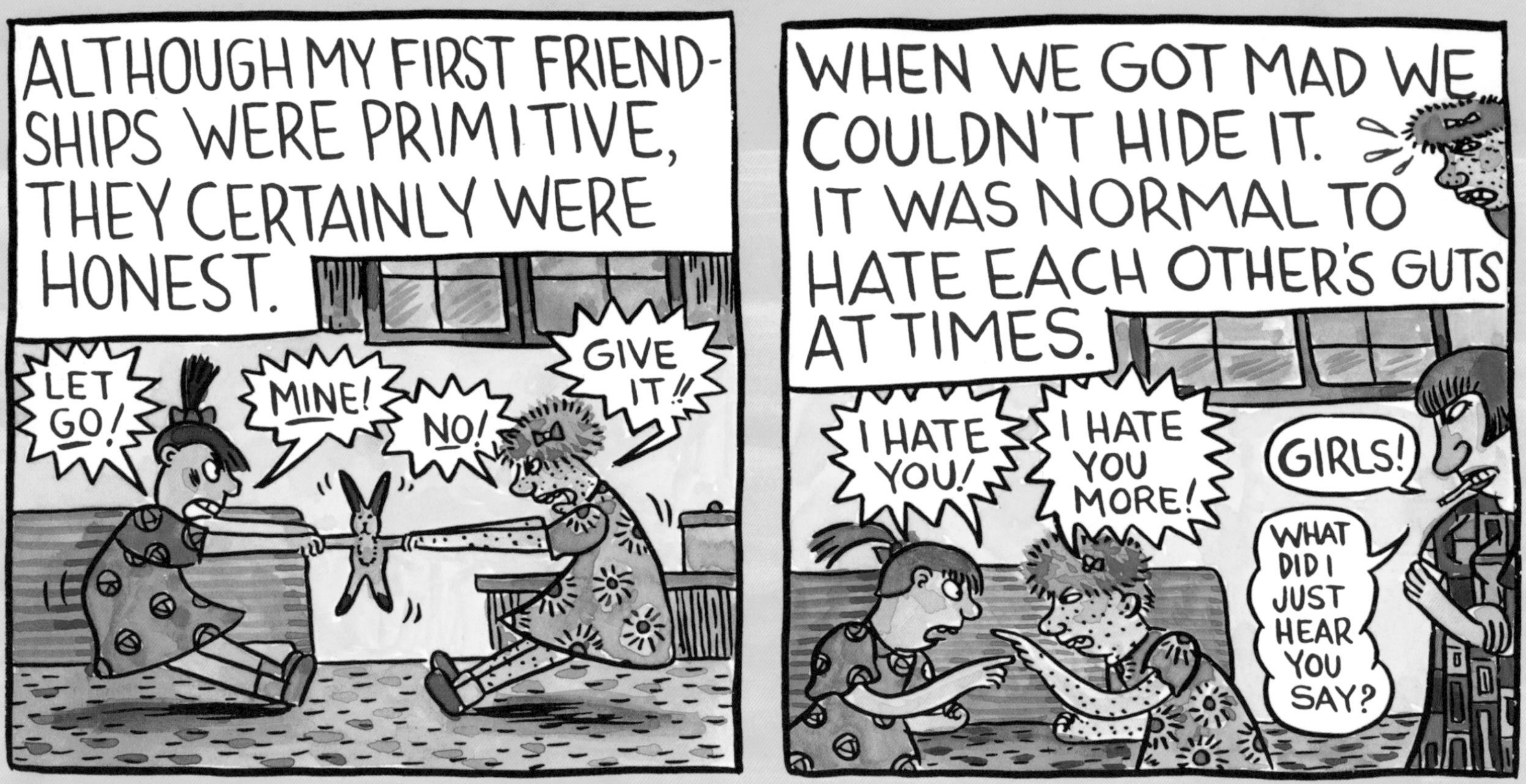
ALTHOUGH MY FIRST FRIENDSHIPS WERE PRIMITIVE, THEY CERTAINLY WERE HONEST.
LET GO!
MINE!
NO!
GIVE IT!!
WHEN WE GOT MAD WE COULDN'T HIDE IT. IT WAS NORMAL TO HATE EACH OTHER'S GUTS AT TIMES.
I HATE YOU!
I HATE YOU MORE!
GIRLS!
WHAT DID I JUST HEAR YOU SAY?

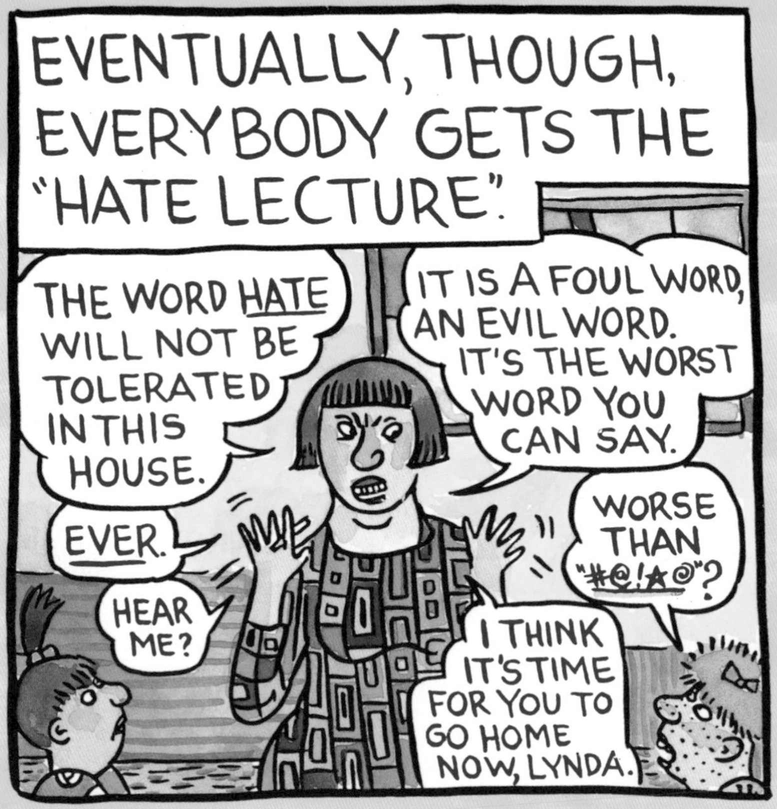
EVENTUALLY, THOUGH, EVERYBODY GETS THE "HATE LECTURE".
THE WORD HATE WILL NOT BE TOLERATED IN THIS HOUSE.
IT IS A FOUL WORD, AN EVIL WORD.
IT'S THE WORST WORD YOU CAN SAY.
EVER.
HEAR ME?
WORSE THAN "#@!★@"?
I THINK IT'S TIME FOR YOU TO GO HOME NOW, LYNDA.

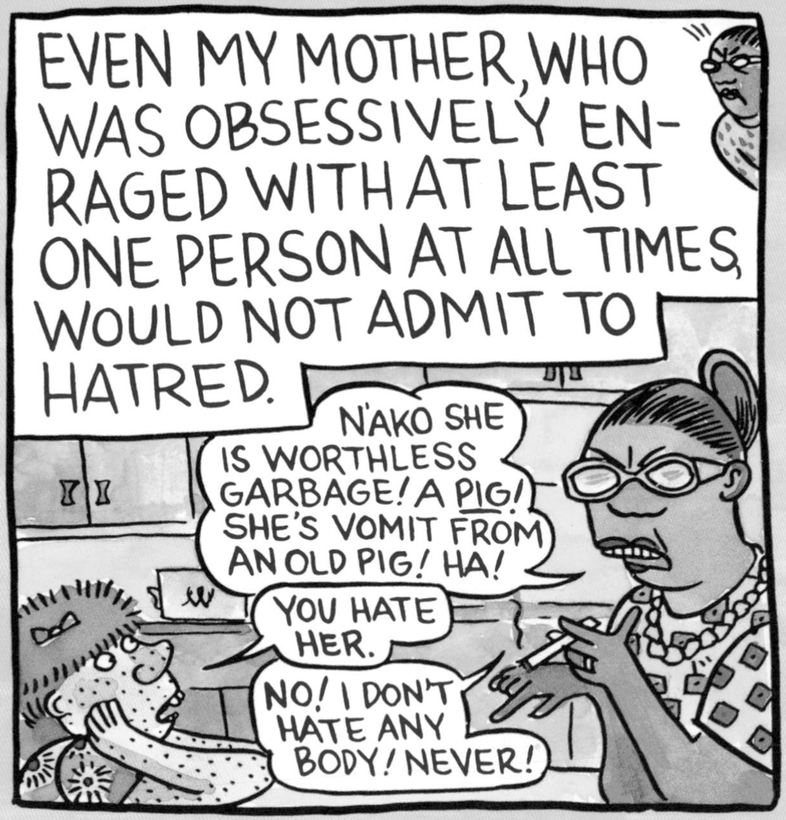
EVEN MY MOTHER, WHO WAS OBSESSIVELY ENRAGED WITH AT LEAST ONE PERSON AT ALL TIMES, WOULD NOT ADMIT TO HATRED.
N'AKO SHE IS WORTHLESS GARBAGE! A PIG! SHE'S VOMIT FROM AN OLD PIG! HA!
YOU HATE HER.
NO! I DON'T HATE ANY BODY! NEVER!

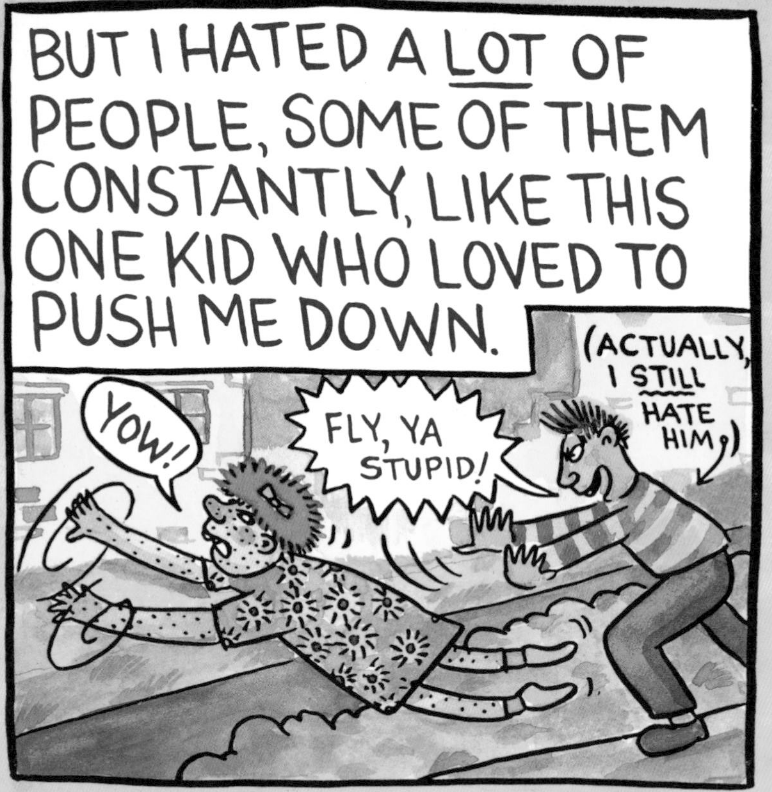
BUT I HATED A LOT OF PEOPLE, SOME OF THEM CONSTANTLY, LIKE THIS ONE KID WHO LOVED TO PUSH ME DOWN.
YOW!
FLY, YA STUPID!
(ACTUALLY, I STILL HATE HIM.)

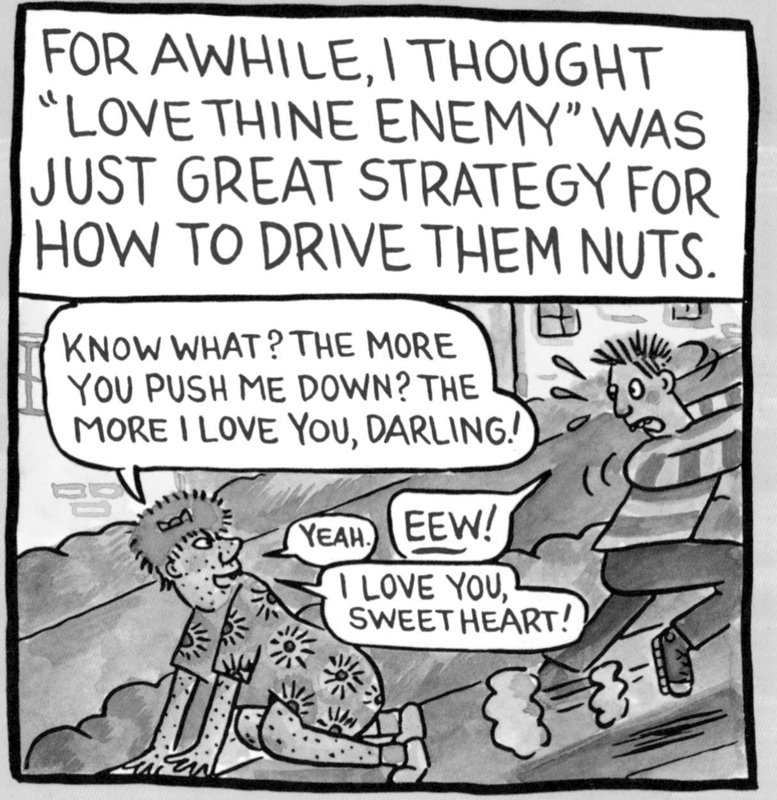
FOR AWHILE, I THOUGHT "LOVE THINE ENEMY" WAS JUST GREAT STRATEGY FOR HOW TO DRIVE THEM NUTS.
KNOW WHAT? THE MORE YOU PUSH ME DOWN? THE MORE I LOVE YOU, DARLING!
EEW!
YEAH.
I LOVE YOU, SWEETHEART!

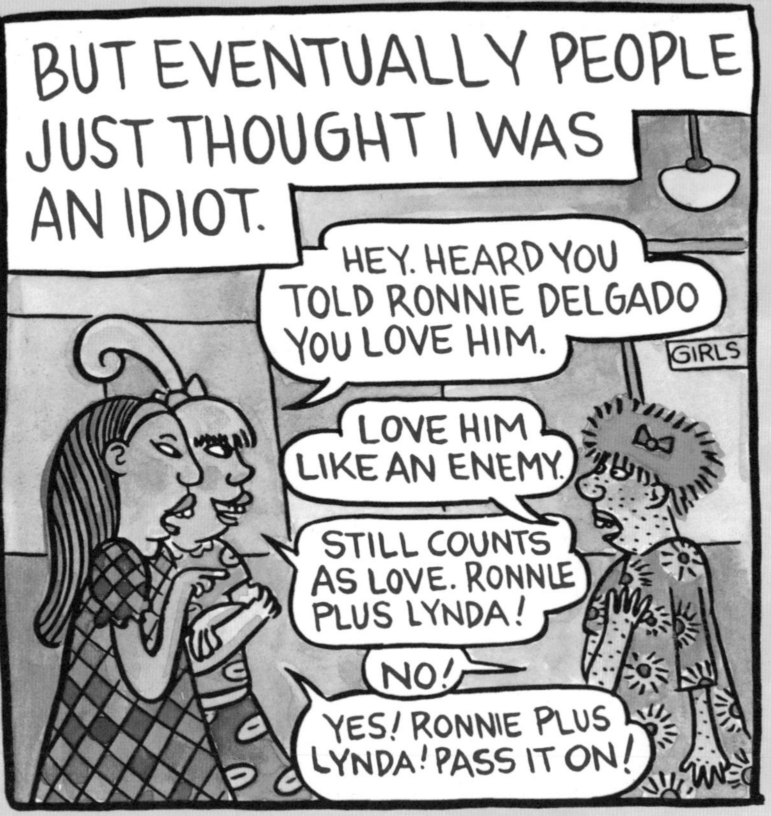
BUT EVENTUALLY PEOPLE JUST THOUGHT I WAS AN IDIOT.
HEY. HEARD YOU TOLD RONNIE DELGADO YOU LOVE HIM.
GIRLS
LOVE HIM LIKE AN ENEMY.
STILL COUNTS AS LOVE. RONNIE PLUS LYNDA!
NO!
YES! RONNIE PLUS LYNDA! PASS IT ON!

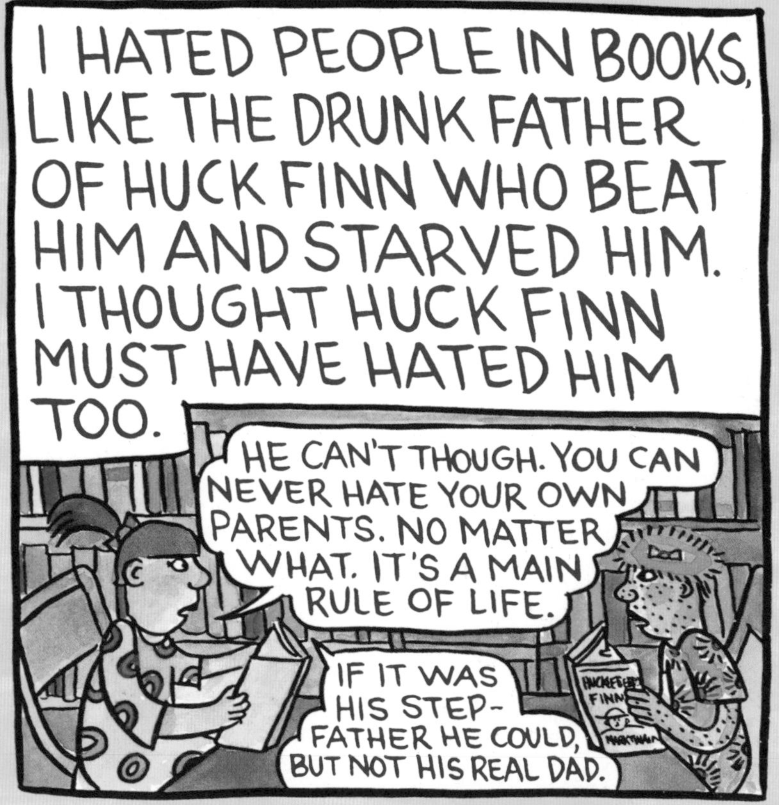
I HATED PEOPLE IN BOOKS, LIKE THE DRUNK FATHER OF HUCK FINN WHO BEAT HIM AND STARVED HIM. I THOUGHT HUCK FINN MUST HAVE HATED HIM TOO.
HE CAN'T THOUGH. YOU CAN NEVER HATE YOUR OWN PARENTS. NO MATTER WHAT. IT'S A MAIN RULE OF LIFE.
IF IT WAS HIS STEP-FATHER HE COULD, BUT NOT HIS REAL DAD.

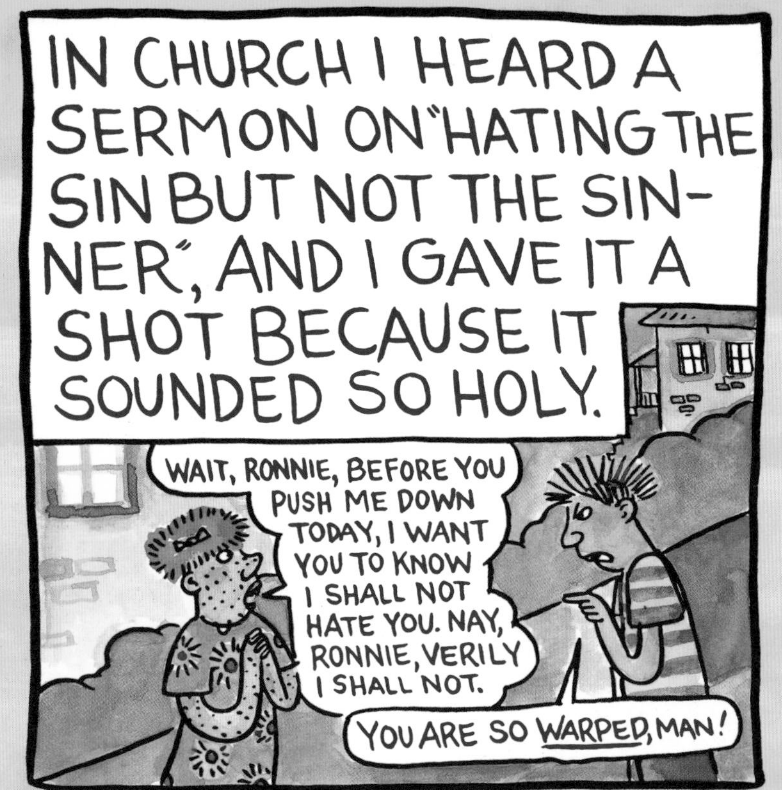
IN CHURCH I HEARD A SERMON ON "HATING THE SIN BUT NOT THE SINNER", AND I GAVE IT A SHOT BECAUSE IT SOUNDED SO HOLY.
WAIT, RONNIE, BEFORE YOU PUSH ME DOWN TODAY, I WANT YOU TO KNOW I SHALL NOT HATE YOU. NAY, RONNIE, VERILY I SHALL NOT.
YOU ARE SO WARPED, MAN!

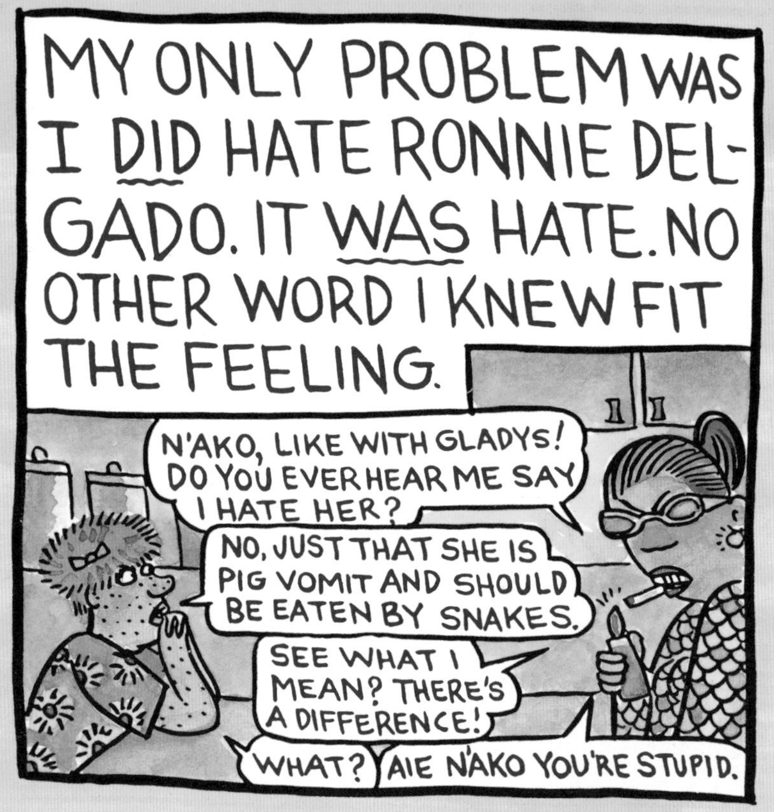
MY ONLY PROBLEM WAS I DID HATE RONNIE DELGADO. IT WAS HATE. NO OTHER WORD I KNEW FIT THE FEELING.
N'AKO, LIKE WITH GLADYS! DO YOU EVER HEAR ME SAY I HATE HER?
NO, JUST THAT SHE IS PIG VOMIT AND SHOULD BE EATEN BY SNAKES.
SEE WHAT I MEAN? THERE'S A DIFFERENCE!
WHAT?
AIE N'AKO YOU'RE STUPID.

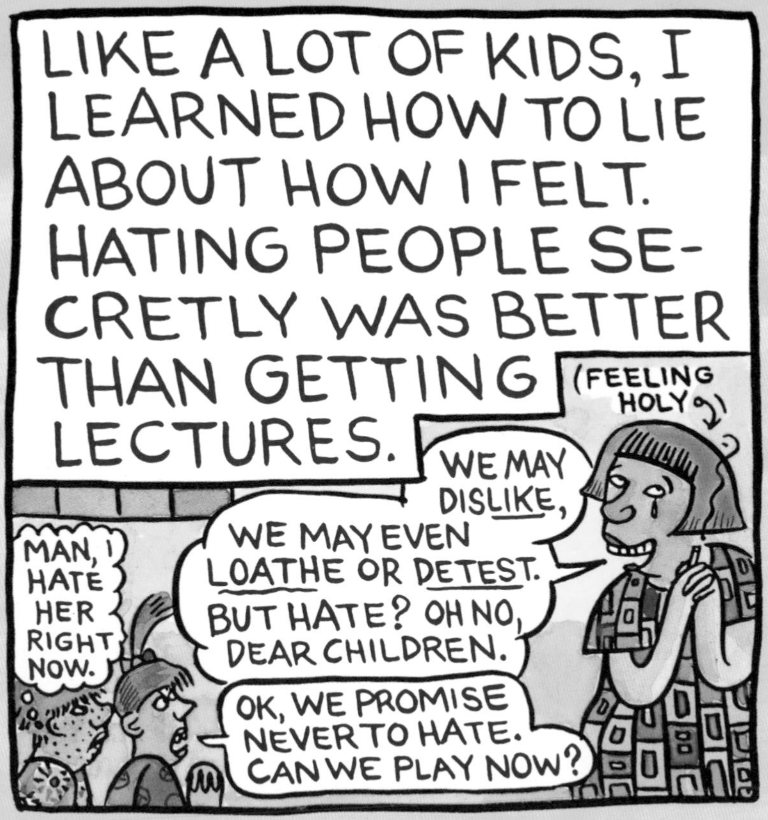
LIKE A LOT OF KIDS, I LEARNED HOW TO LIE ABOUT HOW I FELT. HATING PEOPLE SE-CRETLY WAS BETTER THAN GETTING LECTURES.
(FEELING HOLY)
WE MAY DISLIKE,
WE MAY EVEN LOATHE OR DETEST. BUT HATE? OH NO, DEAR CHILDREN.
MAN, I HATE HER RIGHT NOW.
OK, WE PROMISE NEVER TO HATE. CAN WE PLAY NOW?

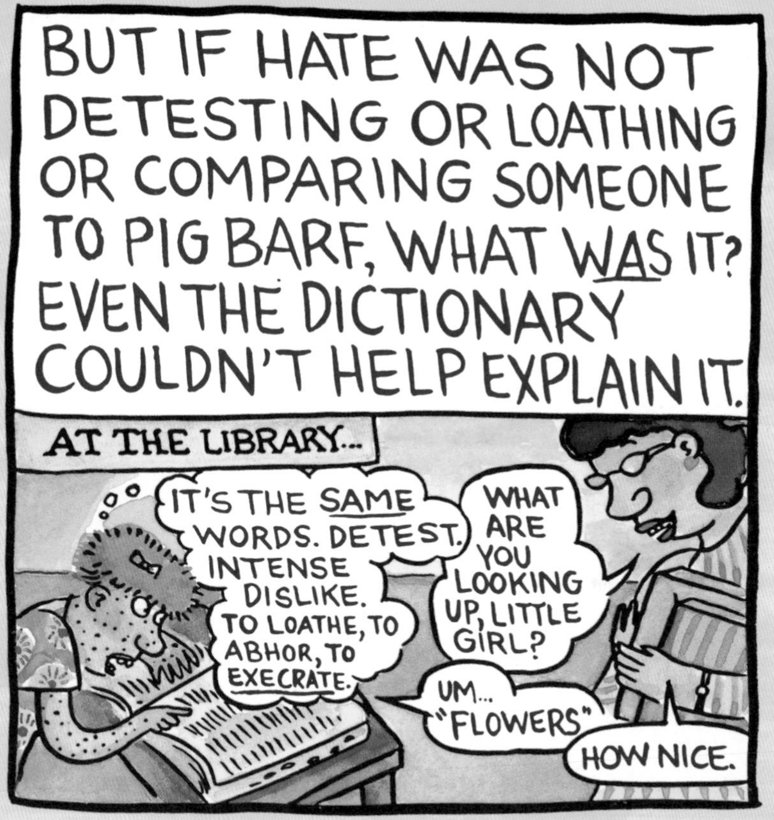
BUT IF HATE WAS NOT DETESTING OR LOATHING OR COMPARING SOMEONE TO PIG BARF, WHAT WAS IT? EVEN THE DICTIONARY COULDN'T HELP EXPLAIN IT.
AT THE LIBRARY...
IT'S THE SAME WORDS. DETEST. INTENSE DISLIKE. TO LOATHE, TO ABHOR, TO EXECRATE.
WHAT ARE YOU LOOKING UP, LITTLE GIRL?
UM... "FLOWERS"
HOW NICE.

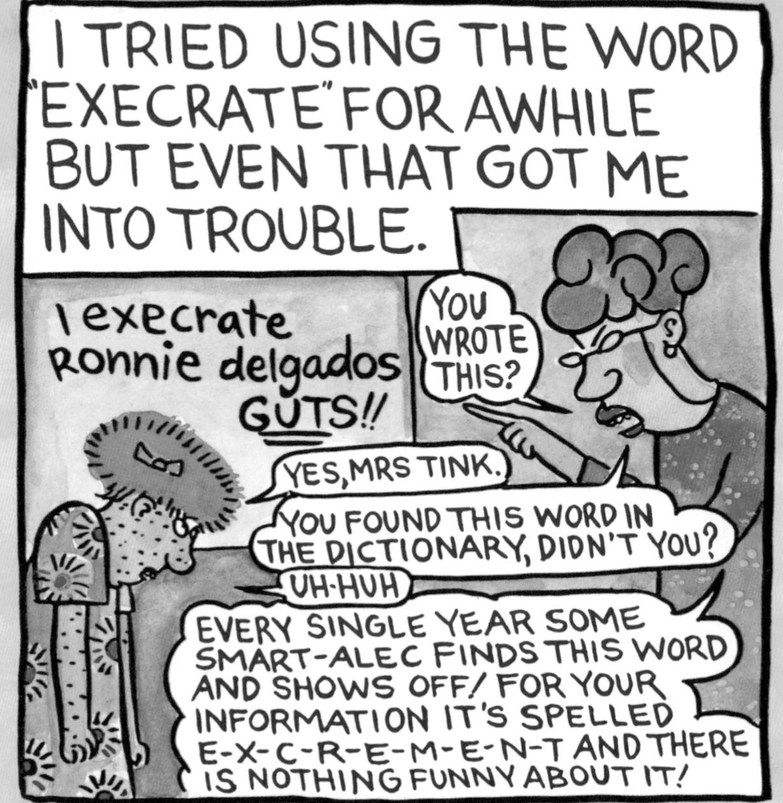
I TRIED USING THE WORD "EXECRATE" FOR AWHILE BUT EVEN THAT GOT ME INTO TROUBLE.
I execrate ronnie delgados GUTS!!
YOU WROTE THIS?
YES, MRS TINK.
YOU FOUND THIS WORD IN THE DICTIONARY, DIDN'T YOU?
UH-HUH
EVERY SINGLE YEAR SOME SMART-ALEC FINDS THIS WORD AND SHOWS OFF! FOR YOUR INFORMATION IT'S SPELLED E-X-C-R-E-M-E-N-T AND THERE IS NOTHING FUNNY ABOUT IT!

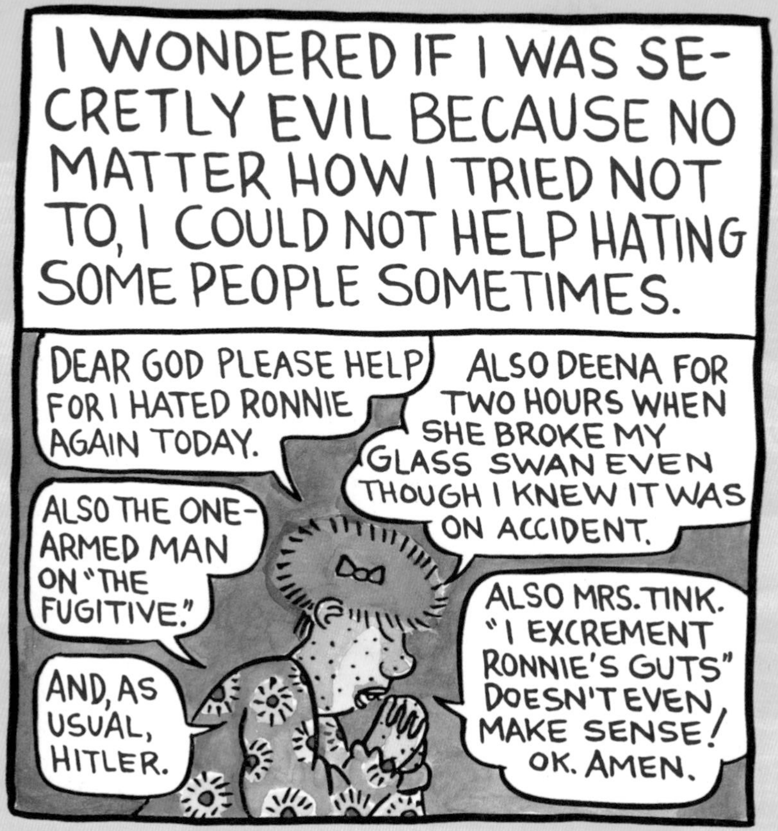
I WONDERED IF I WAS SECRETLY EVIL BECAUSE NO MATTER HOW I TRIED NOT TO, I COULD NOT HELP HATING SOME PEOPLE SOMETIMES.
DEAR GOD PLEASE HELP FOR I HATED RONNIE AGAIN TODAY.
ALSO THE ONE-ARMED MAN ON "THE FUGITIVE."
AND, AS USUAL, HITLER.
ALSO DEENA FOR TWO HOURS WHEN SHE BROKE MY GLASS SWAN EVEN THOUGH I KNEW IT WAS ON ACCIDENT.
ALSO MRS. TINK. "I EXCREMENT RONNIE'S GUTS" DOESN'T EVEN MAKE SENSE! OK. AMEN.

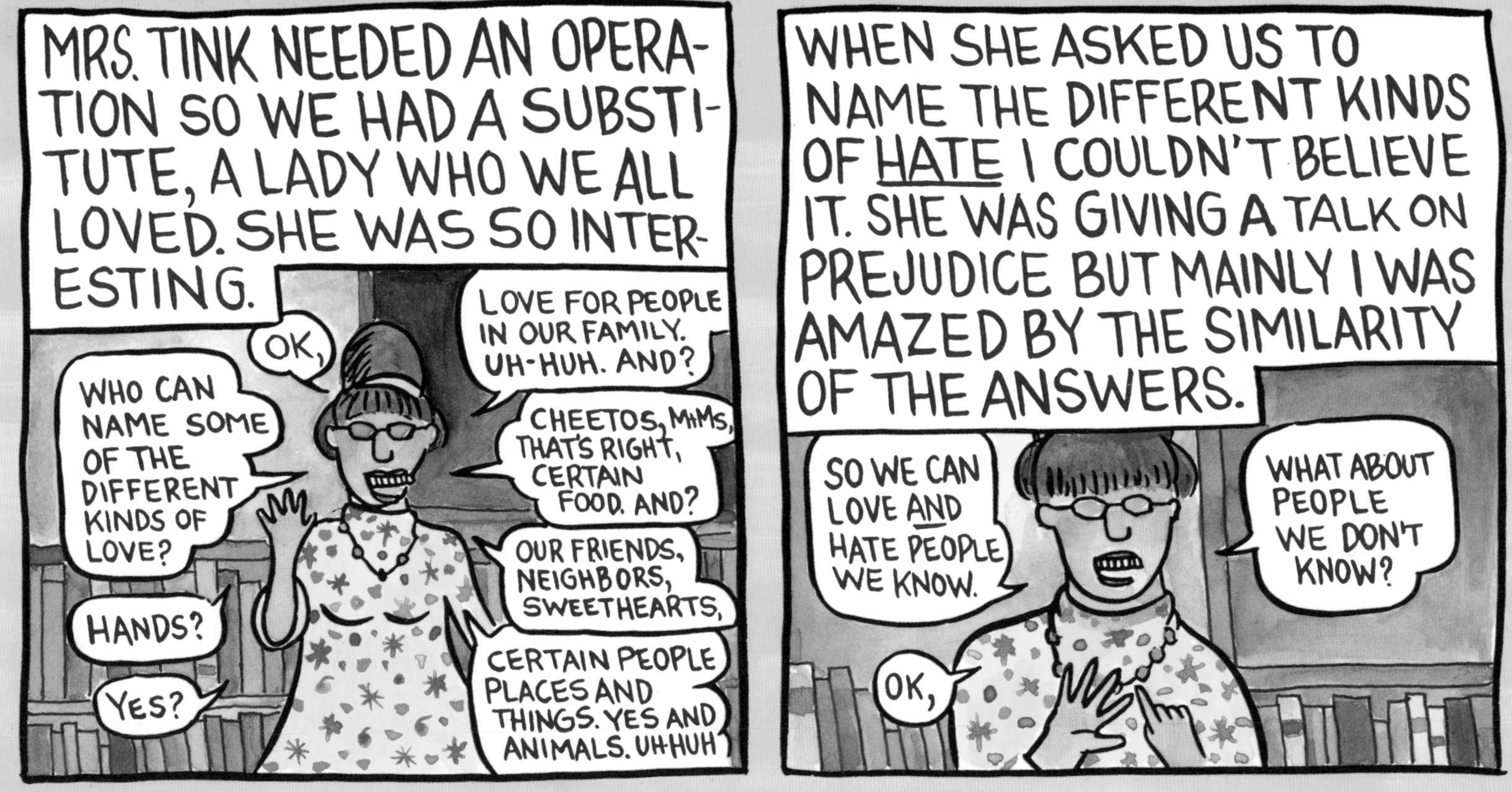
MRS. TINK NEEDED AN OPERATION SO WE HAD A SUBSTITUTE, A LADY WHO WE ALL LOVED. SHE WAS SO INTERESTING.
WHO CAN NAME SOME OF THE DIFFERENT KINDS OF LOVE?
HANDS?
YES?
OK,
LOVE FOR PEOPLE IN OUR FAMILY. UH-HUH. AND?
CHEETOS, M&MS, THAT'S RIGHT, CERTAIN FOOD. AND?
OUR FRIENDS, NEIGHBORS, SWEETHEARTS,
CERTAIN PEOPLE PLACES AND THINGS. YES AND ANIMALS. UH-HUH
WHEN SHE ASKED US TO NAME THE DIFFERENT KINDS OF HATE I COULDN'T BELIEVE IT. SHE WAS GIVING A TALK ON PREJUDICE BUT MAINLY I WAS AMAZED BY THE SIMILARITY OF THE ANSWERS.
SO WE CAN LOVE AND HATE PEOPLE WE KNOW.
OK,
WHAT ABOUT PEOPLE WE DON'T KNOW?

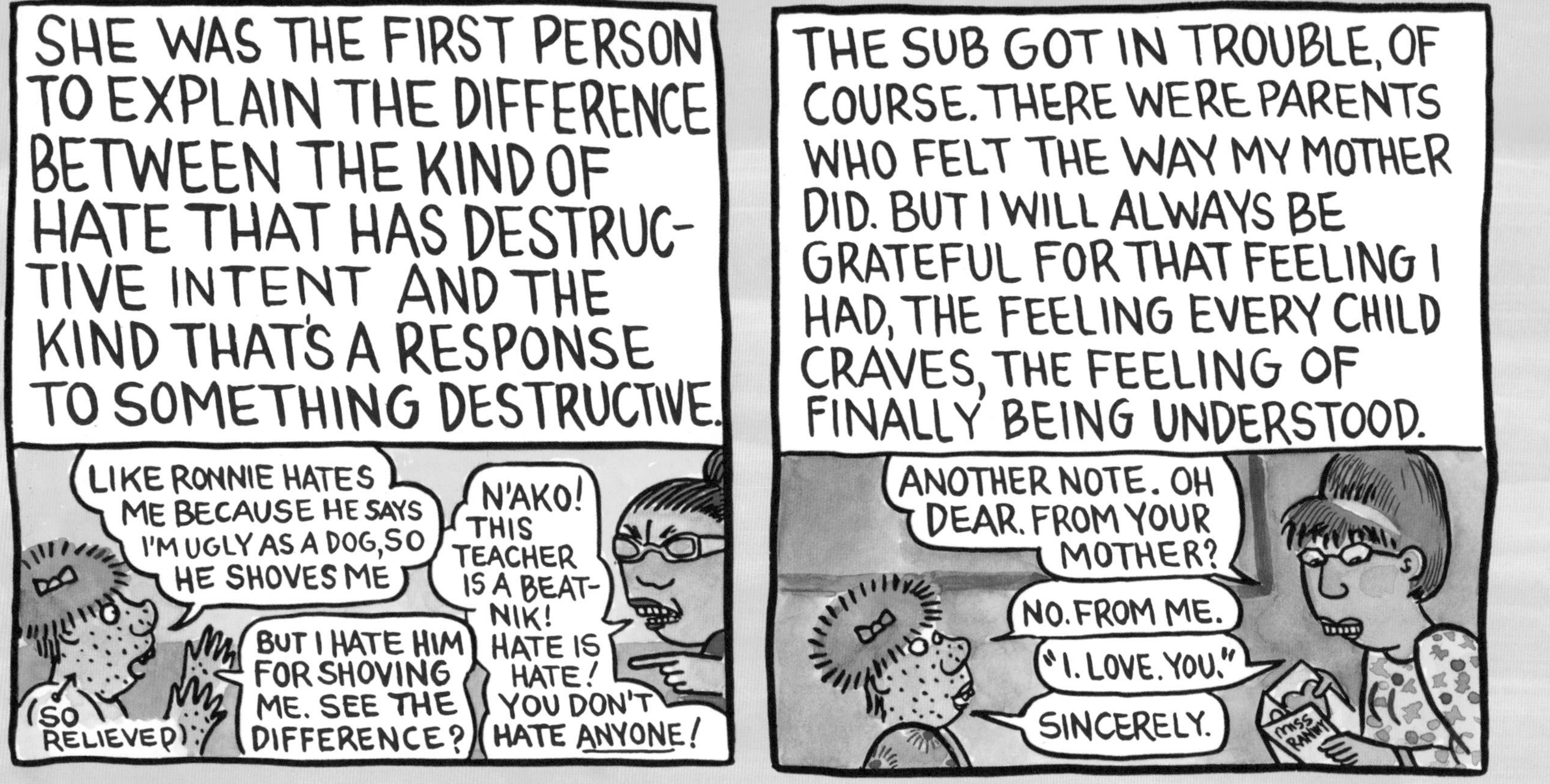
SHE WAS THE FIRST PERSON TO EXPLAIN THE DIFFERENCE BETWEEN THE KIND OF HATE THAT HAS DESTRUCTIVE INTENT AND THE KIND THAT'S A RESPONSE TO SOMETHING DESTRUCTIVE.
LIKE RONNIE HATES ME BECAUSE HE SAYS I'M UGLY AS A DOG, SO HE SHOVES ME
BUT I HATE HIM FOR SHOVING ME. SEE THE DIFFERENCE?
(SO RELIEVED)
N'AKO! THIS TEACHER IS A BEATNIK! HATE IS HATE! YOU DON'T HATE ANYONE!
THE SUB GOT IN TROUBLE, OF COURSE. THERE WERE PARENTS WHO FELT THE WAY MY MOTHER DID. BUT I WILL ALWAYS BE GRATEFUL FOR THAT FEELING I HAD, THE FEELING EVERY CHILD CRAVES, THE FEELING OF FINALLY BEING UNDERSTOOD.
ANOTHER NOTE. OH DEAR. FROM YOUR MOTHER?
NO. FROM ME.
"I. LOVE. YOU."
SINCERELY.

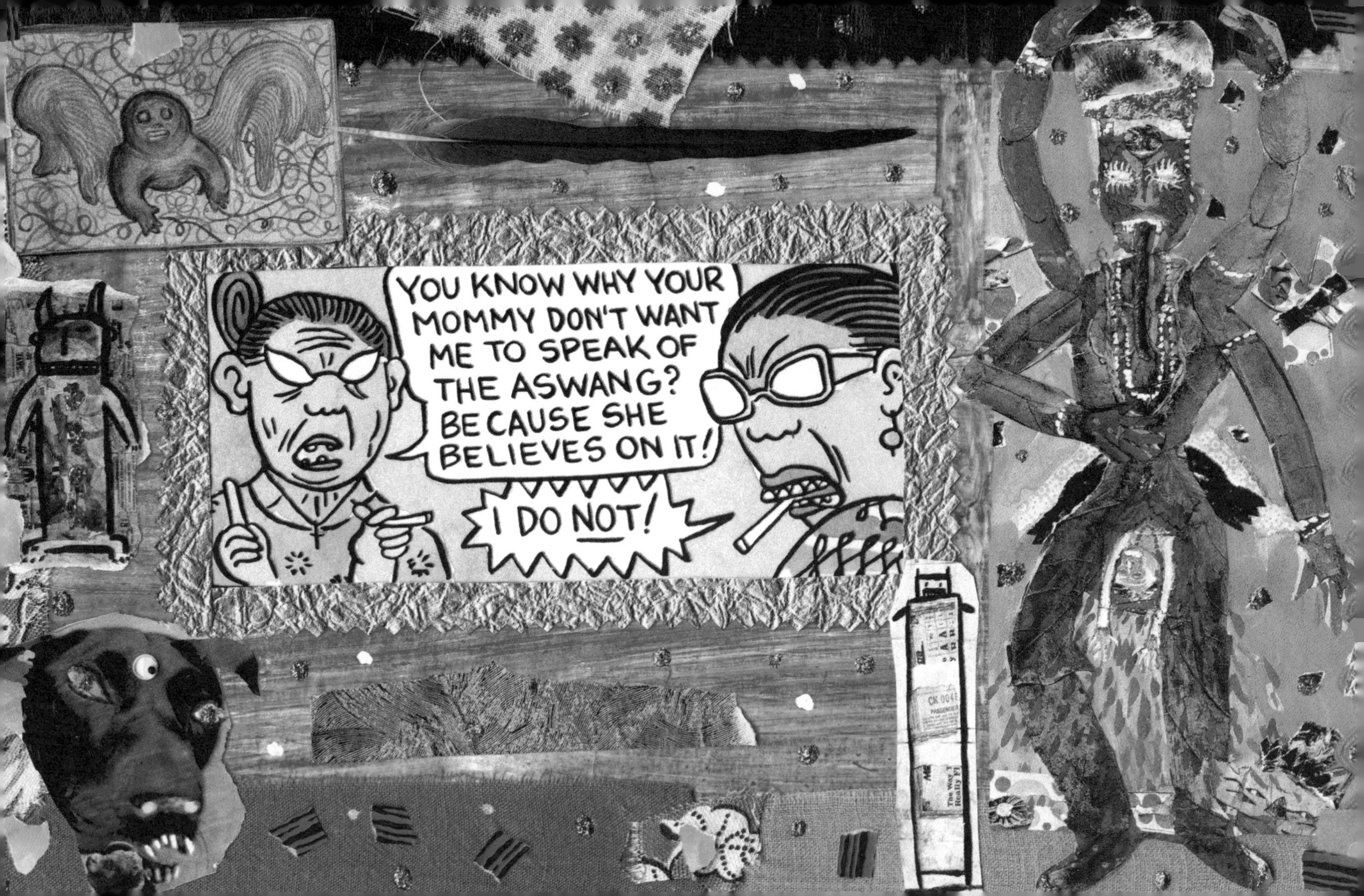
YOU KNOW WHY YOUR MOMMY DON'T WANT ME TO SPEAK OF THE ASWANG? BECAUSE SHE BELIEVES ON IT!
I DO NOT!
CK 0049
PASSENGER

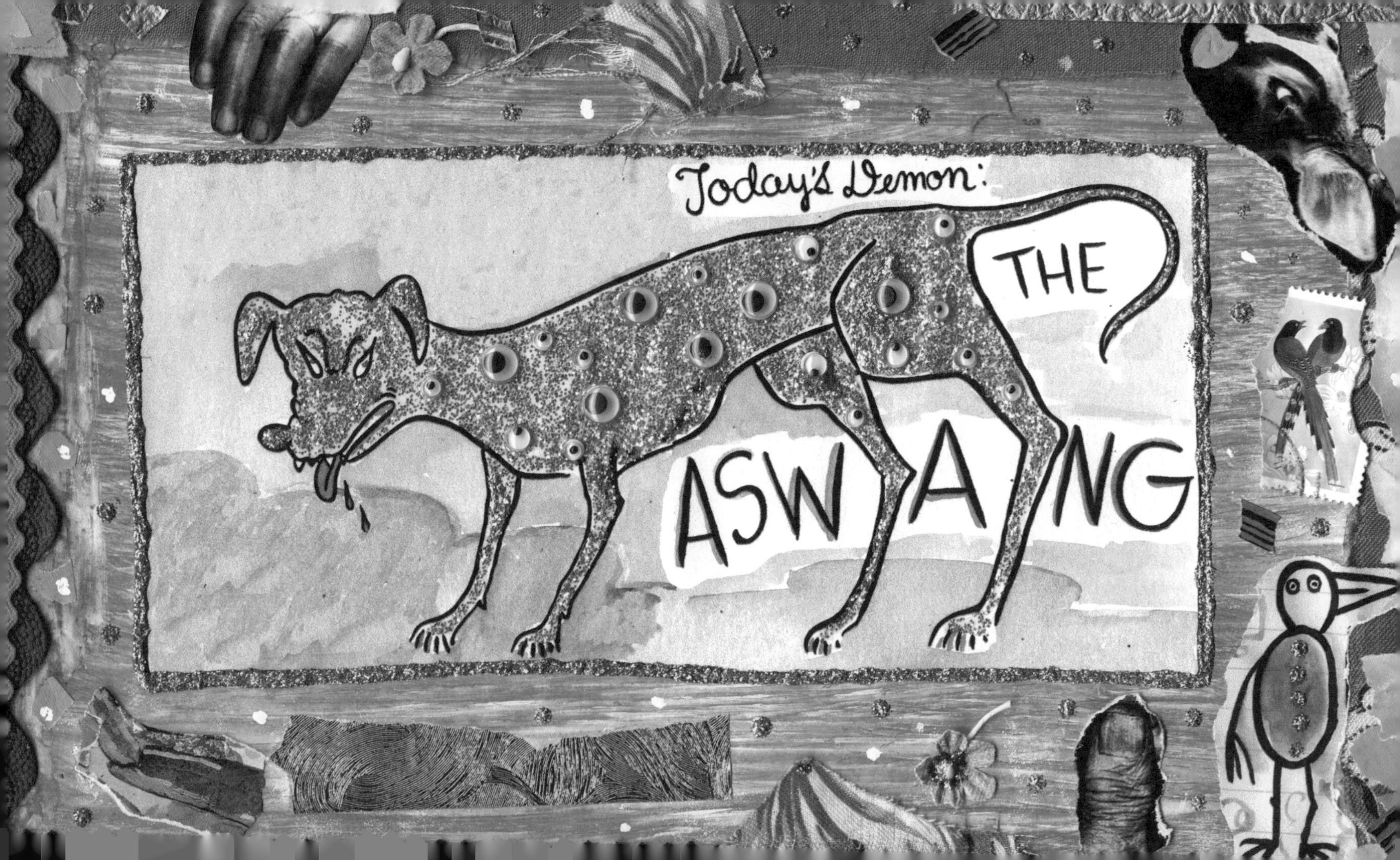
Today's Demon:
THE
ASWANG

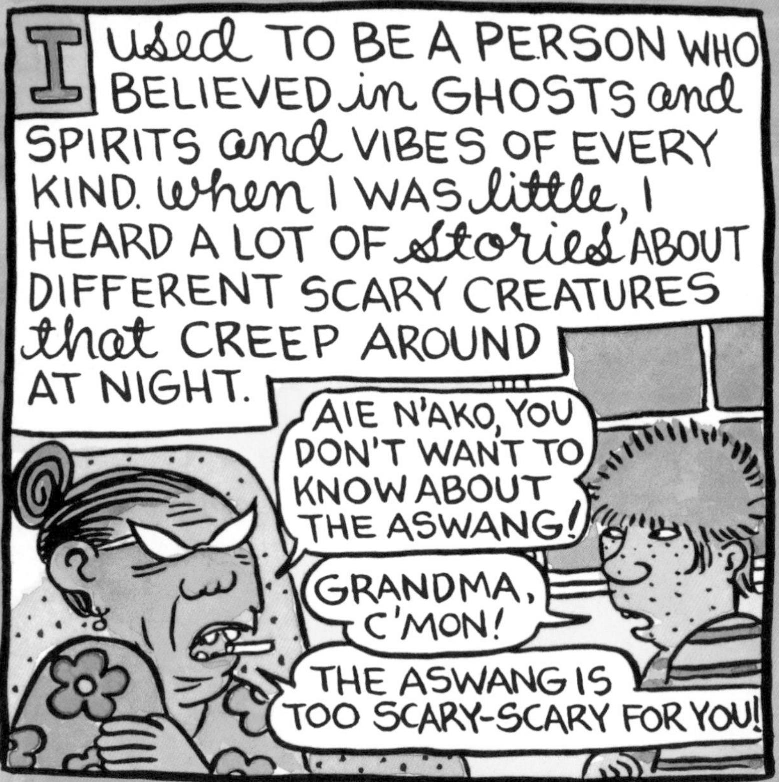
I used TO BE A PERSON WHO BELIEVED in GHOSTS and SPIRITS and VIBES OF EVERY KIND. When I WAS little, I HEARD A LOT OF stories ABOUT DIFFERENT SCARY CREATURES that CREEP AROUND AT NIGHT.
AIE N'AKO, YOU DON'T WANT TO KNOW ABOUT THE ASWANG!
GRANDMA, C'MON!
THE ASWANG IS TOO SCARY-SCARY FOR YOU!

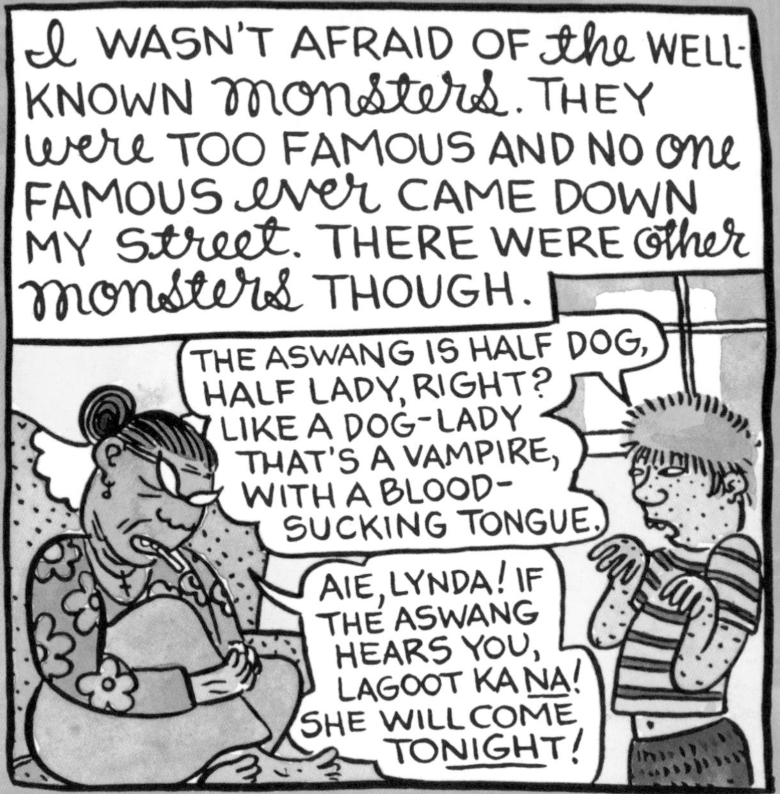
I WASN'T AFRAID OF the WELL-KNOWN monsters. THEY were TOO FAMOUS AND NO one FAMOUS ever CAME DOWN MY street. THERE WERE other monsters THOUGH.
THE ASWANG IS HALF DOG, HALF LADY, RIGHT? LIKE A DOG-LADY THAT'S A VAMPIRE, WITH A BLOOD-SUCKING TONGUE.
AIE, LYNDA! IF THE ASWANG HEARS YOU, LAGOOT KA NA! SHE WILL COME TONIGHT!

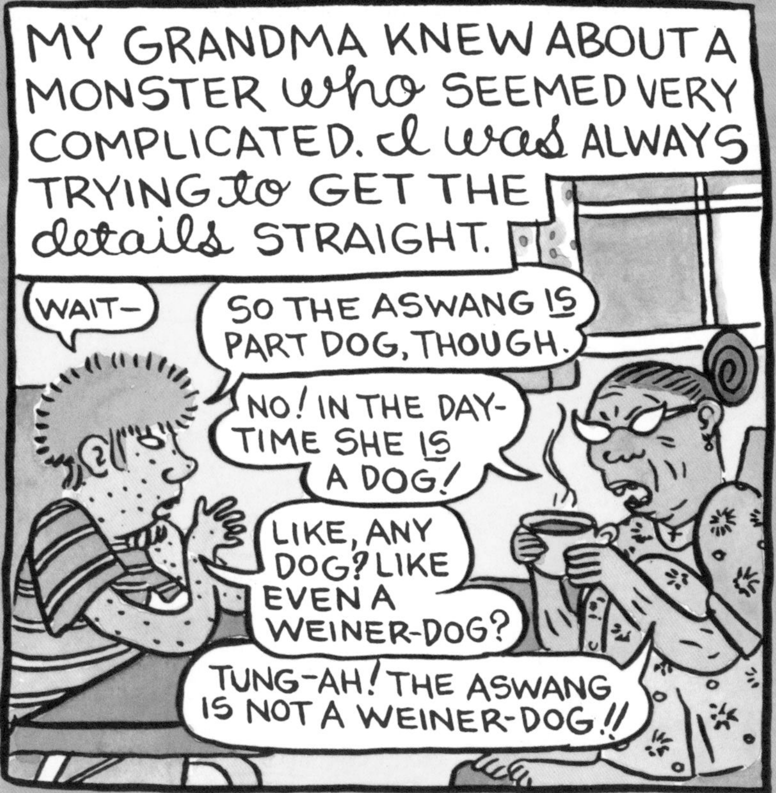
MY GRANDMA KNEW ABOUT A MONSTER who SEEMED VERY COMPLICATED. I was ALWAYS TRYING to GET THE details STRAIGHT.
WAIT—
SO THE ASWANG IS PART DOG, THOUGH.
NO! IN THE DAY-TIME SHE IS A DOG!
LIKE, ANY DOG? LIKE EVEN A WEINER-DOG?
TUNG-AH! THE ASWANG IS NOT A WEINER-DOG!!

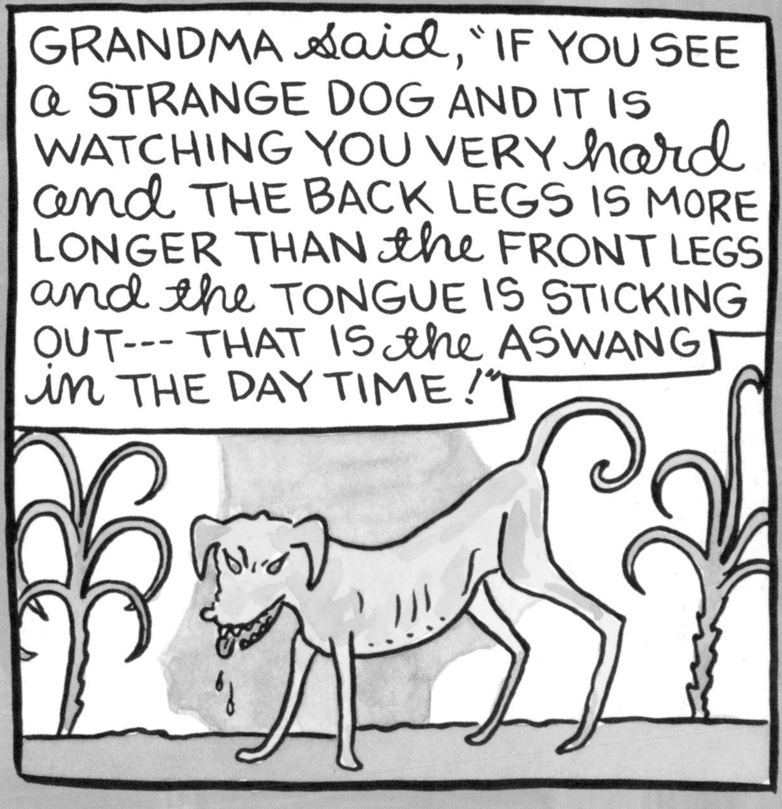
GRANDMA said, "IF YOU SEE a STRANGE DOG AND IT IS WATCHING YOU VERY hard and THE BACK LEGS IS MORE LONGER THAN the FRONT LEGS and the TONGUE IS STICKING OUT--- THAT IS the ASWANG in THE DAY TIME!"

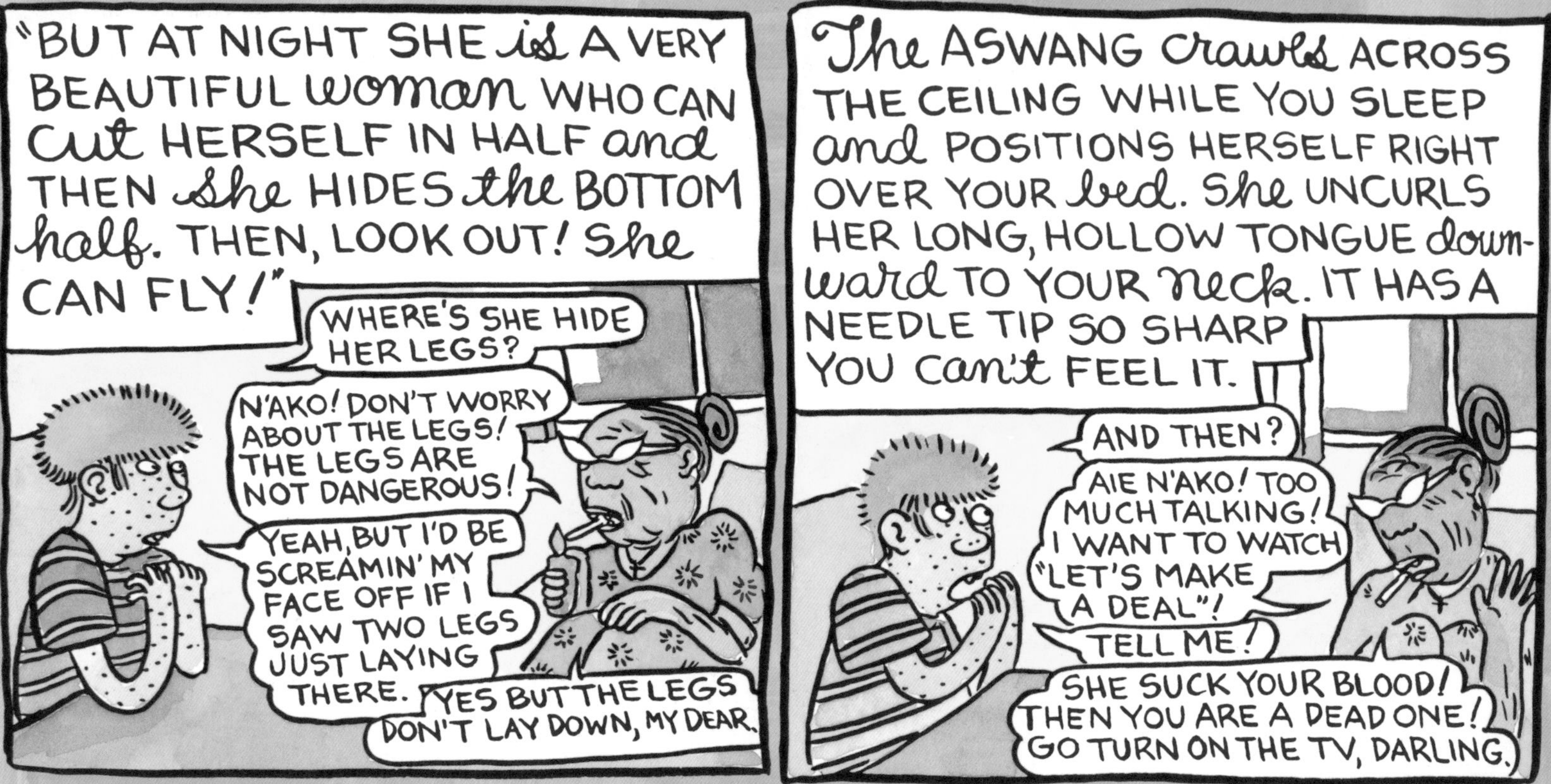
"BUT AT NIGHT SHE is A VERY BEAUTIFUL woman WHO CAN cut HERSELF IN HALF and THEN she HIDES the BOTTOM half. THEN, LOOK OUT! She CAN FLY!"
WHERE'S SHE HIDE HER LEGS?
N'AKO! DON'T WORRY ABOUT THE LEGS! THE LEGS ARE NOT DANGEROUS!
YEAH, BUT I'D BE SCREAMIN' MY FACE OFF IF I SAW TWO LEGS JUST LAYING THERE.
YES BUT THE LEGS DON'T LAY DOWN, MY DEAR.
The ASWANG crawls ACROSS THE CEILING WHILE YOU SLEEP and POSITIONS HERSELF RIGHT OVER YOUR bed. She UNCURLS HER LONG, HOLLOW TONGUE downward TO YOUR neck. IT HAS A NEEDLE TIP SO SHARP YOU can't FEEL IT.
AND THEN?
AIE N'AKO! TOO MUCH TALKING! I WANT TO WATCH "LET'S MAKE A DEAL"!
TELL ME!
SHE SUCK YOUR BLOOD! THEN YOU ARE A DEAD ONE! GO TURN ON THE TV, DARLING.

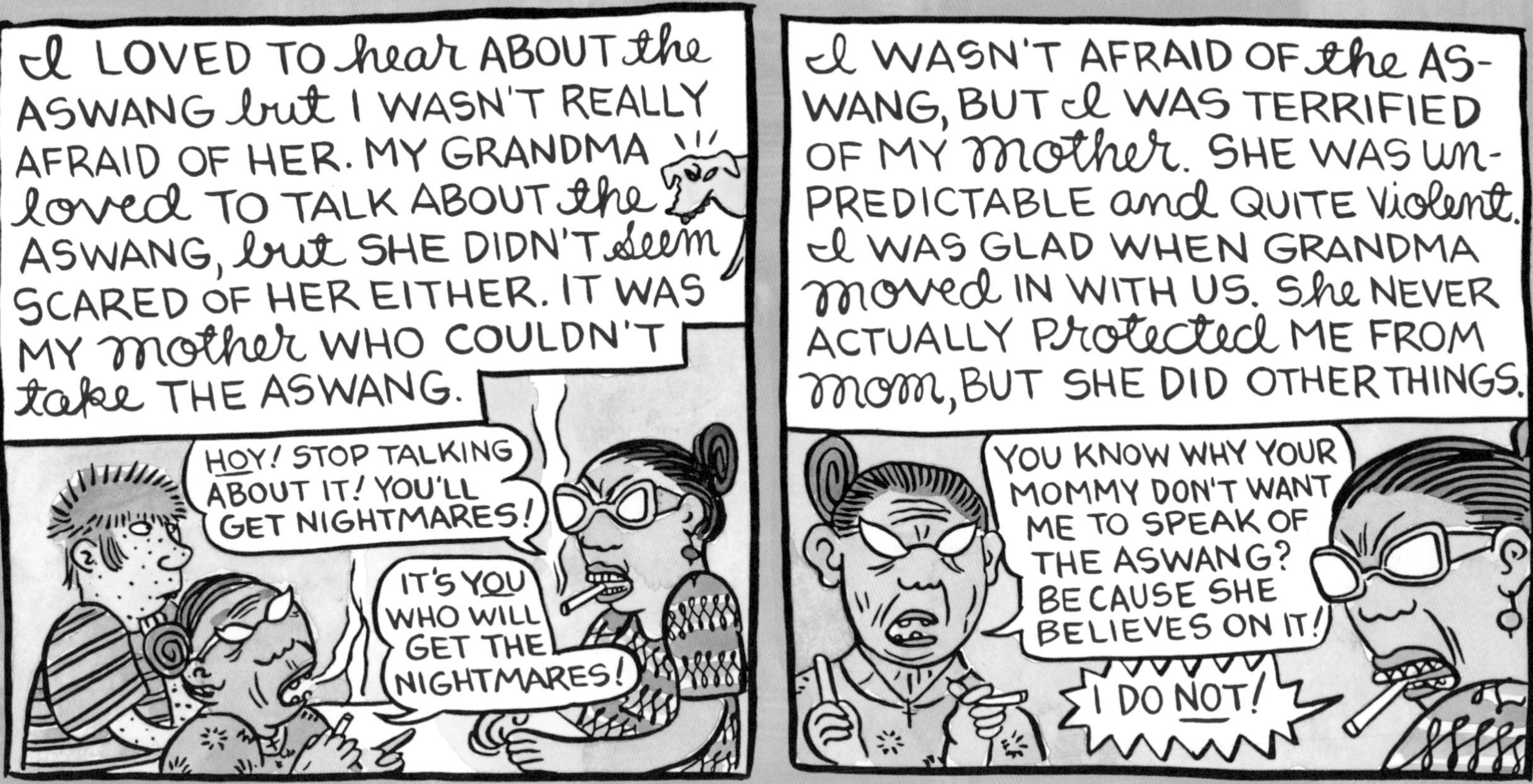
I LOVED TO hear ABOUT the ASWANG but I WASN'T REALLY AFRAID OF HER. MY GRANDMA loved TO TALK ABOUT the ASWANG, but SHE DIDN'T seem SCARED OF HER EITHER. IT WAS MY mother WHO COULDN'T take THE ASWANG.
HOY! STOP TALKING ABOUT IT! YOU'LL GET NIGHTMARES!
IT'S YOU WHO WILL GET THE NIGHTMARES!
I WASN'T AFRAID OF the AS-WANG, BUT I WAS TERRIFIED OF MY mother. SHE WAS un-PREDICTABLE and QUITE violent. I WAS GLAD WHEN GRANDMA moved IN WITH US. She NEVER ACTUALLY protected ME FROM mom, BUT SHE DID OTHER THINGS.
YOU KNOW WHY YOUR MOMMY DON'T WANT ME TO SPEAK OF THE ASWANG? BECAUSE SHE BELIEVES ON IT!
I DO NOT!

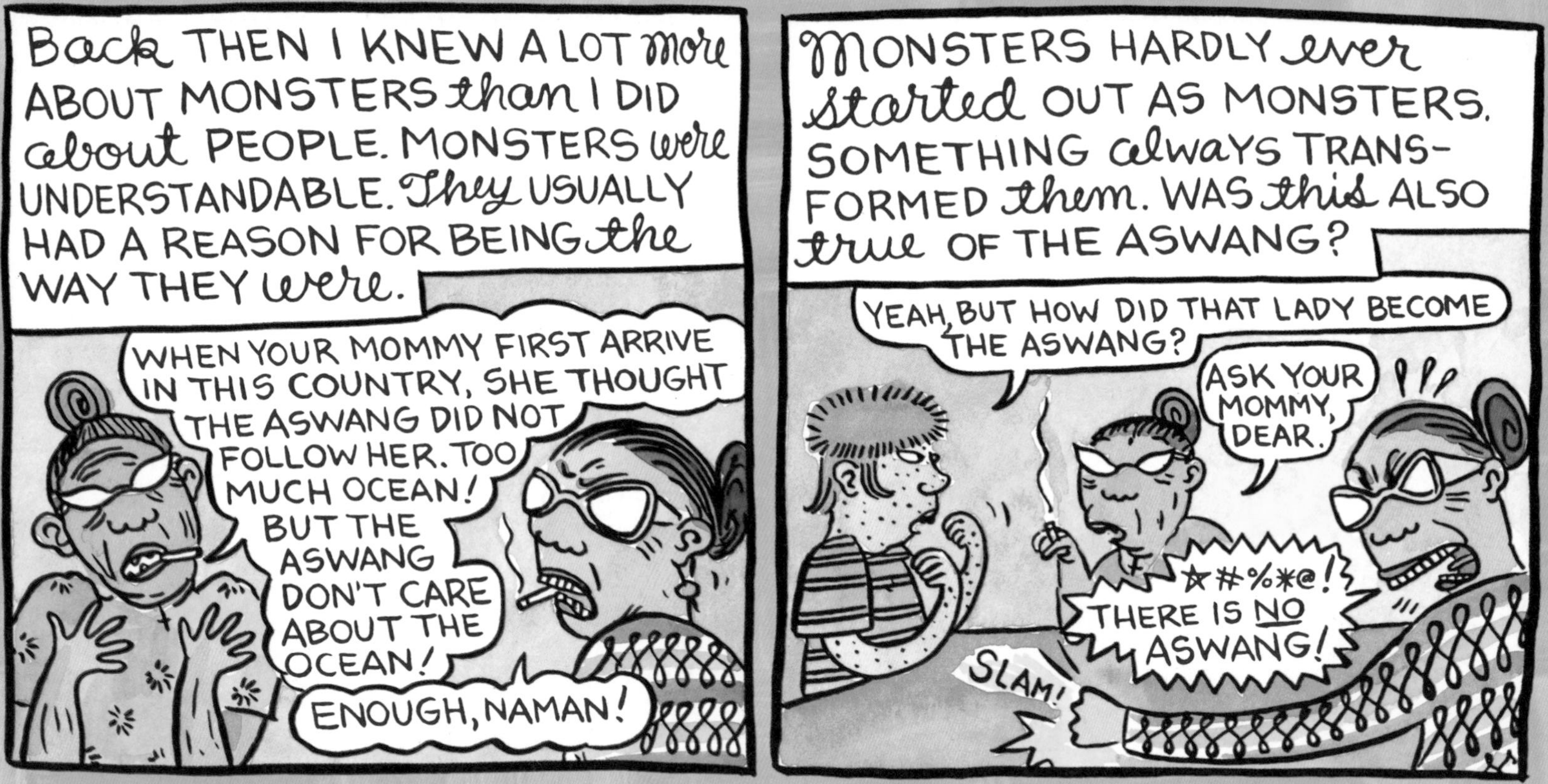

Back THEN I KNEW A LOT more ABOUT MONSTERS than I DID about PEOPLE. MONSTERS were UNDERSTANDABLE. They USUALLY HAD A REASON FOR BEING the WAY THEY were.
WHEN YOUR MOMMY FIRST ARRIVE IN THIS COUNTRY, SHE THOUGHT THE ASWANG DID NOT FOLLOW HER. TOO MUCH OCEAN! BUT THE ASWANG DON'T CARE ABOUT THE OCEAN!
ENOUGH, NAMAN!
MONSTERS HARDLY ever started OUT AS MONSTERS. SOMETHING always TRANS-FORMED them. WAS this ALSO true OF THE ASWANG?
YEAH, BUT HOW DID THAT LADY BECOME THE ASWANG?
ASK YOUR MOMMY, DEAR.
☆#%✱@! THERE IS NO ASWANG!
SLAM!

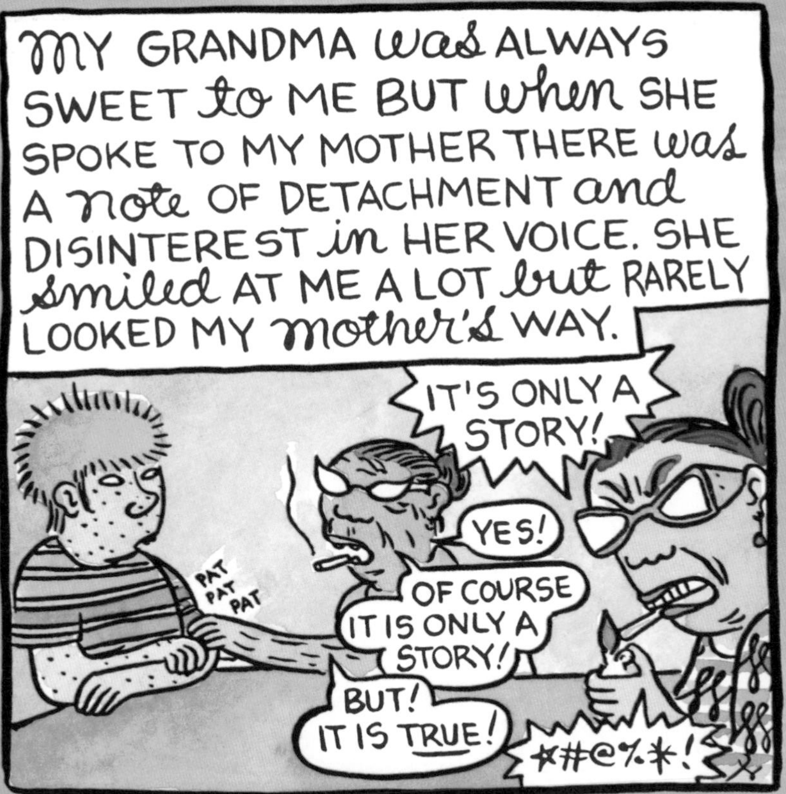
MY GRANDMA WAS ALWAYS SWEET TO ME BUT WHEN SHE SPOKE TO MY MOTHER THERE WAS A NOTE OF DETACHMENT AND DISINTEREST IN HER VOICE. SHE SMILED AT ME A LOT BUT RARELY LOOKED MY MOTHER'S WAY.
IT'S ONLY A STORY!
YES!
PAT PAT PAT
OF COURSE IT IS ONLY A STORY!
BUT! IT IS TRUE!
#@%!

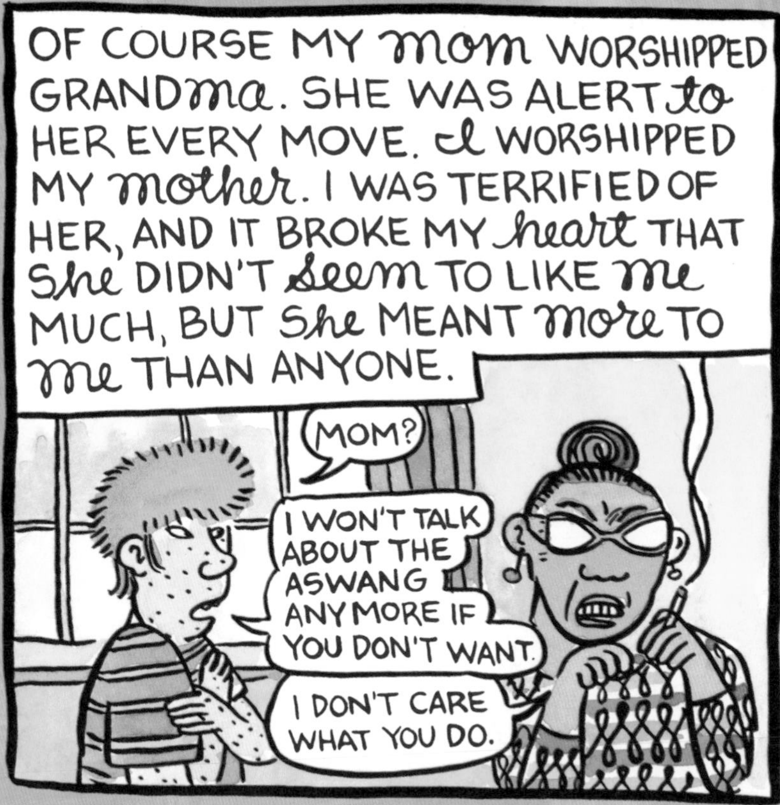
OF COURSE MY MOM WORSHIPPED GRANDMA. SHE WAS ALERT TO HER EVERY MOVE. I WORSHIPPED MY MOTHER. I WAS TERRIFIED OF HER, AND IT BROKE MY HEART THAT SHE DIDN'T SEEM TO LIKE ME MUCH, BUT SHE MEANT MORE TO ME THAN ANYONE.
MOM?
I WON'T TALK ABOUT THE ASWANG ANYMORE IF YOU DON'T WANT.
I DON'T CARE WHAT YOU DO.

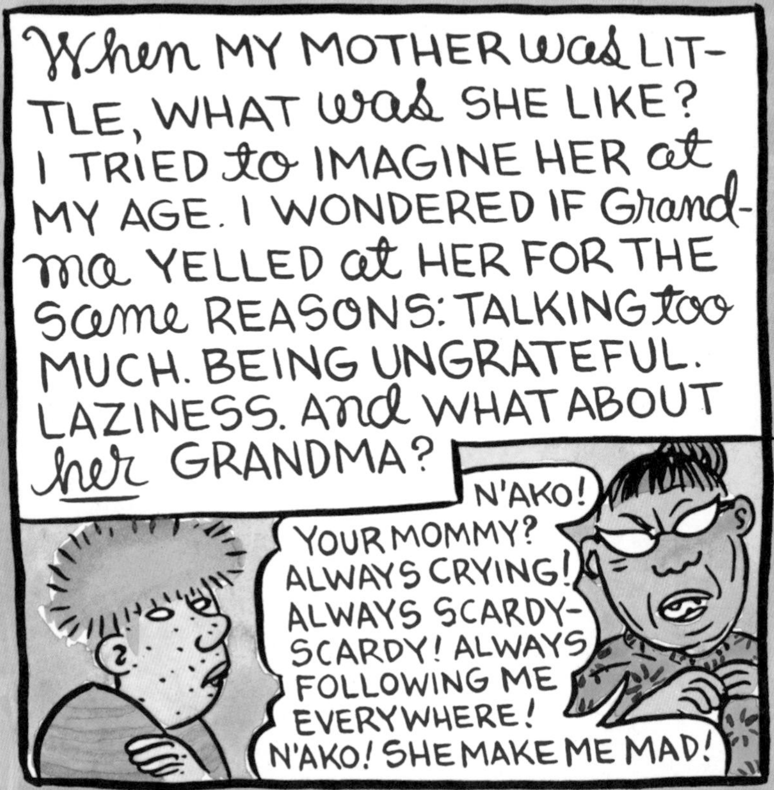
When MY MOTHER was LITTLE, WHAT was SHE LIKE? I TRIED to IMAGINE HER at MY AGE. I WONDERED IF Grandma YELLED at HER FOR THE same REASONS: TALKING too MUCH. BEING UNGRATEFUL. LAZINESS. And WHAT ABOUT her GRANDMA?
N'AKO!
YOUR MOMMY? ALWAYS CRYING! ALWAYS SCARDY-SCARDY! ALWAYS FOLLOWING ME EVERYWHERE! N'AKO! SHE MAKE ME MAD!

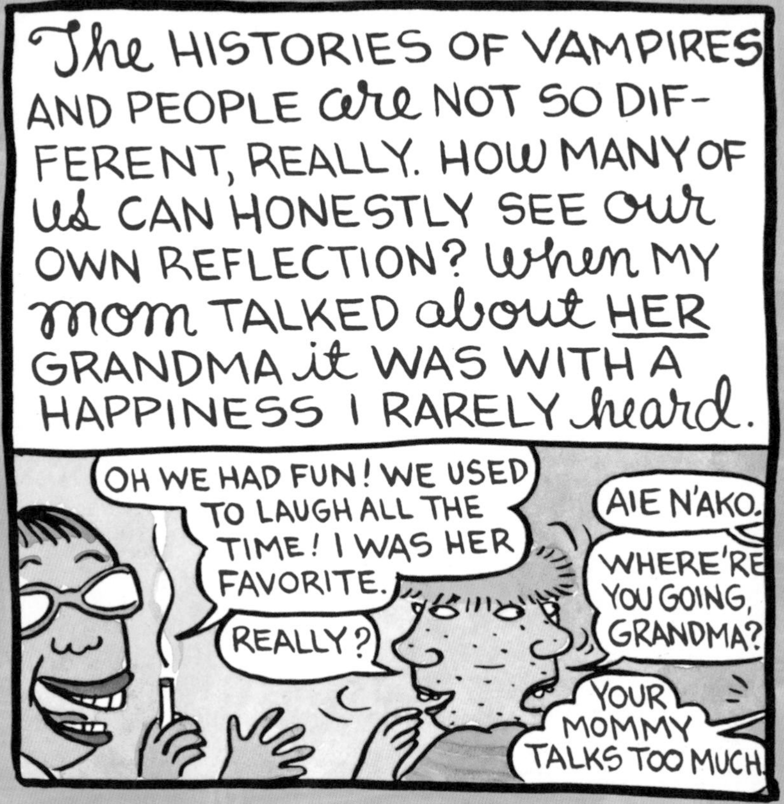
The HISTORIES OF VAMPIRES AND PEOPLE are NOT SO DIFFERENT, REALLY. HOW MANY OF us CAN HONESTLY SEE our OWN REFLECTION? When MY mom TALKED about HER GRANDMA it WAS WITH A HAPPINESS I RARELY heard.
OH WE HAD FUN! WE USED TO LAUGH ALL THE TIME! I WAS HER FAVORITE.
REALLY?
AIE N'AKO.
WHERE'RE YOU GOING, GRANDMA?
YOUR MOMMY TALKS TOO MUCH!

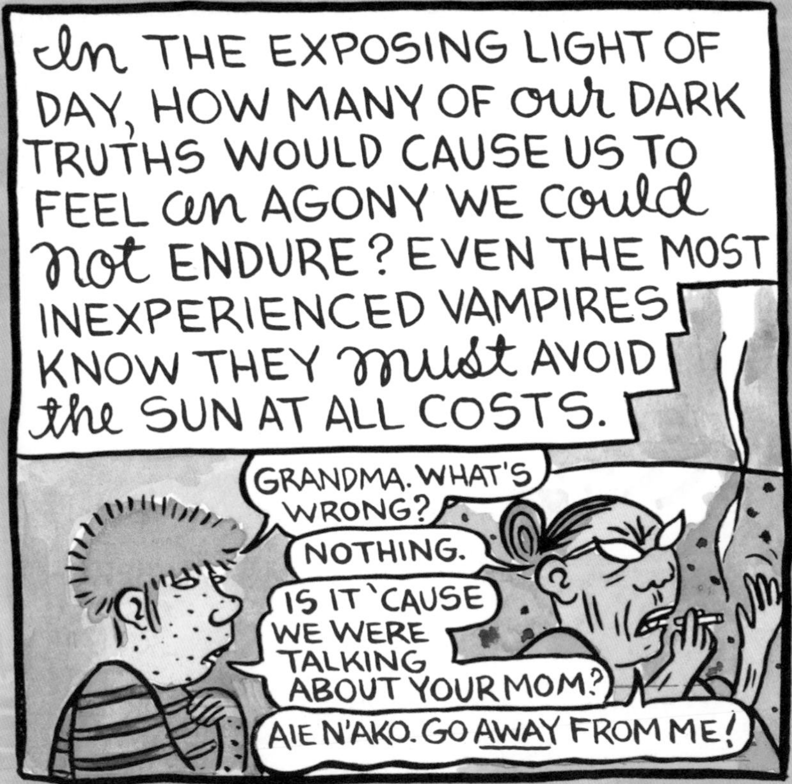

In THE EXPOSING LIGHT OF DAY, HOW MANY OF our DARK TRUTHS WOULD CAUSE US TO FEEL an AGONY WE could not ENDURE? EVEN THE MOST INEXPERIENCED VAMPIRES KNOW THEY must AVOID the SUN AT ALL COSTS.
GRANDMA. WHAT'S WRONG?
NOTHING.
IS IT 'CAUSE WE WERE TALKING ABOUT YOUR MOM?
AIE N'AKO. GO AWAY FROM ME!

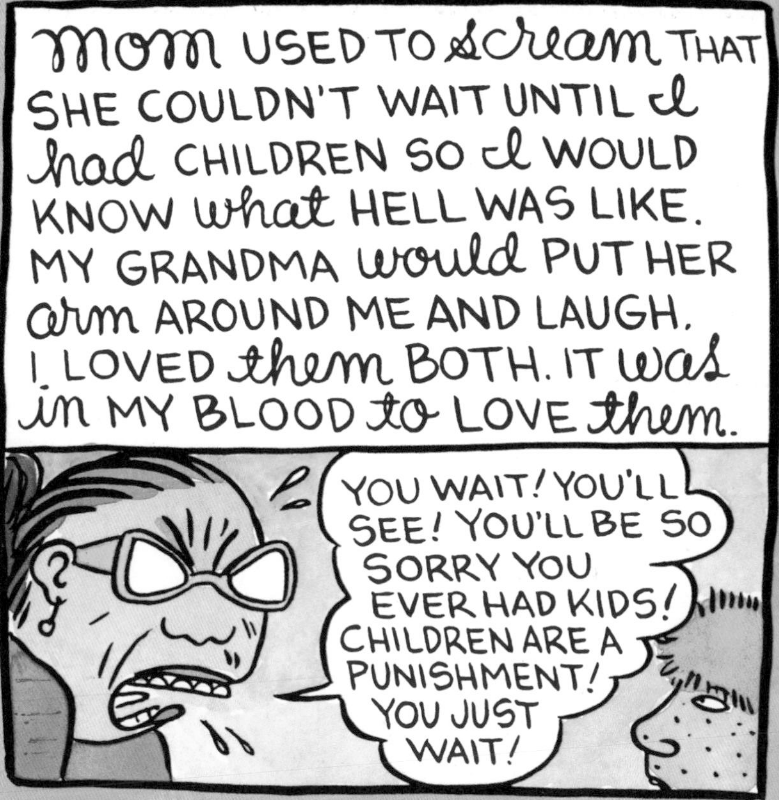

Mom USED TO scream THAT SHE COULDN'T WAIT UNTIL I had CHILDREN SO I WOULD KNOW what HELL WAS LIKE. MY GRANDMA would PUT HER arm AROUND ME AND LAUGH. I LOVED them BOTH. IT was in MY BLOOD to LOVE them.
YOU WAIT! YOU'LL SEE! YOU'LL BE SO SORRY YOU EVER HAD KIDS! CHILDREN ARE A PUNISHMENT! YOU JUST WAIT!

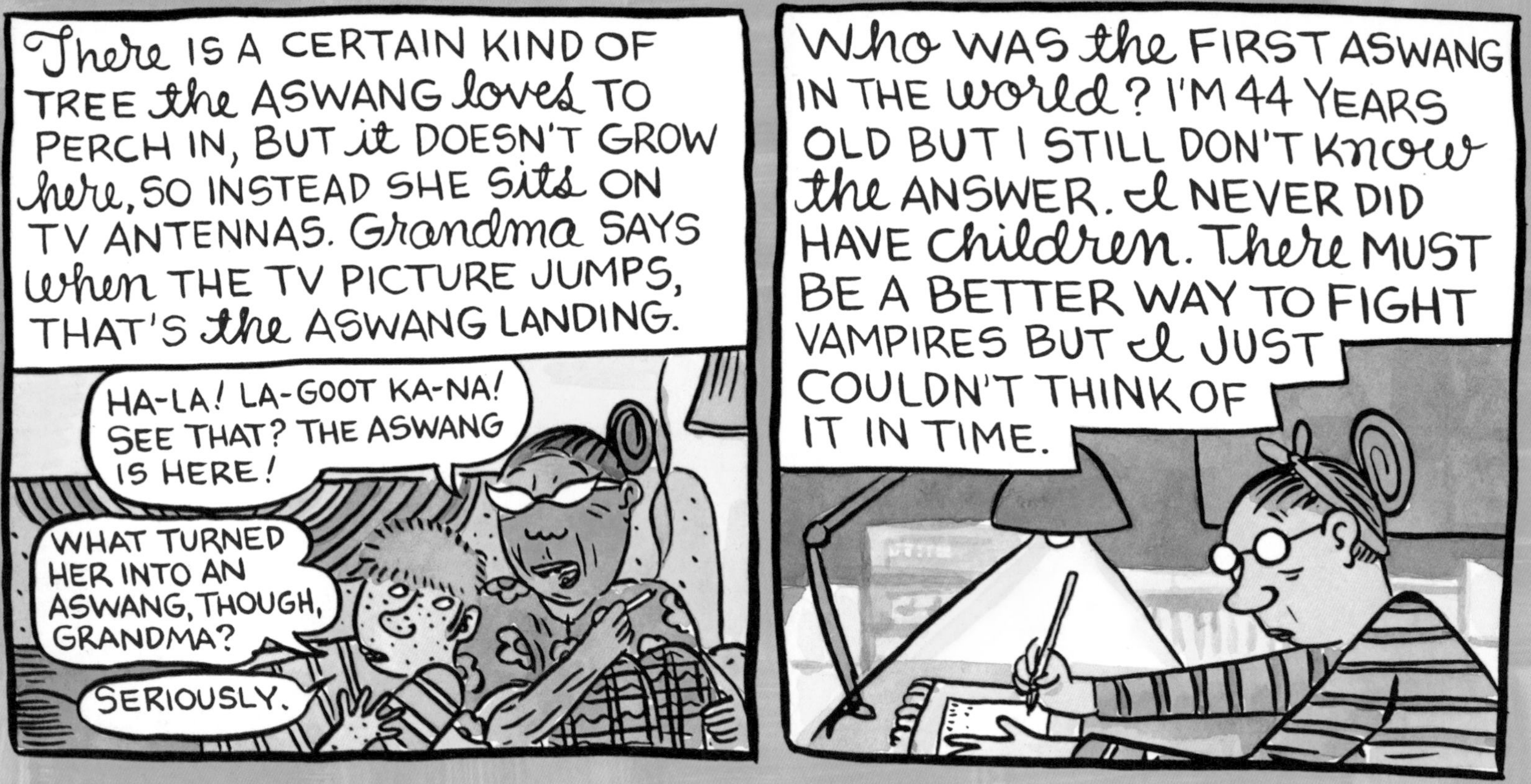
There IS A CERTAIN KIND OF TREE the ASWANG loves TO PERCH IN, BUT it DOESN'T GROW here, SO INSTEAD SHE Sits ON TV ANTENNAS. Grandma SAYS when THE TV PICTURE JUMPS, THAT'S the ASWANG LANDING.
HA-LA! LA-GOOT KA-NA! SEE THAT? THE ASWANG IS HERE!
WHAT TURNED HER INTO AN ASWANG, THOUGH, GRANDMA?
SERIOUSLY.
Who WAS the FIRST ASWANG IN THE world? I'M 44 YEARS OLD BUT I STILL DON'T know the ANSWER. I NEVER DID HAVE children. There MUST BE A BETTER WAY TO FIGHT VAMPIRES BUT I JUST COULDN'T THINK OF IT IN TIME.

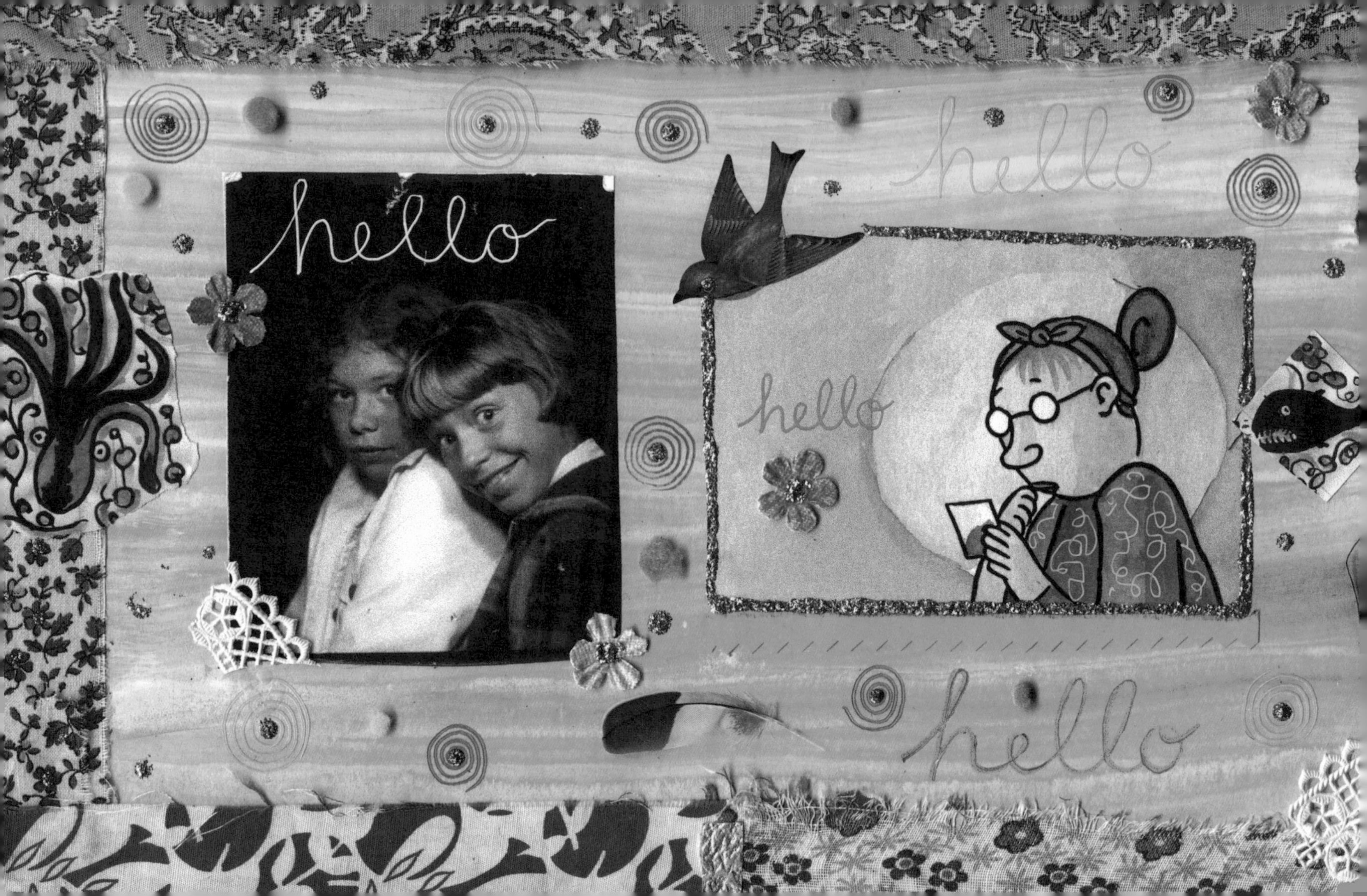
hello
hello
hello
hello

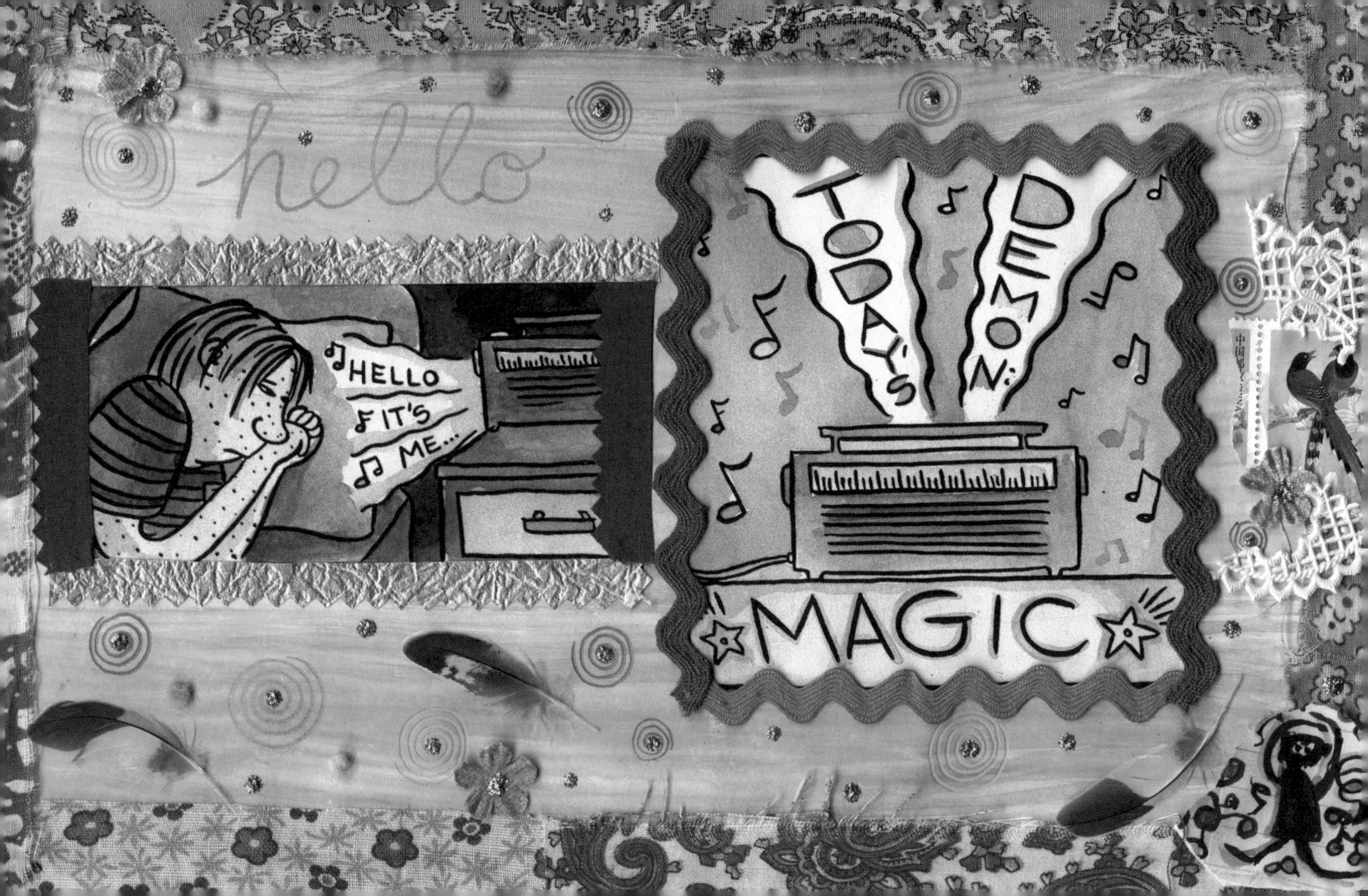
hello
HELLO
IT'S
ME...
TODAY'S
DEMON:
MAGIC

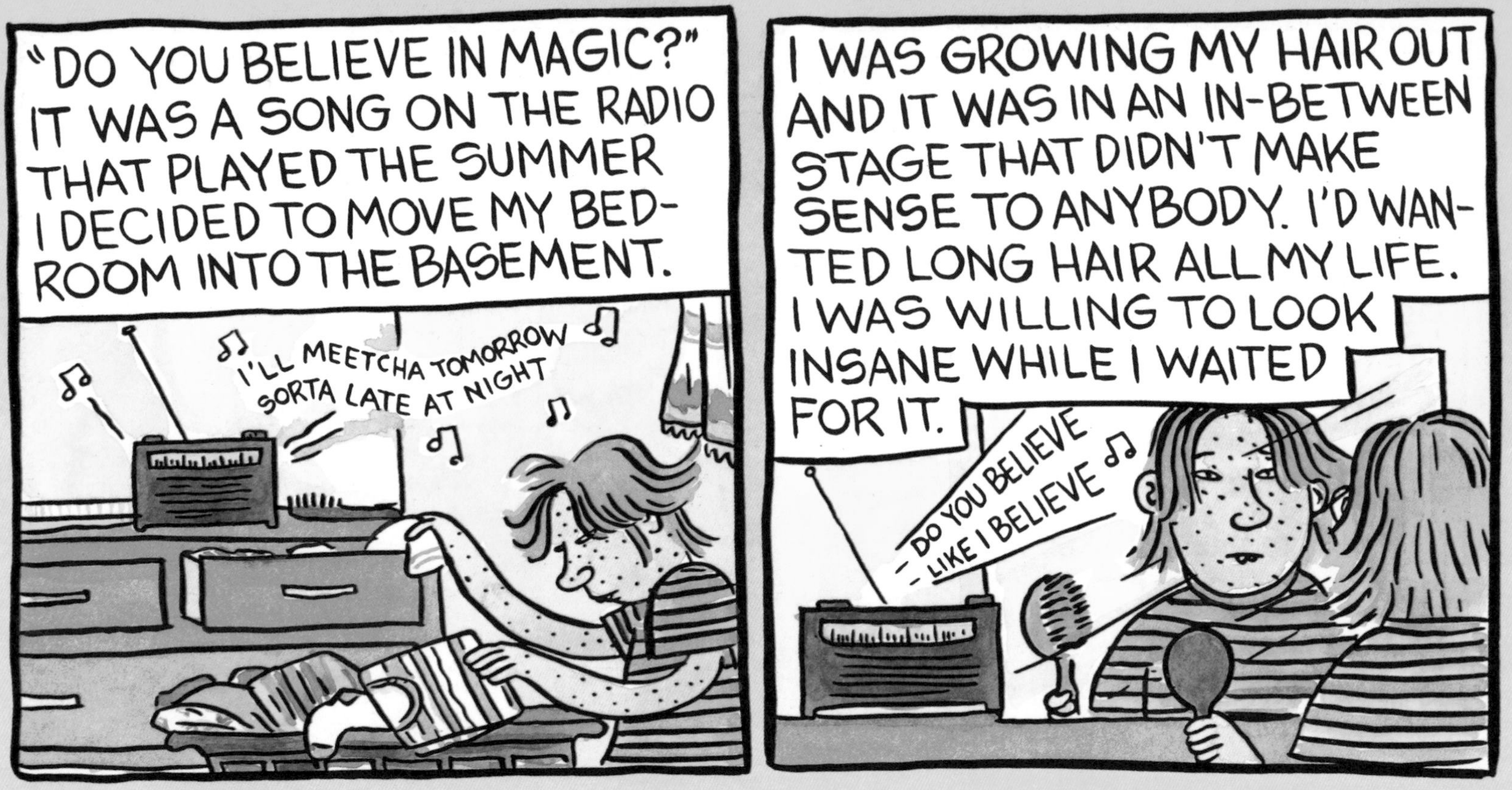
"DO YOU BELIEVE IN MAGIC?" IT WAS A SONG ON THE RADIO THAT PLAYED THE SUMMER I DECIDED TO MOVE MY BED-ROOM INTO THE BASEMENT.
I'LL MEETCHA TOMORROW SORTA LATE AT NIGHT
I WAS GROWING MY HAIR OUT AND IT WAS IN AN IN-BETWEEN STAGE THAT DIDN'T MAKE SENSE TO ANYBODY. I'D WAN-TED LONG HAIR ALL MY LIFE. I WAS WILLING TO LOOK INSANE WHILE I WAITED FOR IT.
- DO YOU BELIEVE - LIKE I BELIEVE

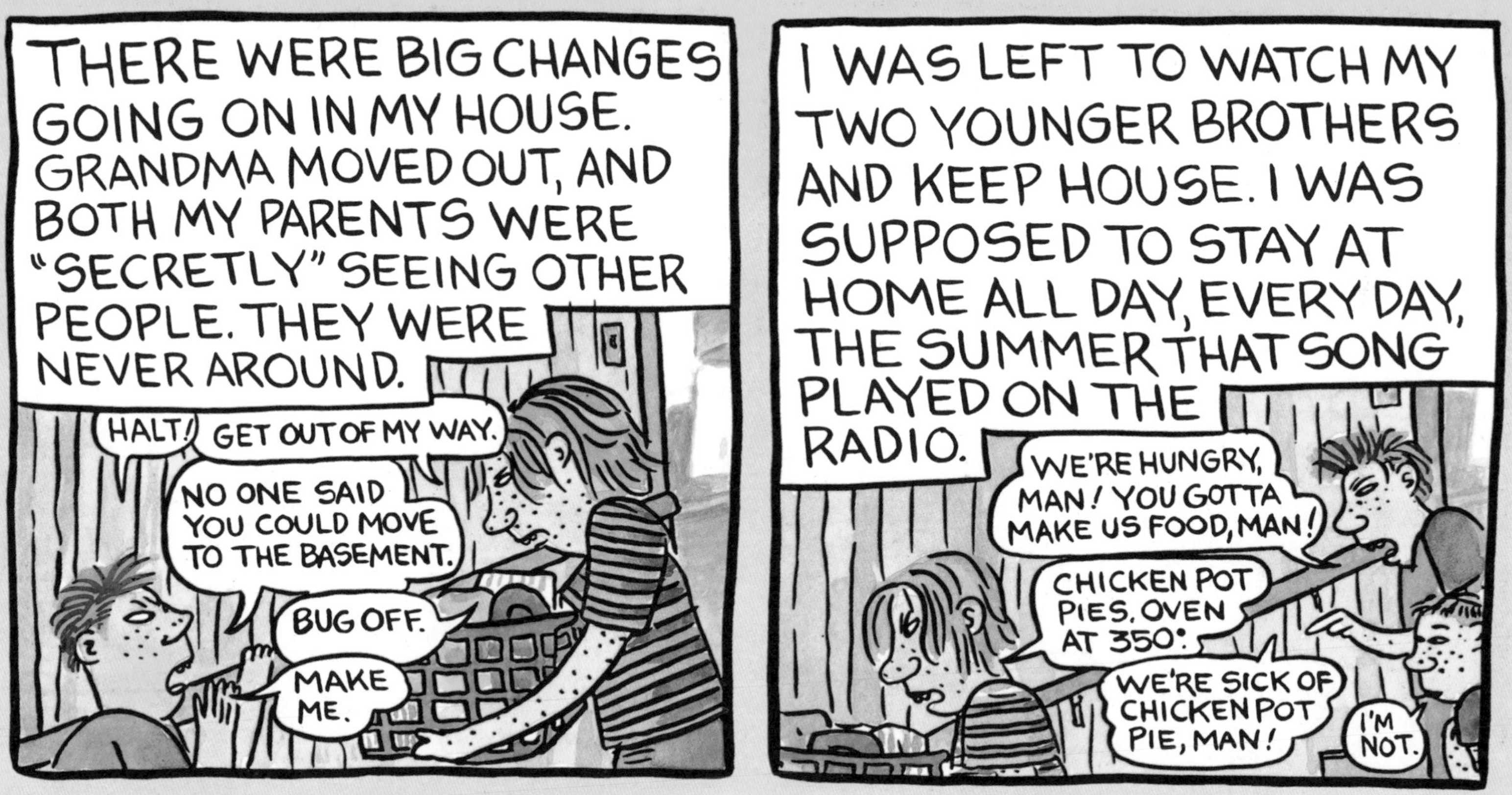
THERE WERE BIG CHANGES GOING ON IN MY HOUSE. GRANDMA MOVED OUT, AND BOTH MY PARENTS WERE "SECRETLY" SEEING OTHER PEOPLE. THEY WERE NEVER AROUND.
HALT!
GET OUT OF MY WAY.
NO ONE SAID YOU COULD MOVE TO THE BASEMENT.
BUG OFF.
MAKE ME.
I WAS LEFT TO WATCH MY TWO YOUNGER BROTHERS AND KEEP HOUSE. I WAS SUPPOSED TO STAY AT HOME ALL DAY, EVERY DAY, THE SUMMER THAT SONG PLAYED ON THE RADIO.
WE'RE HUNGRY, MAN! YOU GOTTA MAKE US FOOD, MAN!
CHICKEN POT PIES. OVEN AT 350°.
WE'RE SICK OF CHICKEN POT PIE, MAN!
I'M NOT.

MY BROTHERS COULD GO WHEREVER THEY WANTED BUT I WAS NEVER ALLOWED TO LEAVE. NOT THAT I HAD ANY PLACE TO GO. I WAS AT AN IN-BETWEEN STAGE IN FRIENDSHIPS.

MY BEST FRIEND, EV, LIVED RIGHT ACROSS THE STREET. SHE WAS AN EXTREMELY KIND AND FUNNY PERSON. WE WERE ALWAYS TOGETHER. SHE WAS TWO YEARS YOUNGER THAN ME BUT IT NEVER MATTERED UNTIL I TURNED 13.

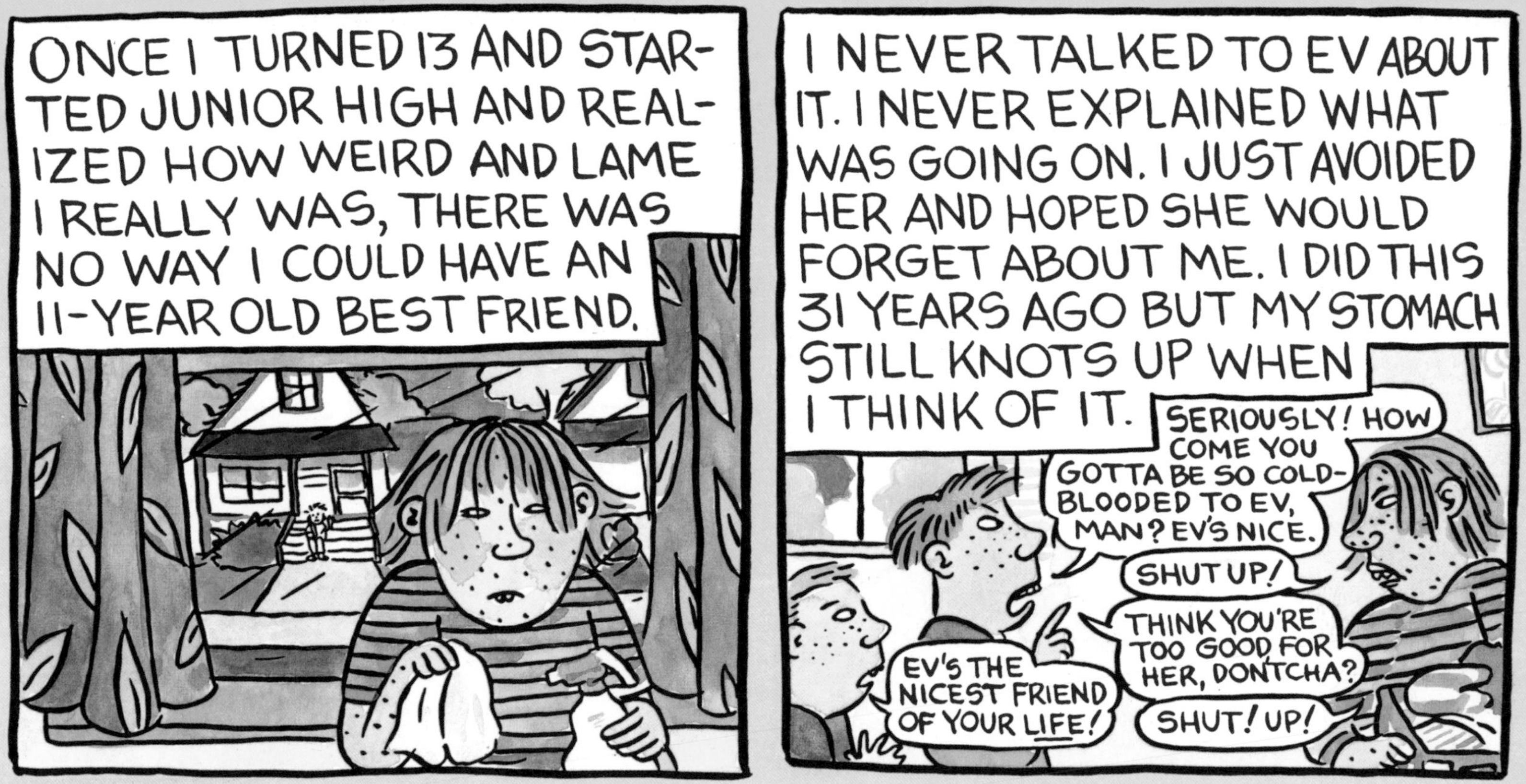
ONCE I TURNED 13 AND STARTED JUNIOR HIGH AND REALIZED HOW WEIRD AND LAME I REALLY WAS, THERE WAS NO WAY I COULD HAVE AN 11-YEAR OLD BEST FRIEND.
I NEVER TALKED TO EV ABOUT IT. I NEVER EXPLAINED WHAT WAS GOING ON. I JUST AVOIDED HER AND HOPED SHE WOULD FORGET ABOUT ME. I DID THIS 31 YEARS AGO BUT MY STOMACH STILL KNOTS UP WHEN I THINK OF IT.
SERIOUSLY! HOW COME YOU GOTTA BE SO COLD-BLOODED TO EV, MAN? EV'S NICE.
SHUT UP!
THINK YOU'RE TOO GOOD FOR HER, DON'TCHA?
EV'S THE NICEST FRIEND OF YOUR LIFE!
SHUT! UP!

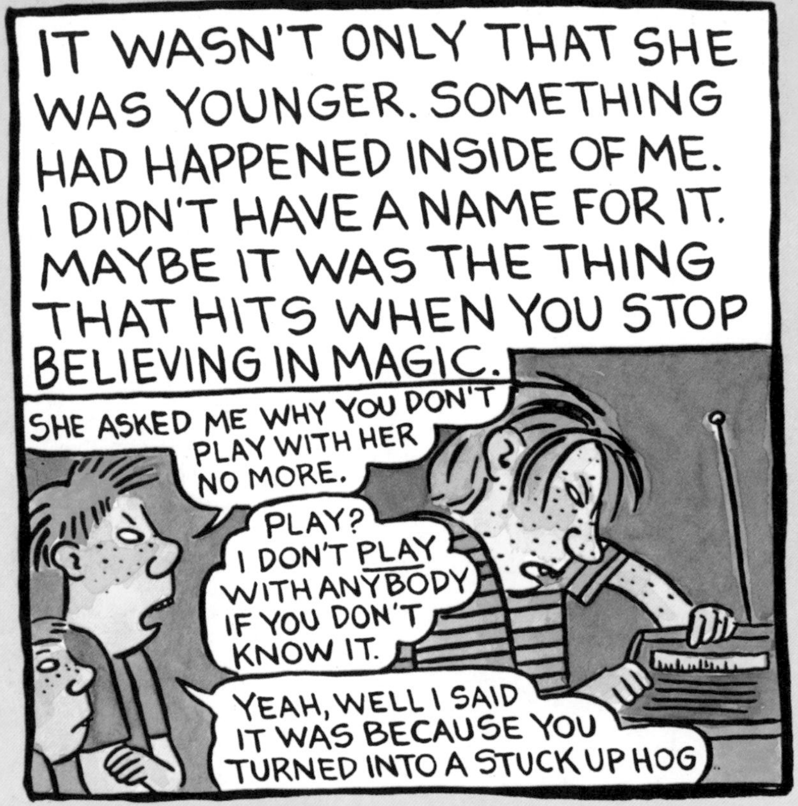
IT WASN'T ONLY THAT SHE WAS YOUNGER. SOMETHING HAD HAPPENED INSIDE OF ME. I DIDN'T HAVE A NAME FOR IT. MAYBE IT WAS THE THING THAT HITS WHEN YOU STOP BELIEVING IN MAGIC.
SHE ASKED ME WHY YOU DON'T PLAY WITH HER NO MORE.
PLAY? I DON'T PLAY WITH ANYBODY IF YOU DON'T KNOW IT.
YEAH, WELL I SAID IT WAS BECAUSE YOU TURNED INTO A STUCK UP HOG

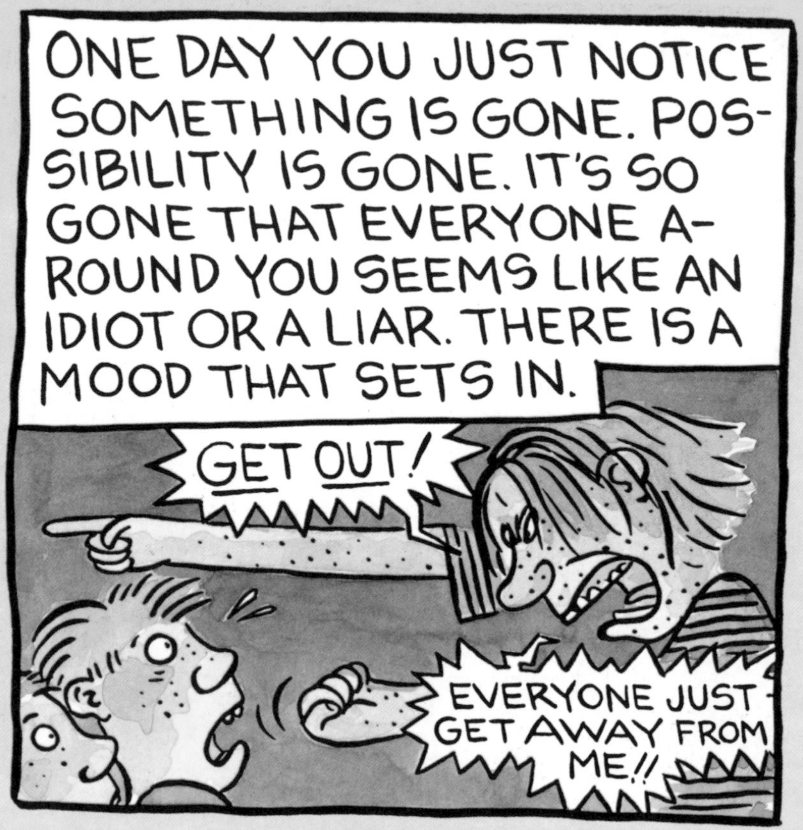
ONE DAY YOU JUST NOTICE SOMETHING IS GONE. POSSIBILITY IS GONE. IT'S SO GONE THAT EVERYONE AROUND YOU SEEMS LIKE AN IDIOT OR A LIAR. THERE IS A MOOD THAT SETS IN.
GET OUT!
EVERYONE JUST GET AWAY FROM ME!!

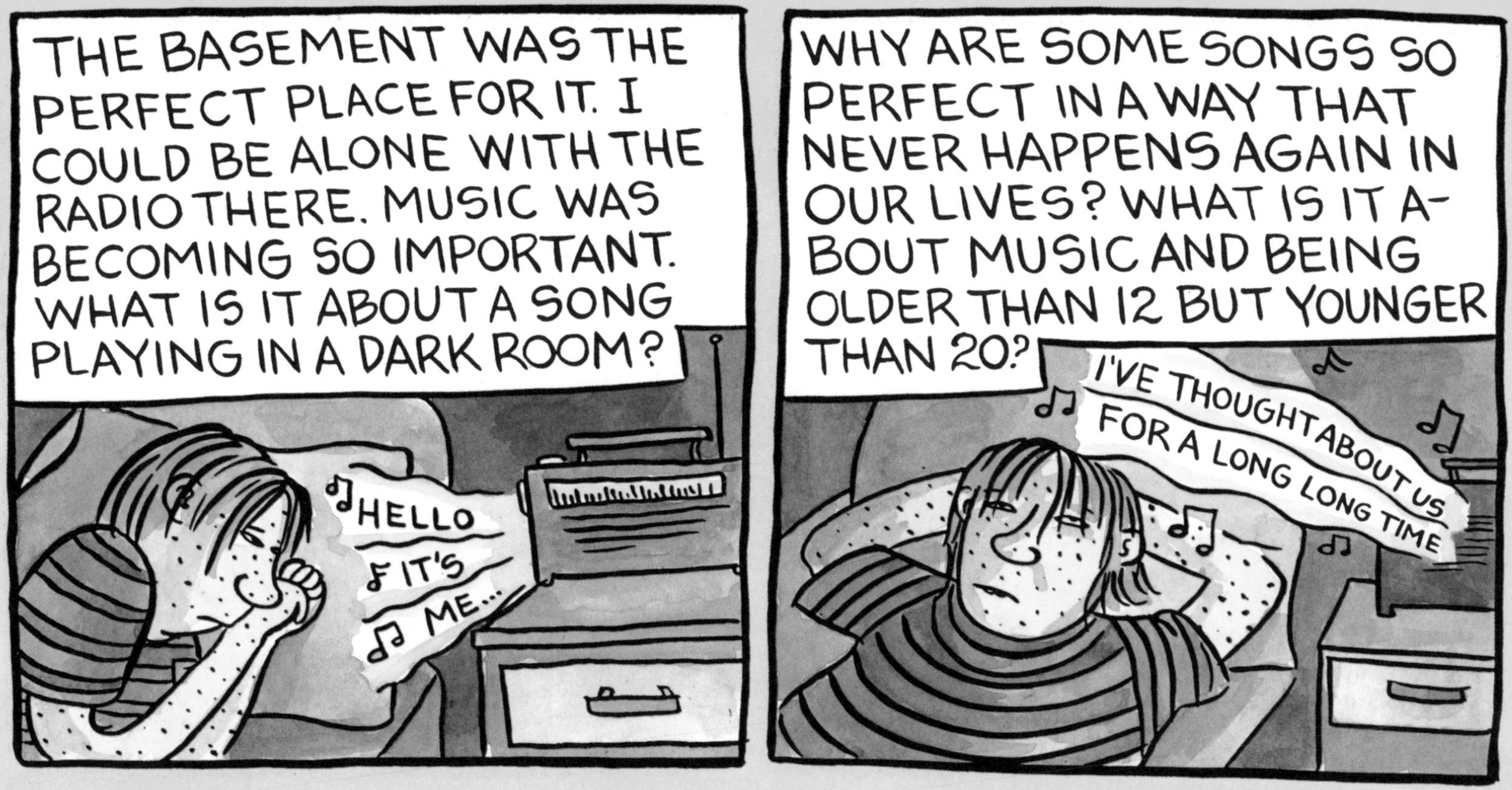
THE BASEMENT WAS THE PERFECT PLACE FOR IT. I COULD BE ALONE WITH THE RADIO THERE. MUSIC WAS BECOMING SO IMPORTANT. WHAT IS IT ABOUT A SONG PLAYING IN A DARK ROOM?
HELLO
IT'S
ME...
WHY ARE SOME SONGS SO PERFECT IN A WAY THAT NEVER HAPPENS AGAIN IN OUR LIVES? WHAT IS IT ABOUT MUSIC AND BEING OLDER THAN 12 BUT YOUNGER THAN 20?
I'VE THOUGHT ABOUT US
FOR A LONG LONG TIME

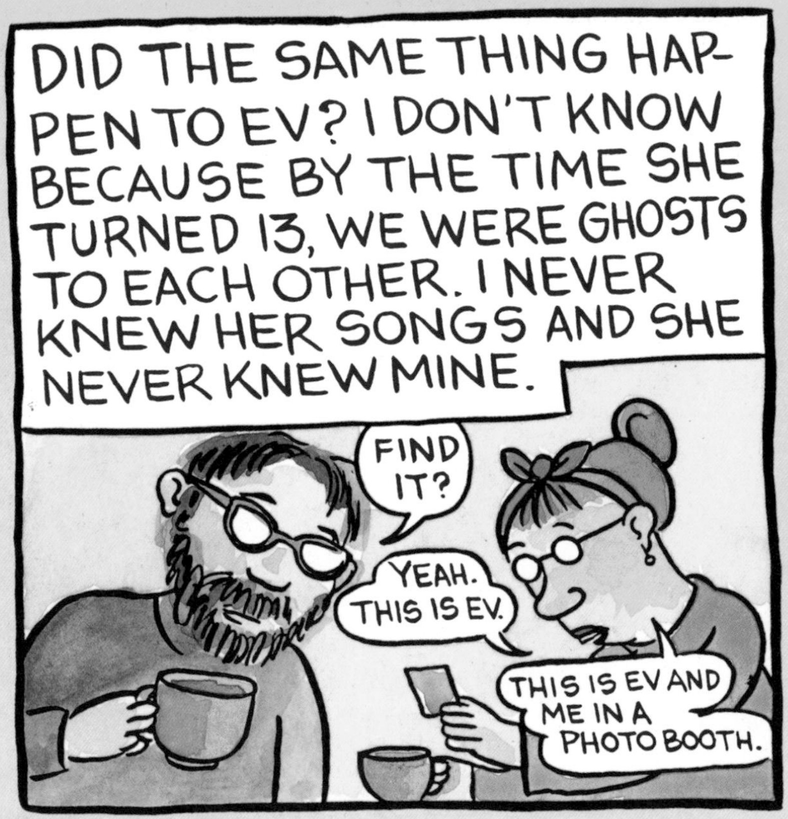
DID THE SAME THING HAPPEN TO EV? I DON'T KNOW BECAUSE BY THE TIME SHE TURNED 13, WE WERE GHOSTS TO EACH OTHER. I NEVER KNEW HER SONGS AND SHE NEVER KNEW MINE.
FIND IT?
YEAH. THIS IS EV.
THIS IS EV AND ME IN A PHOTO BOOTH.

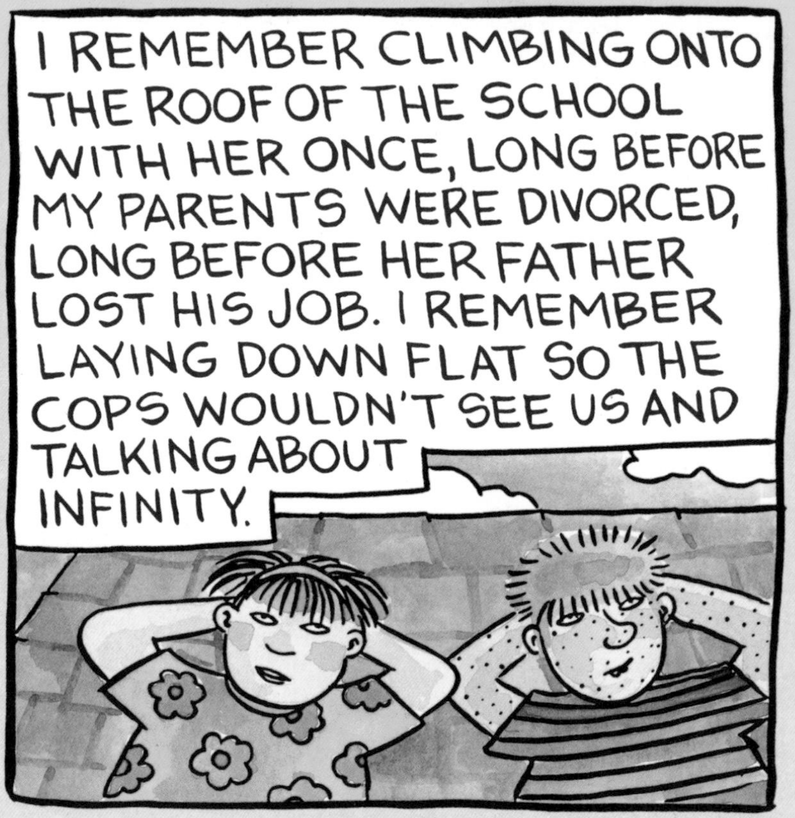
I REMEMBER CLIMBING ONTO THE ROOF OF THE SCHOOL WITH HER ONCE, LONG BEFORE MY PARENTS WERE DIVORCED, LONG BEFORE HER FATHER LOST HIS JOB. I REMEMBER LAYING DOWN FLAT SO THE COPS WOULDN'T SEE US AND TALKING ABOUT INFINITY.

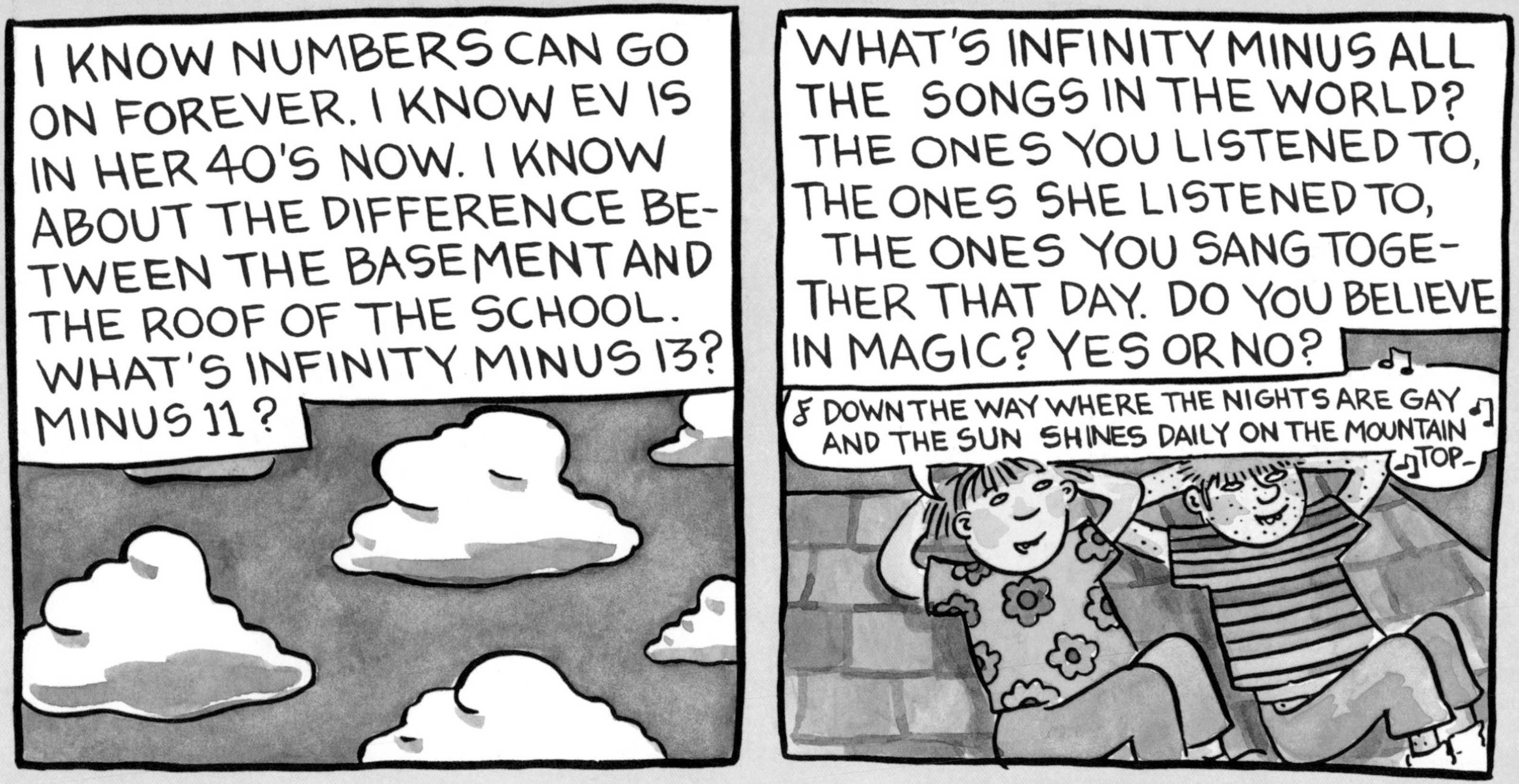
I KNOW NUMBERS CAN GO ON FOREVER. I KNOW EV IS IN HER 40'S NOW. I KNOW ABOUT THE DIFFERENCE BETWEEN THE BASEMENT AND THE ROOF OF THE SCHOOL. WHAT'S INFINITY MINUS 13? MINUS 11?
WHAT'S INFINITY MINUS ALL THE SONGS IN THE WORLD? THE ONES YOU LISTENED TO, THE ONES SHE LISTENED TO, THE ONES YOU SANG TOGETHER THAT DAY. DO YOU BELIEVE IN MAGIC? YES OR NO?
DOWN THE WAY WHERE THE NIGHTS ARE GAY AND THE SUN SHINES DAILY ON THE MOUNTAIN TOP-

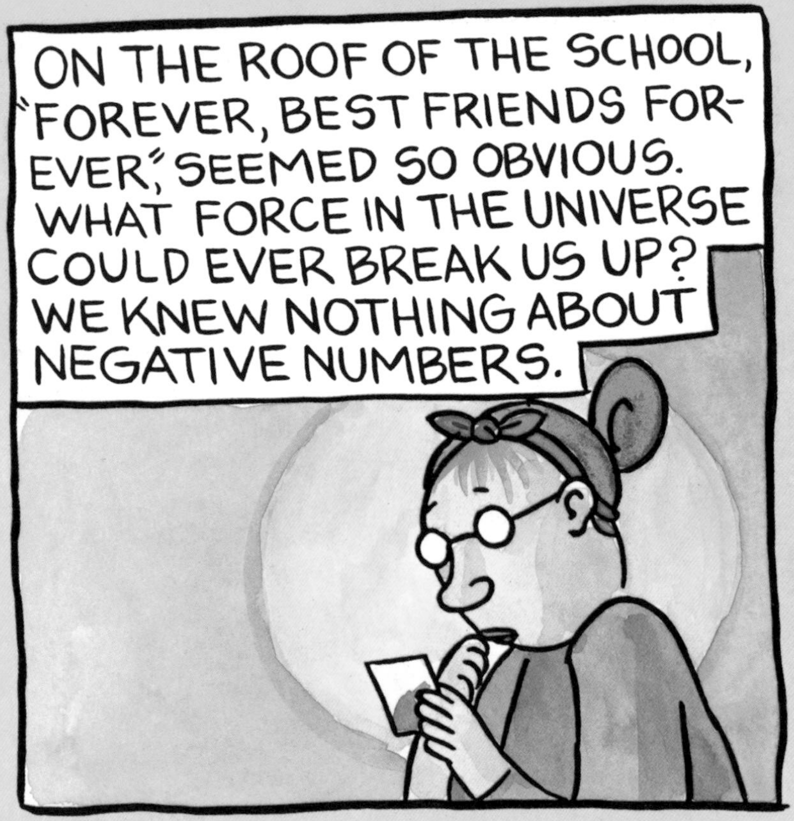
ON THE ROOF OF THE SCHOOL, "FOREVER, BEST FRIENDS FOR-EVER," SEEMED SO OBVIOUS. WHAT FORCE IN THE UNIVERSE COULD EVER BREAK US UP? WE KNEW NOTHING ABOUT NEGATIVE NUMBERS.

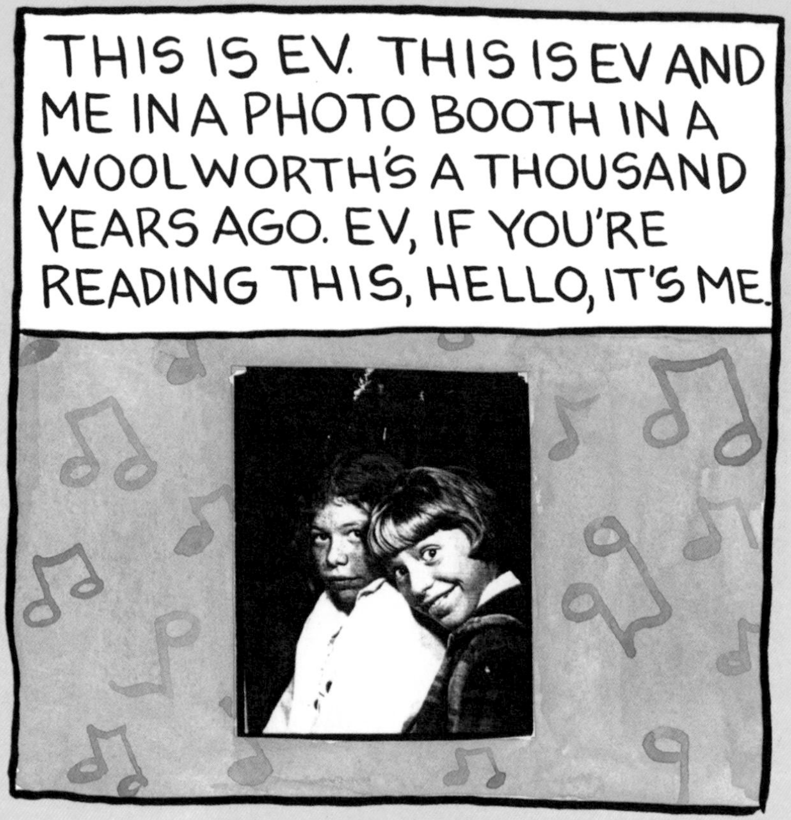
THIS IS EV. THIS IS EV AND ME IN A PHOTO BOOTH IN A WOOLWORTH'S A THOUSAND YEARS AGO. EV, IF YOU'RE READING THIS, HELLO, IT'S ME.

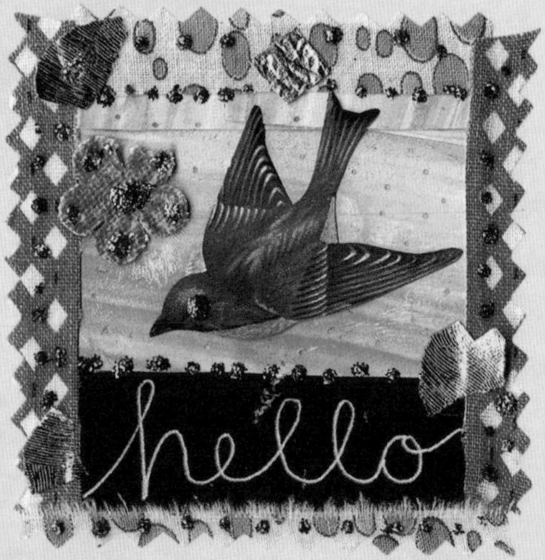
hello

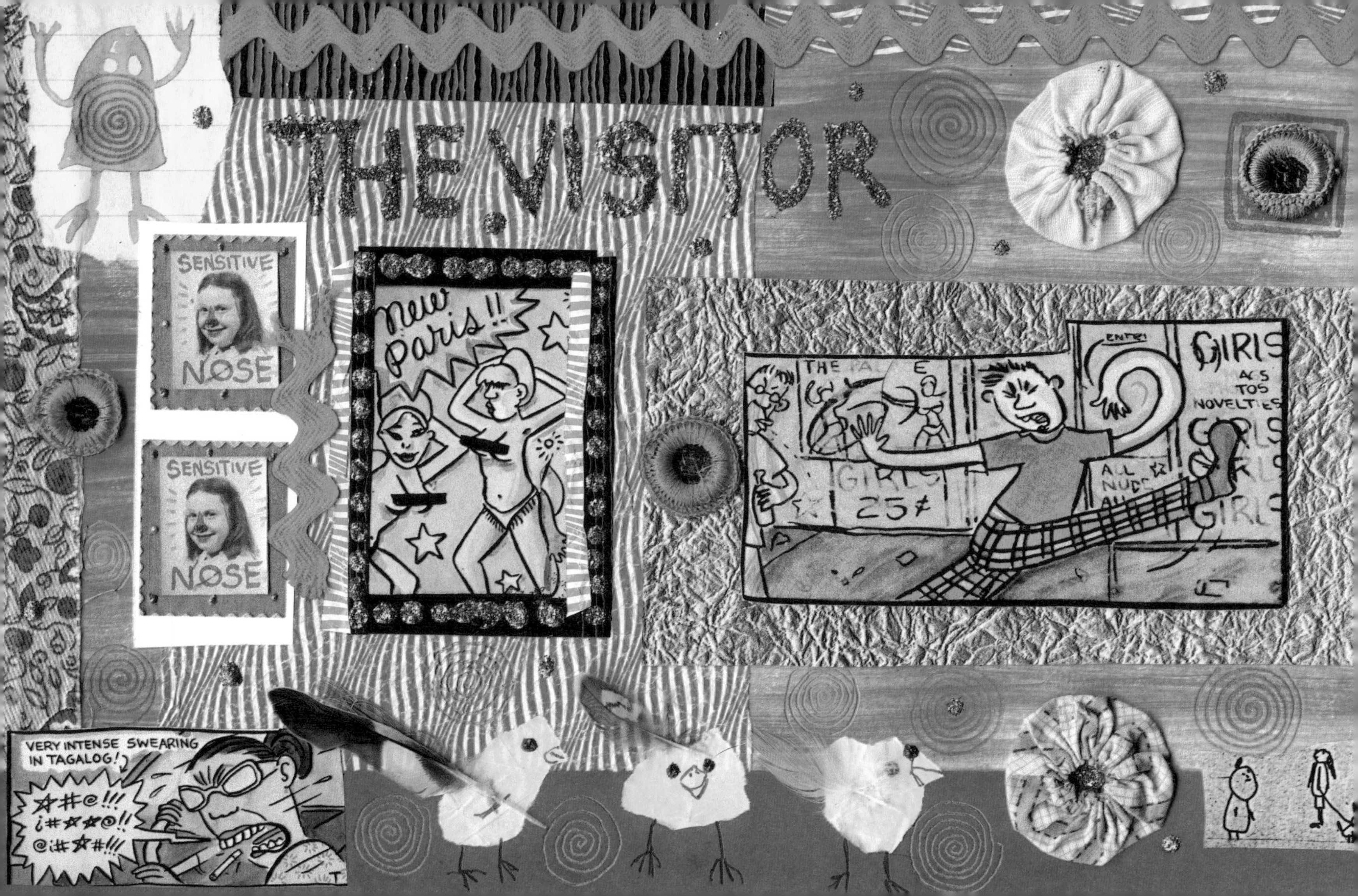

THE VISITOR
SENSITIVE NOSE
SENSITIVE NOSE
new Paris!!
GIRLS
NOVELTIES
GIRLS 25¢
VERY INTENSE SWEARING IN TAGALOG!

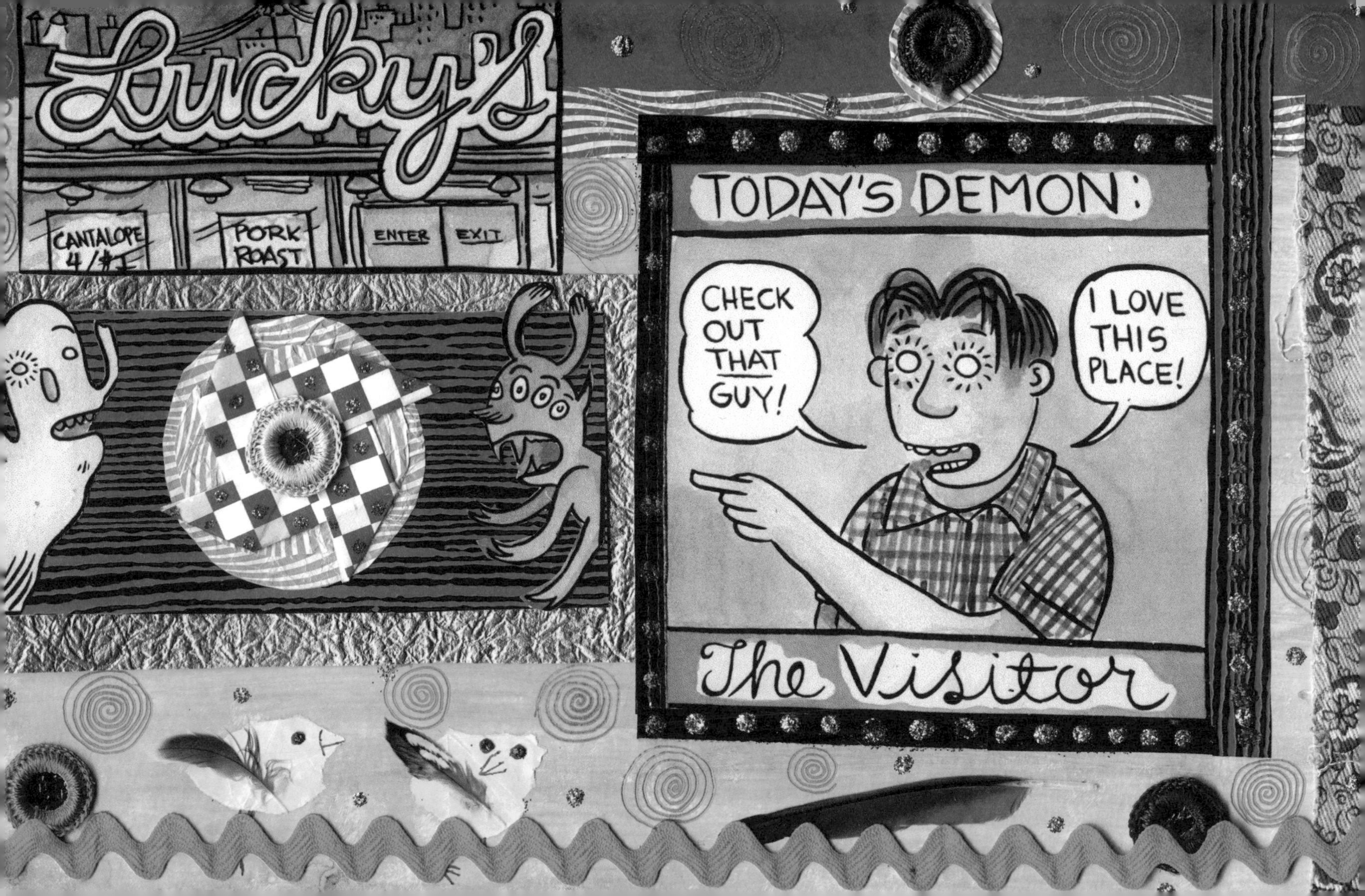
Lucky's
CANTALOPE 4/$1
PORK ROAST
ENTER
EXIT
TODAY'S DEMON:
CHECK OUT THAT GUY!
I LOVE THIS PLACE!
The Visitor

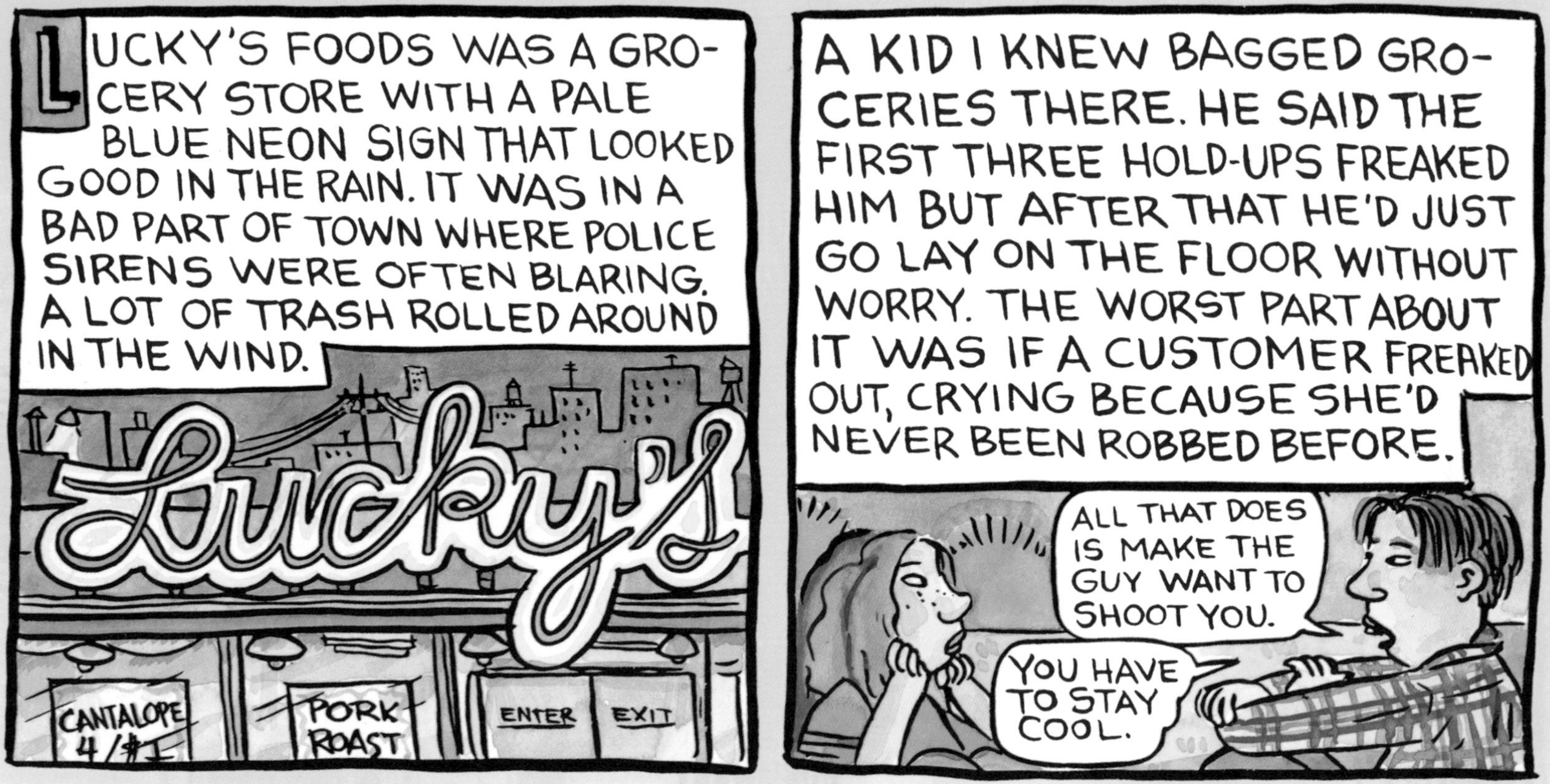
LUCKY'S FOODS WAS A GROCERY STORE WITH A PALE BLUE NEON SIGN THAT LOOKED GOOD IN THE RAIN. IT WAS IN A BAD PART OF TOWN WHERE POLICE SIRENS WERE OFTEN BLARING. A LOT OF TRASH ROLLED AROUND IN THE WIND.
Lucky's
CANTALOPE
PORK ROAST
ENTER
EXIT
A KID I KNEW BAGGED GROCERIES THERE. HE SAID THE FIRST THREE HOLD-UPS FREAKED HIM BUT AFTER THAT HE'D JUST GO LAY ON THE FLOOR WITHOUT WORRY. THE WORST PART ABOUT IT WAS IF A CUSTOMER FREAKED OUT, CRYING BECAUSE SHE'D NEVER BEEN ROBBED BEFORE.
ALL THAT DOES IS MAKE THE GUY WANT TO SHOOT YOU.
YOU HAVE TO STAY COOL.

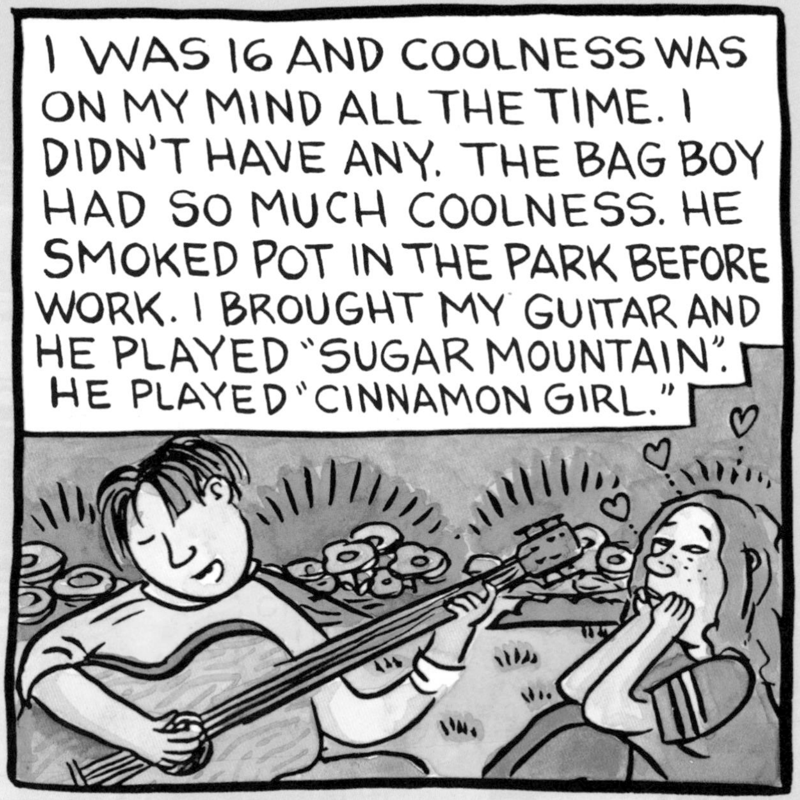
I WAS 16 AND COOLNESS WAS ON MY MIND ALL THE TIME. I DIDN'T HAVE ANY. THE BAG BOY HAD SO MUCH COOLNESS. HE SMOKED POT IN THE PARK BEFORE WORK. I BROUGHT MY GUITAR AND HE PLAYED "SUGAR MOUNTAIN". HE PLAYED "CINNAMON GIRL."

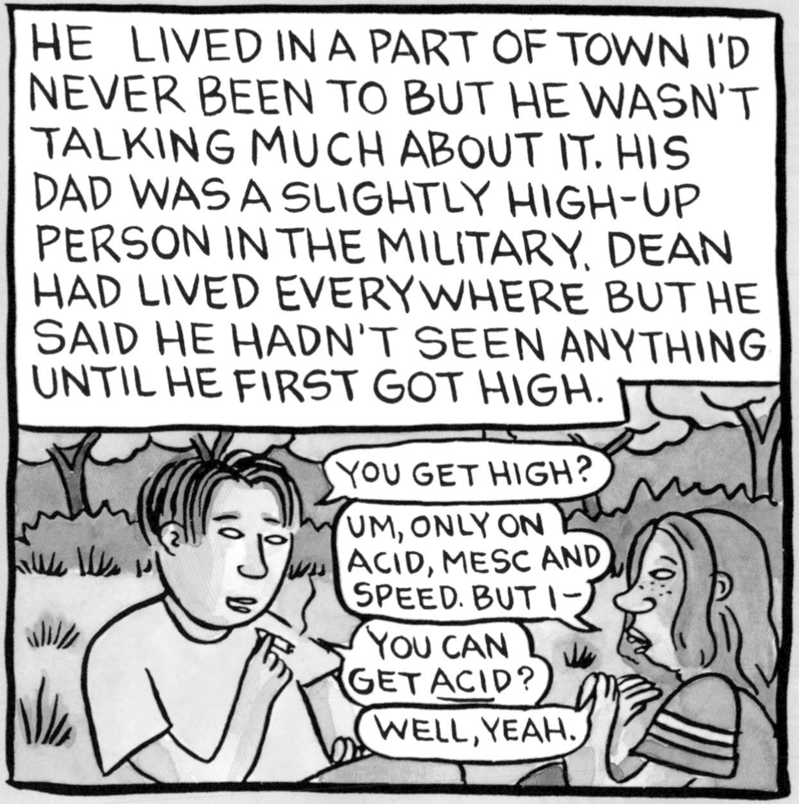
HE LIVED IN A PART OF TOWN I'D NEVER BEEN TO BUT HE WASN'T TALKING MUCH ABOUT IT. HIS DAD WAS A SLIGHTLY HIGH-UP PERSON IN THE MILITARY. DEAN HAD LIVED EVERYWHERE BUT HE SAID HE HADN'T SEEN ANYTHING UNTIL HE FIRST GOT HIGH.
YOU GET HIGH?
UM, ONLY ON ACID, MESC AND SPEED. BUT I-
YOU CAN GET ACID?
WELL, YEAH.

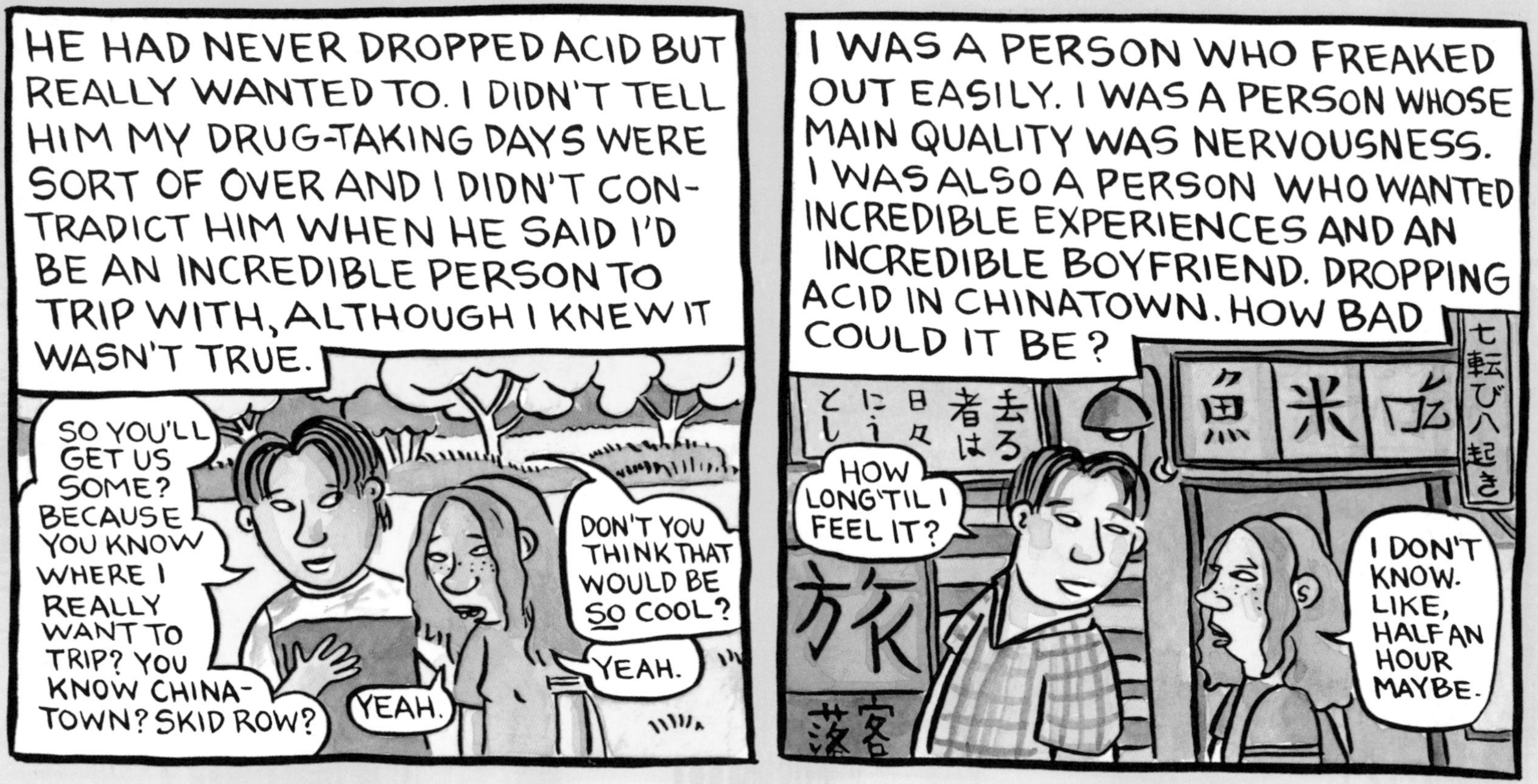
HE HAD NEVER DROPPED ACID BUT REALLY WANTED TO. I DIDN'T TELL HIM MY DRUG-TAKING DAYS WERE SORT OF OVER AND I DIDN'T CONTRADICT HIM WHEN HE SAID I'D BE AN INCREDIBLE PERSON TO TRIP WITH, ALTHOUGH I KNEW IT WASN'T TRUE.
SO YOU'LL GET US SOME? BECAUSE YOU KNOW WHERE I REALLY WANT TO TRIP? YOU KNOW CHINATOWN? SKID ROW?
YEAH.
DON'T YOU THINK THAT WOULD BE SO COOL?
YEAH.
I WAS A PERSON WHO FREAKED OUT EASILY. I WAS A PERSON WHOSE MAIN QUALITY WAS NERVOUSNESS. I WAS ALSO A PERSON WHO WANTED INCREDIBLE EXPERIENCES AND AN INCREDIBLE BOYFRIEND. DROPPING ACID IN CHINATOWN. HOW BAD COULD IT BE?
去る者は日々にうとし
魚 米
七転び八起き
HOW LONG 'TIL I FEEL IT?
I DON'T KNOW. LIKE, HALF AN HOUR MAYBE.
旅

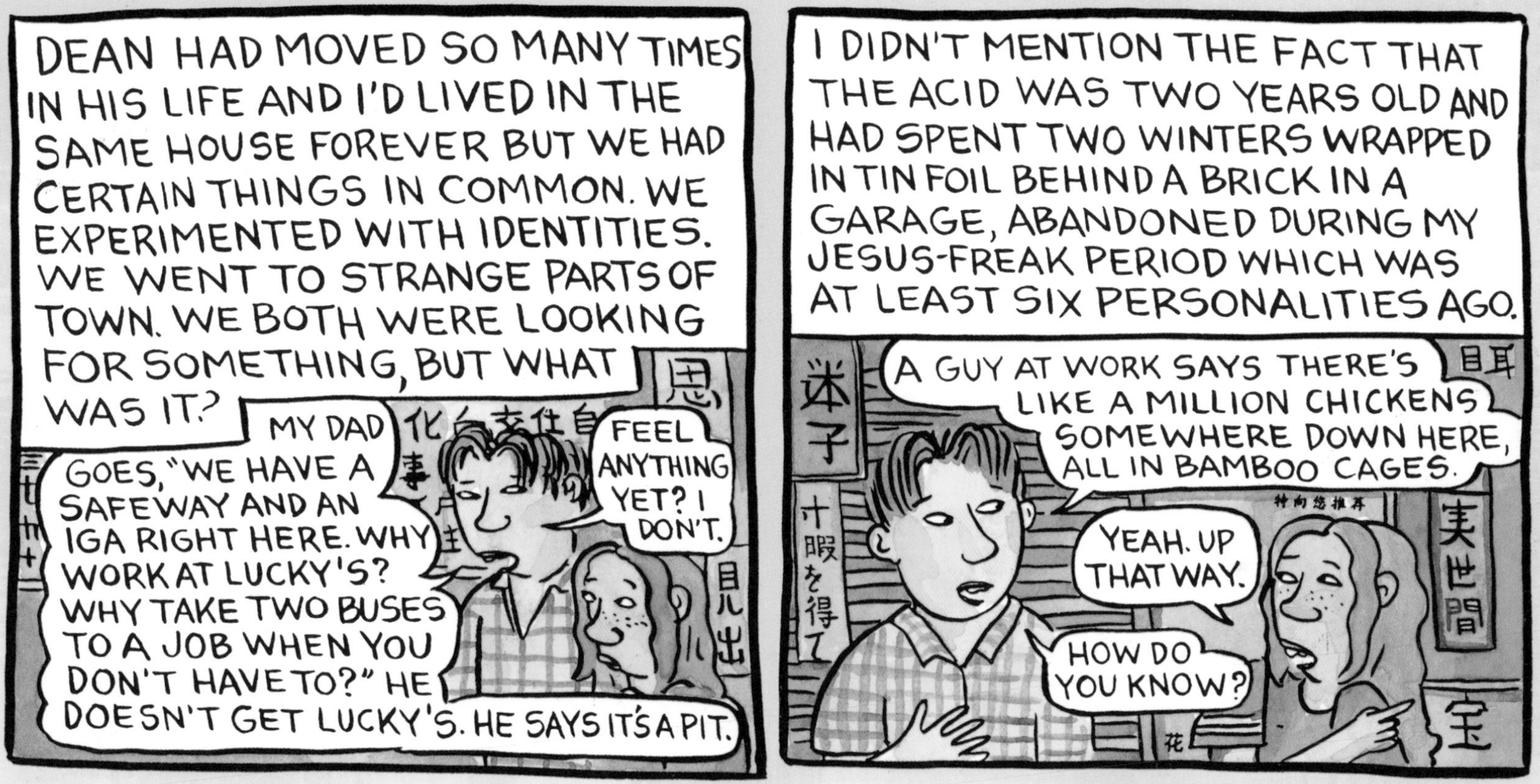
DEAN HAD MOVED SO MANY TIMES IN HIS LIFE AND I'D LIVED IN THE SAME HOUSE FOREVER BUT WE HAD CERTAIN THINGS IN COMMON. WE EXPERIMENTED WITH IDENTITIES. WE WENT TO STRANGE PARTS OF TOWN. WE BOTH WERE LOOKING FOR SOMETHING, BUT WHAT WAS IT?
MY DAD GOES, "WE HAVE A SAFEWAY AND AN IGA RIGHT HERE. WHY WORK AT LUCKY'S? WHY TAKE TWO BUSES TO A JOB WHEN YOU DON'T HAVE TO?" HE DOESN'T GET LUCKY'S. HE SAYS IT'S A PIT.
FEEL ANYTHING YET? I DON'T.
I DIDN'T MENTION THE FACT THAT THE ACID WAS TWO YEARS OLD AND HAD SPENT TWO WINTERS WRAPPED IN TIN FOIL BEHIND A BRICK IN A GARAGE, ABANDONED DURING MY JESUS-FREAK PERIOD WHICH WAS AT LEAST SIX PERSONALITIES AGO.
A GUY AT WORK SAYS THERE'S LIKE A MILLION CHICKENS SOMEWHERE DOWN HERE, ALL IN BAMBOO CAGES.
YEAH. UP THAT WAY.
HOW DO YOU KNOW?

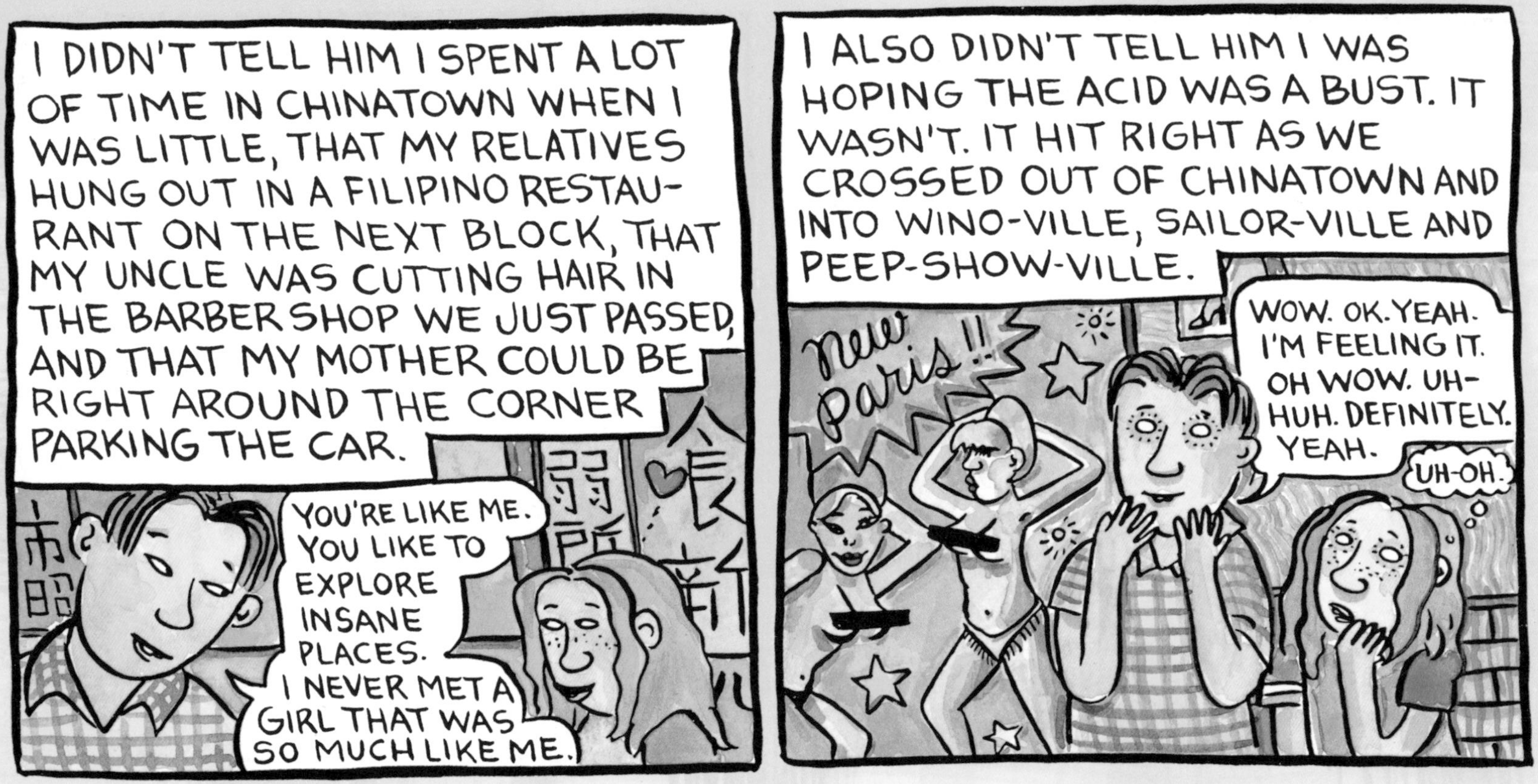
I DIDN'T TELL HIM I SPENT A LOT OF TIME IN CHINATOWN WHEN I WAS LITTLE, THAT MY RELATIVES HUNG OUT IN A FILIPINO RESTAURANT ON THE NEXT BLOCK, THAT MY UNCLE WAS CUTTING HAIR IN THE BARBER SHOP WE JUST PASSED, AND THAT MY MOTHER COULD BE RIGHT AROUND THE CORNER PARKING THE CAR.
YOU'RE LIKE ME. YOU LIKE TO EXPLORE INSANE PLACES. I NEVER MET A GIRL THAT WAS SO MUCH LIKE ME.
I ALSO DIDN'T TELL HIM I WAS HOPING THE ACID WAS A BUST. IT WASN'T. IT HIT RIGHT AS WE CROSSED OUT OF CHINATOWN AND INTO WINO-VILLE, SAILOR-VILLE AND PEEP-SHOW-VILLE.
new Paris!!
WOW. OK. YEAH. I'M FEELING IT. OH WOW. UH-HUH. DEFINITELY. YEAH.
UH-OH.

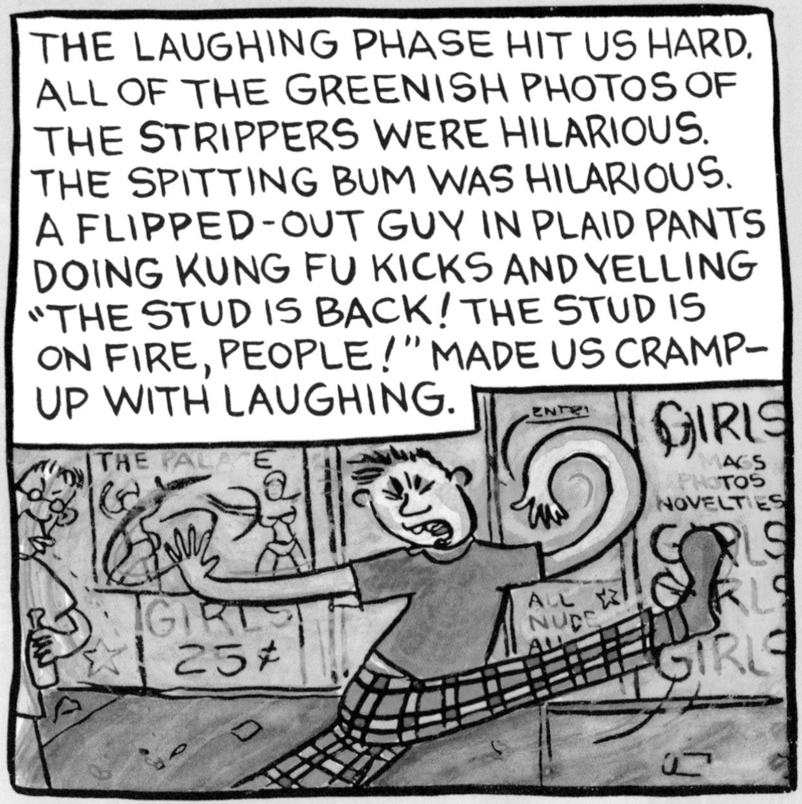
THE LAUGHING PHASE HIT US HARD. ALL OF THE GREENISH PHOTOS OF THE STRIPPERS WERE HILARIOUS. THE SPITTING BUM WAS HILARIOUS. A FLIPPED-OUT GUY IN PLAID PANTS DOING KUNG FU KICKS AND YELLING "THE STUD IS BACK! THE STUD IS ON FIRE, PEOPLE!" MADE US CRAMP-UP WITH LAUGHING.
GIRLS
NOVELTIES
GIRLS
25¢
ALL NUDE

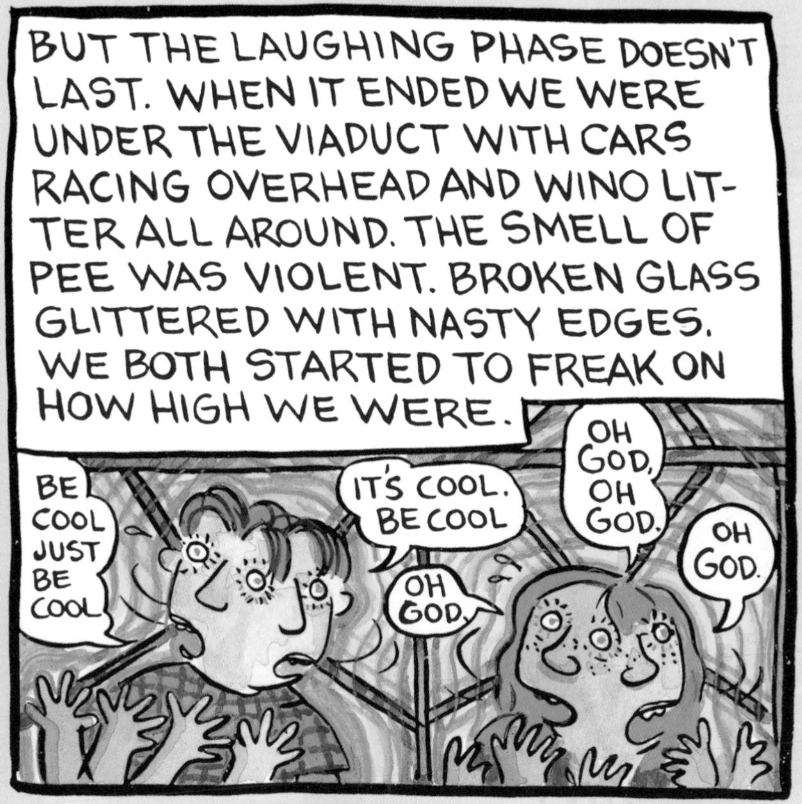
BUT THE LAUGHING PHASE DOESN'T LAST. WHEN IT ENDED WE WERE UNDER THE VIADUCT WITH CARS RACING OVERHEAD AND WINO LITTER ALL AROUND. THE SMELL OF PEE WAS VIOLENT. BROKEN GLASS GLITTERED WITH NASTY EDGES. WE BOTH STARTED TO FREAK ON HOW HIGH WE WERE.
BE COOL JUST BE COOL
IT'S COOL. BE COOL
OH GOD.
OH GOD, OH GOD.
OH GOD.

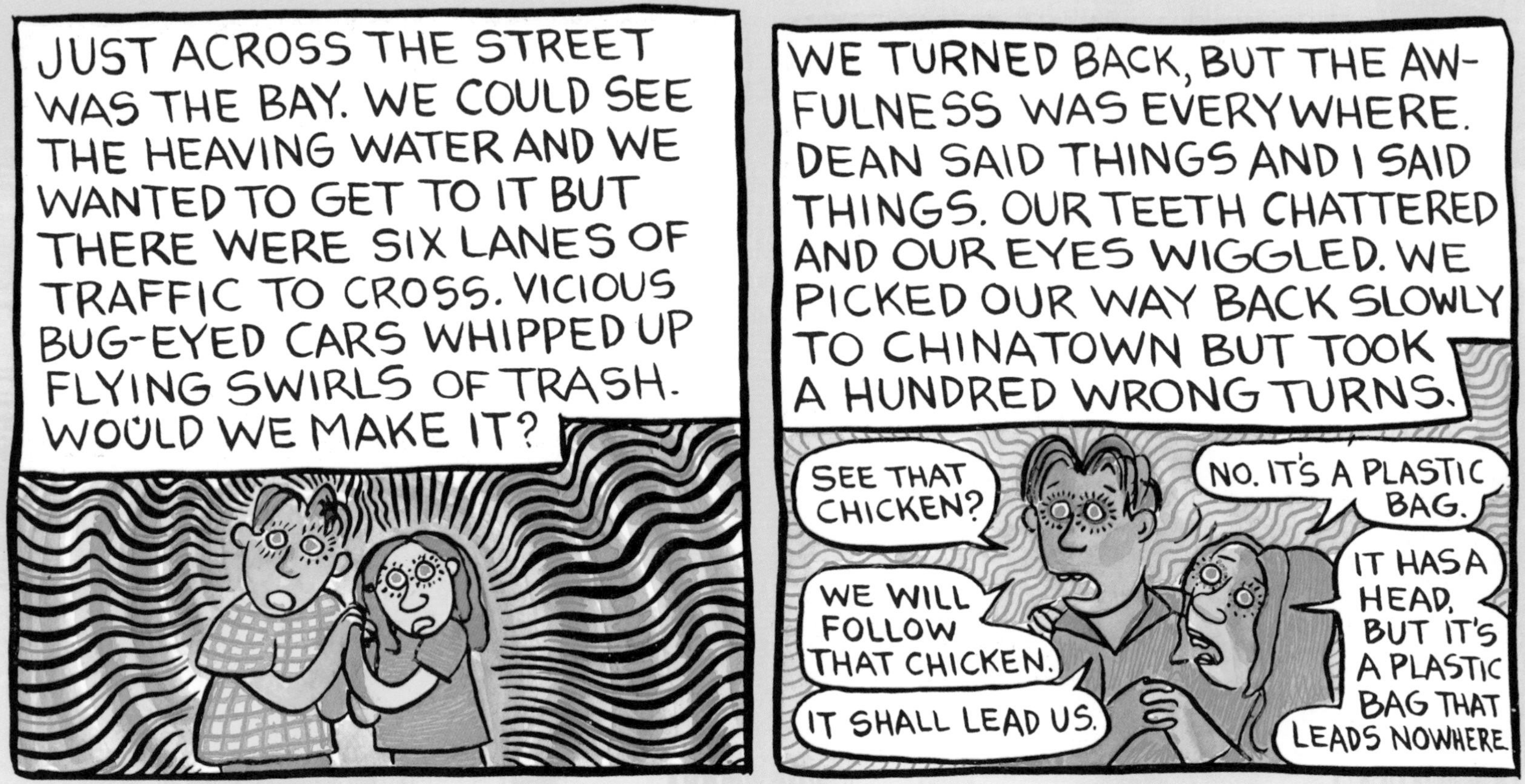
JUST ACROSS THE STREET WAS THE BAY. WE COULD SEE THE HEAVING WATER AND WE WANTED TO GET TO IT BUT THERE WERE SIX LANES OF TRAFFIC TO CROSS. VICIOUS BUG-EYED CARS WHIPPED UP FLYING SWIRLS OF TRASH. WOULD WE MAKE IT?
WE TURNED BACK, BUT THE AWFULNESS WAS EVERYWHERE. DEAN SAID THINGS AND I SAID THINGS. OUR TEETH CHATTERED AND OUR EYES WIGGLED. WE PICKED OUR WAY BACK SLOWLY TO CHINATOWN BUT TOOK A HUNDRED WRONG TURNS.
SEE THAT CHICKEN?
NO. IT'S A PLASTIC BAG.
WE WILL FOLLOW THAT CHICKEN.
IT HAS A HEAD, BUT IT'S A PLASTIC BAG THAT LEADS NOWHERE.
IT SHALL LEAD US.

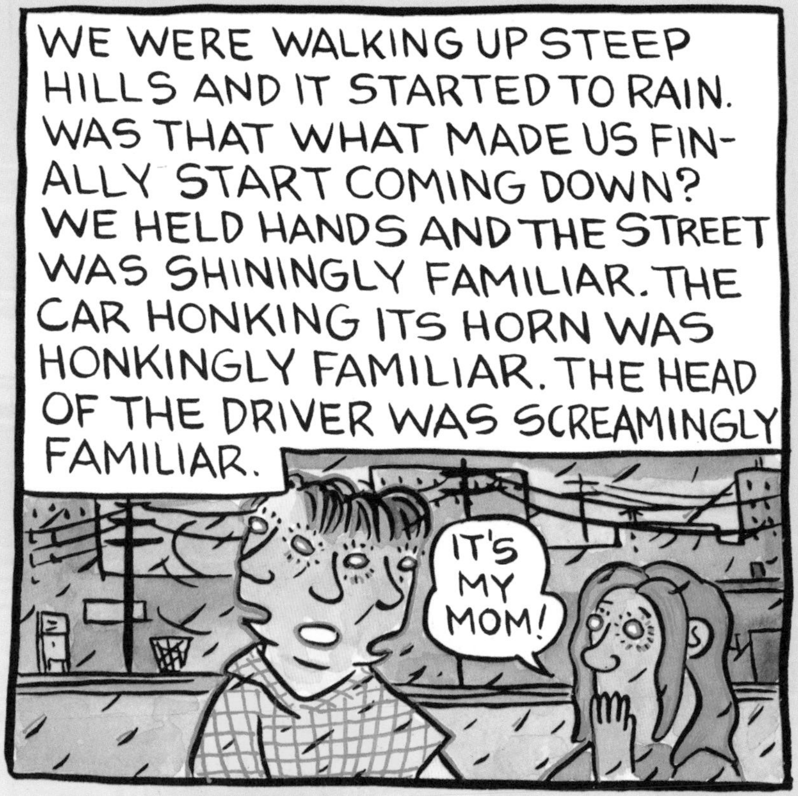
WE WERE WALKING UP STEEP HILLS AND IT STARTED TO RAIN. WAS THAT WHAT MADE US FINALLY START COMING DOWN? WE HELD HANDS AND THE STREET WAS SHININGLY FAMILIAR. THE CAR HONKING ITS HORN WAS HONKINGLY FAMILIAR. THE HEAD OF THE DRIVER WAS SCREAMINGLY FAMILIAR.
IT'S MY MOM!

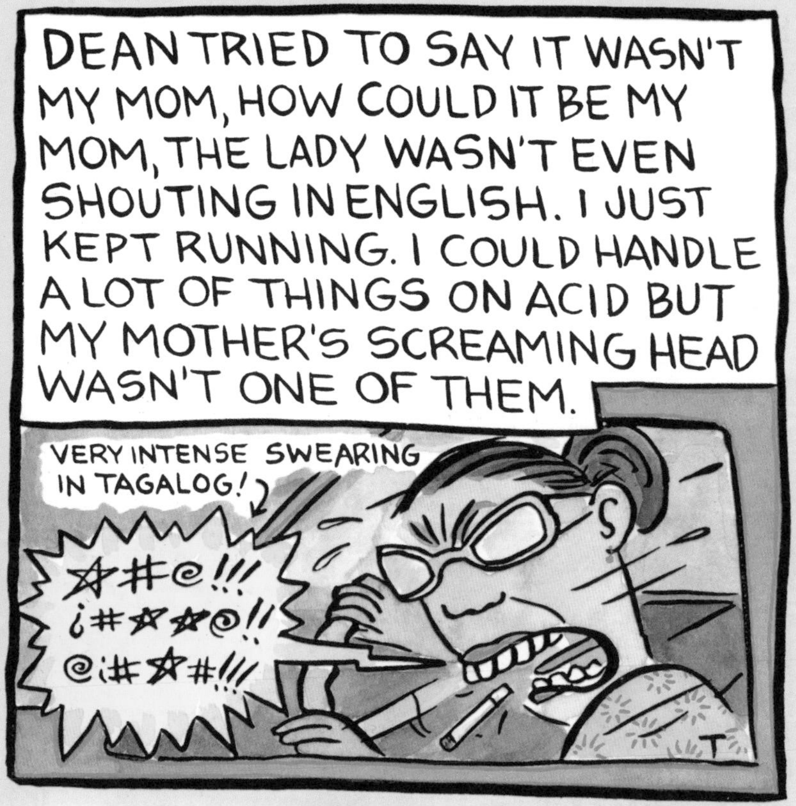
DEAN TRIED TO SAY IT WASN'T MY MOM, HOW COULD IT BE MY MOM, THE LADY WASN'T EVEN SHOUTING IN ENGLISH. I JUST KEPT RUNNING. I COULD HANDLE A LOT OF THINGS ON ACID BUT MY MOTHER'S SCREAMING HEAD WASN'T ONE OF THEM.
VERY INTENSE SWEARING IN TAGALOG!
☆#@!!! ¡#☆☆@!! @¡#☆#!!!

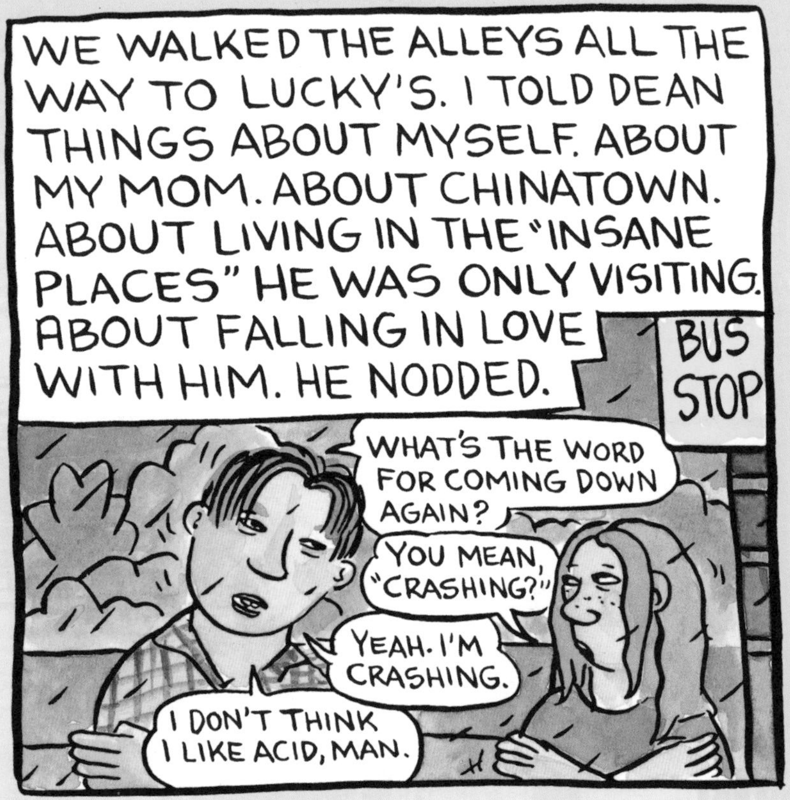
WE WALKED THE ALLEYS ALL THE WAY TO LUCKY'S. I TOLD DEAN THINGS ABOUT MYSELF. ABOUT MY MOM. ABOUT CHINATOWN. ABOUT LIVING IN THE "INSANE PLACES" HE WAS ONLY VISITING. ABOUT FALLING IN LOVE WITH HIM. HE NODDED.
BUS STOP
WHAT'S THE WORD FOR COMING DOWN AGAIN?
YOU MEAN, "CRASHING?"
YEAH. I'M CRASHING.
I DON'T THINK I LIKE ACID, MAN.

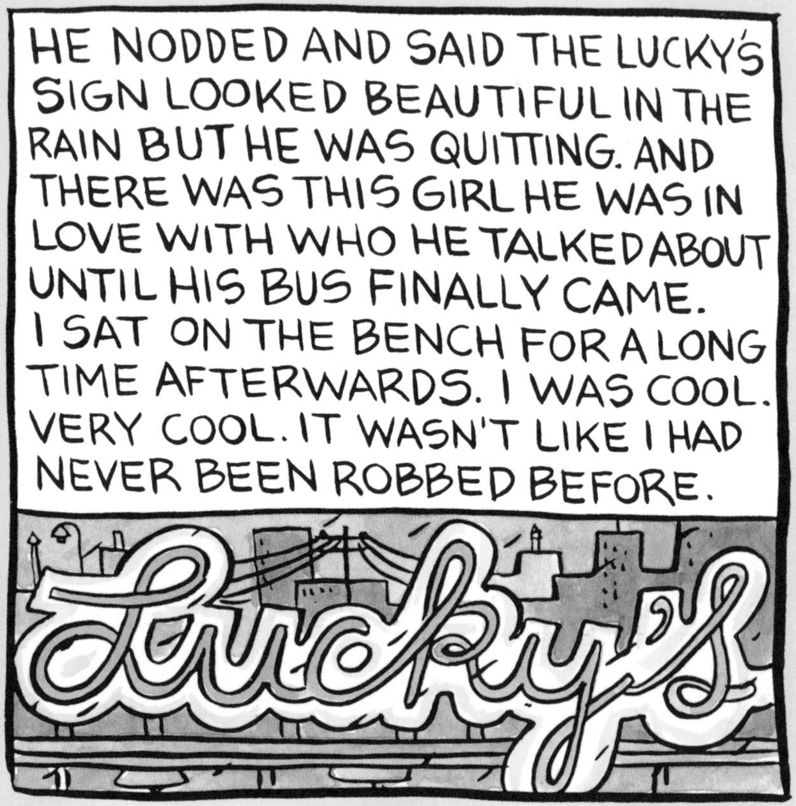
HE NODDED AND SAID THE LUCKY'S SIGN LOOKED BEAUTIFUL IN THE RAIN BUT HE WAS QUITTING. AND THERE WAS THIS GIRL HE WAS IN LOVE WITH WHO HE TALKED ABOUT UNTIL HIS BUS FINALLY CAME. I SAT ON THE BENCH FOR A LONG TIME AFTERWARDS. I WAS COOL. VERY COOL. IT WASN'T LIKE I HAD NEVER BEEN ROBBED BEFORE.
Lucky's

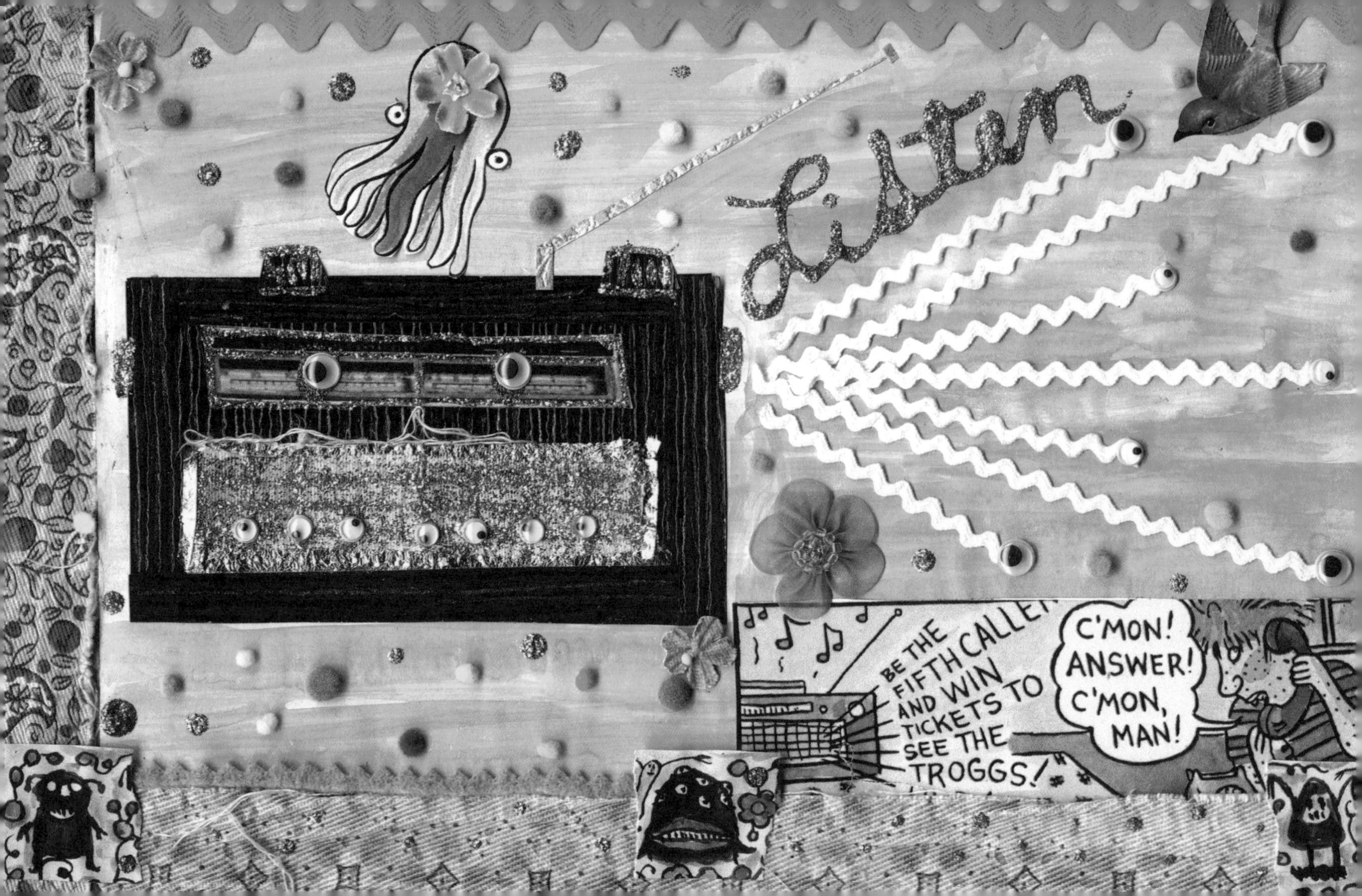
Listen
BE THE FIFTH CALLER AND WIN TICKETS TO SEE THE TROGGS!
C'MON! ANSWER! C'MON, MAN!

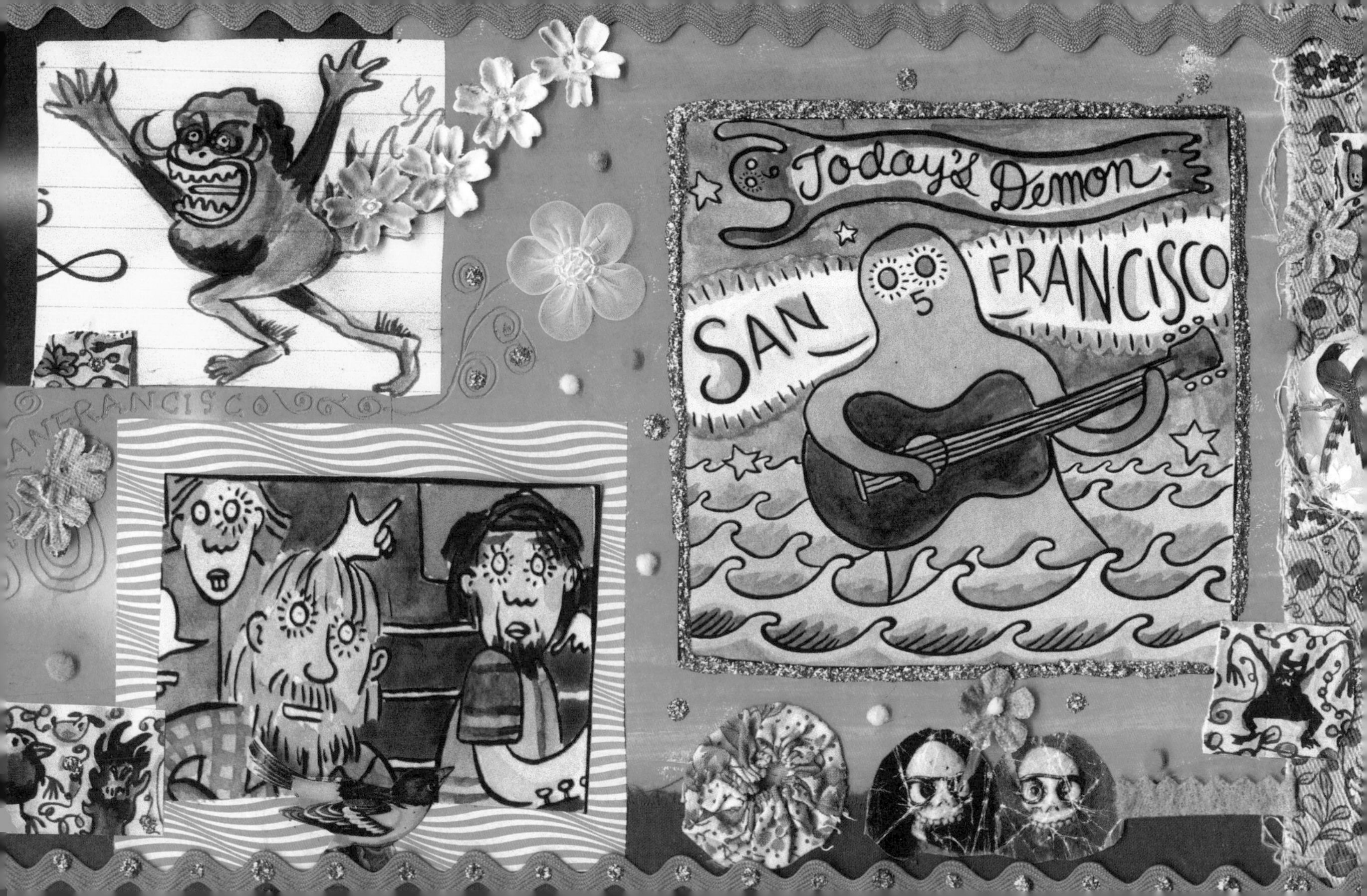

Today's Demon
SAN
FRANCISCO
5

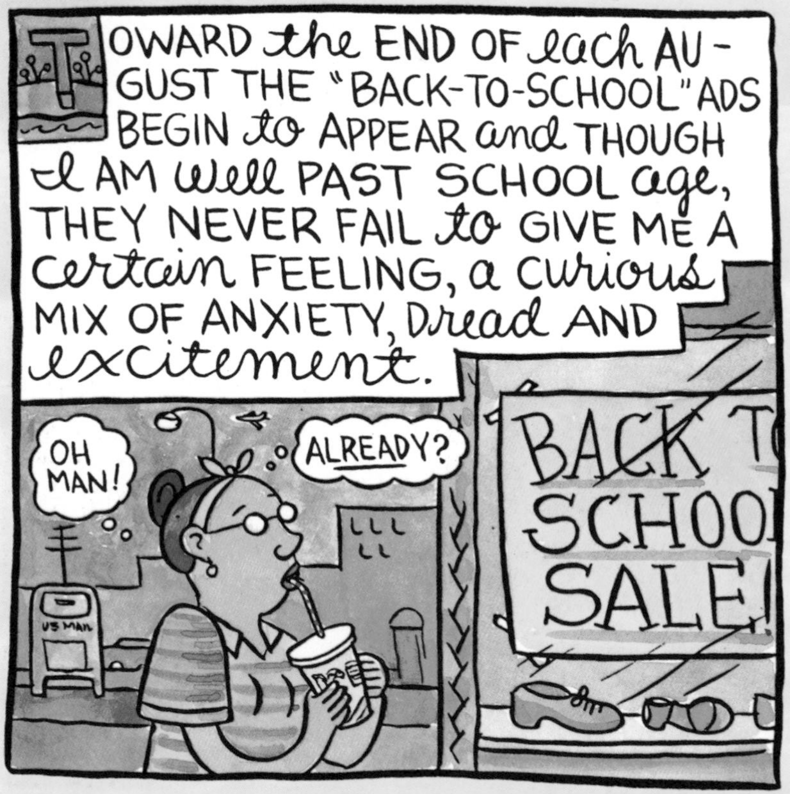
TOWARD the END OF each AUGUST THE "BACK-TO-SCHOOL" ADS BEGIN to APPEAR and THOUGH I AM well PAST SCHOOL age, THEY NEVER FAIL to GIVE ME A certain FEELING, a curious MIX OF ANXIETY, Dread AND excitement.
OH MAN!
ALREADY?
US MAIL
BACK T
SCHOO
SALE

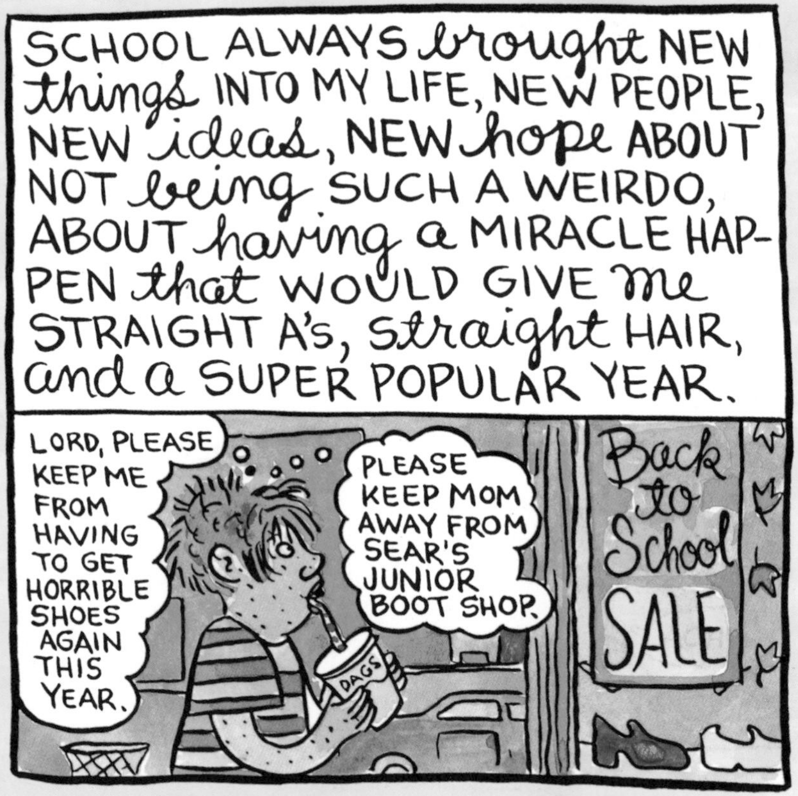
SCHOOL ALWAYS brought NEW things INTO MY LIFE, NEW PEOPLE, NEW ideas, NEW hope ABOUT NOT being SUCH A WEIRDO, ABOUT having a MIRACLE HAPPEN that WOULD GIVE me STRAIGHT A's, straight HAIR, and a SUPER POPULAR YEAR.
LORD, PLEASE KEEP ME FROM HAVING TO GET HORRIBLE SHOES AGAIN THIS YEAR.
PLEASE KEEP MOM AWAY FROM SEAR'S JUNIOR BOOT SHOP.
DAGS
Back to School
SALE

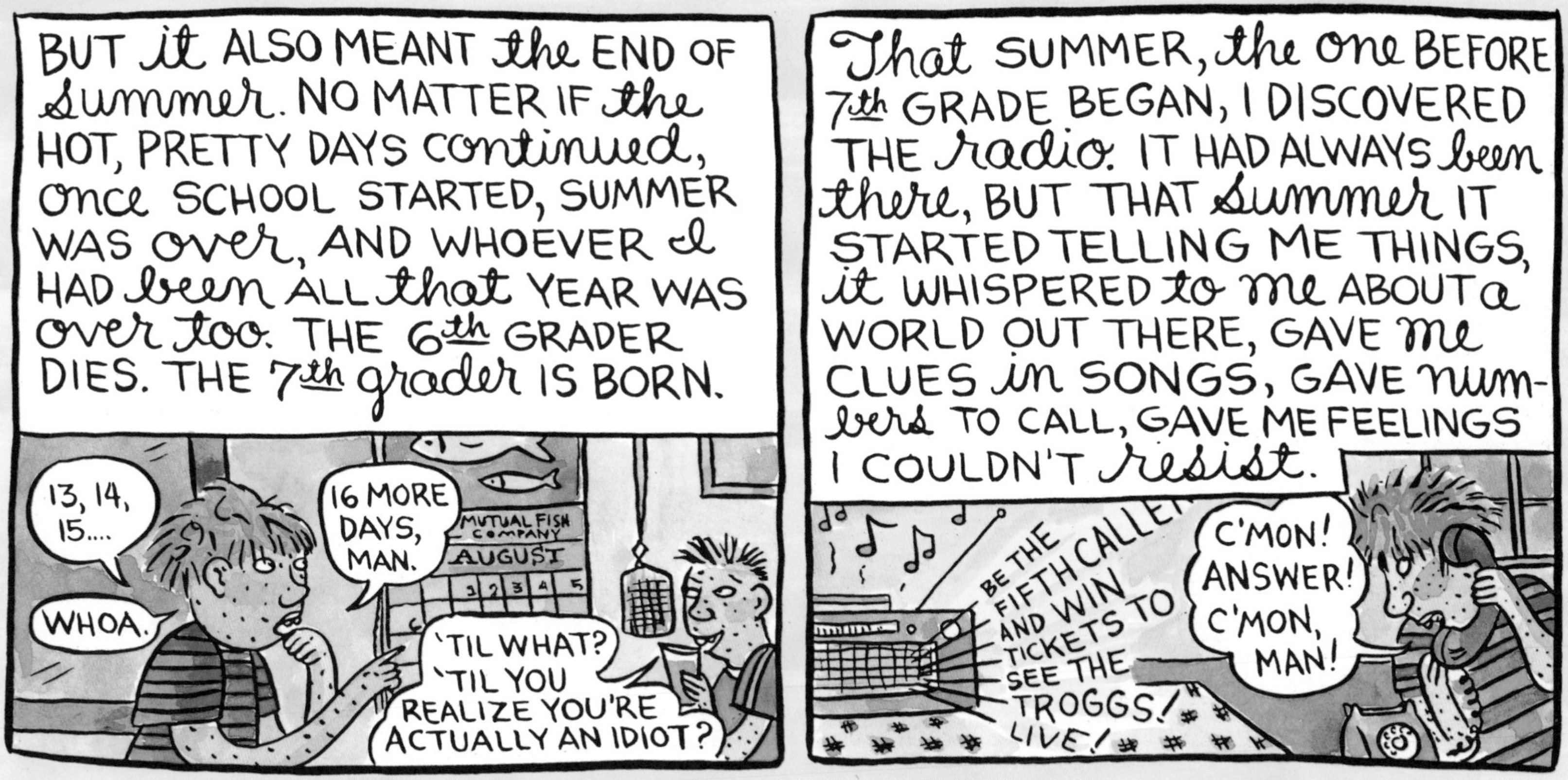
BUT it ALSO MEANT the END OF Summer. NO MATTER IF the HOT, PRETTY DAYS continued, once SCHOOL STARTED, SUMMER WAS over, AND WHOEVER I HAD been ALL that YEAR WAS over too. THE 6th GRADER DIES. THE 7th grader IS BORN.
13, 14, 15....
WHOA.
16 MORE DAYS, MAN.
MUTUAL FISH COMPANY
AUGUST
`TIL WHAT? `TIL YOU REALIZE YOU'RE ACTUALLY AN IDIOT?
That SUMMER, the one BEFORE 7th GRADE BEGAN, I DISCOVERED THE radio. IT HAD ALWAYS been there, BUT THAT Summer IT STARTED TELLING ME THINGS, it WHISPERED to me ABOUT a WORLD OUT THERE, GAVE me CLUES in SONGS, GAVE numbers TO CALL, GAVE ME FEELINGS I COULDN'T resist.
BE THE FIFTH CALLER AND WIN TICKETS TO SEE THE TROGGS! LIVE!
C'MON! ANSWER! C'MON, MAN!

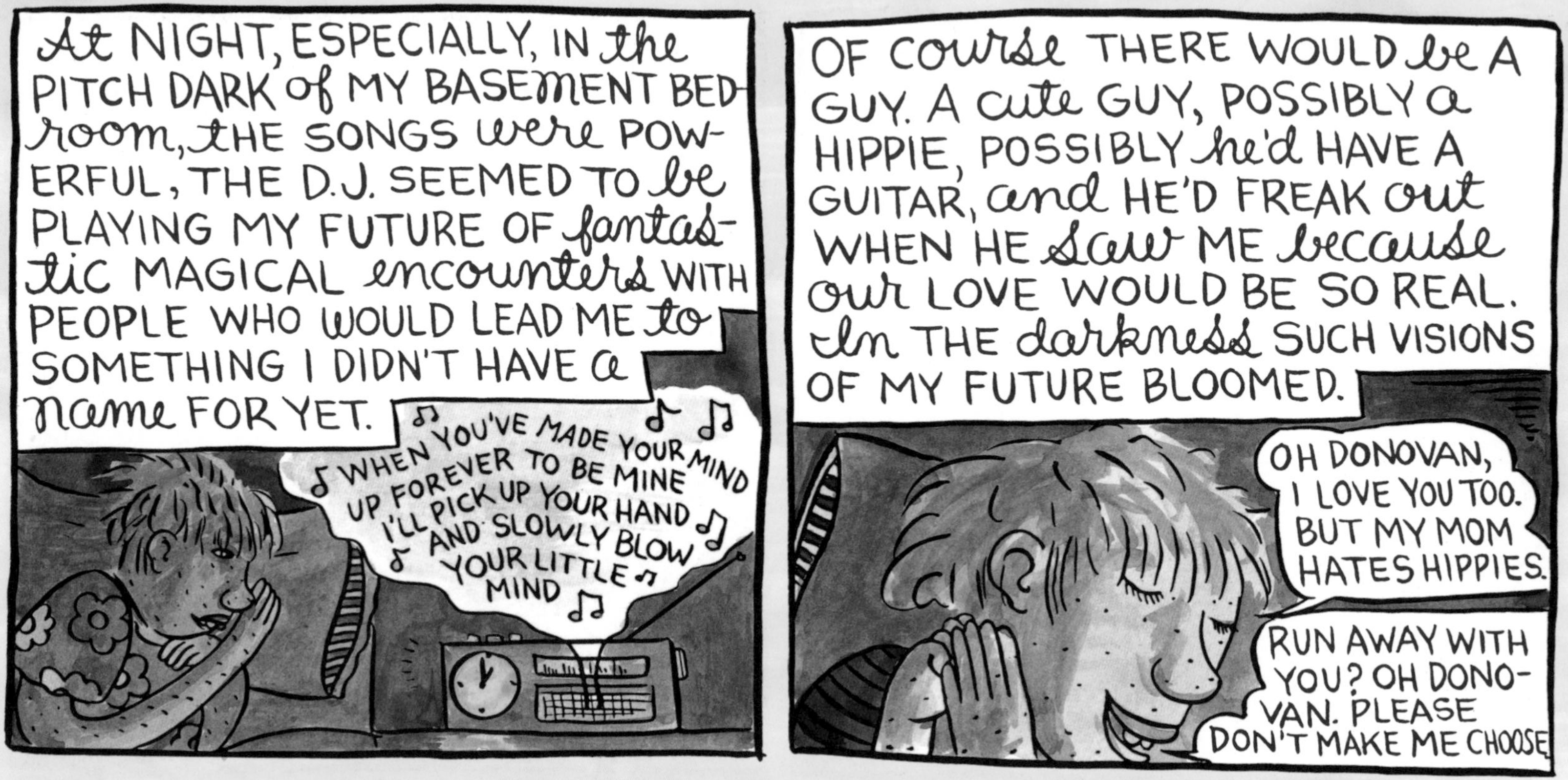
At NIGHT, ESPECIALLY, IN the PITCH DARK of MY BASEMENT BEDroom, the SONGS were POWERFUL, THE D.J. SEEMED TO be PLAYING MY FUTURE OF fantastic MAGICAL encounters WITH PEOPLE WHO WOULD LEAD ME to SOMETHING I DIDN'T HAVE a name FOR YET.
WHEN YOU'VE MADE YOUR MIND UP FOREVER TO BE MINE I'LL PICK UP YOUR HAND AND SLOWLY BLOW YOUR LITTLE MIND
OF course THERE WOULD be A GUY. A cute GUY, POSSIBLY a HIPPIE, POSSIBLY he'd HAVE A GUITAR, and HE'D FREAK out WHEN HE saw ME because our LOVE WOULD BE SO REAL. In THE darkness SUCH VISIONS OF MY FUTURE BLOOMED.
OH DONOVAN, I LOVE YOU TOO. BUT MY MOM HATES HIPPIES.
RUN AWAY WITH YOU? OH DONOVAN. PLEASE DON'T MAKE ME CHOOSE.

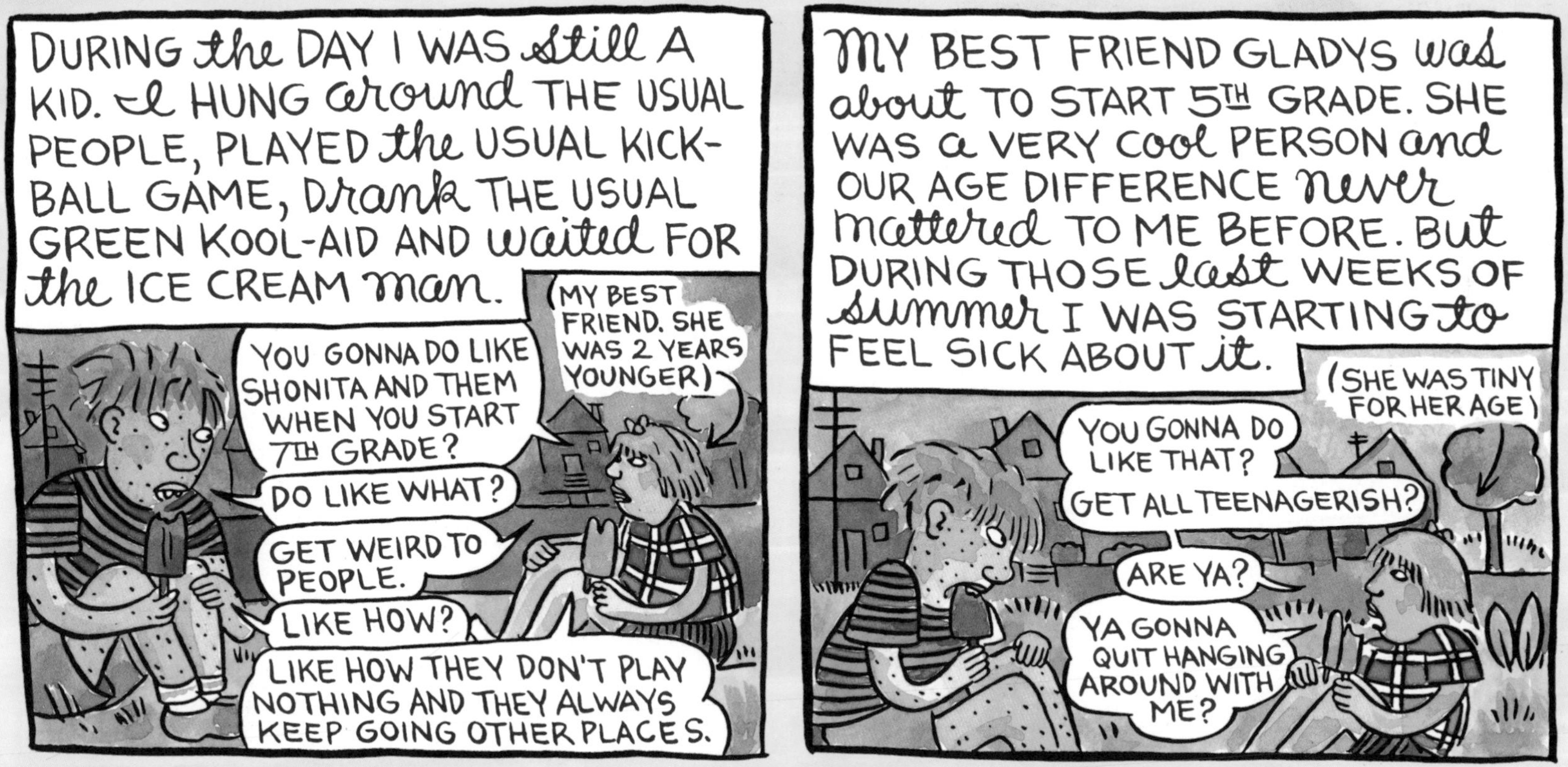
DURING the DAY I WAS still A KID. I HUNG around THE USUAL PEOPLE, PLAYED the USUAL KICK-BALL GAME, drank THE USUAL GREEN KOOL-AID AND waited FOR the ICE CREAM man.
(MY BEST FRIEND. SHE WAS 2 YEARS YOUNGER)
YOU GONNA DO LIKE SHONITA AND THEM WHEN YOU START 7TH GRADE?
DO LIKE WHAT?
GET WEIRD TO PEOPLE.
LIKE HOW?
LIKE HOW THEY DON'T PLAY NOTHING AND THEY ALWAYS KEEP GOING OTHER PLACES.
MY BEST FRIEND GLADYS was about TO START 5TH GRADE. SHE WAS a VERY cool PERSON and OUR AGE DIFFERENCE never mattered TO ME BEFORE. But DURING THOSE last WEEKS OF summer I WAS STARTING to FEEL SICK ABOUT it.
(SHE WAS TINY FOR HER AGE)
YOU GONNA DO LIKE THAT?
GET ALL TEENAGERISH?
ARE YA?
YA GONNA QUIT HANGING AROUND WITH ME?

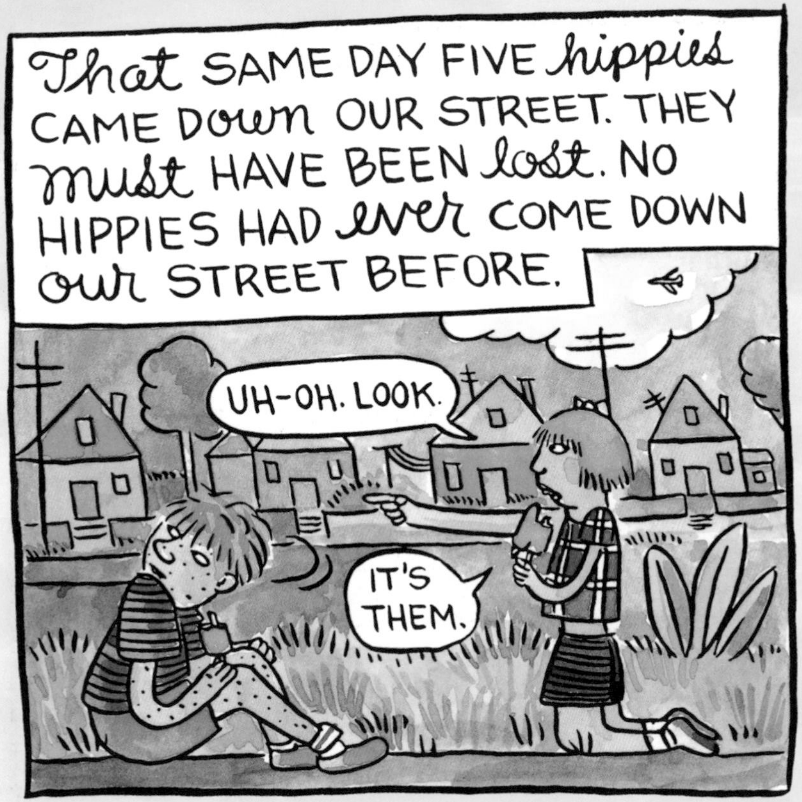
That SAME DAY FIVE hippies CAME DOWN OUR STREET. THEY must HAVE BEEN lost. NO HIPPIES HAD ever COME DOWN our STREET BEFORE.
UH-OH. LOOK.
IT'S THEM.

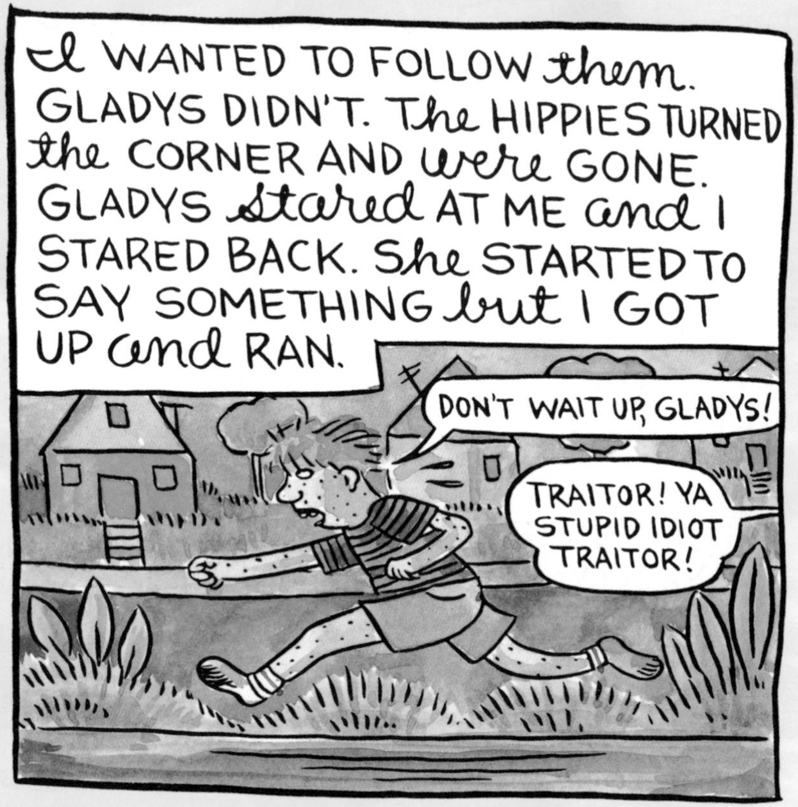
I WANTED TO FOLLOW them. GLADYS DIDN'T. The HIPPIES TURNED the CORNER AND were GONE. GLADYS stared AT ME and I STARED BACK. She STARTED TO SAY SOMETHING but I GOT UP and RAN.
DON'T WAIT UP, GLADYS!
TRAITOR! YA STUPID IDIOT TRAITOR!

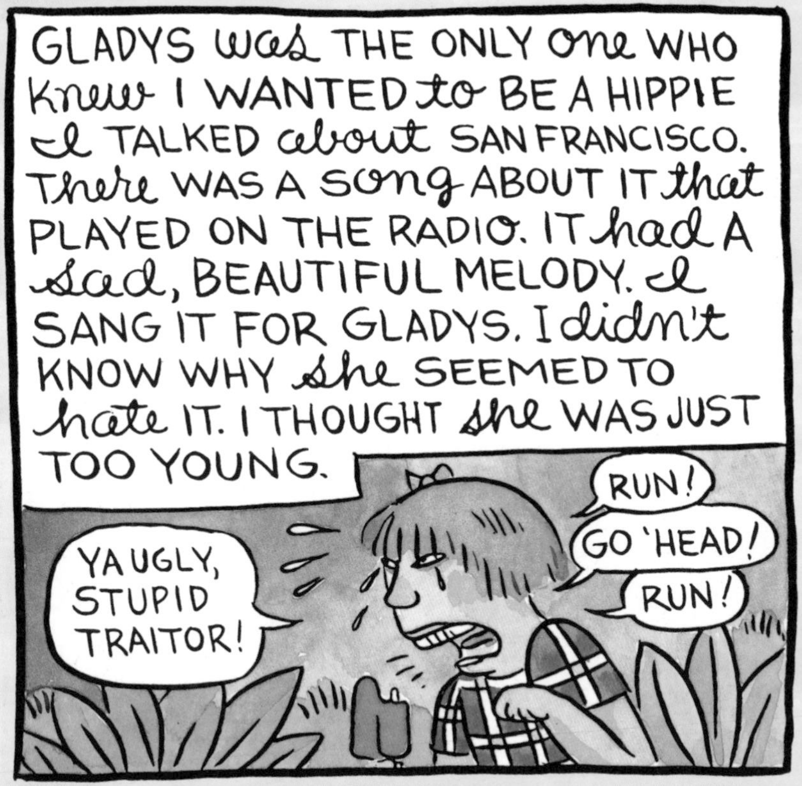
GLADYS was THE ONLY one WHO Knew I WANTED to BE A HIPPIE I TALKED about SAN FRANCISCO. There WAS A song ABOUT IT that PLAYED ON THE RADIO. IT had A sad, BEAUTIFUL MELODY. I SANG IT FOR GLADYS. I didn't KNOW WHY she SEEMED TO hate IT. I THOUGHT she WAS JUST TOO YOUNG.
YA UGLY, STUPID TRAITOR!
RUN!
GO 'HEAD!
RUN!

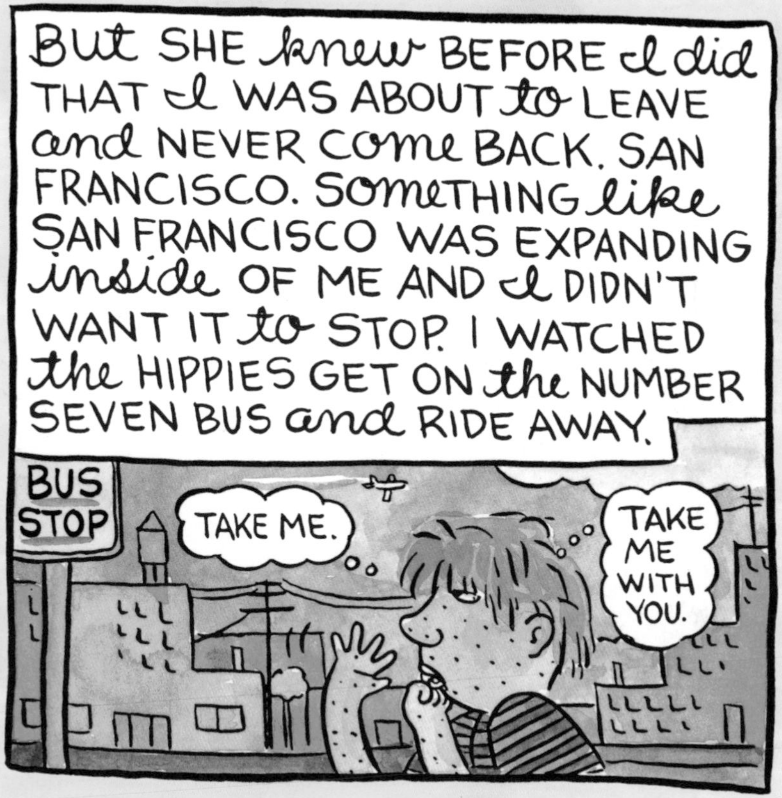
But SHE knew BEFORE I did THAT I WAS ABOUT to LEAVE and NEVER come BACK. SAN FRANCISCO. Something like SAN FRANCISCO WAS EXPANDING inside OF ME AND I DIDN'T WANT IT to STOP. I WATCHED the HIPPIES GET ON the NUMBER SEVEN BUS and RIDE AWAY.
BUS STOP
TAKE ME.
TAKE ME WITH YOU.

The LAST DAYS OF summer ARE ALWAYS SO SAD. FLOWERS lose THEIR PETALS and BECOME HARD SEEDS. I TOOK THE number SEVEN BUS in SEARCH OF THE HIPPIES. I AVOIDED GLADYS.

END OF THE LINE, SWEETHEART. YOU HAVE TO GET OFF.

WHAT DO YOU MEAN?

I DON'T GO NO FURTHER.

BUT WHERE'S THE HIPPIES?

lease n't STURB VER.

I LISTENED to THE RADIO FOR LOCATIONS AND CHANGED buses downtown LOOKING out THE WINDOW FOR "THE HAPPENING," the PLACE WHERE the HIPPIES ALL GROOVED in THE sun. I knew IT WAS OUT THERE. ALL I NEEDED was TO FIND the RIGHT bus.

YOU RIDE THE #27?

EVERYDAY.

YOU EVER SEE WILD LOOKING PEOPLE ACTING MAGICAL WITH STICKING-OUT HAIR, MAYBE WEARING BOOTS AND POSSIBLY CAPES MADE FROM FLAGS?

YOU MEAN THE HALFWAY HOUSE?

BUS STOP

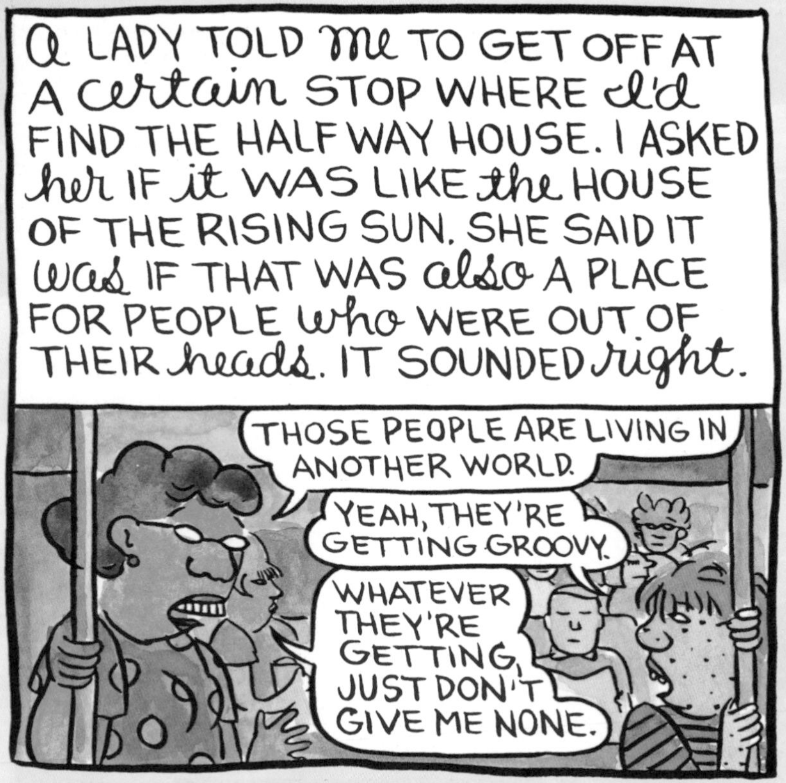
A LADY TOLD ME TO GET OFF AT A CERTAIN STOP WHERE I'D FIND THE HALF WAY HOUSE. I ASKED HER IF IT WAS LIKE THE HOUSE OF THE RISING SUN. SHE SAID IT WAS IF THAT WAS ALSO A PLACE FOR PEOPLE WHO WERE OUT OF THEIR HEADS. IT SOUNDED RIGHT.
THOSE PEOPLE ARE LIVING IN ANOTHER WORLD.
YEAH, THEY'RE GETTING GROOVY.
WHATEVER THEY'RE GETTING, JUST DON'T GIVE ME NONE.

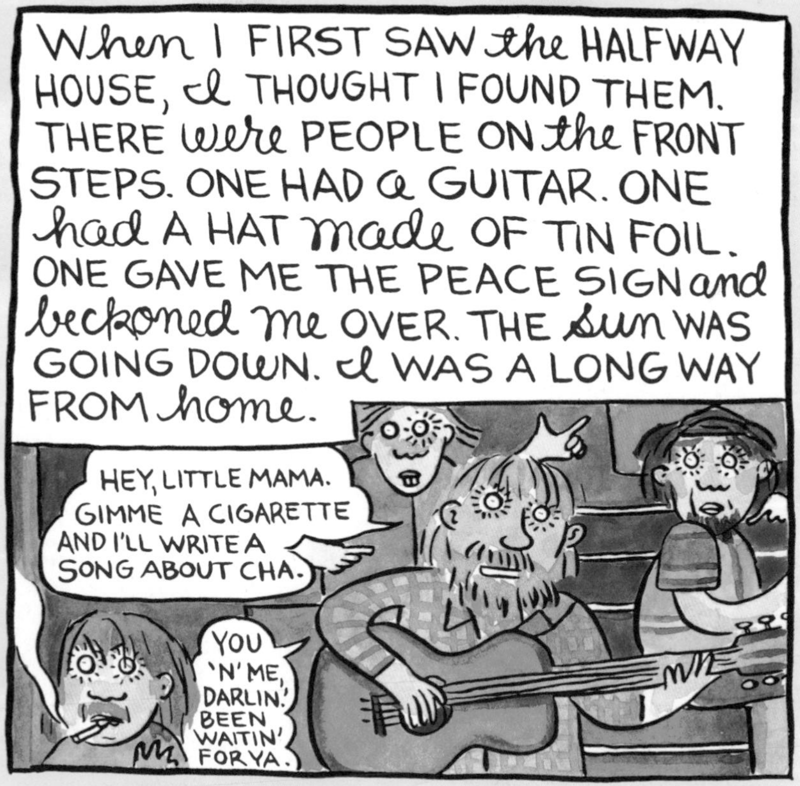
WHEN I FIRST SAW THE HALFWAY HOUSE, I THOUGHT I FOUND THEM. THERE WERE PEOPLE ON THE FRONT STEPS. ONE HAD A GUITAR. ONE HAD A HAT MADE OF TIN FOIL. ONE GAVE ME THE PEACE SIGN AND BECKONED ME OVER. THE SUN WAS GOING DOWN. I WAS A LONG WAY FROM HOME.
HEY, LITTLE MAMA. GIMME A CIGARETTE AND I'LL WRITE A SONG ABOUT CHA.
YOU 'N' ME, DARLIN.' BEEN WAITIN' FOR YA.

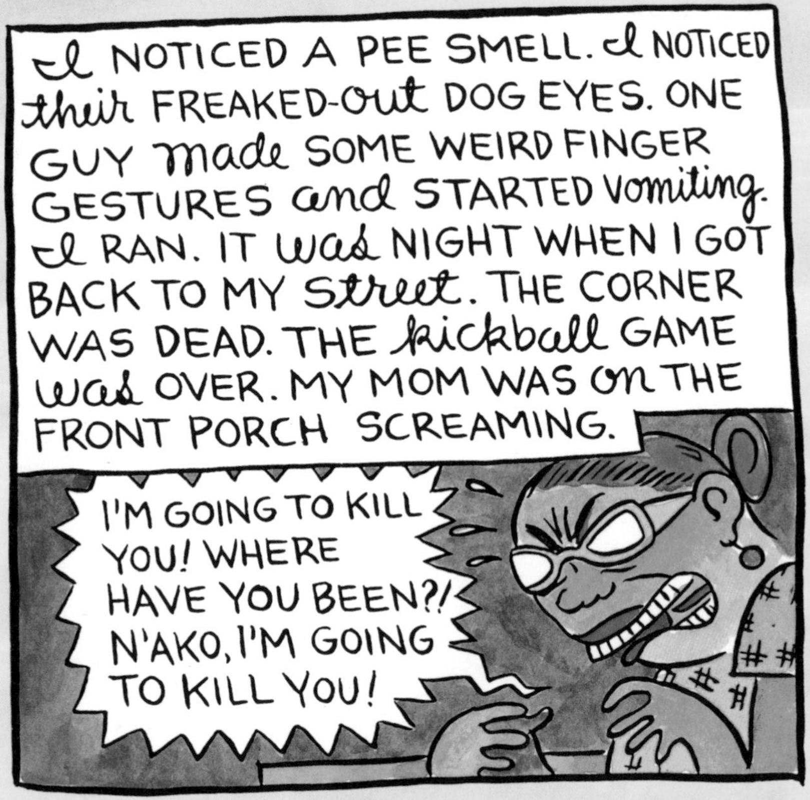
I NOTICED A PEE SMELL. I NOTICED their FREAKED-out DOG EYES. ONE GUY made SOME WEIRD FINGER GESTURES and STARTED vomiting. I RAN. IT was NIGHT WHEN I GOT BACK TO MY Street. THE CORNER WAS DEAD. THE kickball GAME was OVER. MY MOM WAS on THE FRONT PORCH SCREAMING.
I'M GOING TO KILL YOU! WHERE HAVE YOU BEEN?! N'AKO, I'M GOING TO KILL YOU!

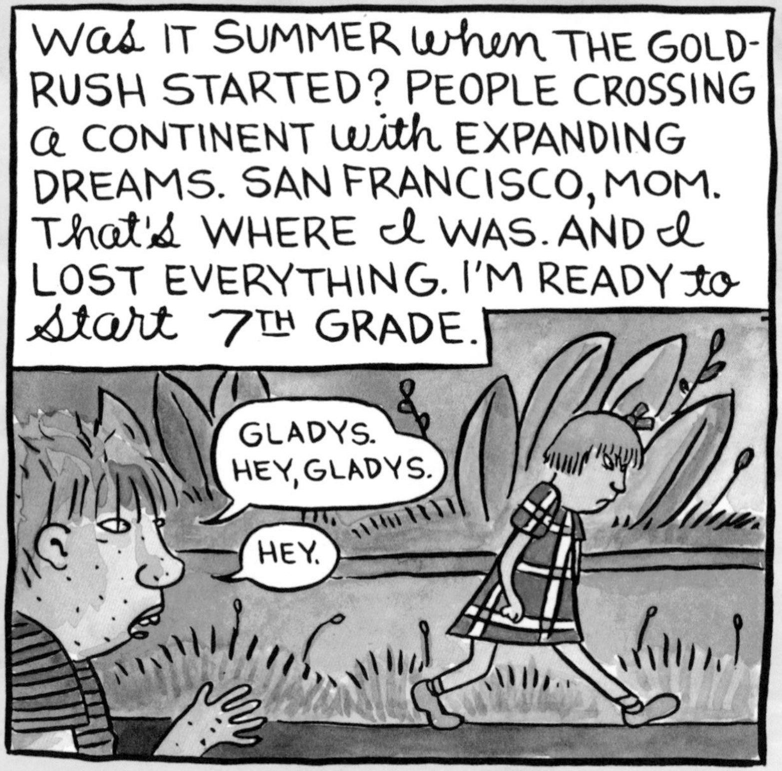
Was IT SUMMER when THE GOLD-RUSH STARTED? PEOPLE CROSSING a CONTINENT with EXPANDING DREAMS. SAN FRANCISCO, MOM. That's WHERE I WAS. AND I LOST EVERYTHING. I'M READY to start 7TH GRADE.
GLADYS. HEY, GLADYS.
HEY.

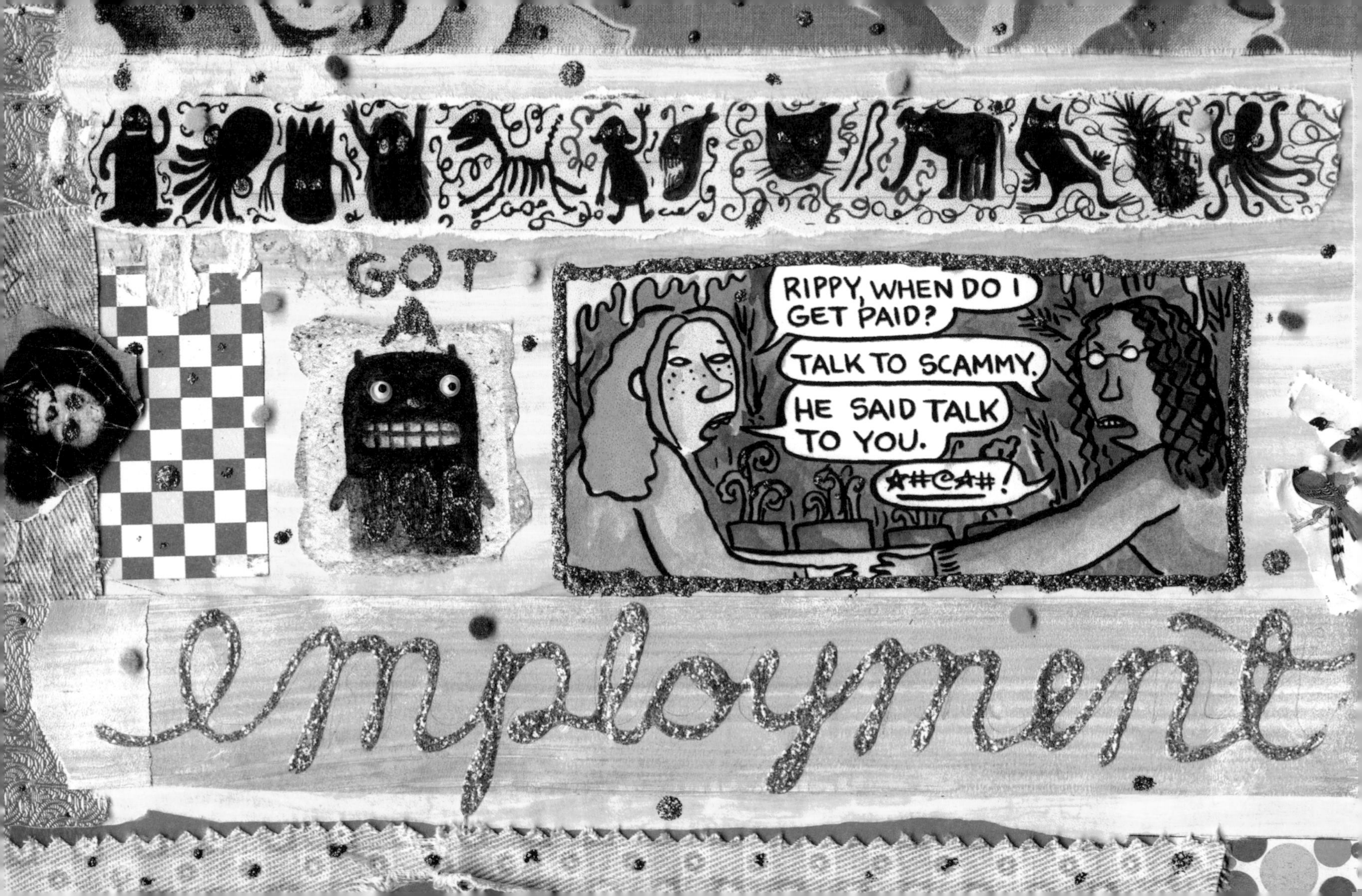
GOT
A
RIPPY, WHEN DO I GET PAID?
TALK TO SCAMMY.
HE SAID TALK TO YOU.
#@#!
employment

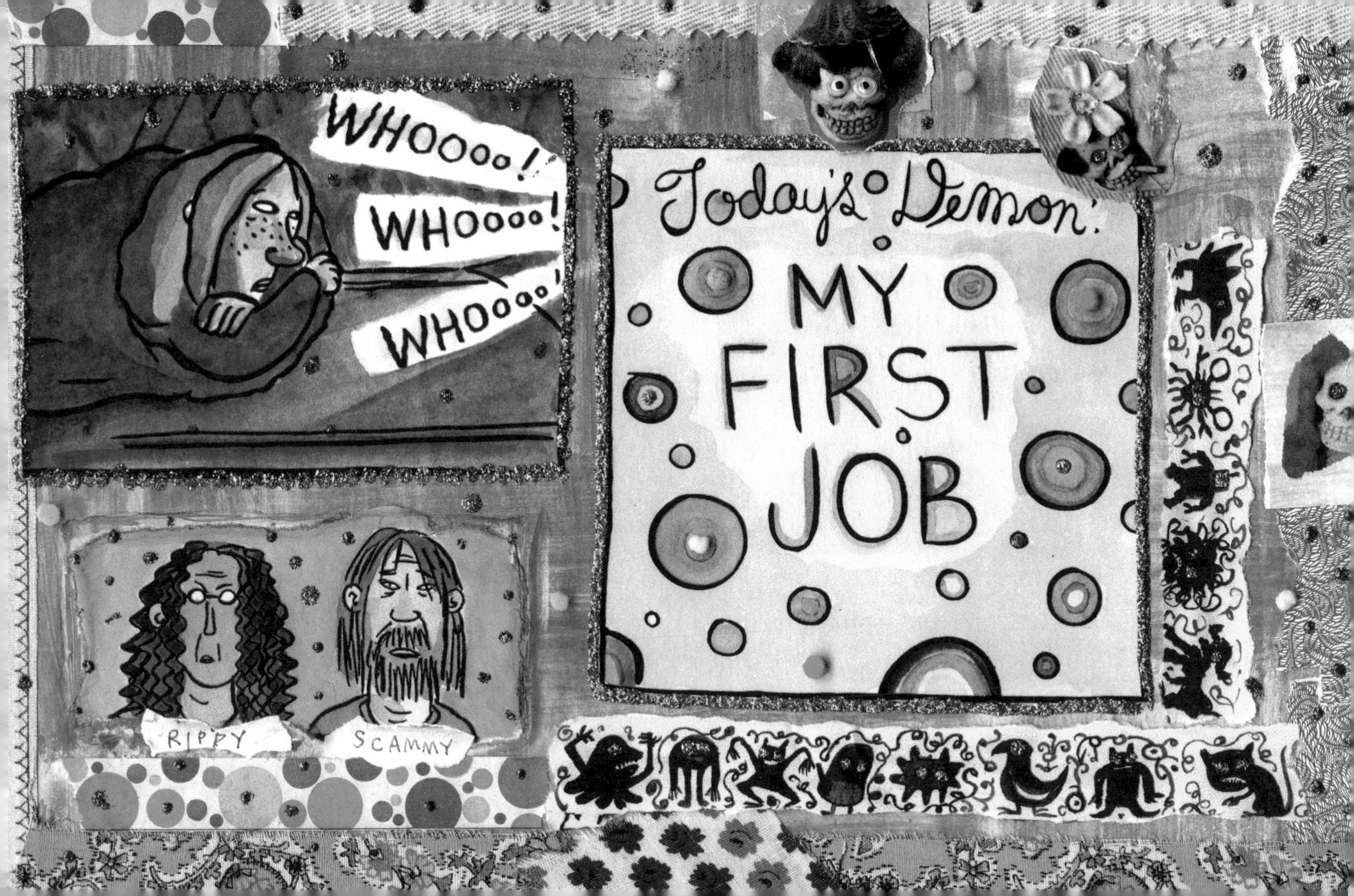
WHOOOO!
WHOOOO!
WHOOOO!
Today's Demon:
MY FIRST JOB
RIPPY
SCAMMY

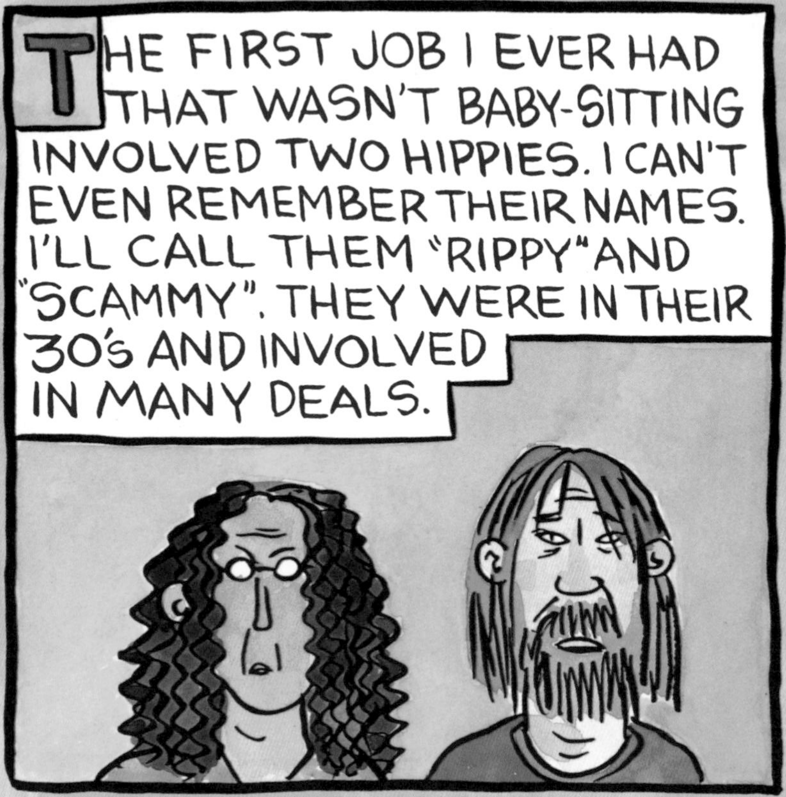
THE FIRST JOB I EVER HAD THAT WASN'T BABY-SITTING INVOLVED TWO HIPPIES. I CAN'T EVEN REMEMBER THEIR NAMES. I'LL CALL THEM "RIPPY" AND "SCAMMY". THEY WERE IN THEIR 30'S AND INVOLVED IN MANY DEALS.

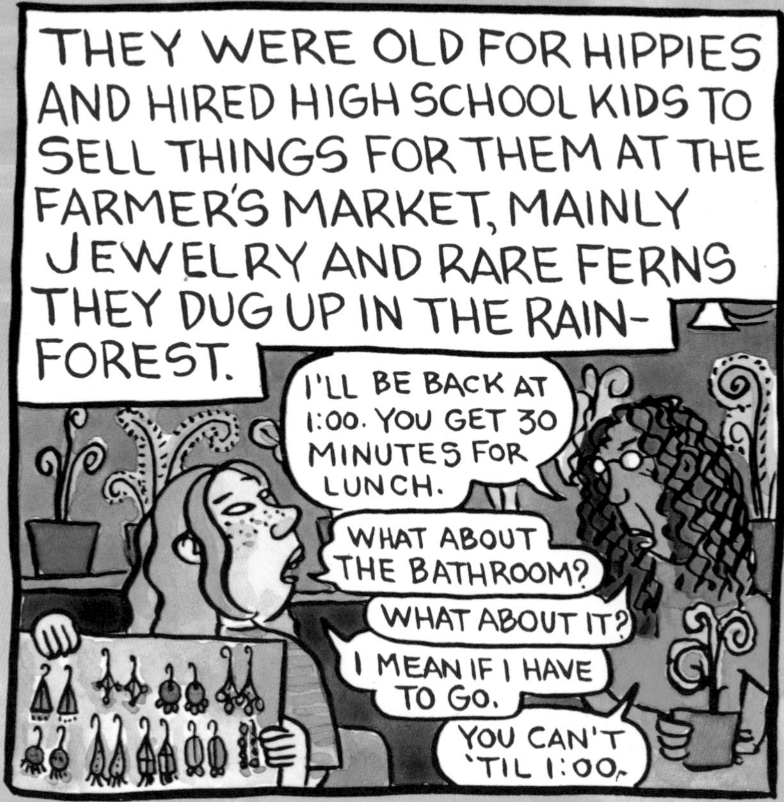
THEY WERE OLD FOR HIPPIES AND HIRED HIGH SCHOOL KIDS TO SELL THINGS FOR THEM AT THE FARMER'S MARKET, MAINLY JEWELRY AND RARE FERNS THEY DUG UP IN THE RAIN-FOREST.
I'LL BE BACK AT 1:00. YOU GET 30 MINUTES FOR LUNCH.
WHAT ABOUT THE BATHROOM?
WHAT ABOUT IT?
I MEAN IF I HAVE TO GO.
YOU CAN'T 'TIL 1:00.

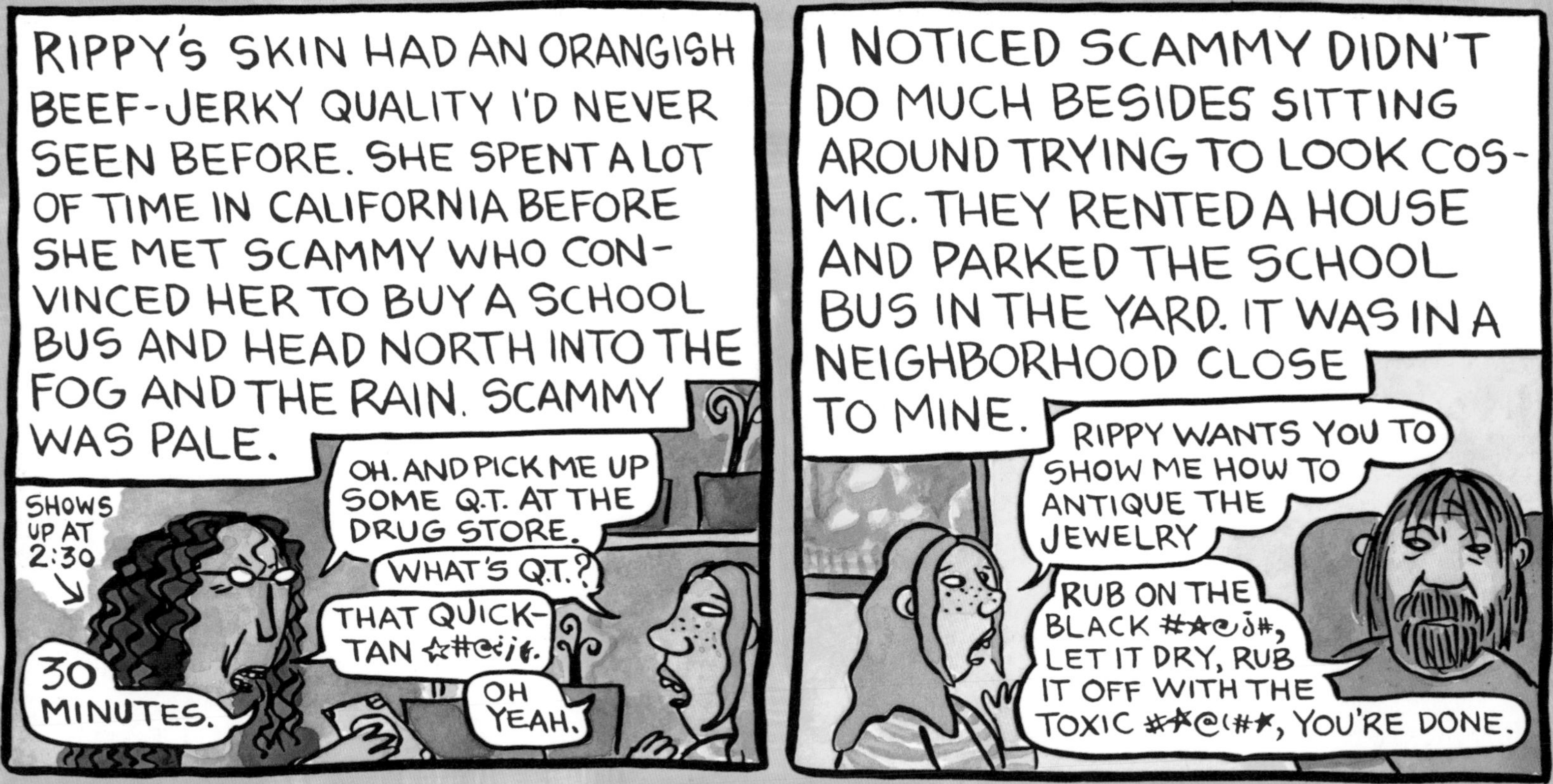
RIPPY'S SKIN HAD AN ORANGISH BEEF-JERKY QUALITY I'D NEVER SEEN BEFORE. SHE SPENT A LOT OF TIME IN CALIFORNIA BEFORE SHE MET SCAMMY WHO CONVINCED HER TO BUY A SCHOOL BUS AND HEAD NORTH INTO THE FOG AND THE RAIN. SCAMMY WAS PALE.
SHOWS UP AT 2:30
OH. AND PICK ME UP SOME Q.T. AT THE DRUG STORE.
WHAT'S Q.T.?
THAT QUICK-TAN ☆#@¡¡.
30 MINUTES.
OH YEAH.
I NOTICED SCAMMY DIDN'T DO MUCH BESIDES SITTING AROUND TRYING TO LOOK COSMIC. THEY RENTED A HOUSE AND PARKED THE SCHOOL BUS IN THE YARD. IT WAS IN A NEIGHBORHOOD CLOSE TO MINE.
RIPPY WANTS YOU TO SHOW ME HOW TO ANTIQUE THE JEWELRY
RUB ON THE BLACK #★@¡#, LET IT DRY, RUB IT OFF WITH THE TOXIC #★@(#★, YOU'RE DONE.

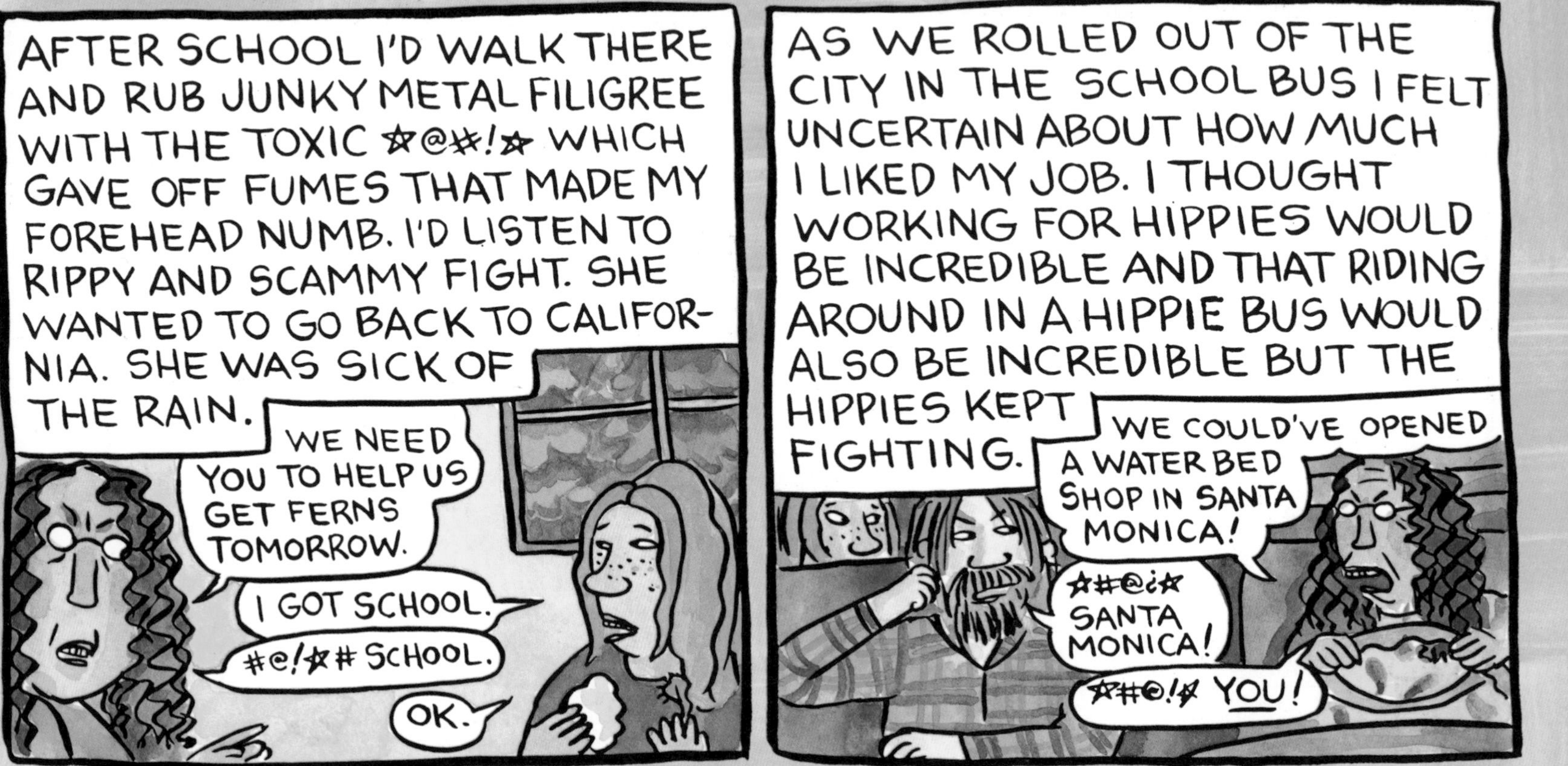
AFTER SCHOOL I'D WALK THERE AND RUB JUNKY METAL FILIGREE WITH THE TOXIC ☆@#!☆ WHICH GAVE OFF FUMES THAT MADE MY FOREHEAD NUMB. I'D LISTEN TO RIPPY AND SCAMMY FIGHT. SHE WANTED TO GO BACK TO CALIFORNIA. SHE WAS SICK OF THE RAIN.
WE NEED YOU TO HELP US GET FERNS TOMORROW.
I GOT SCHOOL.
#@!☆# SCHOOL.
OK.
AS WE ROLLED OUT OF THE CITY IN THE SCHOOL BUS I FELT UNCERTAIN ABOUT HOW MUCH I LIKED MY JOB. I THOUGHT WORKING FOR HIPPIES WOULD BE INCREDIBLE AND THAT RIDING AROUND IN A HIPPIE BUS WOULD ALSO BE INCREDIBLE BUT THE HIPPIES KEPT FIGHTING.
WE COULD'VE OPENED A WATER BED SHOP IN SANTA MONICA!
☆#@¡☆ SANTA MONICA!
☆#©!☆ YOU!

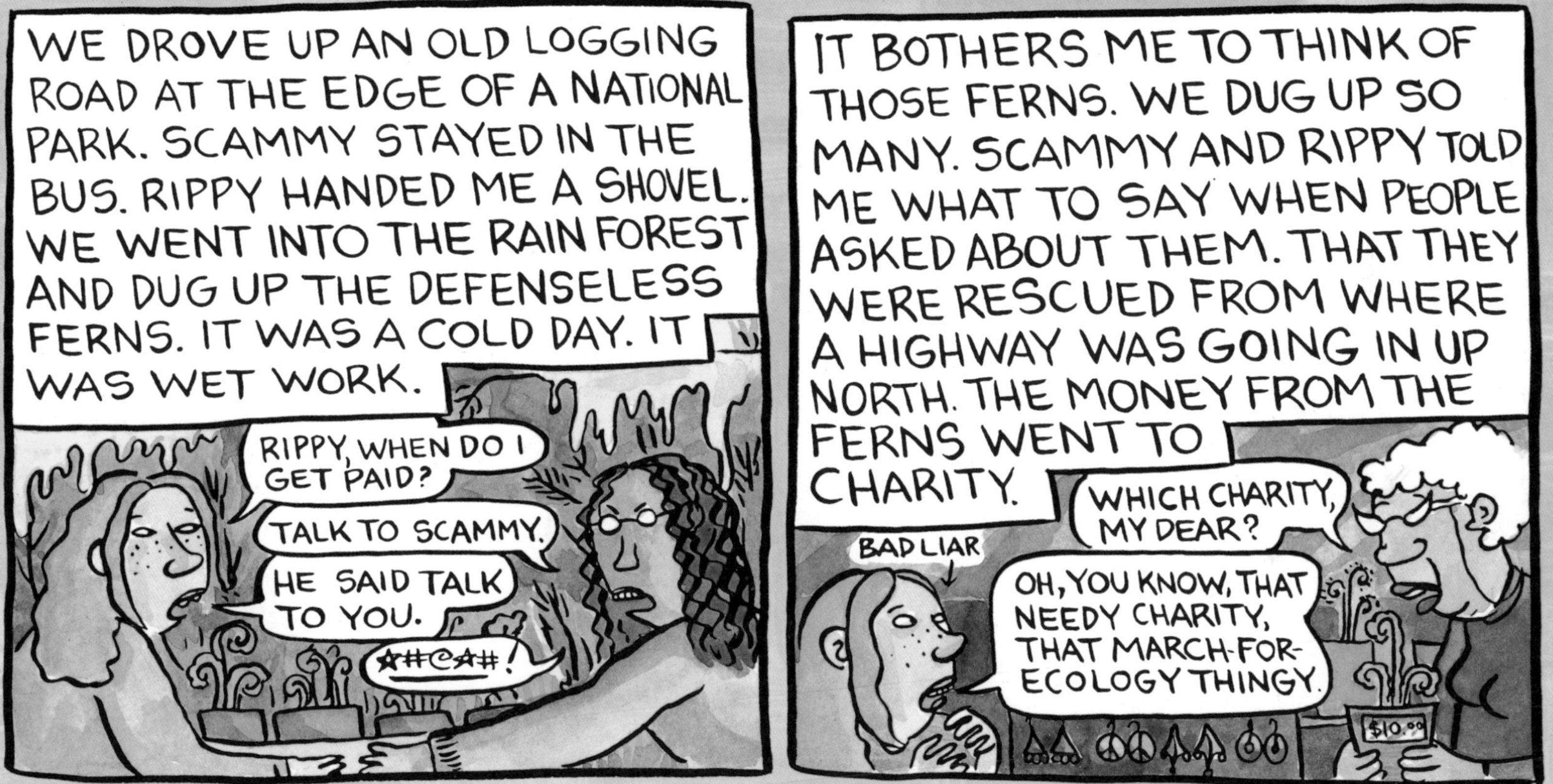

WE DROVE UP AN OLD LOGGING ROAD AT THE EDGE OF A NATIONAL PARK. SCAMMY STAYED IN THE BUS. RIPPY HANDED ME A SHOVEL. WE WENT INTO THE RAIN FOREST AND DUG UP THE DEFENSELESS FERNS. IT WAS A COLD DAY. IT WAS WET WORK.
RIPPY, WHEN DO I GET PAID?
TALK TO SCAMMY.
HE SAID TALK TO YOU.
★#@★#!
IT BOTHERS ME TO THINK OF THOSE FERNS. WE DUG UP SO MANY. SCAMMY AND RIPPY TOLD ME WHAT TO SAY WHEN PEOPLE ASKED ABOUT THEM. THAT THEY WERE RESCUED FROM WHERE A HIGHWAY WAS GOING IN UP NORTH. THE MONEY FROM THE FERNS WENT TO CHARITY.
WHICH CHARITY, MY DEAR?
BAD LIAR
OH, YOU KNOW, THAT NEEDY CHARITY, THAT MARCH-FOR-ECOLOGY THINGY.
$10.00

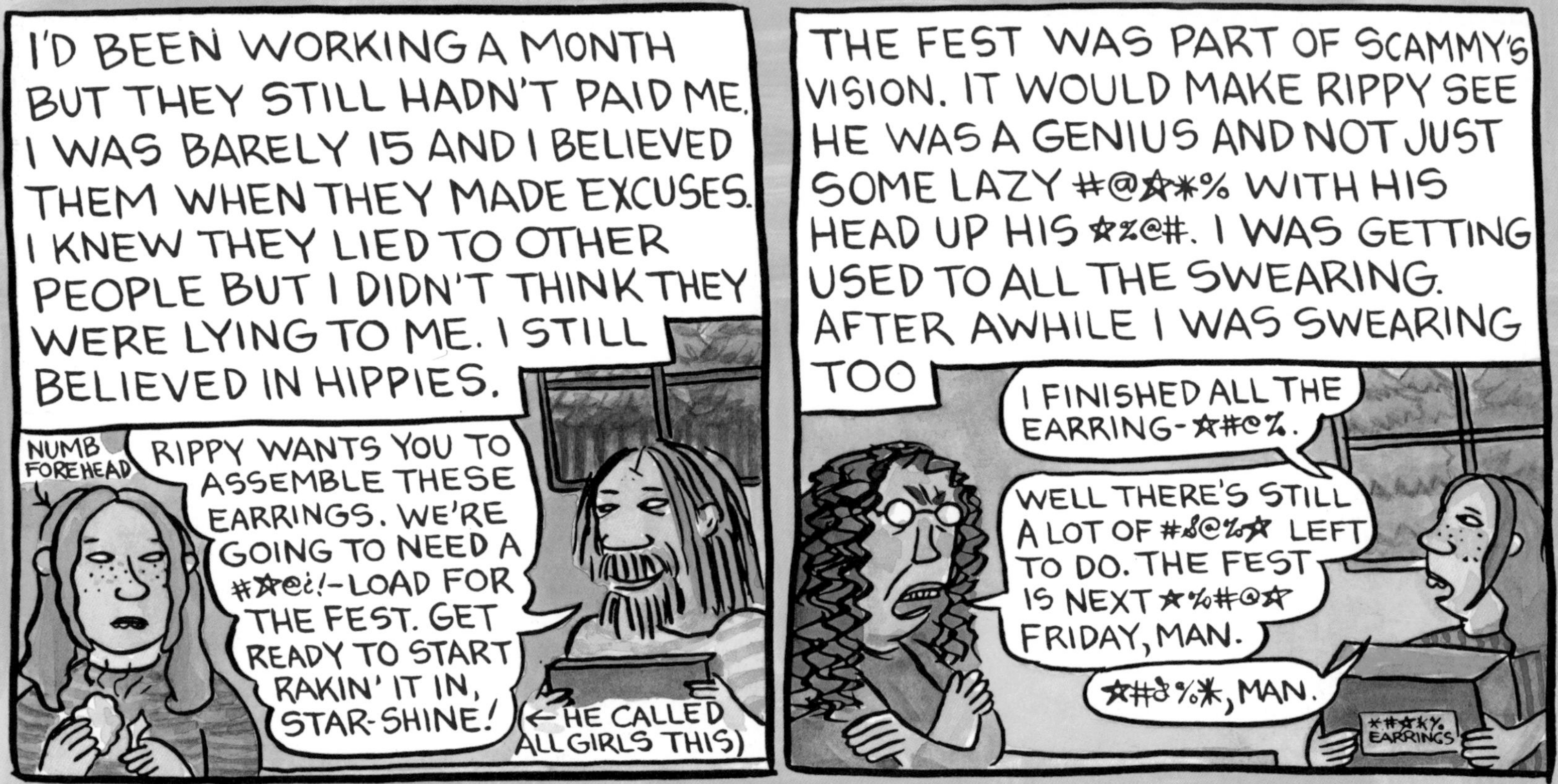
I'D BEEN WORKING A MONTH BUT THEY STILL HADN'T PAID ME. I WAS BARELY 15 AND I BELIEVED THEM WHEN THEY MADE EXCUSES. I KNEW THEY LIED TO OTHER PEOPLE BUT I DIDN'T THINK THEY WERE LYING TO ME. I STILL BELIEVED IN HIPPIES.
NUMB FOREHEAD
RIPPY WANTS YOU TO ASSEMBLE THESE EARRINGS. WE'RE GOING TO NEED A #☆@¿!-LOAD FOR THE FEST. GET READY TO START RAKIN' IT IN, STAR-SHINE!
(← HE CALLED ALL GIRLS THIS)
THE FEST WAS PART OF SCAMMY'S VISION. IT WOULD MAKE RIPPY SEE HE WAS A GENIUS AND NOT JUST SOME LAZY #@☆*% WITH HIS HEAD UP HIS ☆%@#. I WAS GETTING USED TO ALL THE SWEARING. AFTER AWHILE I WAS SWEARING TOO
I FINISHED ALL THE EARRING-☆#@%.
WELL THERE'S STILL A LOT OF #$@%☆ LEFT TO DO. THE FEST IS NEXT ☆%#@☆ FRIDAY, MAN.
☆#$%*, MAN.
#☆% EARRINGS

I'D NEVER HEARD OF THE FEST. IT TURNS OUT THERE WERE LOTS OF FESTS, ALL WITH DIFFERENT NAMES, ALL JUST BASICALLY GATHERINGS OF HIPPIES IN THE WOODS. SOME FESTS HAD THEMES AND COSTUMES.

YOU GOT ANY MEDIEVAL-✳@✳# TO WEAR? AND YOU'LL NEED A SLEEPING BAG.

I GOT A SLEEPING BAG BUT I DON'T KNOW WHAT MEDIEVAL-✳#@✳ LOOKS LIKE.

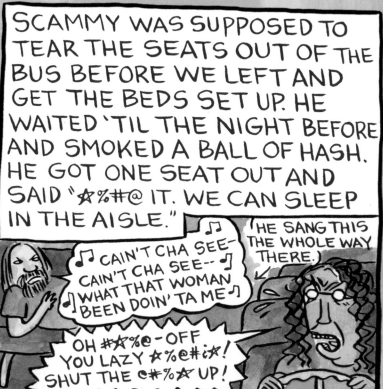

SCAMMY WAS SUPPOSED TO TEAR THE SEATS OUT OF THE BUS BEFORE WE LEFT AND GET THE BEDS SET UP. HE WAITED 'TIL THE NIGHT BEFORE AND SMOKED A BALL OF HASH. HE GOT ONE SEAT OUT AND SAID "✳%#@ IT. WE CAN SLEEP IN THE AISLE."

♫ CAIN'T CHA SEE— CAIN'T CHA SEE-- WHAT THAT WOMAN BEEN DOIN' TA ME ♫

(HE SANG THIS THE WHOLE WAY THERE.)

OH #✳%@-OFF YOU LAZY ✳%@#i✳! SHUT THE ¢#%✳ UP!

141

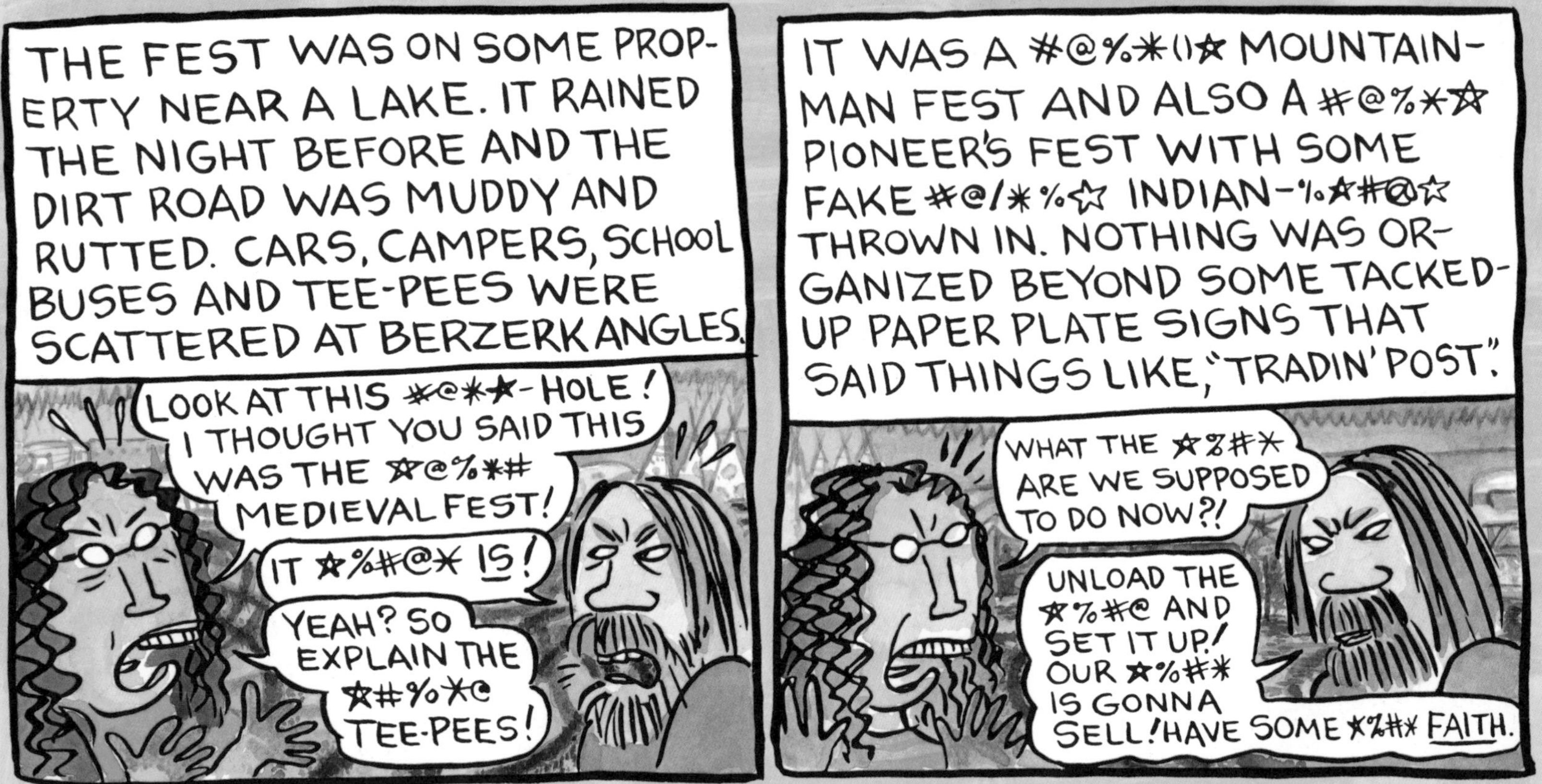
THE FEST WAS ON SOME PROPERTY NEAR A LAKE. IT RAINED THE NIGHT BEFORE AND THE DIRT ROAD WAS MUDDY AND RUTTED. CARS, CAMPERS, SCHOOL BUSES AND TEE-PEES WERE SCATTERED AT BERZERK ANGLES.
LOOK AT THIS *@**-HOLE! I THOUGHT YOU SAID THIS WAS THE ☆@%**# MEDIEVAL FEST!
IT ☆%#@* IS!
YEAH? SO EXPLAIN THE ☆#%*@ TEE-PEES!
IT WAS A #@%*()☆ MOUNTAIN-MAN FEST AND ALSO A #@%*☆ PIONEER'S FEST WITH SOME FAKE #@/*%☆ INDIAN-%☆#@☆ THROWN IN. NOTHING WAS ORGANIZED BEYOND SOME TACKED-UP PAPER PLATE SIGNS THAT SAID THINGS LIKE, "TRADIN' POST".
WHAT THE ☆%#* ARE WE SUPPOSED TO DO NOW?!
UNLOAD THE ☆%#@ AND SET IT UP! OUR ☆%#* IS GONNA SELL! HAVE SOME *%#* FAITH.

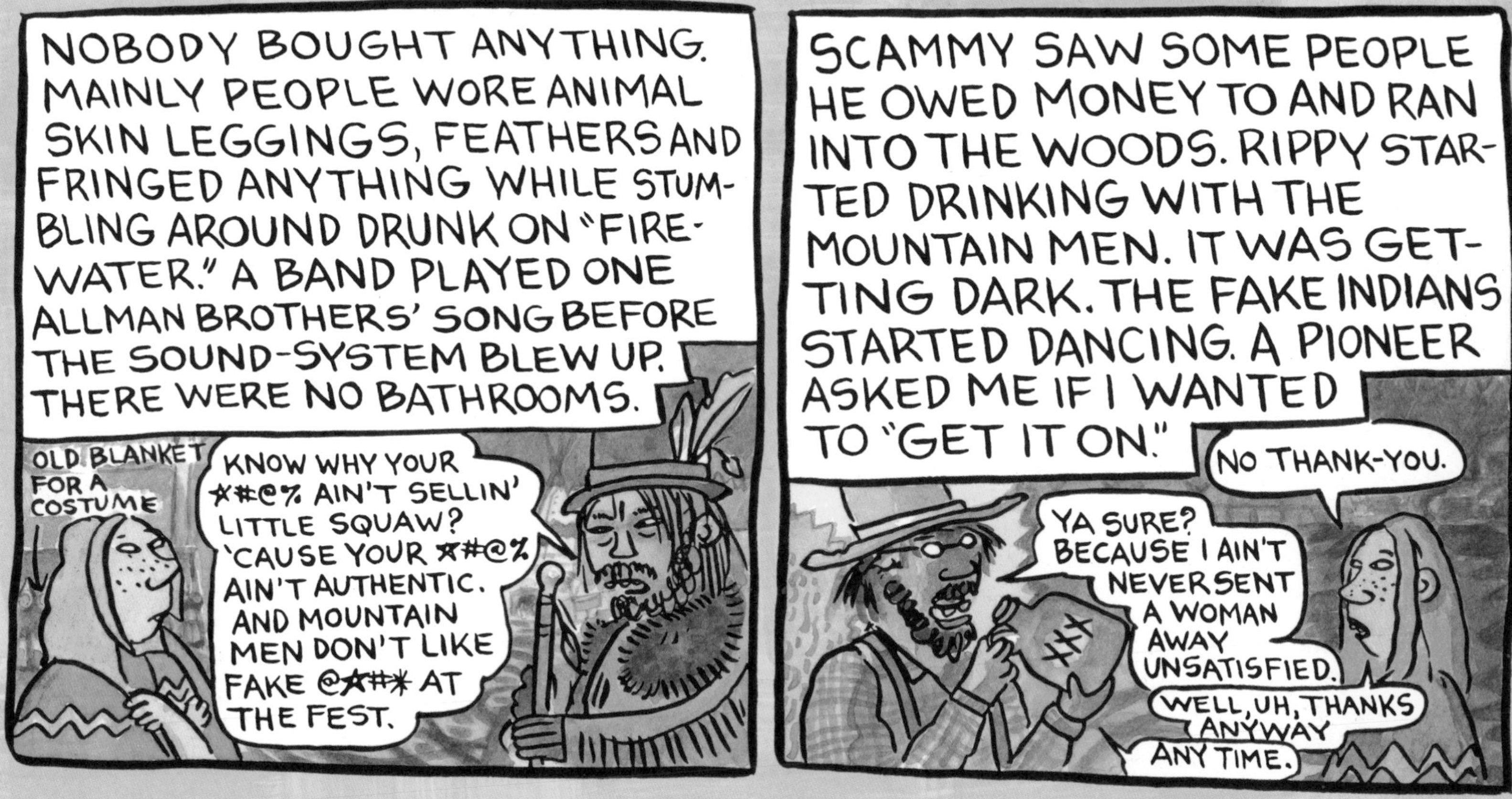
NOBODY BOUGHT ANYTHING. MAINLY PEOPLE WORE ANIMAL SKIN LEGGINGS, FEATHERS AND FRINGED ANYTHING WHILE STUMBLING AROUND DRUNK ON "FIRE-WATER." A BAND PLAYED ONE ALLMAN BROTHERS' SONG BEFORE THE SOUND-SYSTEM BLEW UP. THERE WERE NO BATHROOMS.
OLD BLANKET FOR A COSTUME
KNOW WHY YOUR ☆#@% AIN'T SELLIN' LITTLE SQUAW? 'CAUSE YOUR ☆#@% AIN'T AUTHENTIC. AND MOUNTAIN MEN DON'T LIKE FAKE @☆#* AT THE FEST.
SCAMMY SAW SOME PEOPLE HE OWED MONEY TO AND RAN INTO THE WOODS. RIPPY STARTED DRINKING WITH THE MOUNTAIN MEN. IT WAS GETTING DARK. THE FAKE INDIANS STARTED DANCING. A PIONEER ASKED ME IF I WANTED TO "GET IT ON."
NO THANK-YOU.
YA SURE? BECAUSE I AIN'T NEVER SENT A WOMAN AWAY UNSATISFIED.
XXX
WELL, UH, THANKS ANYWAY
ANY TIME.

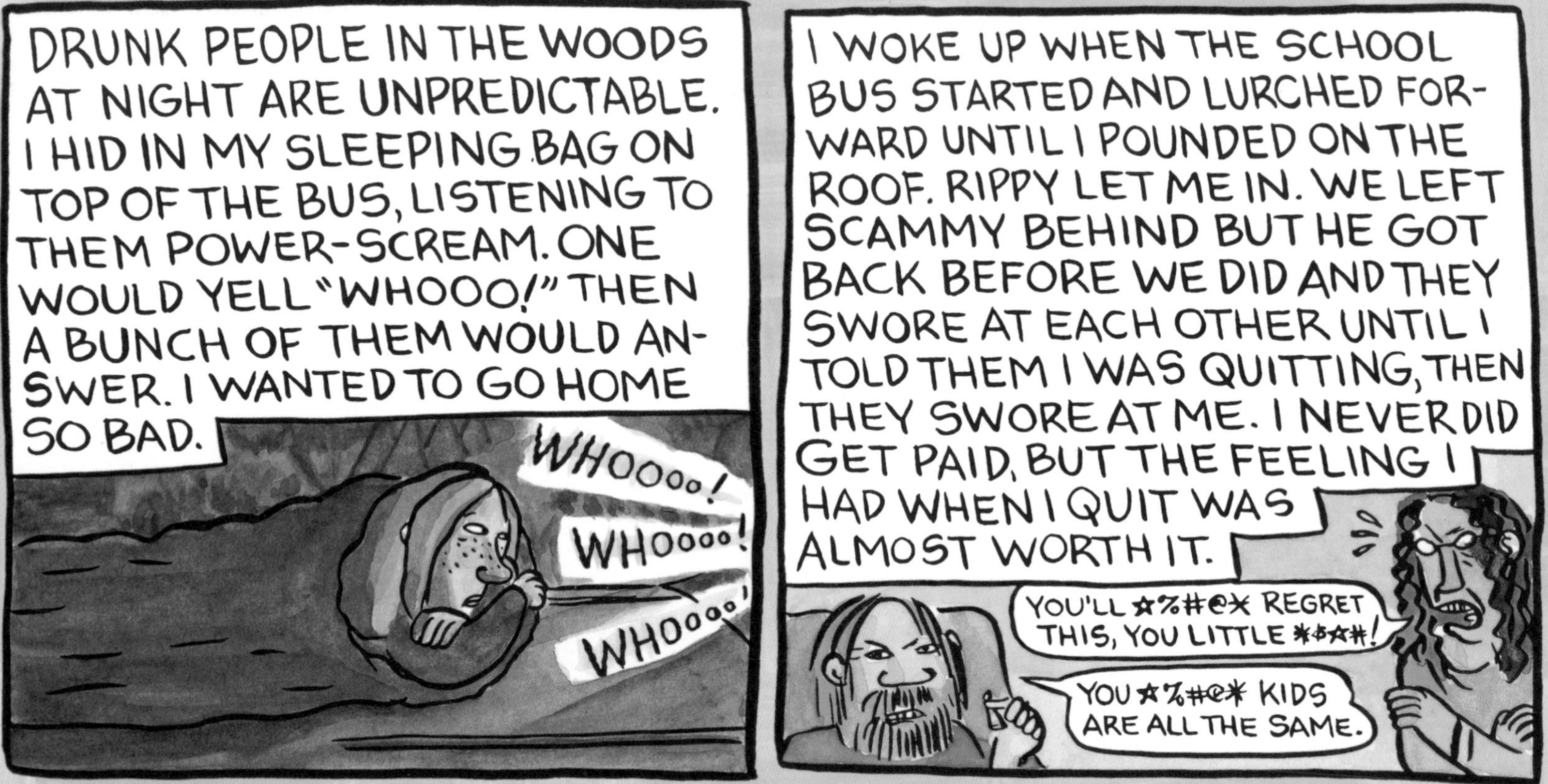
DRUNK PEOPLE IN THE WOODS AT NIGHT ARE UNPREDICTABLE. I HID IN MY SLEEPING BAG ON TOP OF THE BUS, LISTENING TO THEM POWER-SCREAM. ONE WOULD YELL "WHOOO!" THEN A BUNCH OF THEM WOULD ANSWER. I WANTED TO GO HOME SO BAD.
WHOOOO!
WHOOOO!
WHOOOO!
I WOKE UP WHEN THE SCHOOL BUS STARTED AND LURCHED FORWARD UNTIL I POUNDED ON THE ROOF. RIPPY LET ME IN. WE LEFT SCAMMY BEHIND BUT HE GOT BACK BEFORE WE DID AND THEY SWORE AT EACH OTHER UNTIL I TOLD THEM I WAS QUITTING, THEN THEY SWORE AT ME. I NEVER DID GET PAID, BUT THE FEELING I HAD WHEN I QUIT WAS ALMOST WORTH IT.
YOU'LL ★%#@✱ REGRET THIS, YOU LITTLE ✱$★#!
YOU ★%#@✱ KIDS ARE ALL THE SAME.

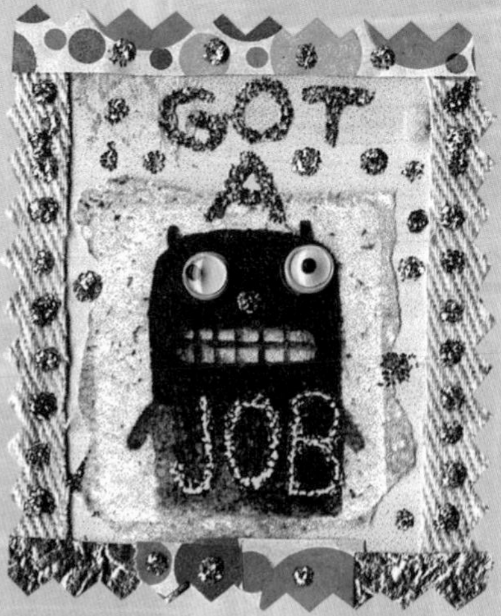
GOT
A
JOB

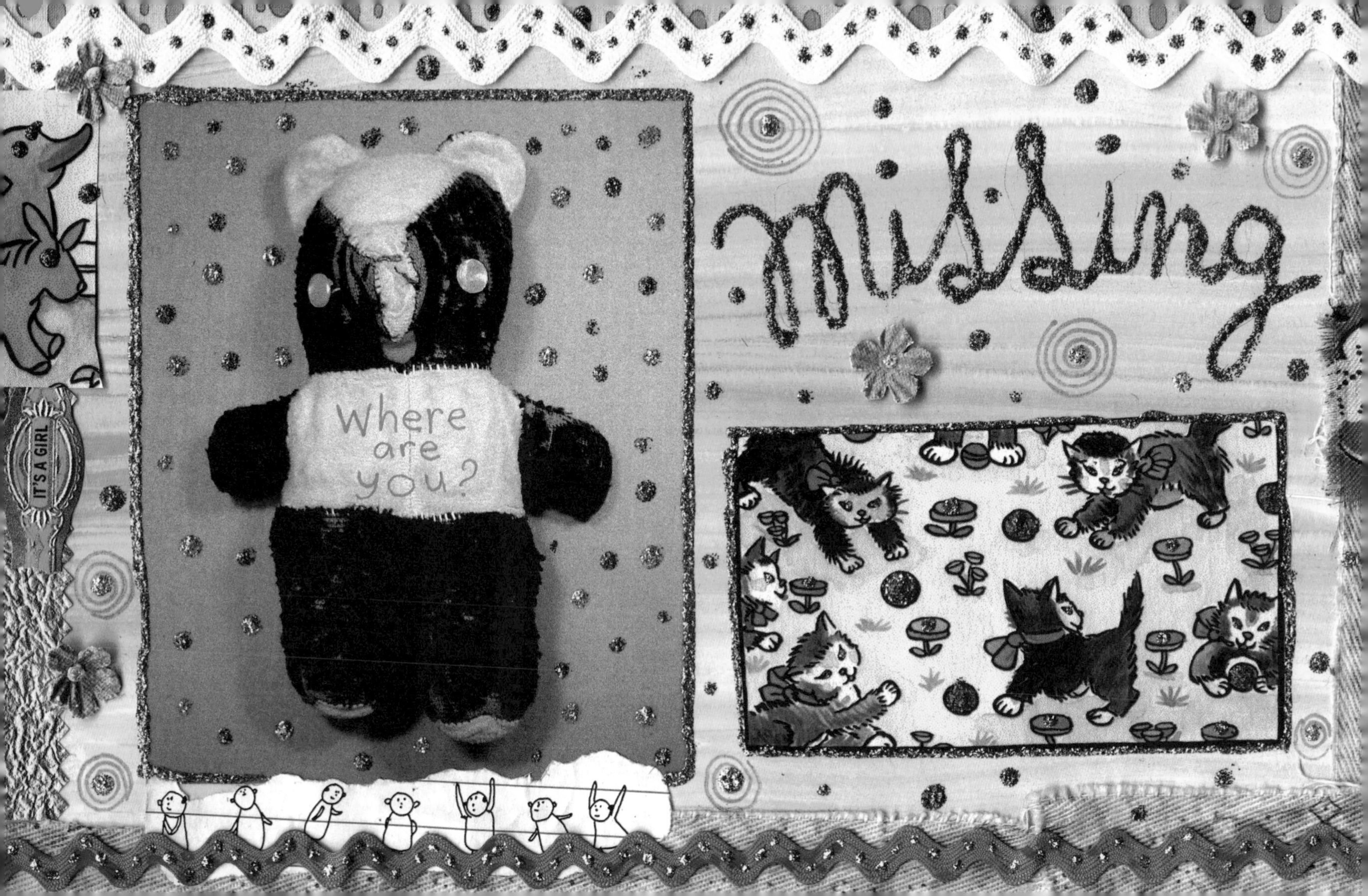
IT'S A GIRL
Where are you?
Missing

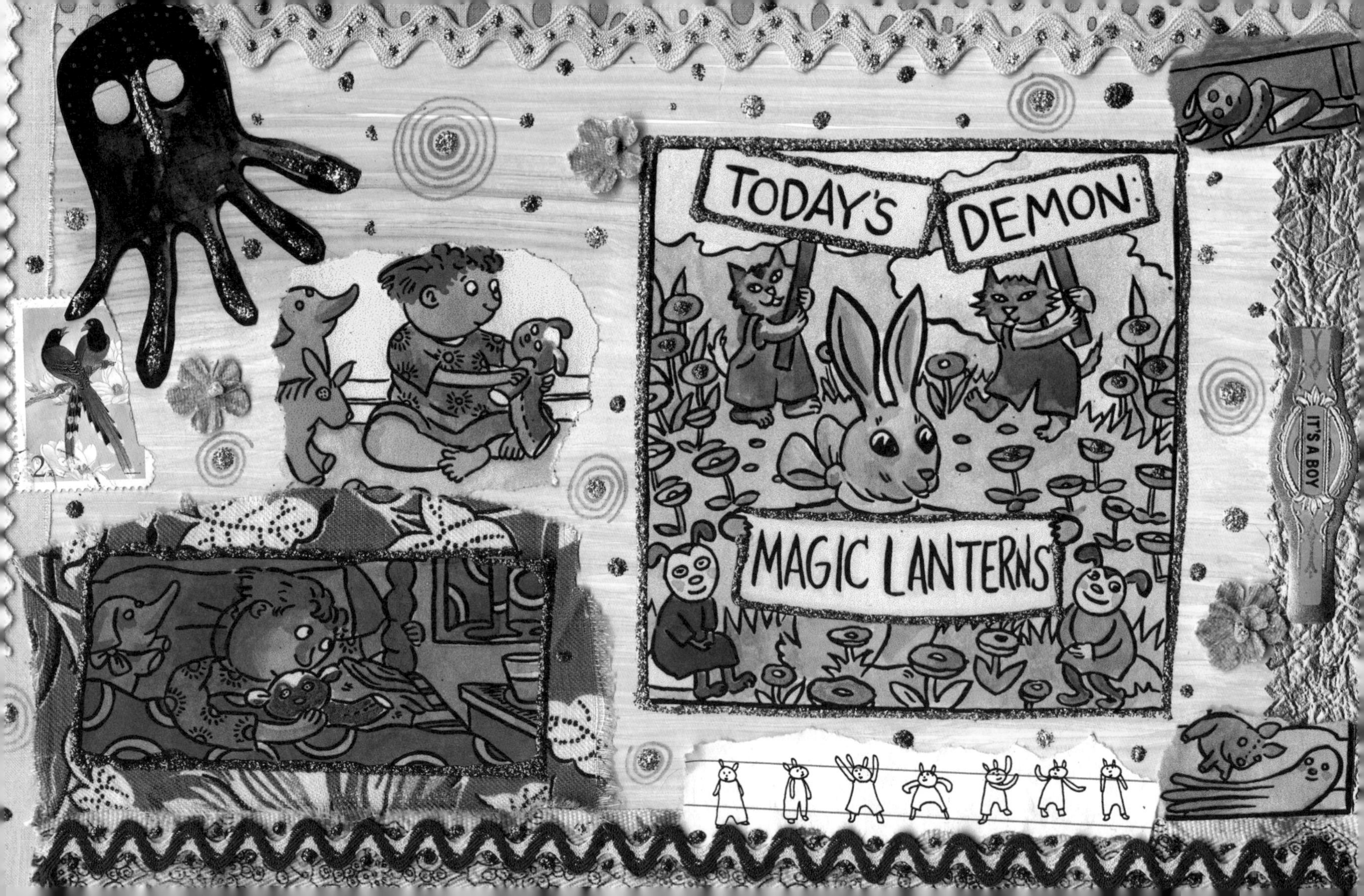

TODAY'S
DEMON:
MAGIC LANTERNS
IT'S A BOY
2

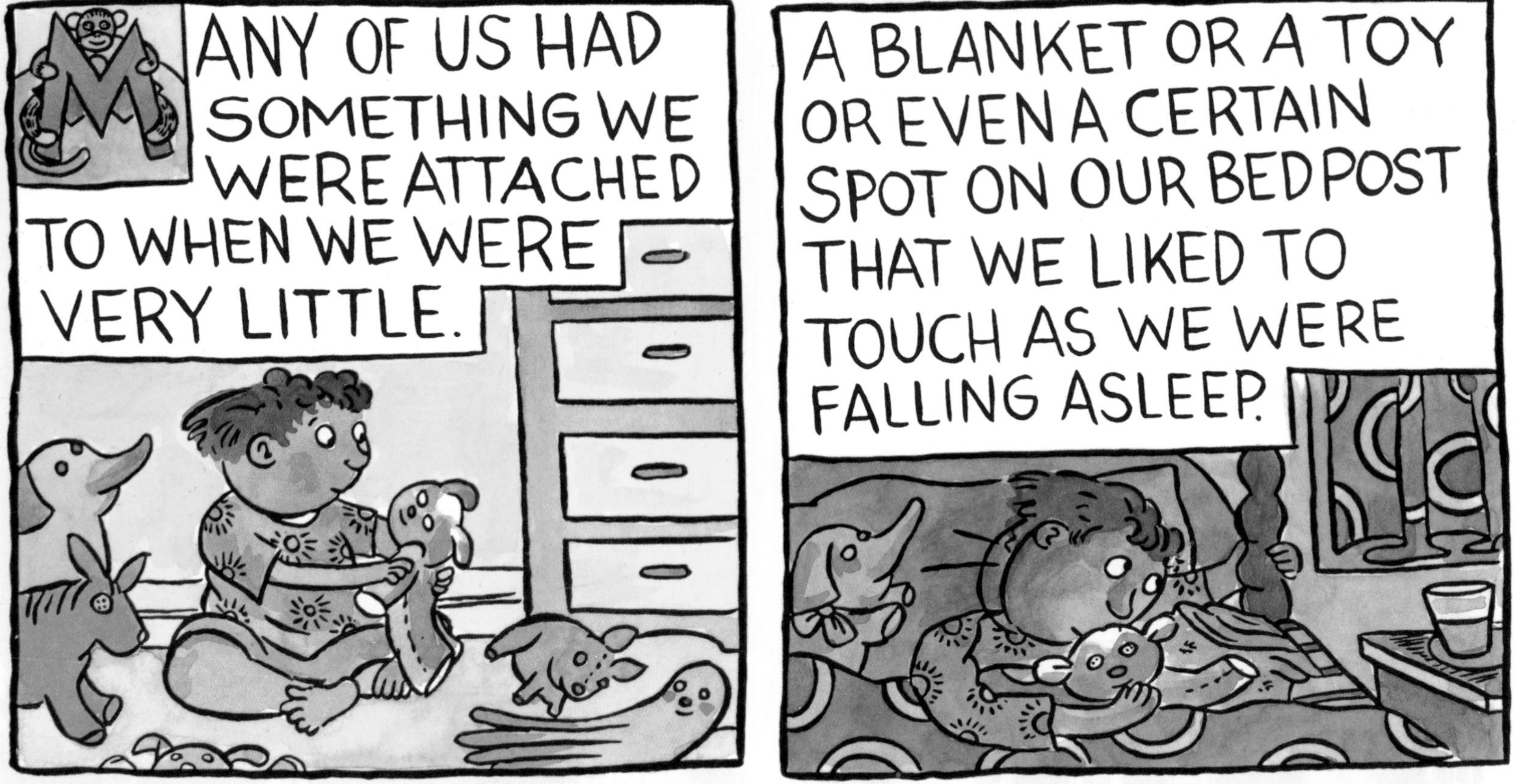
MANY OF US HAD SOMETHING WE WERE ATTACHED TO WHEN WE WERE VERY LITTLE.
A BLANKET OR A TOY OR EVEN A CERTAIN SPOT ON OUR BEDPOST THAT WE LIKED TO TOUCH AS WE WERE FALLING ASLEEP.

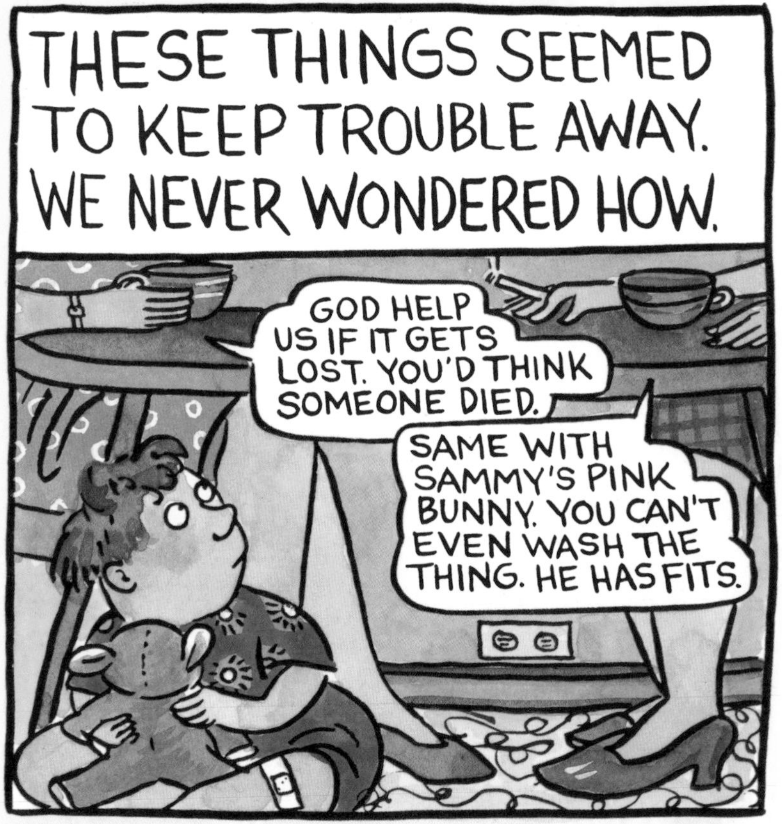
THESE THINGS SEEMED TO KEEP TROUBLE AWAY. WE NEVER WONDERED HOW.
GOD HELP US IF IT GETS LOST. YOU'D THINK SOMEONE DIED.
SAME WITH SAMMY'S PINK BUNNY. YOU CAN'T EVEN WASH THE THING. HE HAS FITS.

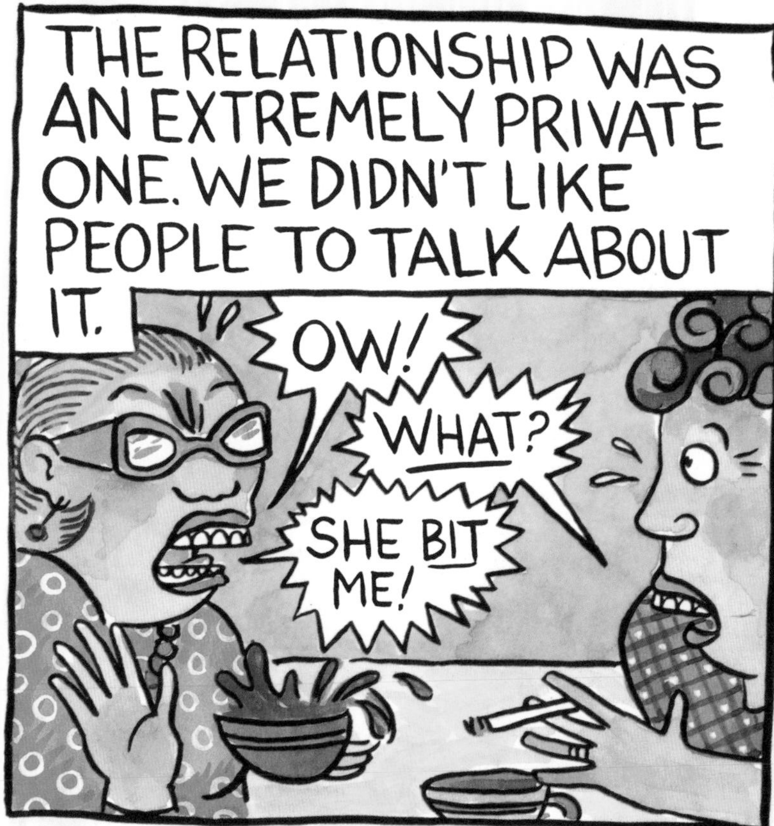
THE RELATIONSHIP WAS AN EXTREMELY PRIVATE ONE. WE DIDN'T LIKE PEOPLE TO TALK ABOUT IT.
OW!
WHAT?
SHE BIT ME!

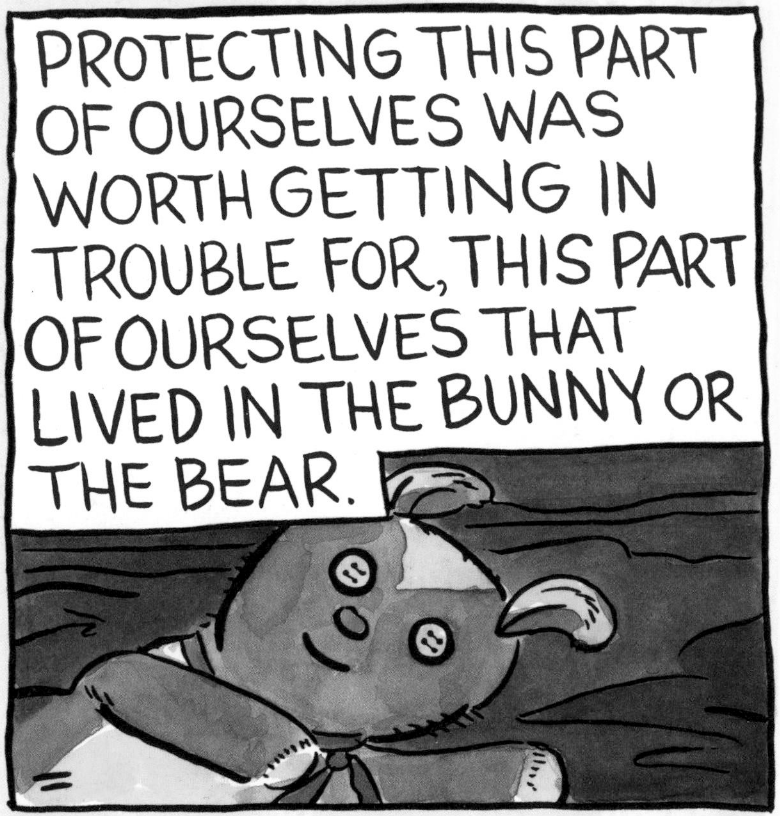
PROTECTING THIS PART OF OURSELVES WAS WORTH GETTING IN TROUBLE FOR, THIS PART OF OURSELVES THAT LIVED IN THE BUNNY OR THE BEAR.

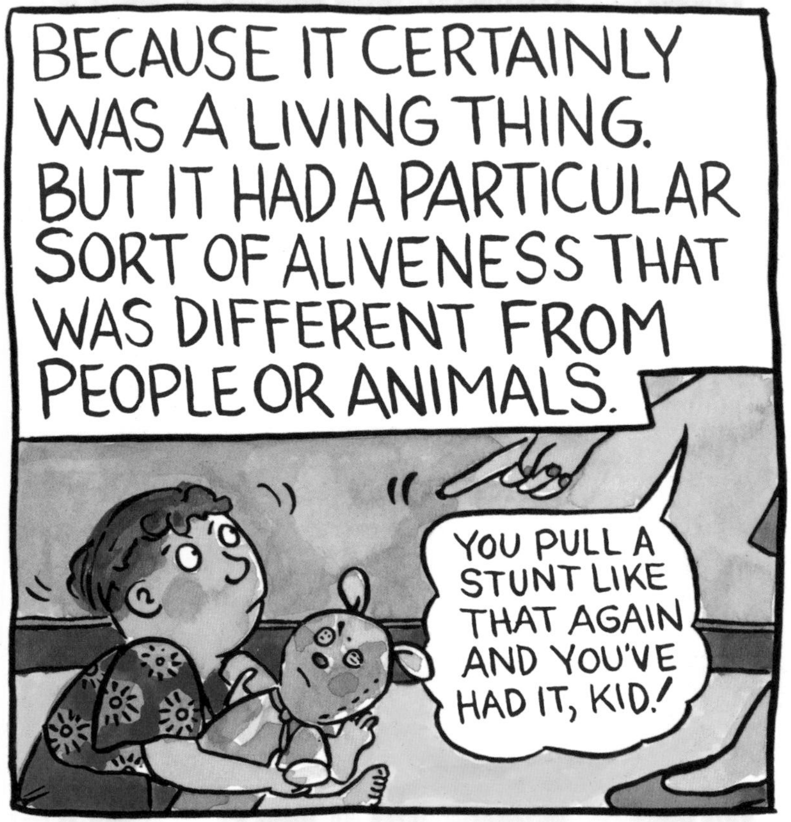
BECAUSE IT CERTAINLY WAS A LIVING THING. BUT IT HAD A PARTICULAR SORT OF ALIVENESS THAT WAS DIFFERENT FROM PEOPLE OR ANIMALS.
YOU PULL A STUNT LIKE THAT AGAIN AND YOU'VE HAD IT, KID!

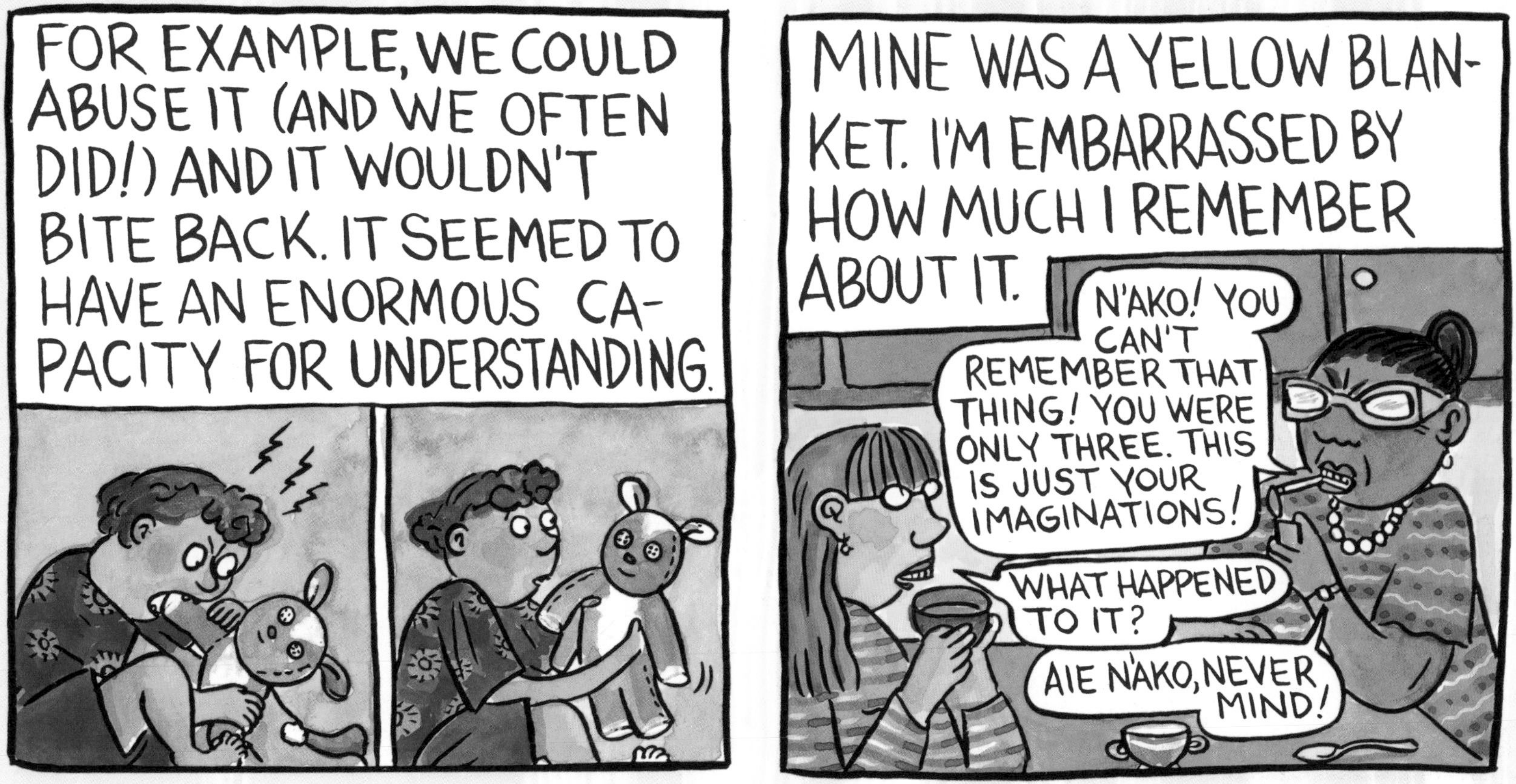
FOR EXAMPLE, WE COULD ABUSE IT (AND WE OFTEN DID!) AND IT WOULDN'T BITE BACK. IT SEEMED TO HAVE AN ENORMOUS CAPACITY FOR UNDERSTANDING.
MINE WAS A YELLOW BLANKET. I'M EMBARRASSED BY HOW MUCH I REMEMBER ABOUT IT.
N'AKO! YOU CAN'T REMEMBER THAT THING! YOU WERE ONLY THREE. THIS IS JUST YOUR IMAGINATIONS!
WHAT HAPPENED TO IT?
AIE N'AKO, NEVER MIND!

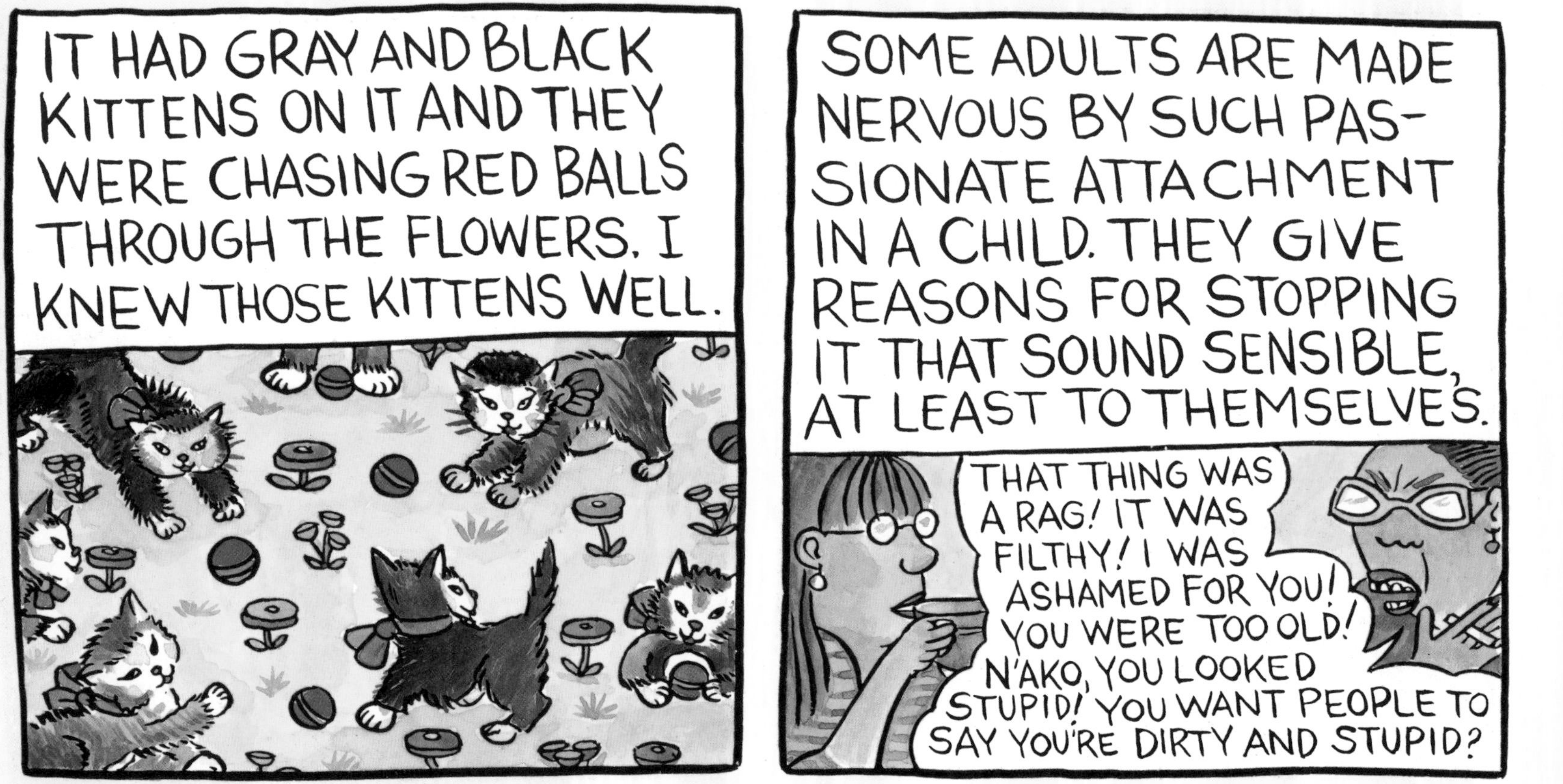
IT HAD GRAY AND BLACK KITTENS ON IT AND THEY WERE CHASING RED BALLS THROUGH THE FLOWERS. I KNEW THOSE KITTENS WELL.
SOME ADULTS ARE MADE NERVOUS BY SUCH PAS-SIONATE ATTACHMENT IN A CHILD. THEY GIVE REASONS FOR STOPPING IT THAT SOUND SENSIBLE, AT LEAST TO THEMSELVES.
THAT THING WAS A RAG! IT WAS FILTHY! I WAS ASHAMED FOR YOU! YOU WERE TOO OLD! N'AKO, YOU LOOKED STUPID! YOU WANT PEOPLE TO SAY YOU'RE DIRTY AND STUPID?

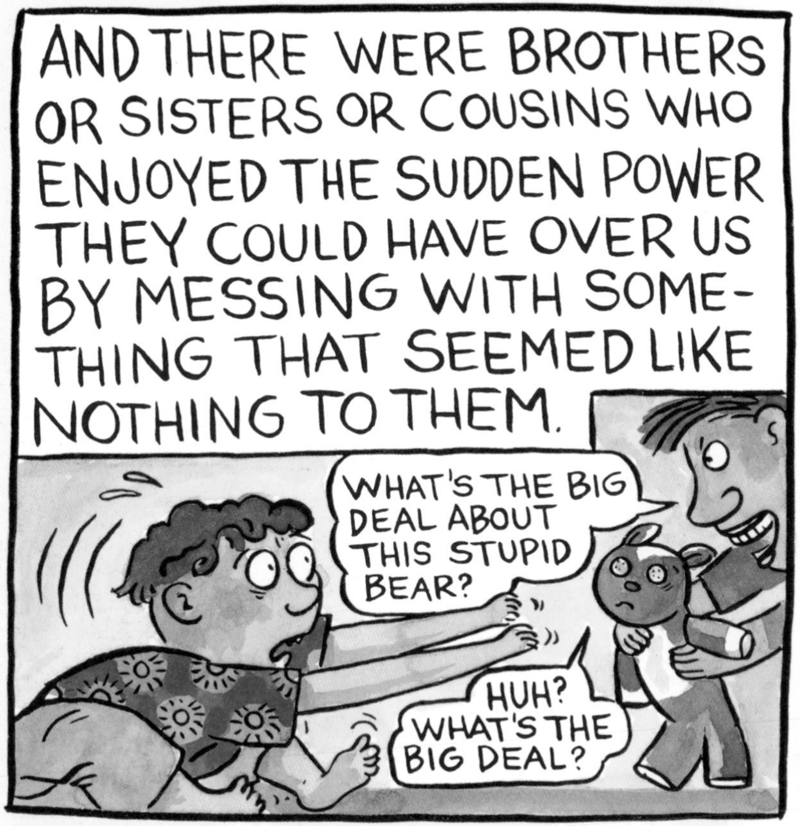
AND THERE WERE BROTHERS OR SISTERS OR COUSINS WHO ENJOYED THE SUDDEN POWER THEY COULD HAVE OVER US BY MESSING WITH SOME-THING THAT SEEMED LIKE NOTHING TO THEM.
WHAT'S THE BIG DEAL ABOUT THIS STUPID BEAR?
HUH? WHAT'S THE BIG DEAL?

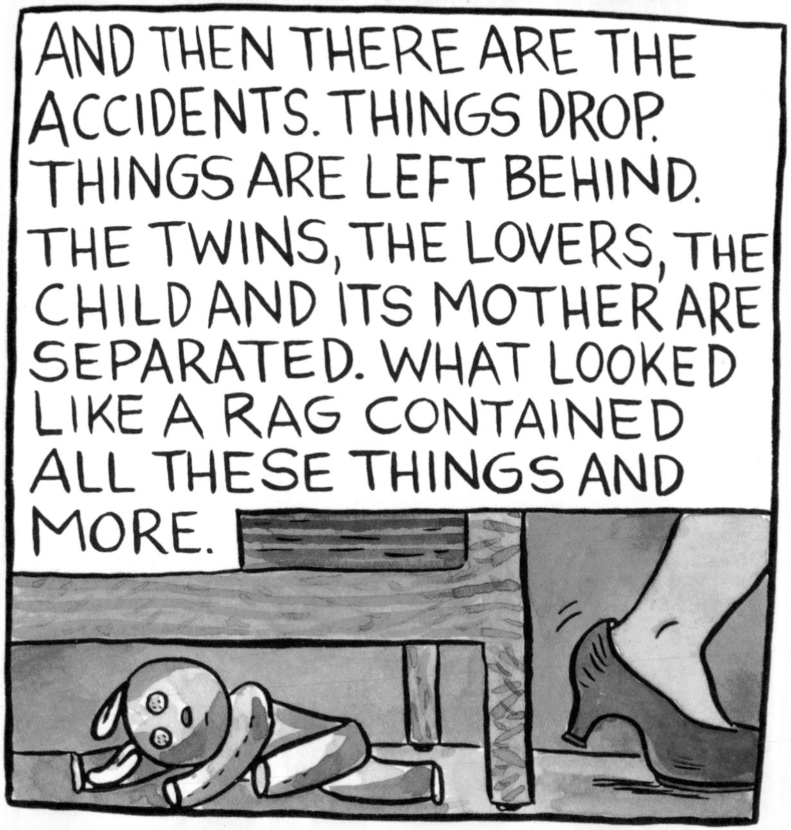
AND THEN THERE ARE THE ACCIDENTS. THINGS DROP. THINGS ARE LEFT BEHIND. THE TWINS, THE LOVERS, THE CHILD AND ITS MOTHER ARE SEPARATED. WHAT LOOKED LIKE A RAG CONTAINED ALL THESE THINGS AND MORE.

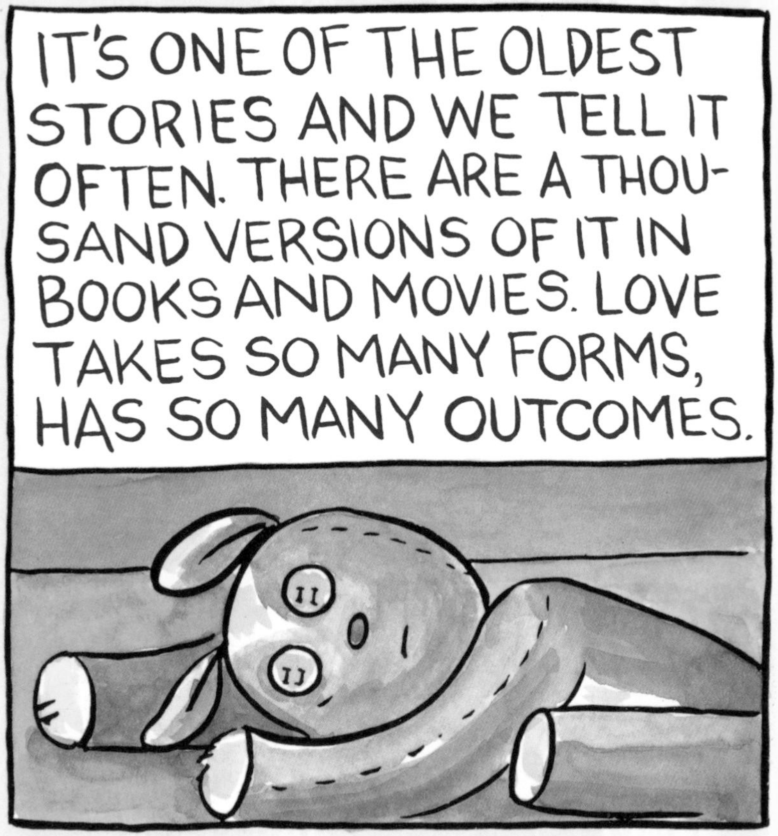
IT'S ONE OF THE OLDEST STORIES AND WE TELL IT OFTEN. THERE ARE A THOUSAND VERSIONS OF IT IN BOOKS AND MOVIES. LOVE TAKES SO MANY FORMS, HAS SO MANY OUTCOMES.

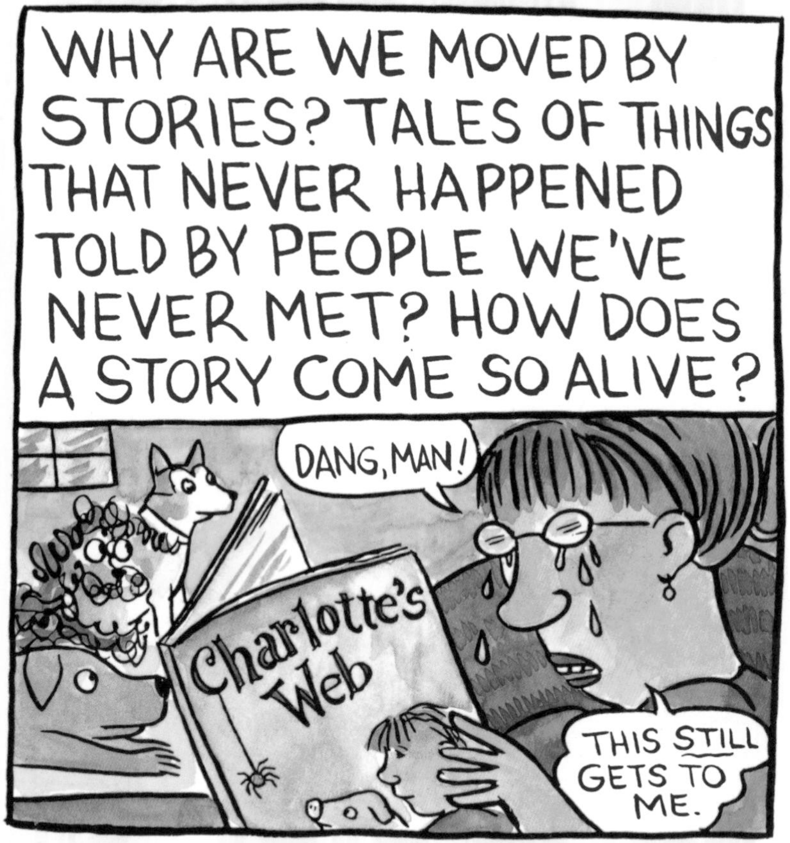
WHY ARE WE MOVED BY STORIES? TALES OF THINGS THAT NEVER HAPPENED TOLD BY PEOPLE WE'VE NEVER MET? HOW DOES A STORY COME SO ALIVE?
DANG, MAN!
Charlotte's Web
THIS STILL GETS TO ME.

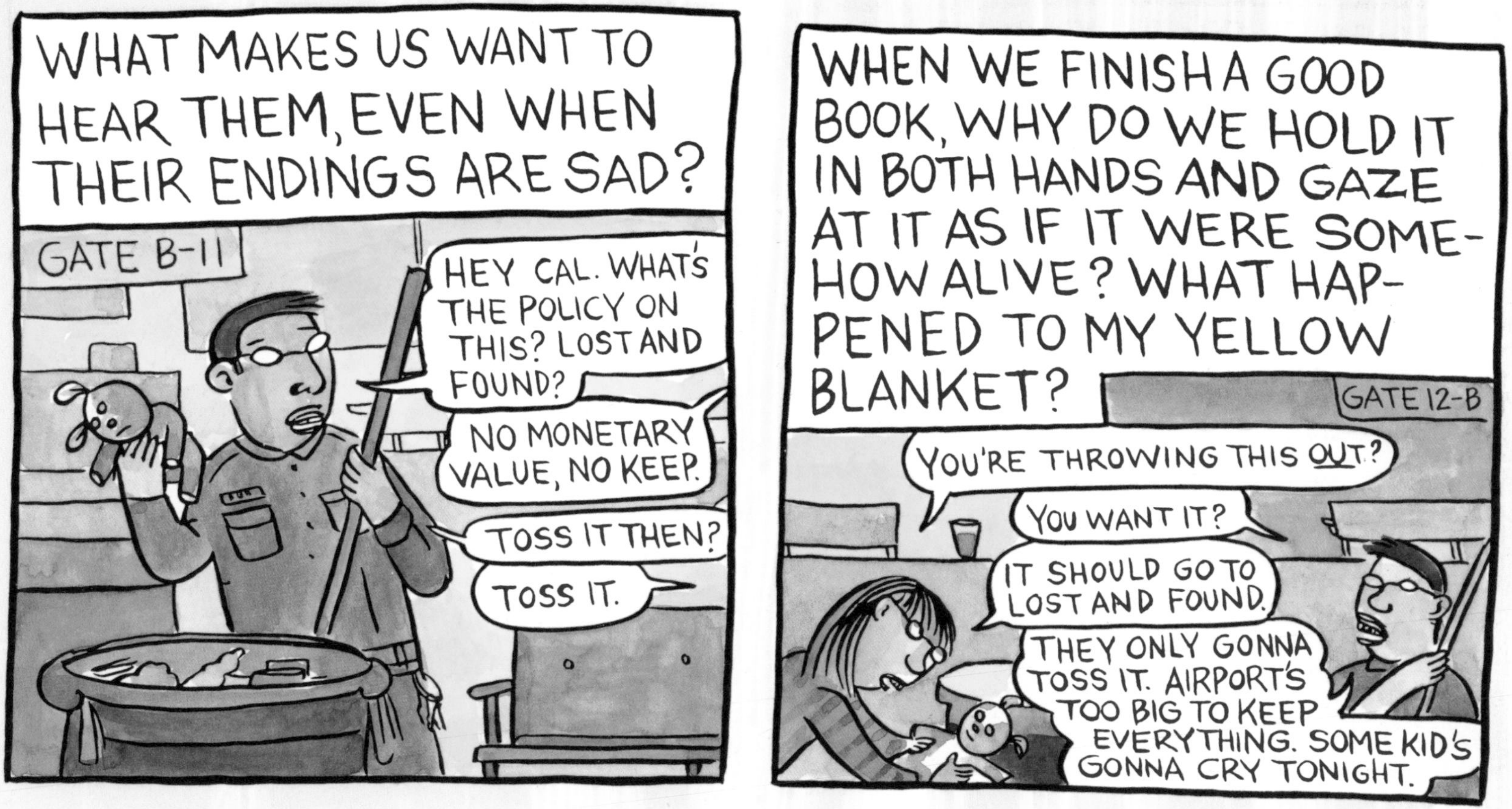
WHAT MAKES US WANT TO HEAR THEM, EVEN WHEN THEIR ENDINGS ARE SAD?
GATE B-11
HEY CAL. WHAT'S THE POLICY ON THIS? LOST AND FOUND?
NO MONETARY VALUE, NO KEEP.
TOSS IT THEN?
TOSS IT.
WHEN WE FINISH A GOOD BOOK, WHY DO WE HOLD IT IN BOTH HANDS AND GAZE AT IT AS IF IT WERE SOME-HOW ALIVE? WHAT HAP-PENED TO MY YELLOW BLANKET?
GATE 12-B
YOU'RE THROWING THIS OUT?
YOU WANT IT?
IT SHOULD GO TO LOST AND FOUND.
THEY ONLY GONNA TOSS IT. AIRPORT'S TOO BIG TO KEEP EVERYTHING. SOME KID'S GONNA CRY TONIGHT.

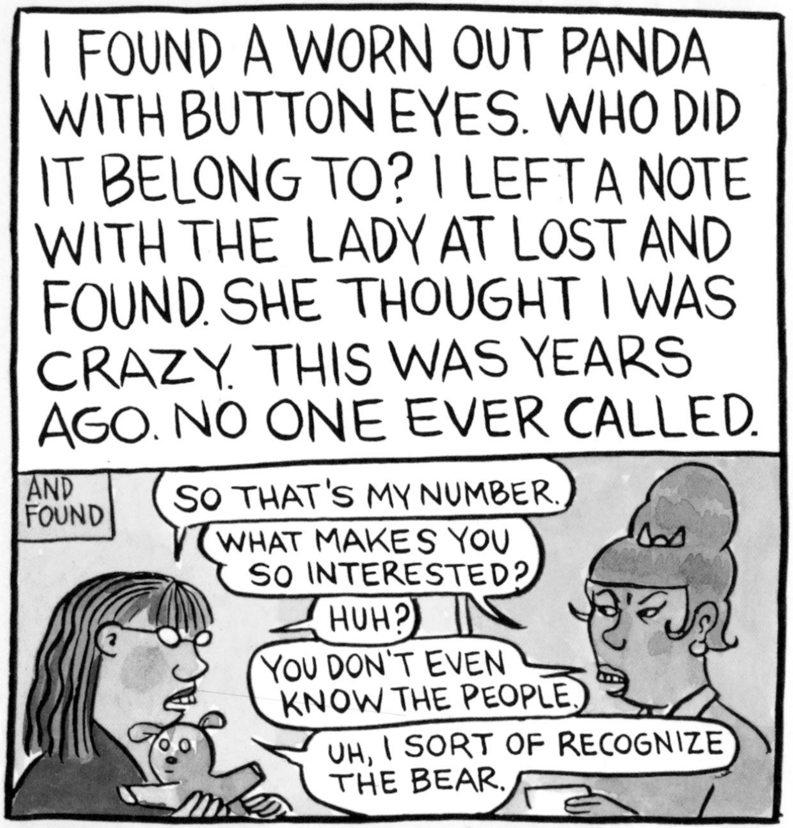
I FOUND A WORN OUT PANDA WITH BUTTON EYES. WHO DID IT BELONG TO? I LEFT A NOTE WITH THE LADY AT LOST AND FOUND. SHE THOUGHT I WAS CRAZY. THIS WAS YEARS AGO. NO ONE EVER CALLED.
AND FOUND
SO THAT'S MY NUMBER.
WHAT MAKES YOU SO INTERESTED?
HUH?
YOU DON'T EVEN KNOW THE PEOPLE.
UH, I SORT OF RECOGNIZE THE BEAR.

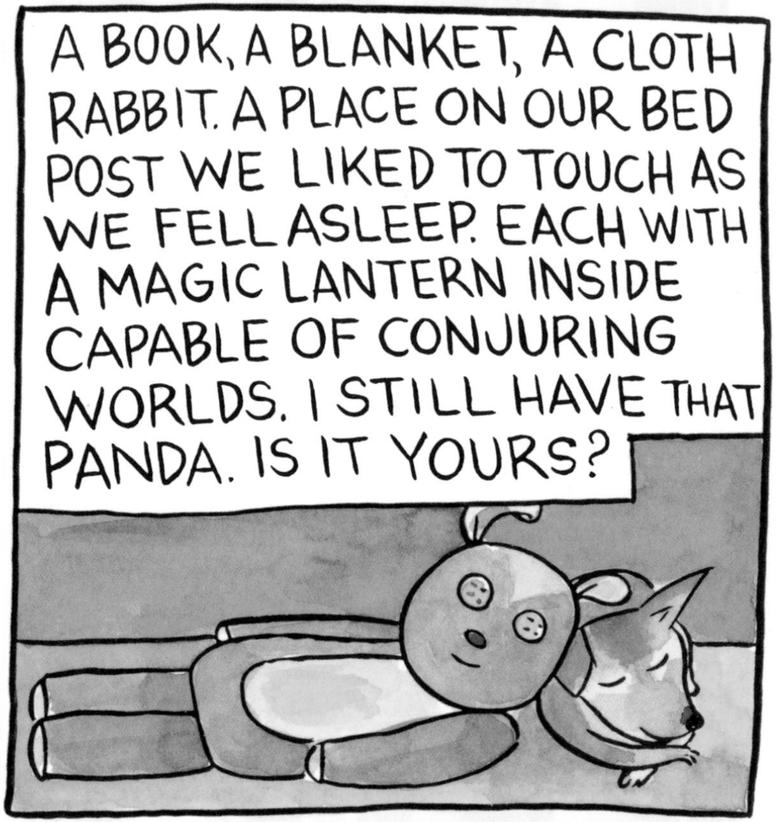
A BOOK, A BLANKET, A CLOTH RABBIT. A PLACE ON OUR BED POST WE LIKED TO TOUCH AS WE FELL ASLEEP. EACH WITH A MAGIC LANTERN INSIDE CAPABLE OF CONJURING WORLDS. I STILL HAVE THAT PANDA. IS IT YOURS?

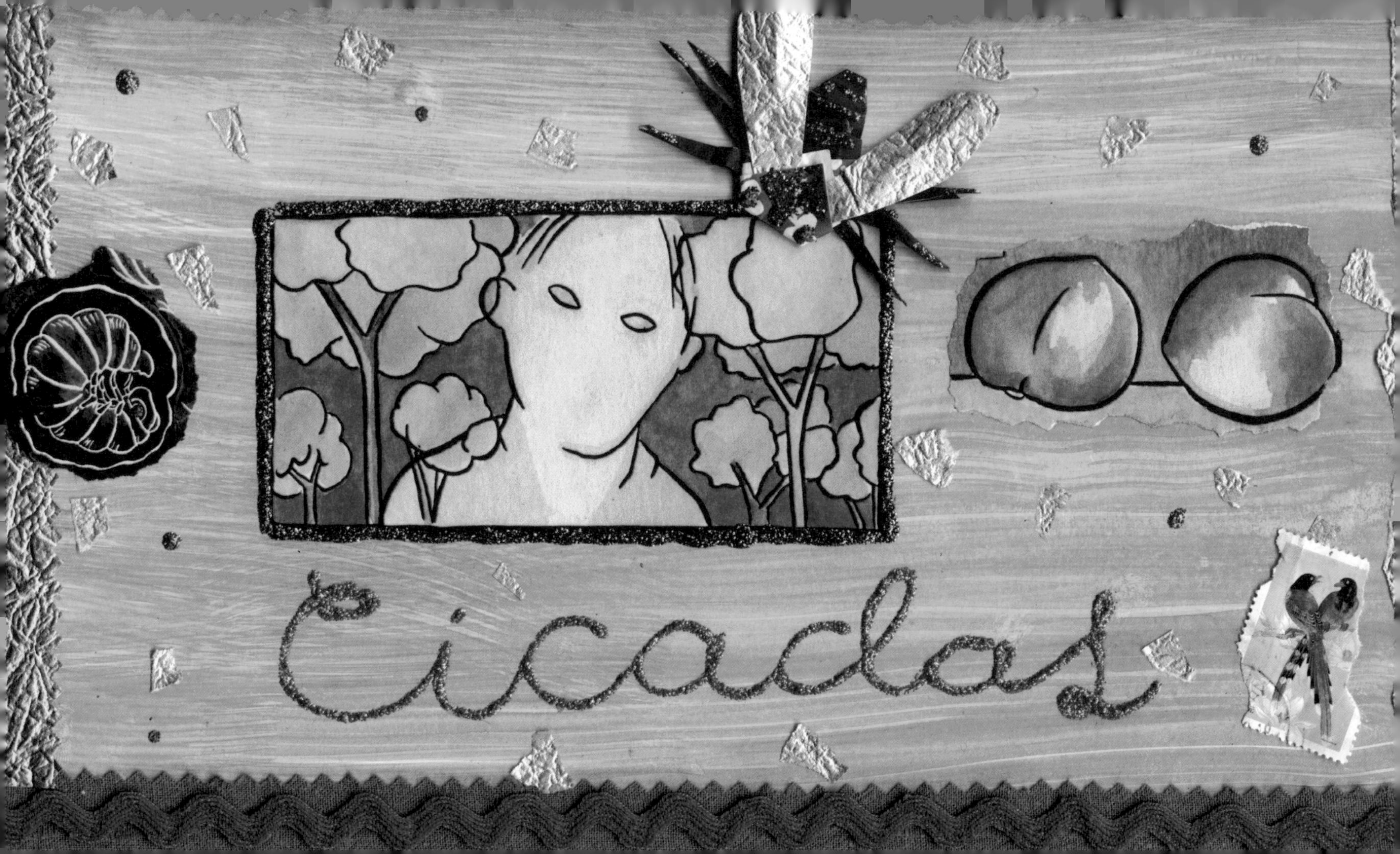
Cicadas

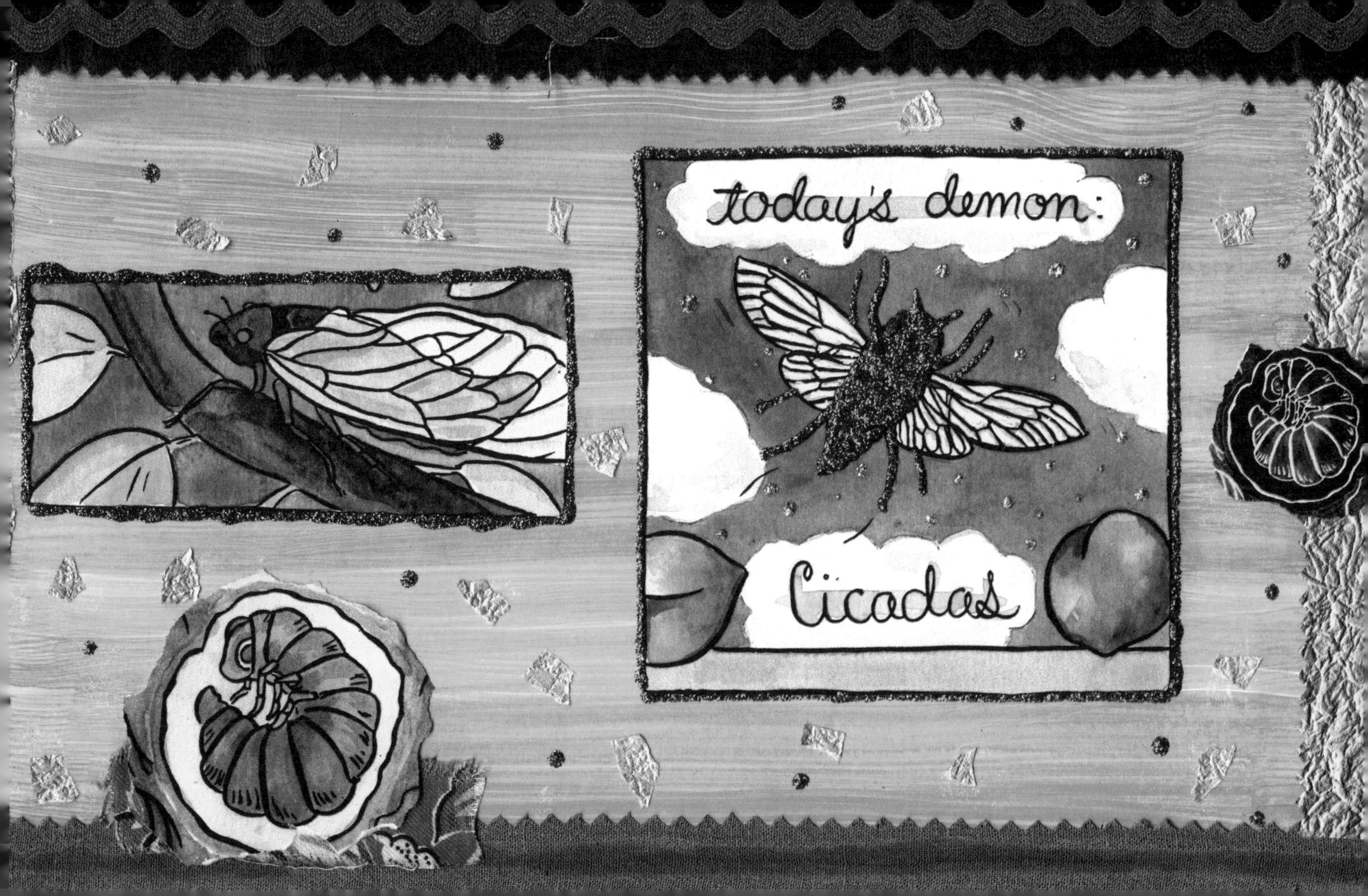
today's demon:
Cicadas

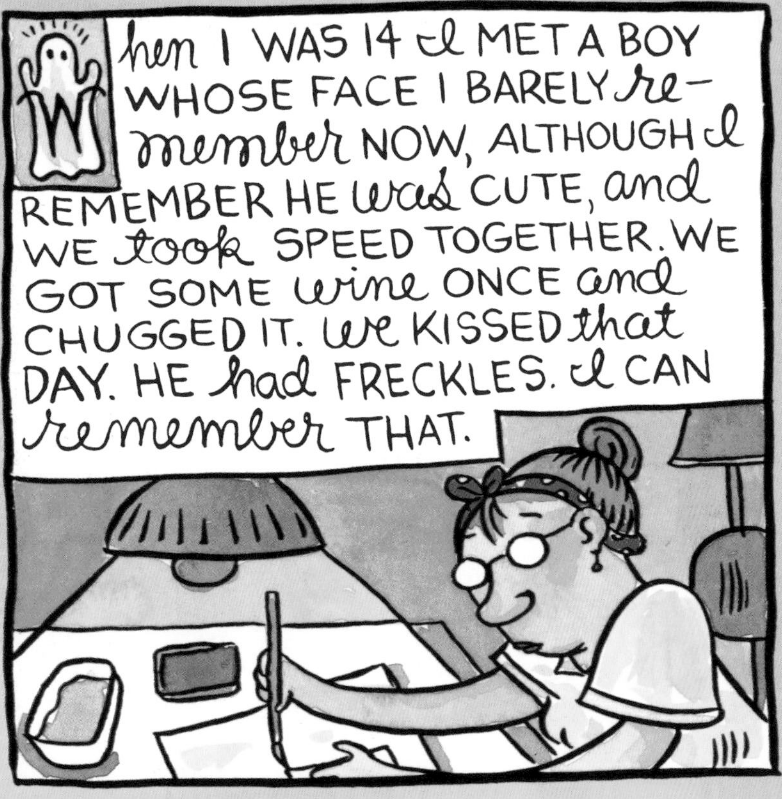
When I WAS 14 I MET A BOY WHOSE FACE I BARELY remember NOW, ALTHOUGH I REMEMBER HE was CUTE, and WE took SPEED TOGETHER. WE GOT SOME wine ONCE and CHUGGED IT. We KISSED that DAY. HE had FRECKLES. I CAN remember THAT.

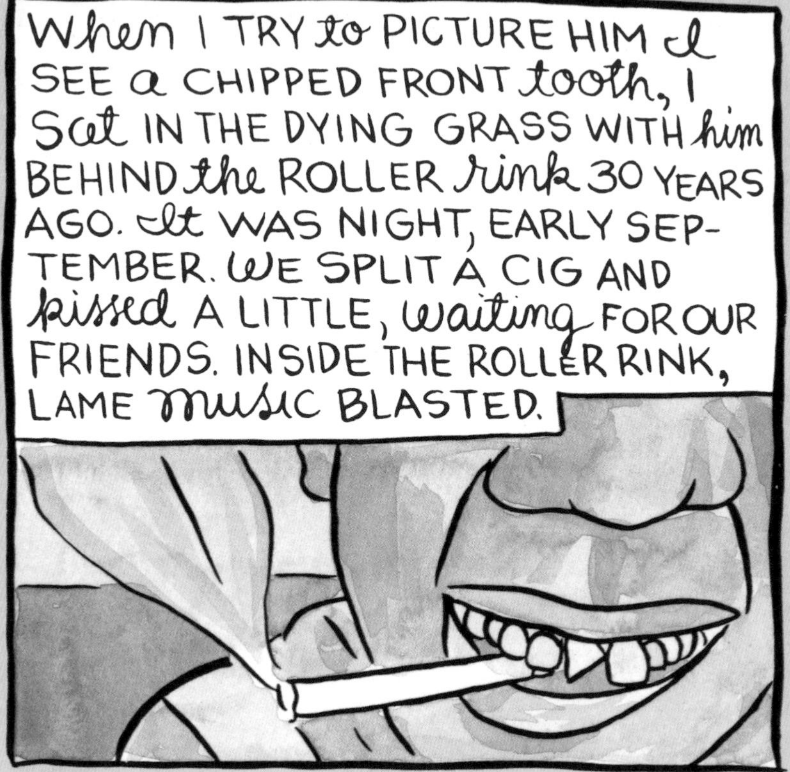
When I TRY to PICTURE HIM I SEE a CHIPPED FRONT tooth, I Sat IN THE DYING GRASS WITH him BEHIND the ROLLER rink 30 YEARS AGO. It WAS NIGHT, EARLY SEPTEMBER. We SPLIT A CIG AND kissed A LITTLE, waiting FOR OUR FRIENDS. INSIDE THE ROLLER RINK, LAME music BLASTED.

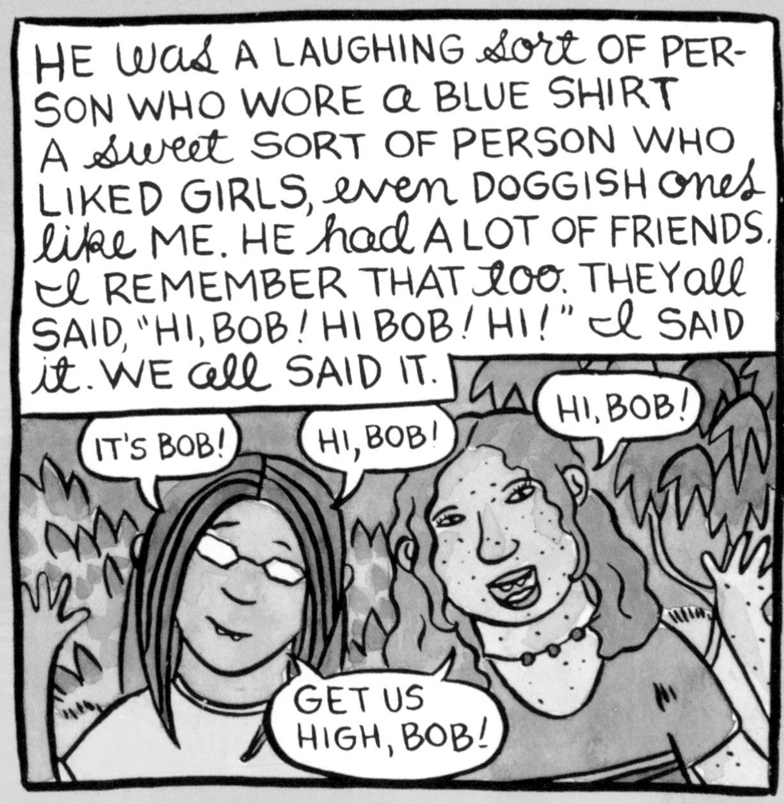
HE WAS A LAUGHING SORT OF PERSON WHO WORE A BLUE SHIRT A SWEET SORT OF PERSON WHO LIKED GIRLS, EVEN DOGGISH ONES LIKE ME. HE HAD A LOT OF FRIENDS. I REMEMBER THAT TOO. THEY ALL SAID, "HI, BOB! HI BOB! HI!" I SAID IT. WE ALL SAID IT.
IT'S BOB!
HI, BOB!
HI, BOB!
GET US HIGH, BOB!

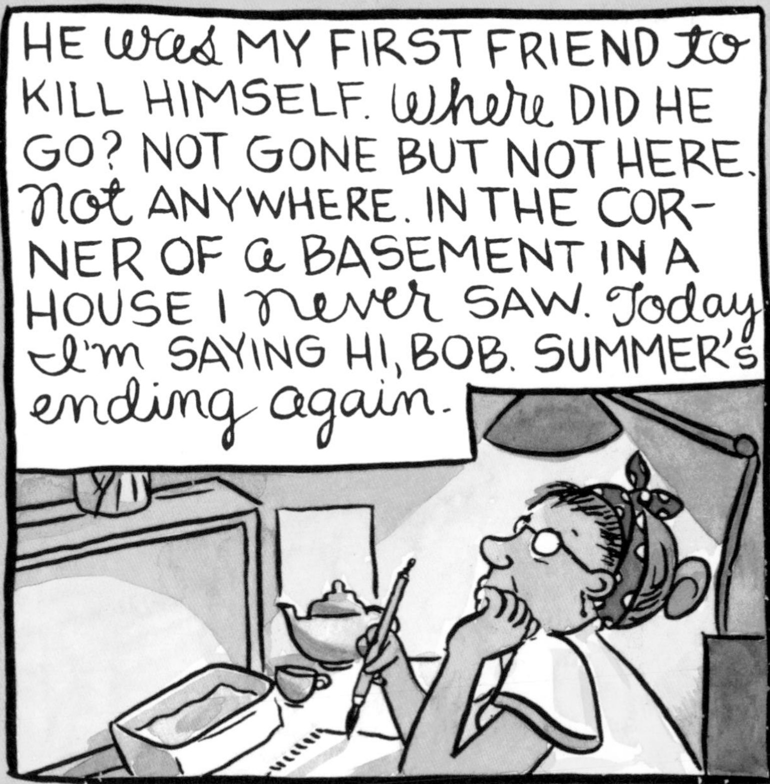
HE WAS MY FIRST FRIEND TO KILL HIMSELF. WHERE DID HE GO? NOT GONE BUT NOT HERE. NOT ANYWHERE. IN THE CORNER OF A BASEMENT IN A HOUSE I NEVER SAW. TODAY I'M SAYING HI, BOB. SUMMER'S ENDING AGAIN.

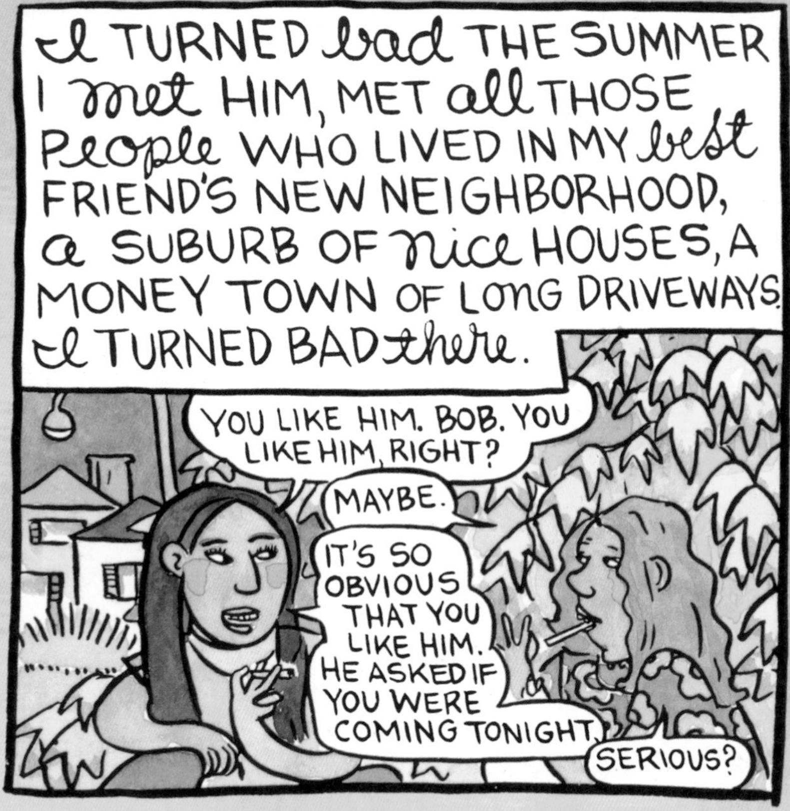
I TURNED bad THE SUMMER I met HIM, MET all THOSE People WHO LIVED IN MY best FRIEND'S NEW NEIGHBORHOOD, a SUBURB OF nice HOUSES, A MONEY TOWN OF LONG DRIVEWAYS. I TURNED BAD there.
YOU LIKE HIM. BOB. YOU LIKE HIM, RIGHT?
MAYBE.
IT'S SO OBVIOUS THAT YOU LIKE HIM. HE ASKED IF YOU WERE COMING TONIGHT.
SERIOUS?

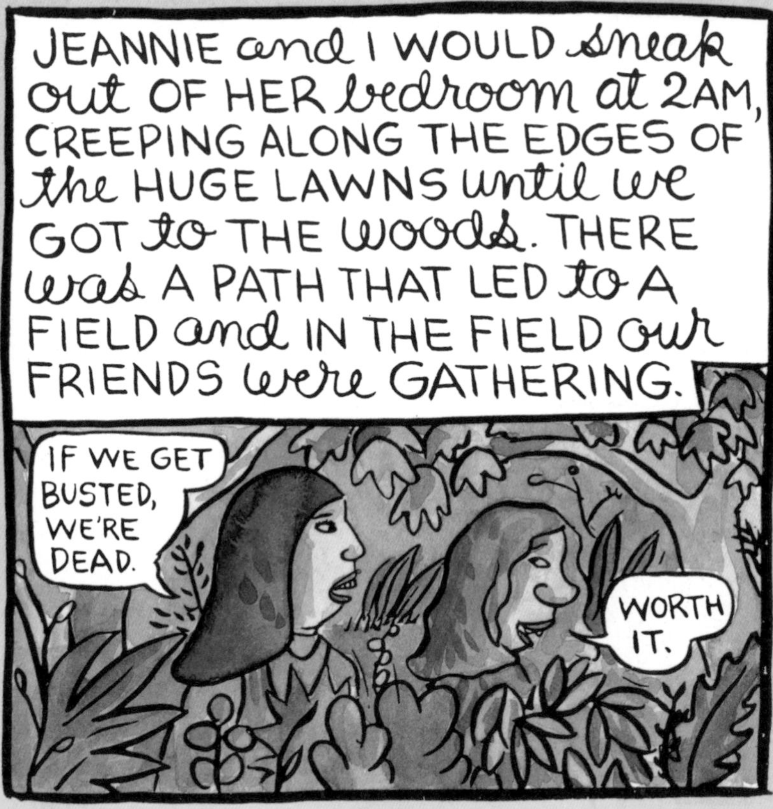
JEANNIE and I WOULD sneak out OF HER bedroom at 2AM, CREEPING ALONG THE EDGES OF the HUGE LAWNS until we GOT to THE woods. THERE was A PATH THAT LED to A FIELD and IN THE FIELD our FRIENDS were GATHERING.
IF WE GET BUSTED, WE'RE DEAD.
WORTH IT.

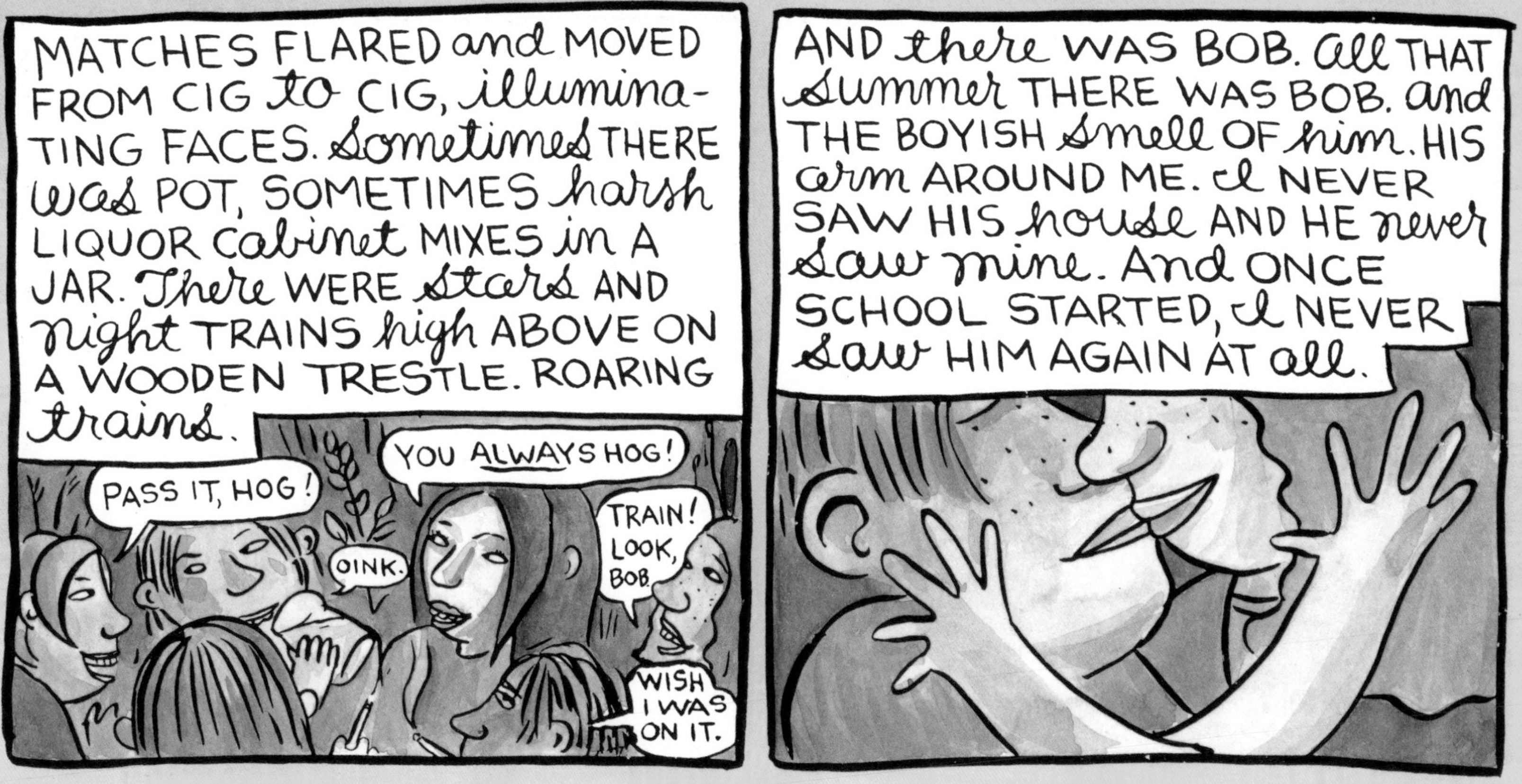
MATCHES FLARED and MOVED FROM CIG to CIG, illuminating FACES. Sometimes THERE was POT, SOMETIMES harsh LIQUOR cabinet MIXES in A JAR. There WERE stars AND night TRAINS high ABOVE ON A WOODEN TRESTLE. ROARING trains.
PASS IT, HOG!
YOU ALWAYS HOG!
OINK.
TRAIN! LOOK, BOB.
WISH I WAS ON IT.
AND there WAS BOB. all THAT summer THERE WAS BOB. and THE BOYISH smell OF him. HIS arm AROUND ME. I NEVER SAW HIS house AND HE never saw mine. And ONCE SCHOOL STARTED, I NEVER saw HIM AGAIN AT all.

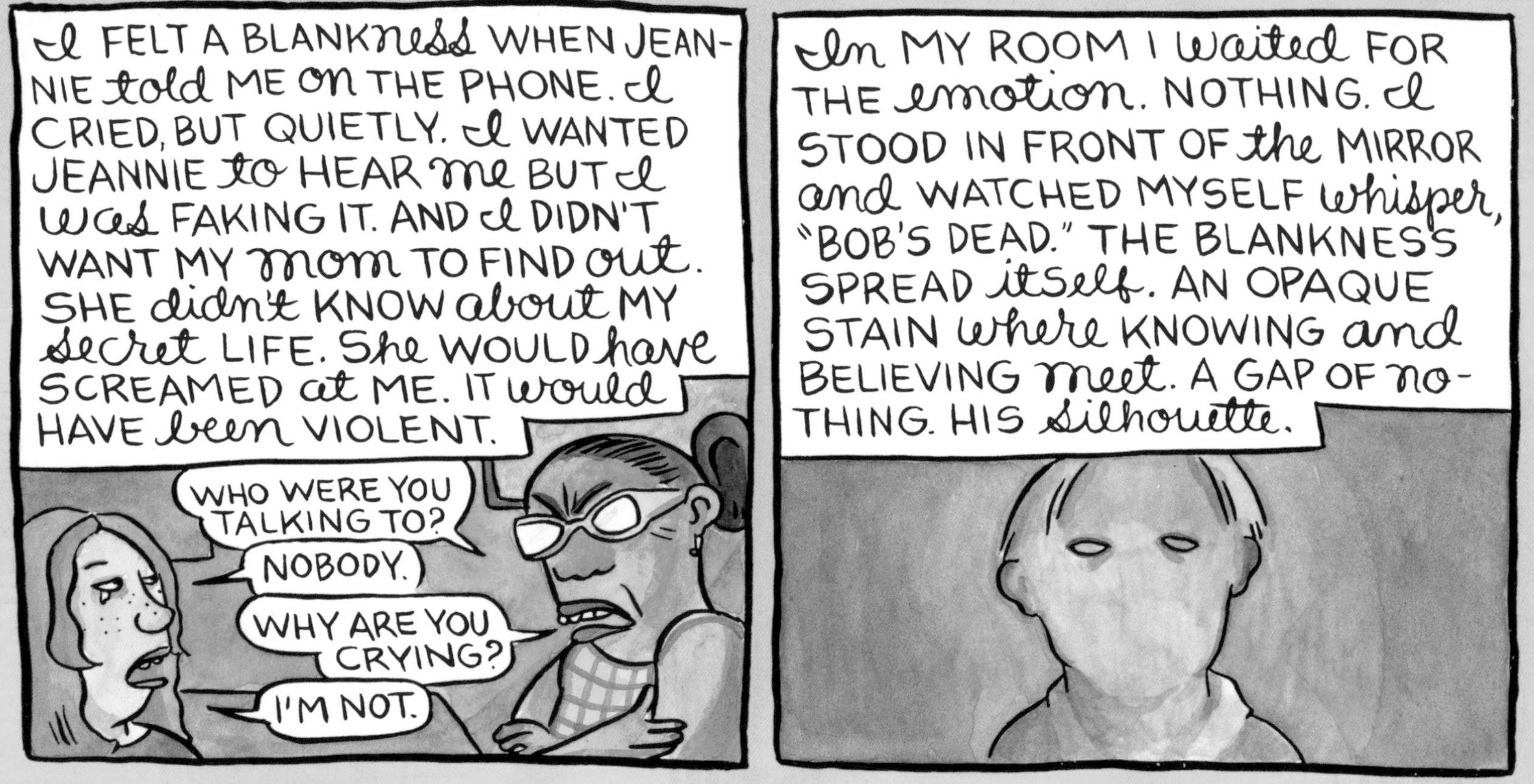
I FELT A BLANKness WHEN JEANNIE told ME ON THE PHONE. I CRIED, BUT QUIETLY. I WANTED JEANNIE to HEAR me BUT I was FAKING IT. AND I DIDN'T WANT MY mom TO FIND out. SHE didn't KNOW about MY secret LIFE. She WOULD have SCREAMED at ME. IT would HAVE been VIOLENT.
WHO WERE YOU TALKING TO?
NOBODY.
WHY ARE YOU CRYING?
I'M NOT.
In MY ROOM I waited FOR THE emotion. NOTHING. I STOOD IN FRONT OF the MIRROR and WATCHED MYSELF whisper, "BOB'S DEAD." THE BLANKNESS SPREAD itself. AN OPAQUE STAIN where KNOWING and BELIEVING meet. A GAP OF nothing. HIS silhouette.

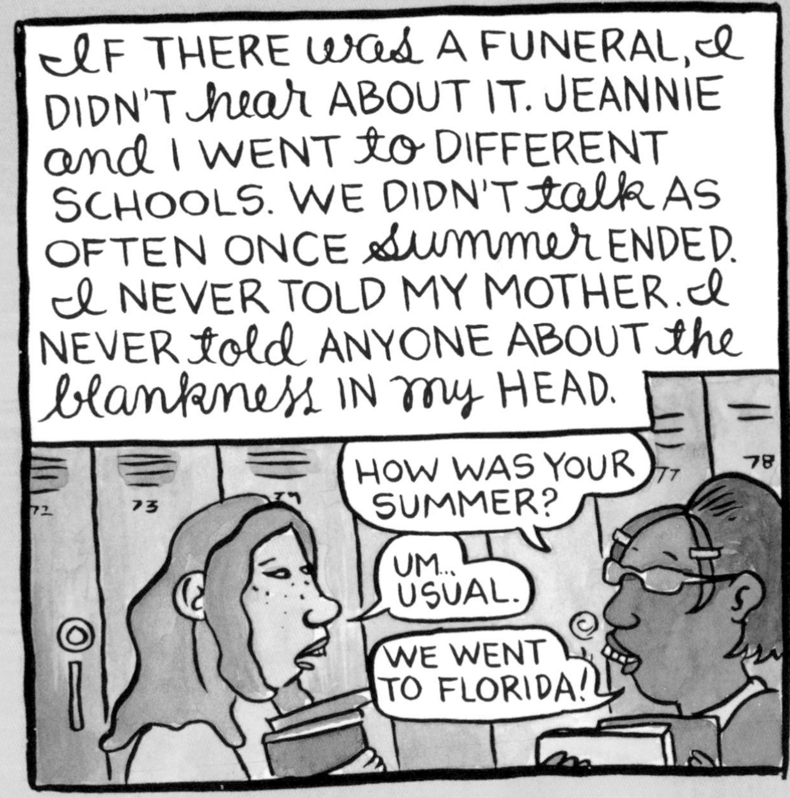
IF THERE WAS A FUNERAL, I DIDN'T HEAR ABOUT IT. JEANNIE AND I WENT TO DIFFERENT SCHOOLS. WE DIDN'T TALK AS OFTEN ONCE SUMMER ENDED. I NEVER TOLD MY MOTHER. I NEVER TOLD ANYONE ABOUT THE BLANKNESS IN MY HEAD.
HOW WAS YOUR SUMMER?
UM... USUAL.
WE WENT TO FLORIDA!

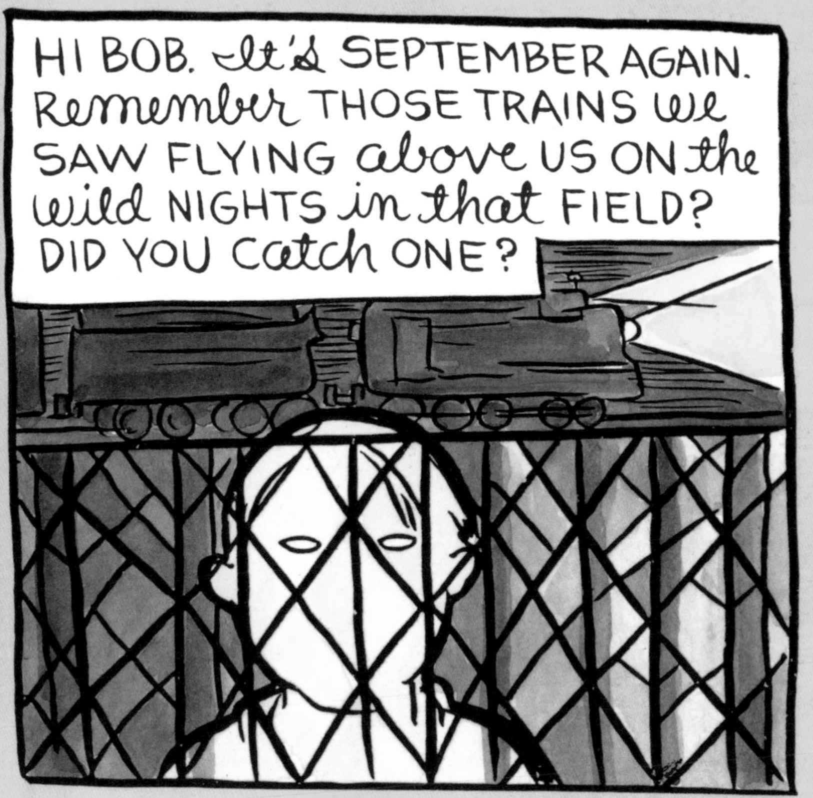
HI BOB. IT'S SEPTEMBER AGAIN. REMEMBER THOSE TRAINS WE SAW FLYING ABOVE US ON THE WILD NIGHTS IN THAT FIELD? DID YOU CATCH ONE?

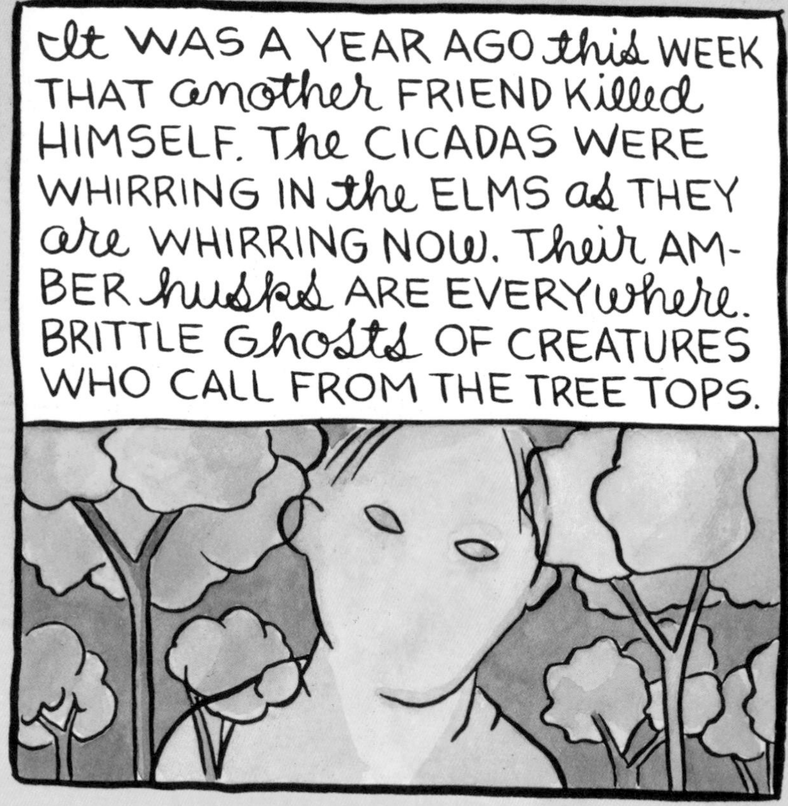
It WAS A YEAR AGO this WEEK THAT another FRIEND Killed HIMSELF. The CICADAS WERE WHIRRING IN the ELMS as THEY are WHIRRING NOW. Their AMBER husks ARE EVERYwhere. BRITTLE Ghosts OF CREATURES WHO CALL FROM THE TREE TOPS.

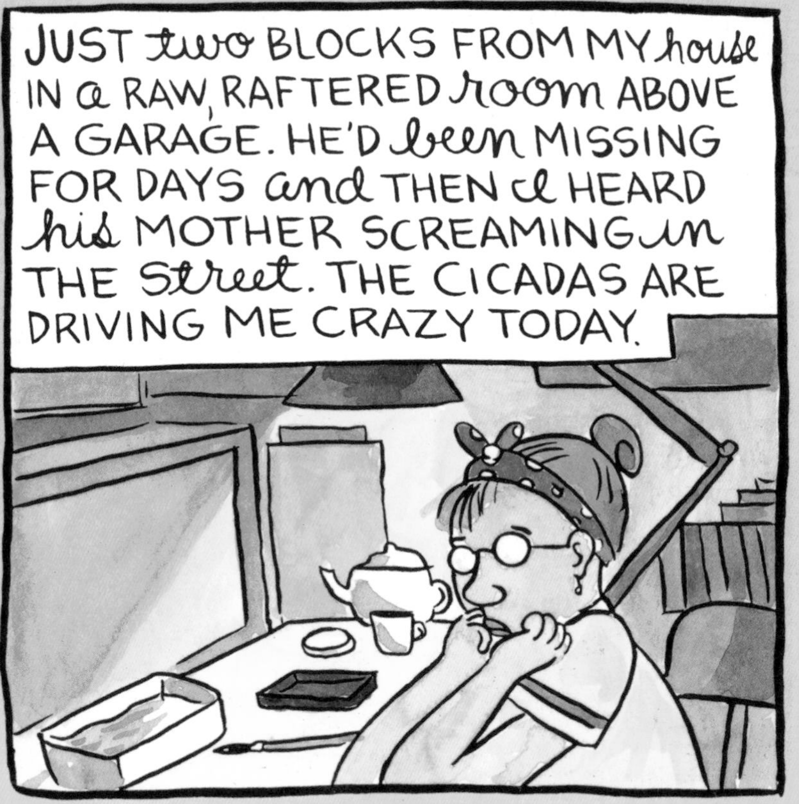
JUST two BLOCKS FROM MY house IN a RAW, RAFTERED room ABOVE A GARAGE. HE'D been MISSING FOR DAYS and THEN I HEARD his MOTHER SCREAMING in THE Street. THE CICADAS ARE DRIVING ME CRAZY TODAY.

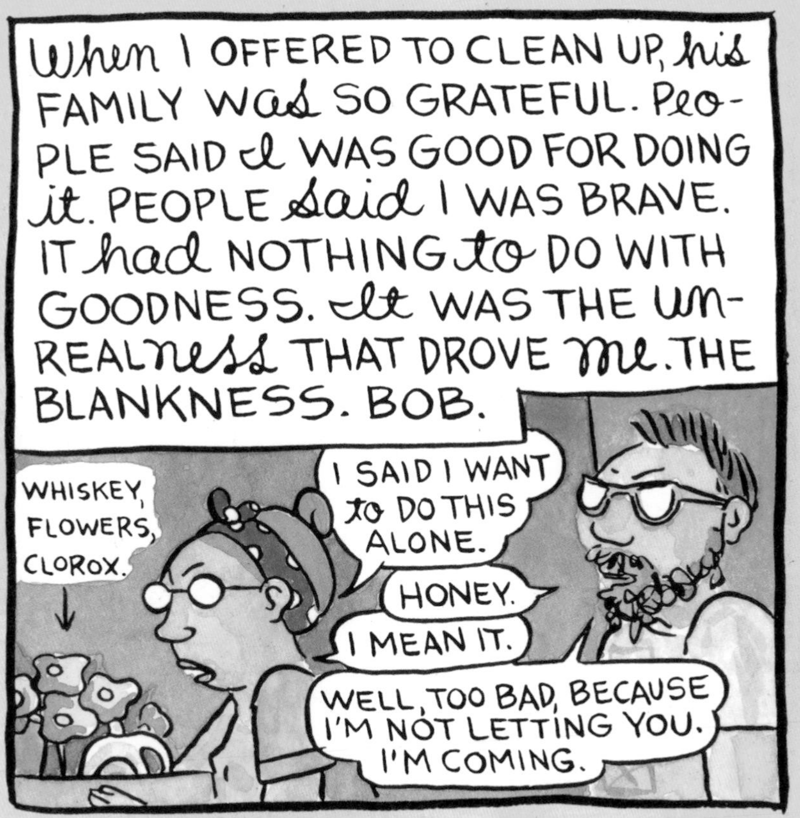
When I OFFERED TO CLEAN UP, his FAMILY was SO GRATEFUL. People SAID I WAS GOOD FOR DOING it. PEOPLE said I WAS BRAVE. IT had NOTHING to DO WITH GOODNESS. It WAS THE unREALness THAT DROVE me. THE BLANKNESS. BOB.
WHISKEY, FLOWERS, CLOROX.
I SAID I WANT to DO THIS ALONE.
HONEY.
I MEAN IT.
WELL, TOO BAD, BECAUSE I'M NOT LETTING YOU. I'M COMING.

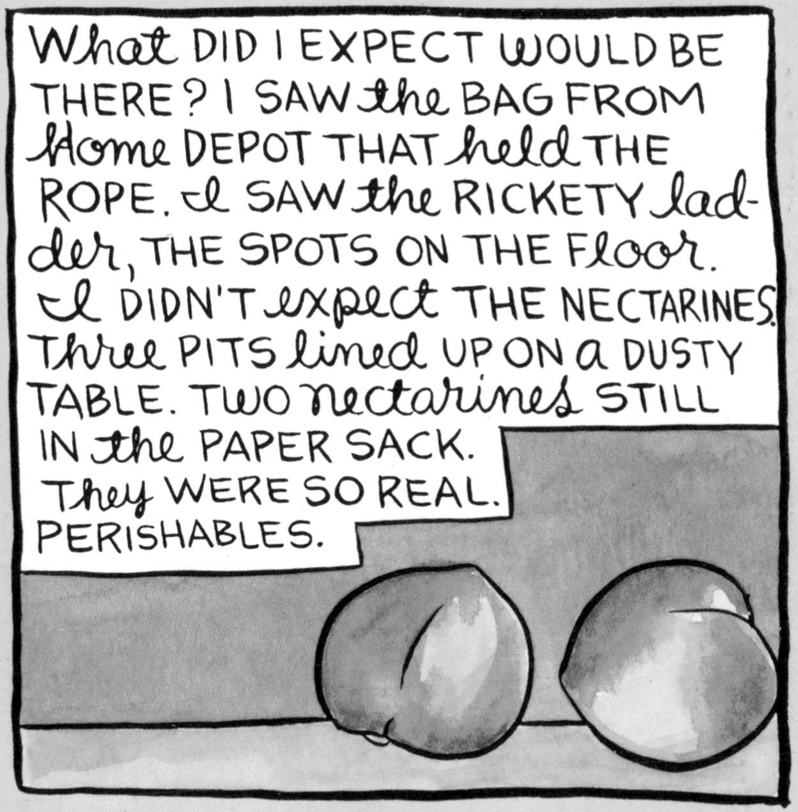
What DID I EXPECT WOULD BE THERE? I SAW the BAG FROM Home DEPOT THAT held THE ROPE. I SAW the RICKETY ladder, THE SPOTS ON THE Floor. I DIDN'T expect THE NECTARINES. Three PITS lined UP ON a DUSTY TABLE. TWO nectarines STILL IN the PAPER SACK. They WERE SO REAL. PERISHABLES.

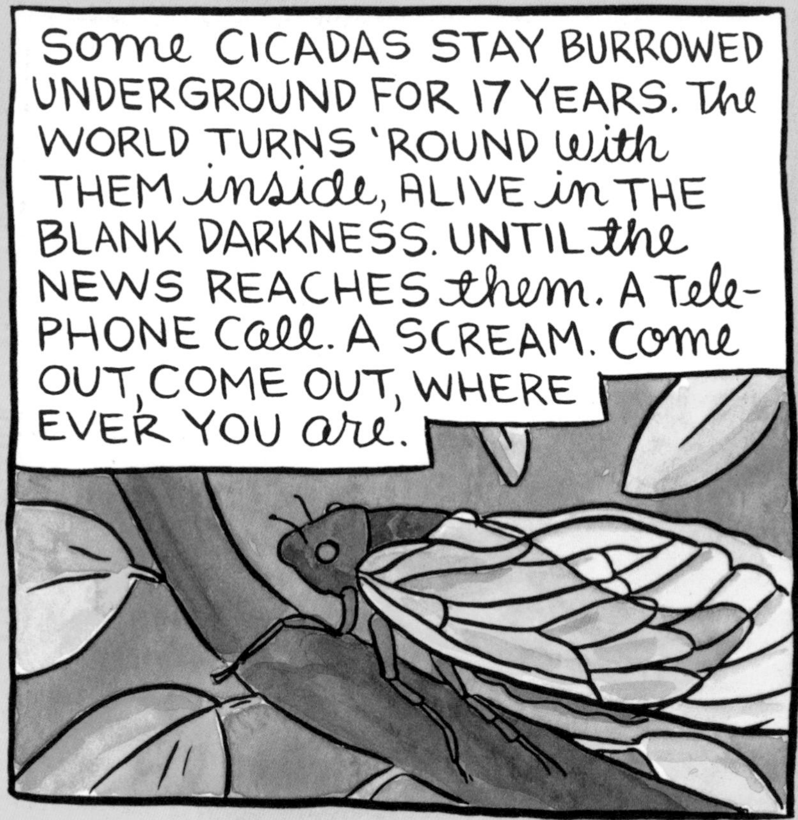
Some CICADAS STAY BURROWED UNDERGROUND FOR 17 YEARS. The WORLD TURNS 'ROUND with THEM inside, ALIVE in THE BLANK DARKNESS. UNTIL the NEWS REACHES them. A Telephone Call. A SCREAM. Come OUT, COME OUT, WHERE EVER YOU are.

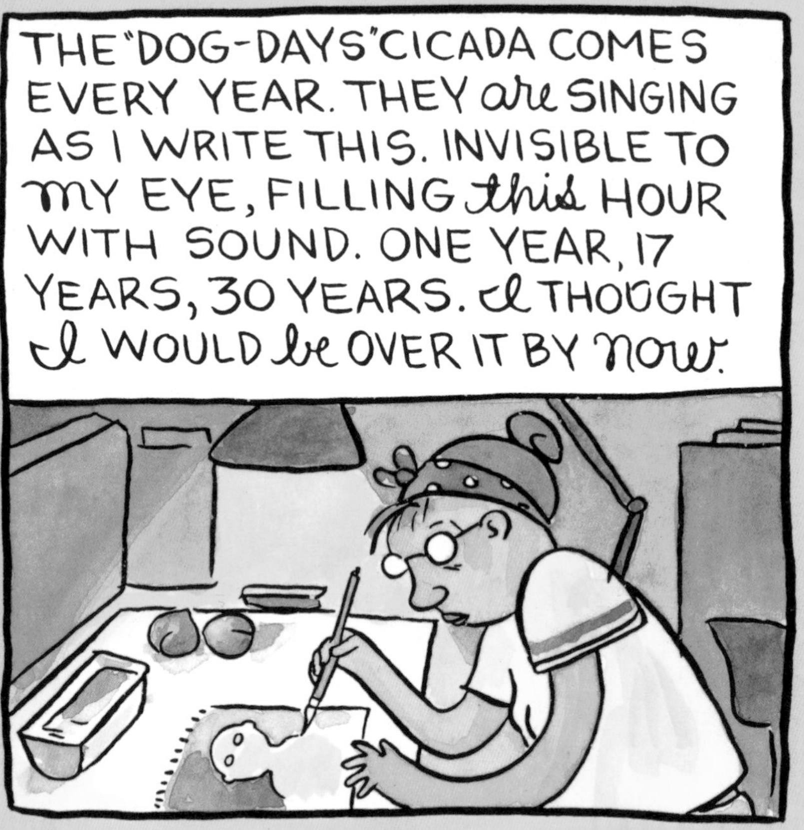
THE "DOG-DAYS" CICADA COMES EVERY YEAR. THEY are SINGING AS I WRITE THIS. INVISIBLE TO my EYE, FILLING this HOUR WITH SOUND. ONE YEAR, 17 YEARS, 30 YEARS. I THOUGHT I WOULD be OVER IT BY now.

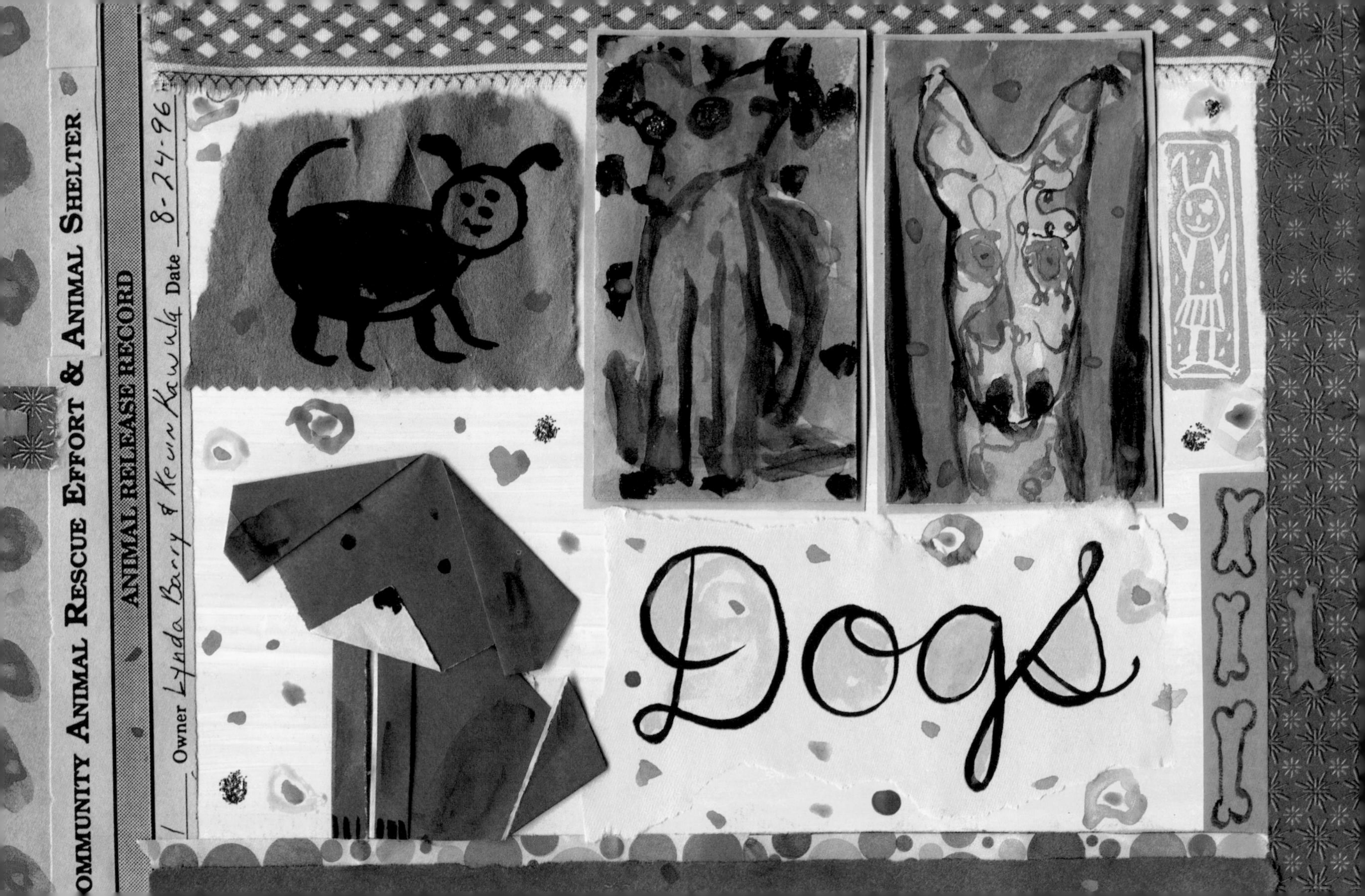
OMMUNITY ANIMAL RESCUE EFFORT & ANIMAL SHELTER
ANIMAL RELEASE RECORD
Owner Lynda Barry & Kevin Kawula Date 8-24-96
Dogs

Dogs

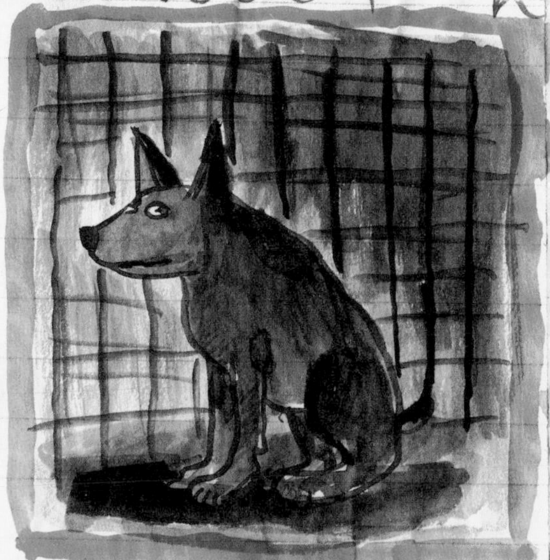

First Pet

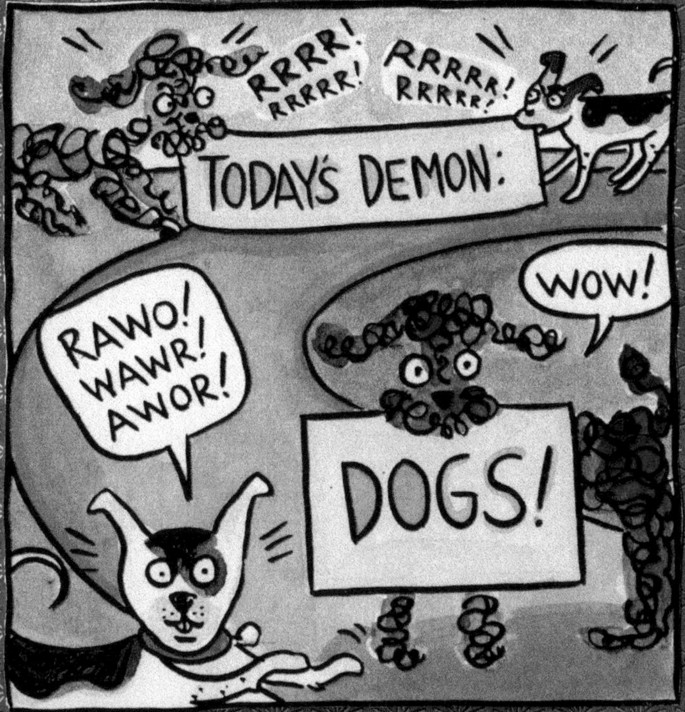
RRRR! RRRRR!
RRRRR! RRRRR!
TODAY'S DEMON:
RAWO! WAWR! AWOR!
WOW!
DOGS!

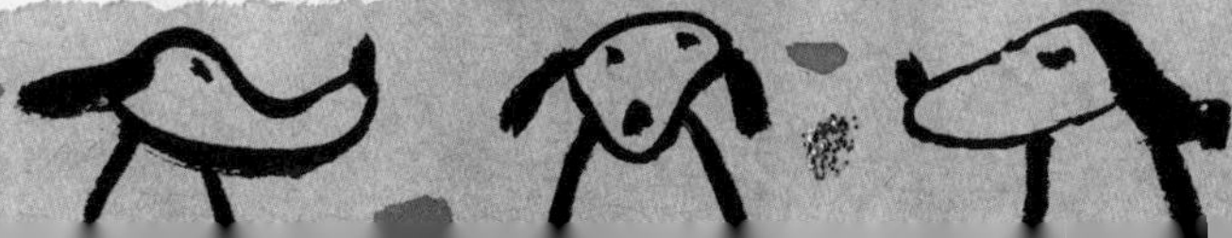

Dog or Cat ?	Gender	Pet's Name	Breed
D ☒ C ☐	M ☐ F ☒	OOOLA	??
Pet License	Tag Order	[illegible] Combo Order	

WE HAVE **THREE**. WHEN THE DOORBELL RINGS, THEY ALL GO BERZERK. THEY DO THIS EVEN IF SOMEONE RINGS A DOORBELL ON TV.

DING DONG! ♪

RAWF! ROWF! RAWF!

KNOCK IT OFF!

RARK! RARK! WROW!

RARK! RARK! RARK!

ROWA! WAOR!

MY RESPONSE, OF COURSE, IS THE WRONG ONE. I YELL AT THEM. LOUDLY. REPEATEDLY. THE DOG BOOKS ALL SAY NEVER SHOUT AND DO NOT REPEAT COMMANDS.

LULU! OOOLA! ED! HEY! KNOCK IT OFF! HEY! STOP THAT! IT'S THE TV, YOU GOOFS!

RAROO! WRRIB! RWARRO! RARR! RARR!

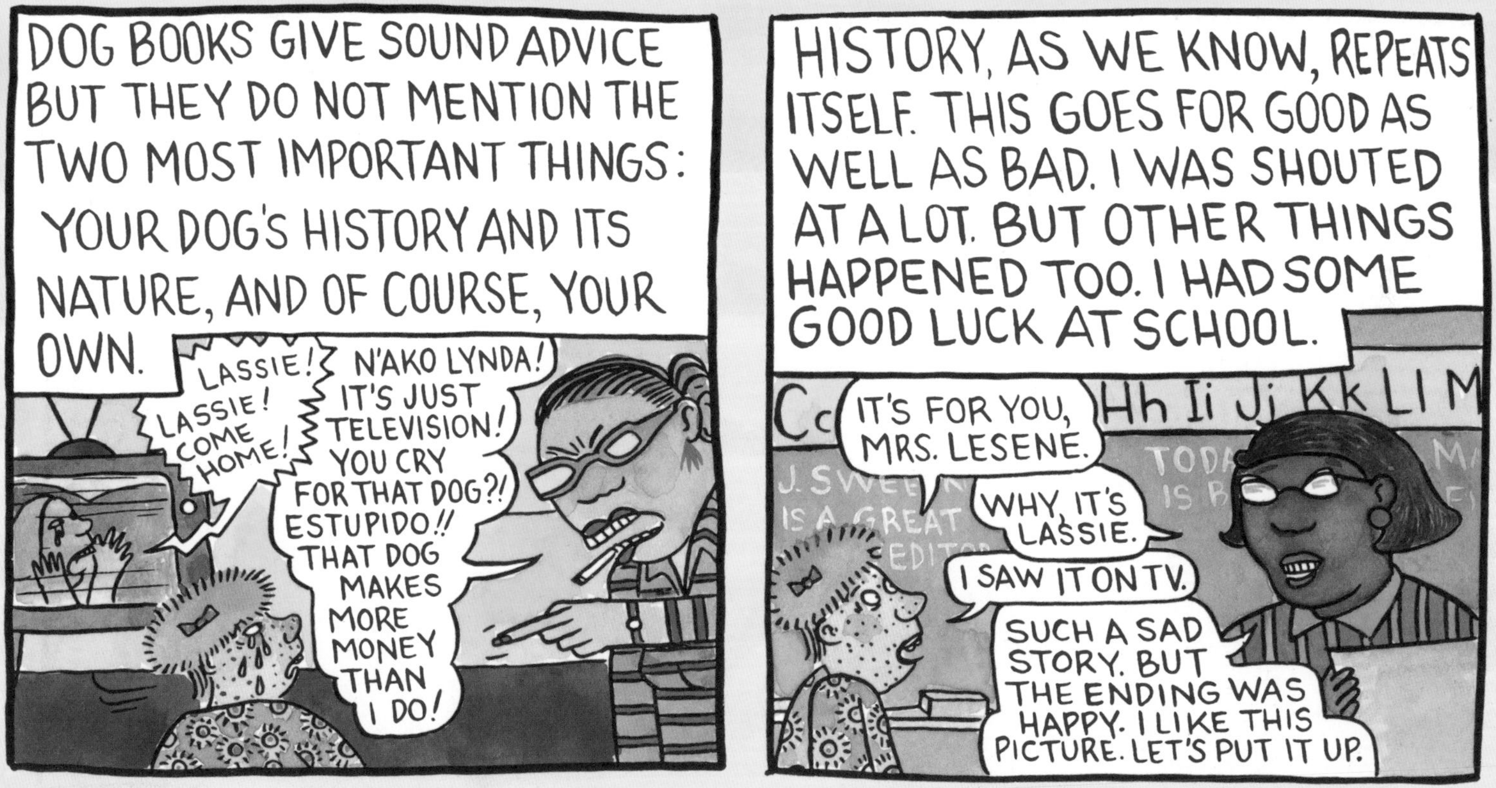
DOG BOOKS GIVE SOUND ADVICE BUT THEY DO NOT MENTION THE TWO MOST IMPORTANT THINGS: YOUR DOG'S HISTORY AND ITS NATURE, AND OF COURSE, YOUR OWN.
LASSIE! LASSIE! COME HOME!
N'AKO LYNDA! IT'S JUST TELEVISION! YOU CRY FOR THAT DOG?! ESTUPIDO!! THAT DOG MAKES MORE MONEY THAN I DO!
HISTORY, AS WE KNOW, REPEATS ITSELF. THIS GOES FOR GOOD AS WELL AS BAD. I WAS SHOUTED AT A LOT. BUT OTHER THINGS HAPPENED TOO. I HAD SOME GOOD LUCK AT SCHOOL.
IT'S FOR YOU, MRS. LESENE.
WHY, IT'S LASSIE.
I SAW IT ON TV.
SUCH A SAD STORY. BUT THE ENDING WAS HAPPY. I LIKE THIS PICTURE. LET'S PUT IT UP.

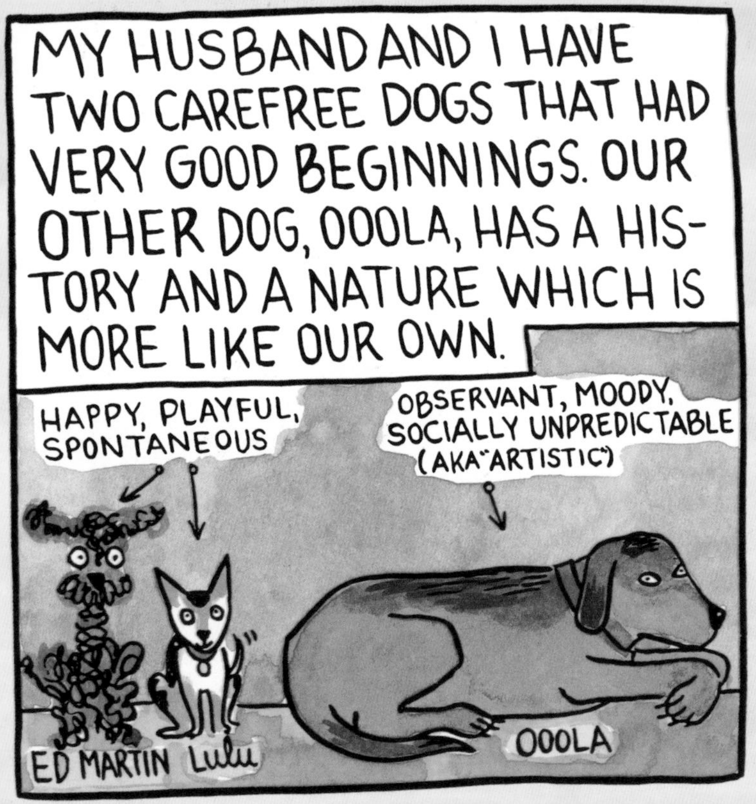
MY HUSBAND AND I HAVE TWO CAREFREE DOGS THAT HAD VERY GOOD BEGINNINGS. OUR OTHER DOG, OOOLA, HAS A HISTORY AND A NATURE WHICH IS MORE LIKE OUR OWN.
HAPPY, PLAYFUL, SPONTANEOUS
OBSERVANT, MOODY, SOCIALLY UNPREDICTABLE (AKA "ARTISTIC")
ED MARTIN
Lulu
OOOLA

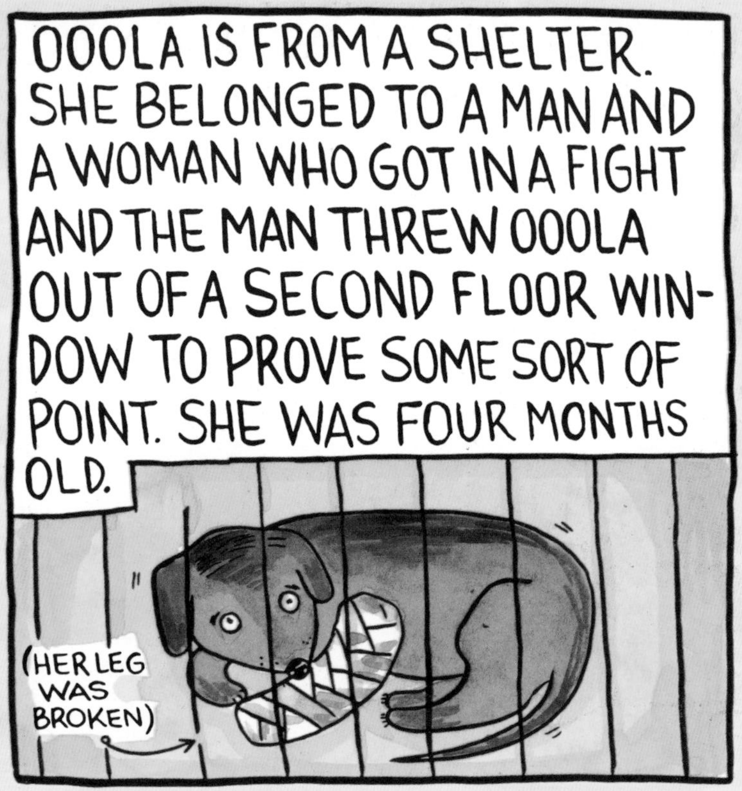
OOOLA IS FROM A SHELTER. SHE BELONGED TO A MAN AND A WOMAN WHO GOT IN A FIGHT AND THE MAN THREW OOOLA OUT OF A SECOND FLOOR WINDOW TO PROVE SOME SORT OF POINT. SHE WAS FOUR MONTHS OLD.
(HER LEG WAS BROKEN)

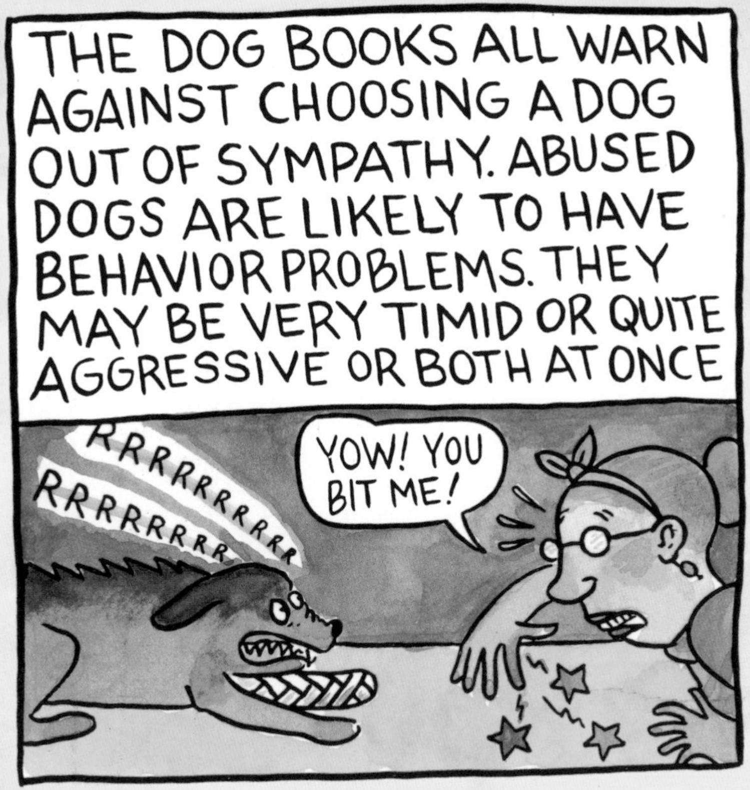
THE DOG BOOKS ALL WARN AGAINST CHOOSING A DOG OUT OF SYMPATHY. ABUSED DOGS ARE LIKELY TO HAVE BEHAVIOR PROBLEMS. THEY MAY BE VERY TIMID OR QUITE AGGRESSIVE OR BOTH AT ONCE
RRRRRRRRRRR
RRRRRRRRRR
YOW! YOU BIT ME!

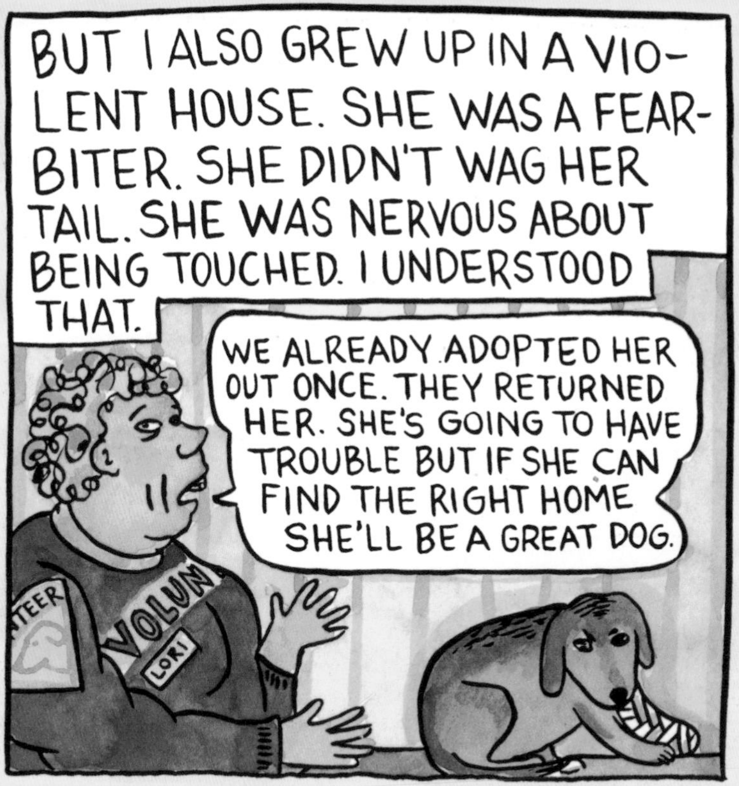
BUT I ALSO GREW UP IN A VIOLENT HOUSE. SHE WAS A FEAR-BITER. SHE DIDN'T WAG HER TAIL. SHE WAS NERVOUS ABOUT BEING TOUCHED. I UNDERSTOOD THAT.
WE ALREADY ADOPTED HER OUT ONCE. THEY RETURNED HER. SHE'S GOING TO HAVE TROUBLE BUT IF SHE CAN FIND THE RIGHT HOME SHE'LL BE A GREAT DOG.
VOLUN
TEER
LORI

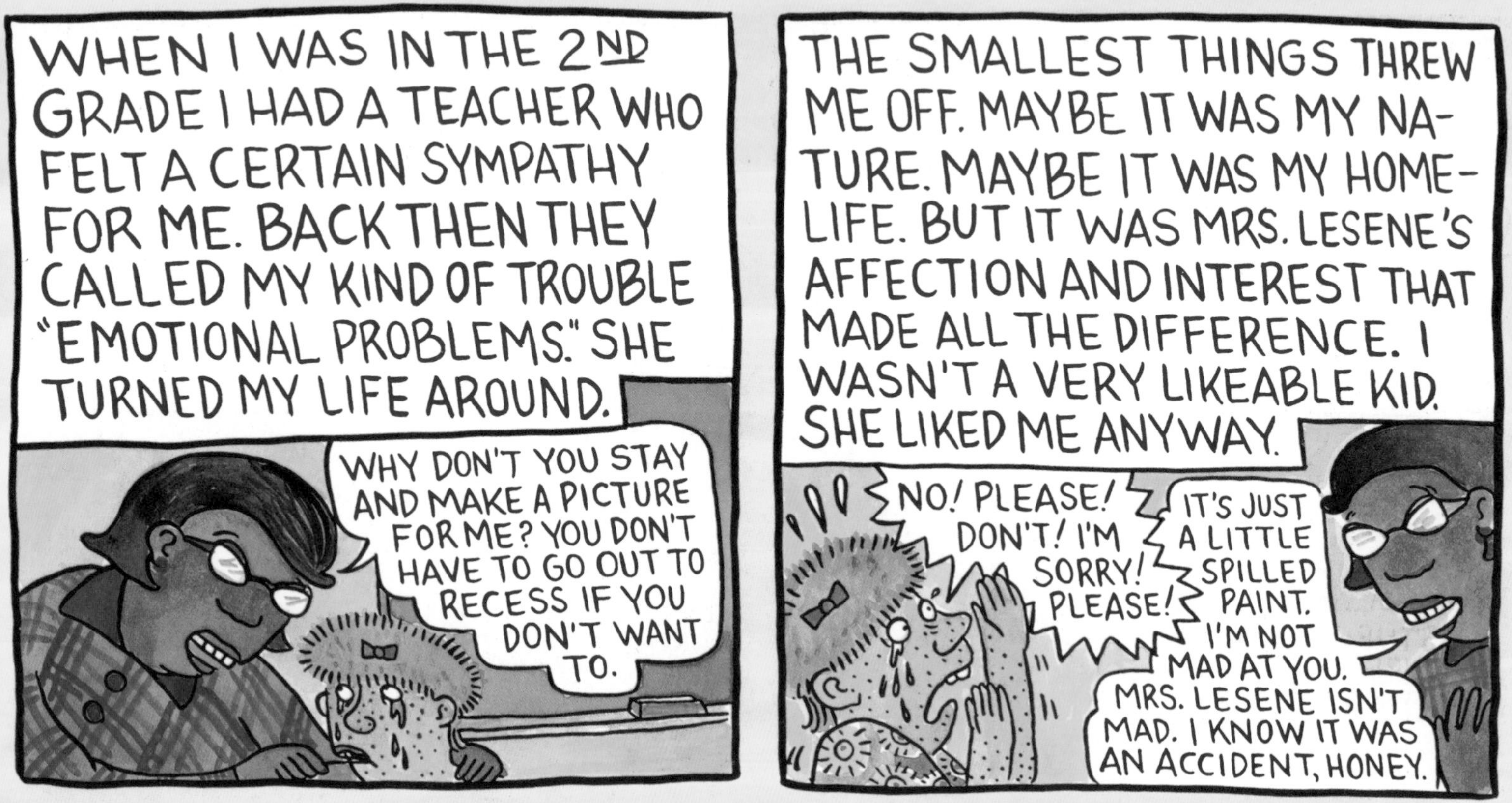
WHEN I WAS IN THE 2ND GRADE I HAD A TEACHER WHO FELT A CERTAIN SYMPATHY FOR ME. BACK THEN THEY CALLED MY KIND OF TROUBLE "EMOTIONAL PROBLEMS." SHE TURNED MY LIFE AROUND.
WHY DON'T YOU STAY AND MAKE A PICTURE FOR ME? YOU DON'T HAVE TO GO OUT TO RECESS IF YOU DON'T WANT TO.
THE SMALLEST THINGS THREW ME OFF. MAYBE IT WAS MY NATURE. MAYBE IT WAS MY HOME-LIFE. BUT IT WAS MRS. LESENE'S AFFECTION AND INTEREST THAT MADE ALL THE DIFFERENCE. I WASN'T A VERY LIKEABLE KID. SHE LIKED ME ANYWAY.
NO! PLEASE! DON'T! I'M SORRY! PLEASE!
IT'S JUST A LITTLE SPILLED PAINT. I'M NOT MAD AT YOU. MRS. LESENE ISN'T MAD. I KNOW IT WAS AN ACCIDENT, HONEY.

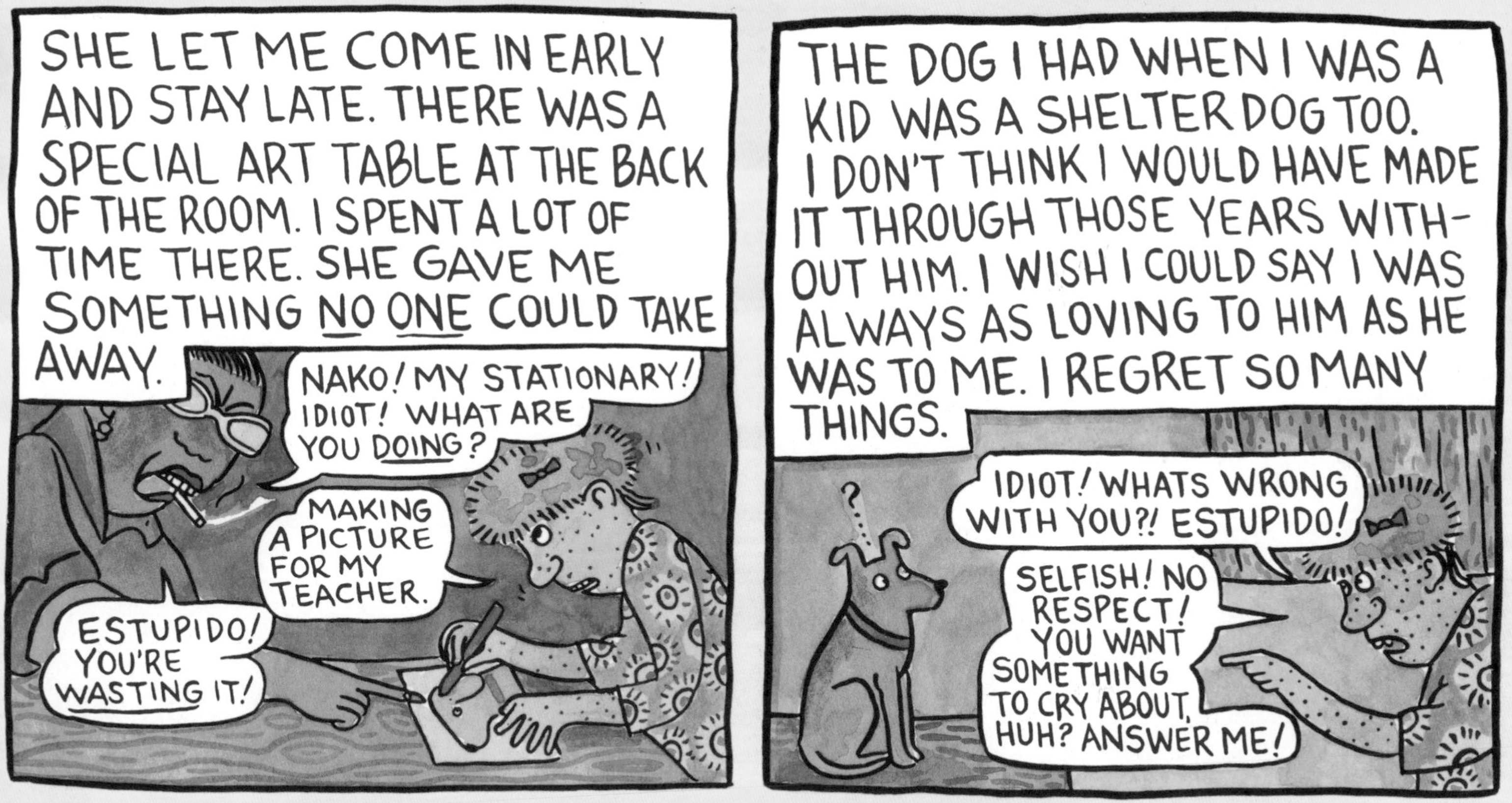
SHE LET ME COME IN EARLY AND STAY LATE. THERE WAS A SPECIAL ART TABLE AT THE BACK OF THE ROOM. I SPENT A LOT OF TIME THERE. SHE GAVE ME SOMETHING NO ONE COULD TAKE AWAY.
NAKO! MY STATIONARY! IDIOT! WHAT ARE YOU DOING?
MAKING A PICTURE FOR MY TEACHER.
ESTUPIDO! YOU'RE WASTING IT!
THE DOG I HAD WHEN I WAS A KID WAS A SHELTER DOG TOO. I DON'T THINK I WOULD HAVE MADE IT THROUGH THOSE YEARS WITHOUT HIM. I WISH I COULD SAY I WAS ALWAYS AS LOVING TO HIM AS HE WAS TO ME. I REGRET SO MANY THINGS.
?
IDIOT! WHATS WRONG WITH YOU?! ESTUPIDO!
SELFISH! NO RESPECT! YOU WANT SOMETHING TO CRY ABOUT, HUH? ANSWER ME!

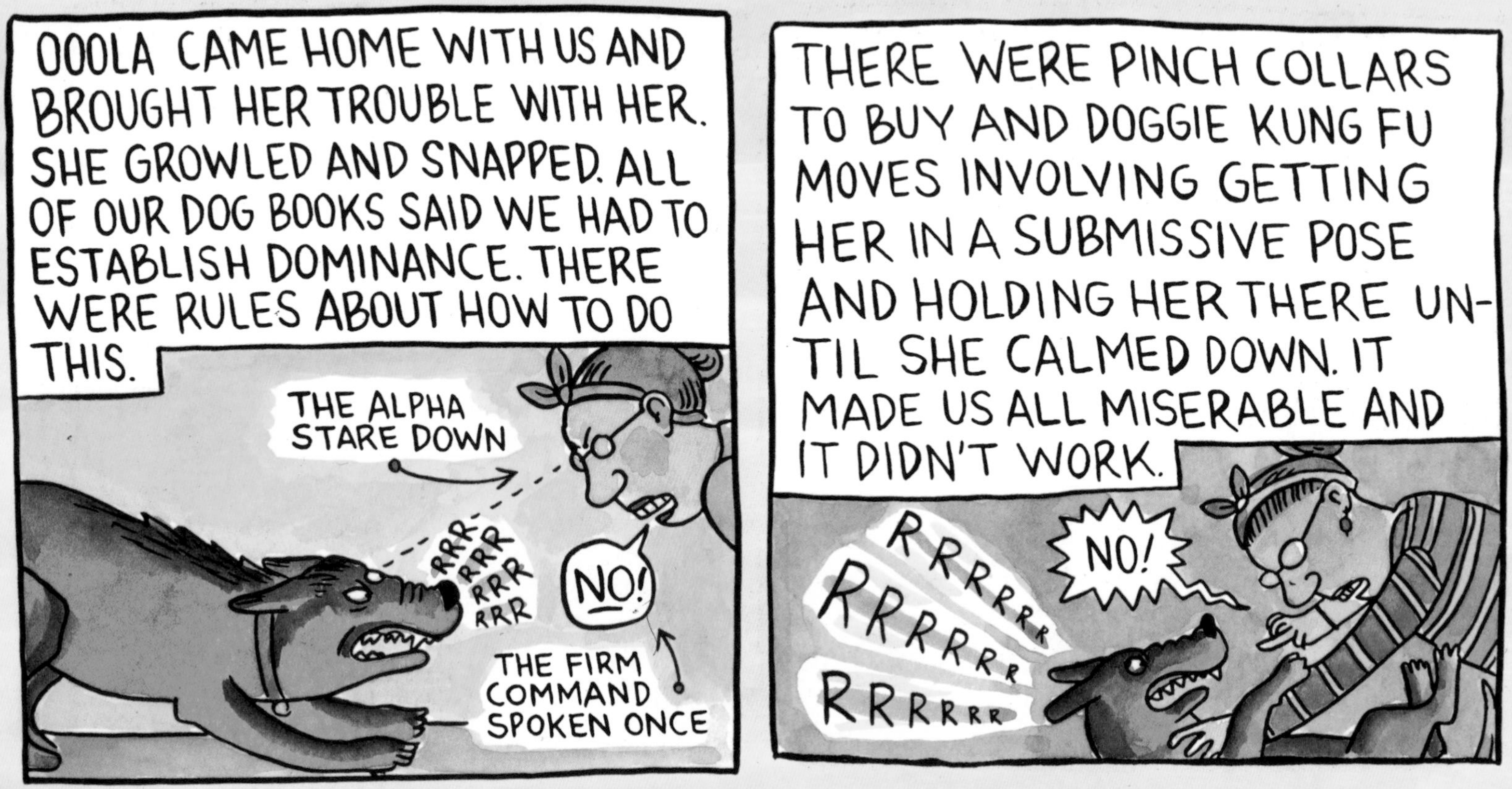
OOOLA CAME HOME WITH US AND BROUGHT HER TROUBLE WITH HER. SHE GROWLED AND SNAPPED. ALL OF OUR DOG BOOKS SAID WE HAD TO ESTABLISH DOMINANCE. THERE WERE RULES ABOUT HOW TO DO THIS.
THE ALPHA STARE DOWN
RRR RRR RRR RRR RRR
NO!
THE FIRM COMMAND SPOKEN ONCE
THERE WERE PINCH COLLARS TO BUY AND DOGGIE KUNG FU MOVES INVOLVING GETTING HER IN A SUBMISSIVE POSE AND HOLDING HER THERE UN-TIL SHE CALMED DOWN. IT MADE US ALL MISERABLE AND IT DIDN'T WORK.
RRRRRRR
RRRRRRR
RRRRRRR
NO!

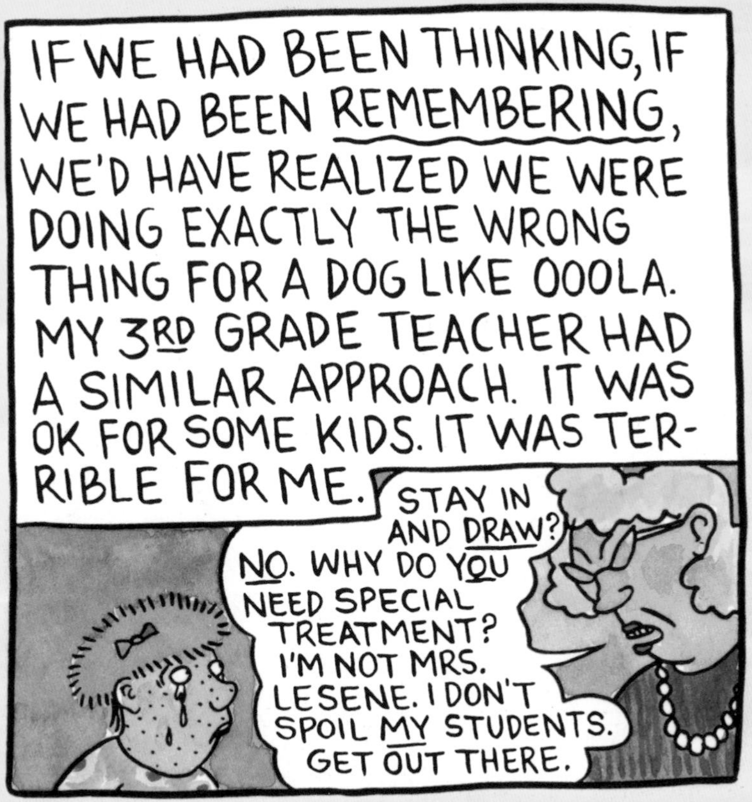
IF WE HAD BEEN THINKING, IF WE HAD BEEN REMEMBERING, WE'D HAVE REALIZED WE WERE DOING EXACTLY THE WRONG THING FOR A DOG LIKE OOOLA. MY 3RD GRADE TEACHER HAD A SIMILAR APPROACH. IT WAS OK FOR SOME KIDS. IT WAS TERRIBLE FOR ME.
STAY IN AND DRAW?
NO. WHY DO YOU NEED SPECIAL TREATMENT? I'M NOT MRS. LESENE. I DON'T SPOIL MY STUDENTS. GET OUT THERE.

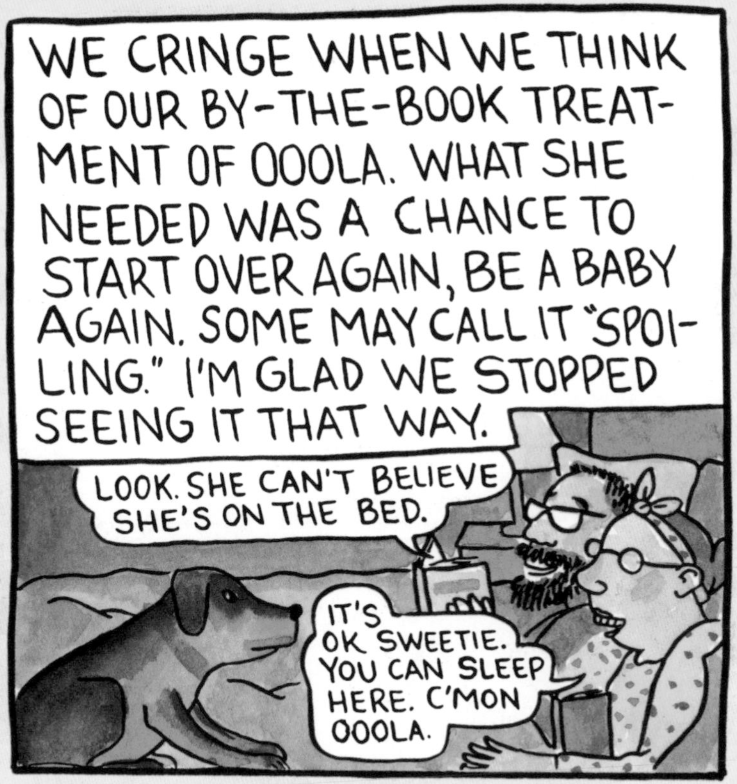
WE CRINGE WHEN WE THINK OF OUR BY-THE-BOOK TREATMENT OF OOOLA. WHAT SHE NEEDED WAS A CHANCE TO START OVER AGAIN, BE A BABY AGAIN. SOME MAY CALL IT "SPOILING." I'M GLAD WE STOPPED SEEING IT THAT WAY.
LOOK. SHE CAN'T BELIEVE SHE'S ON THE BED.
IT'S OK SWEETIE. YOU CAN SLEEP HERE. C'MON OOOLA.

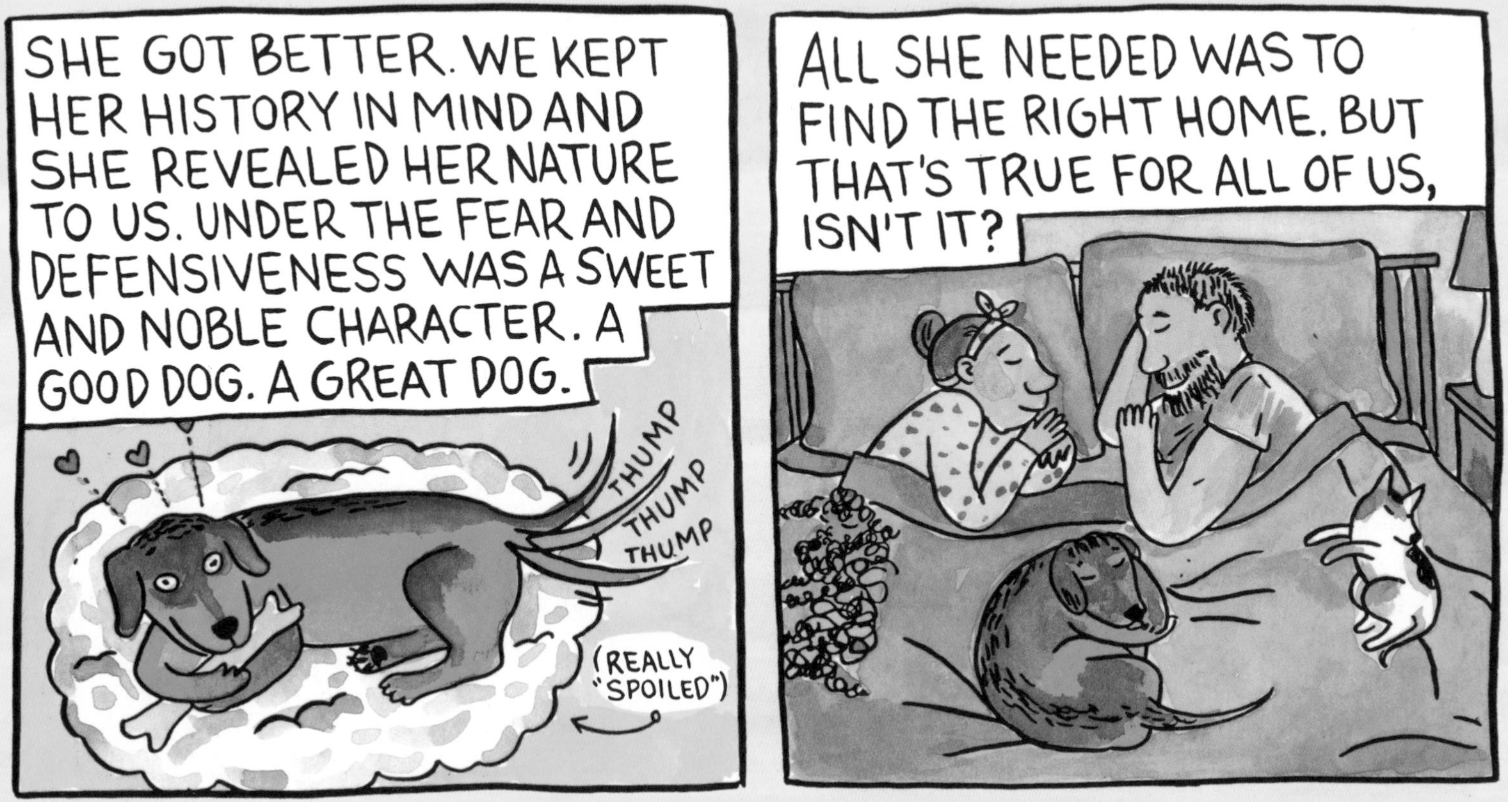
SHE GOT BETTER. WE KEPT HER HISTORY IN MIND AND SHE REVEALED HER NATURE TO US. UNDER THE FEAR AND DEFENSIVENESS WAS A SWEET AND NOBLE CHARACTER. A GOOD DOG. A GREAT DOG.
THUMP THUMP THUMP THUMP
(REALLY "SPOILED")
ALL SHE NEEDED WAS TO FIND THE RIGHT HOME. BUT THAT'S TRUE FOR ALL OF US, ISN'T IT?

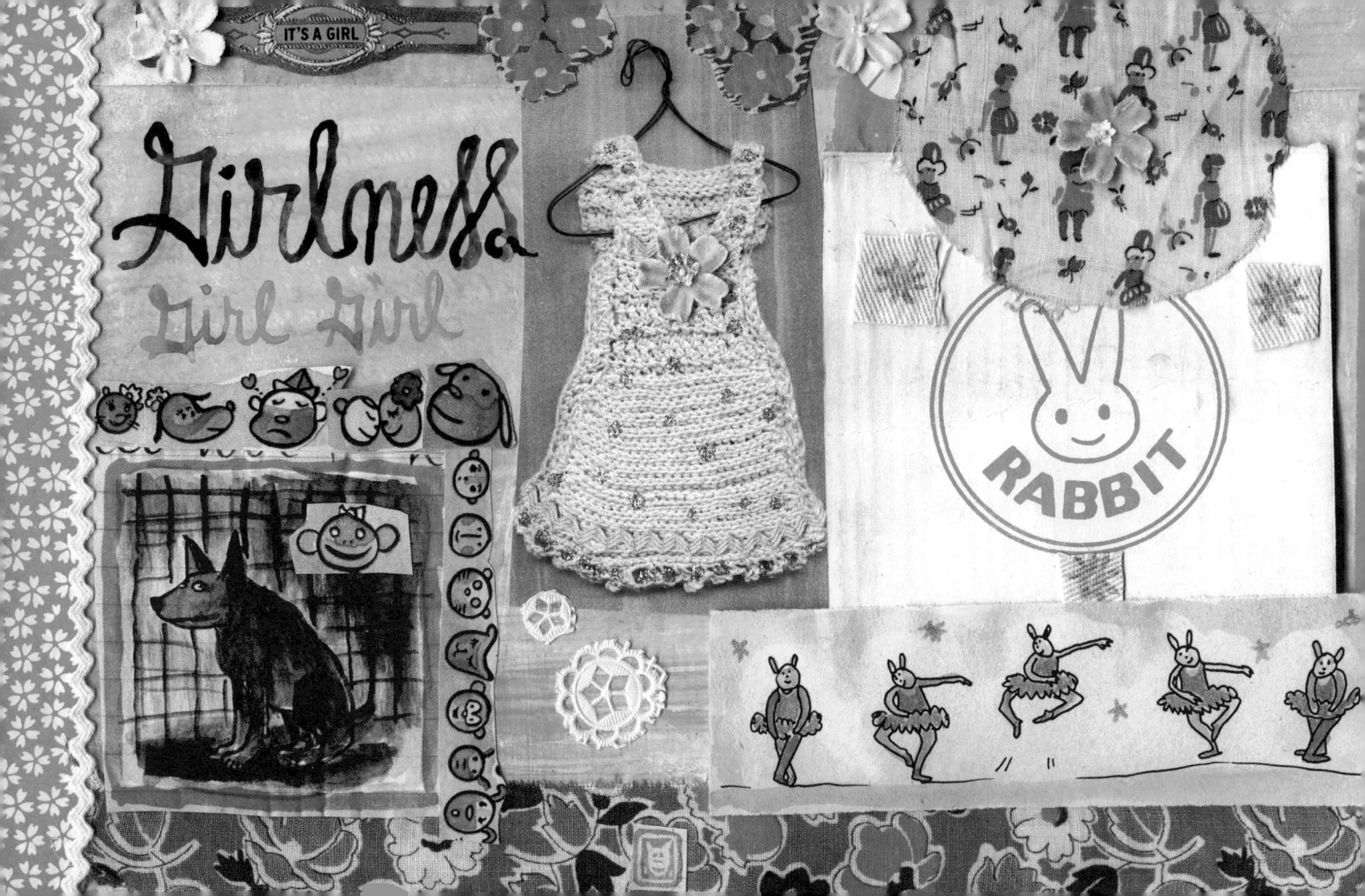
IT'S A GIRL
Girlness
Girl Girl
RABBIT

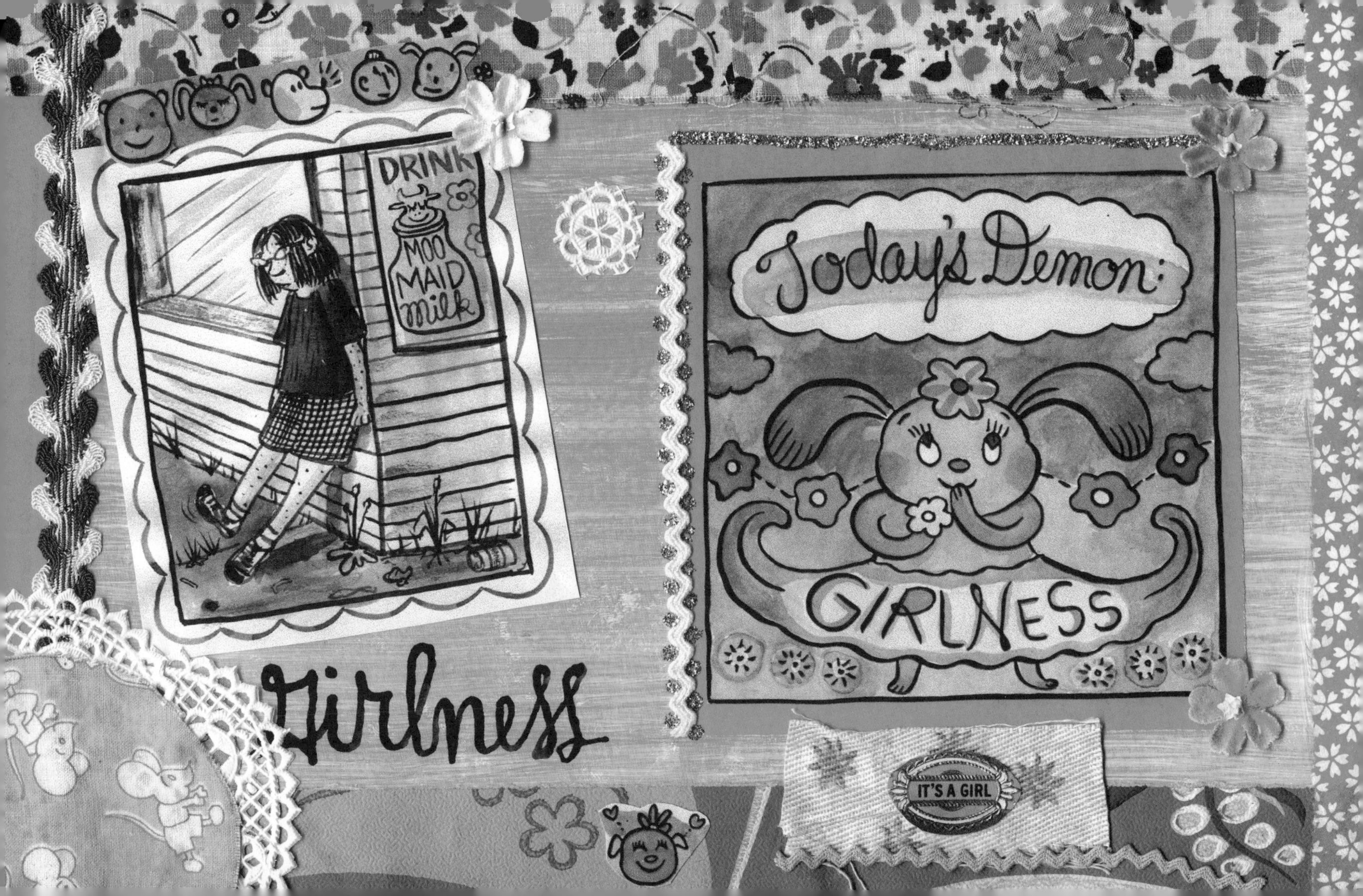
DRINK
MOO MAID milk
Girlness
Today's Demon:
GIRLNESS
IT'S A GIRL

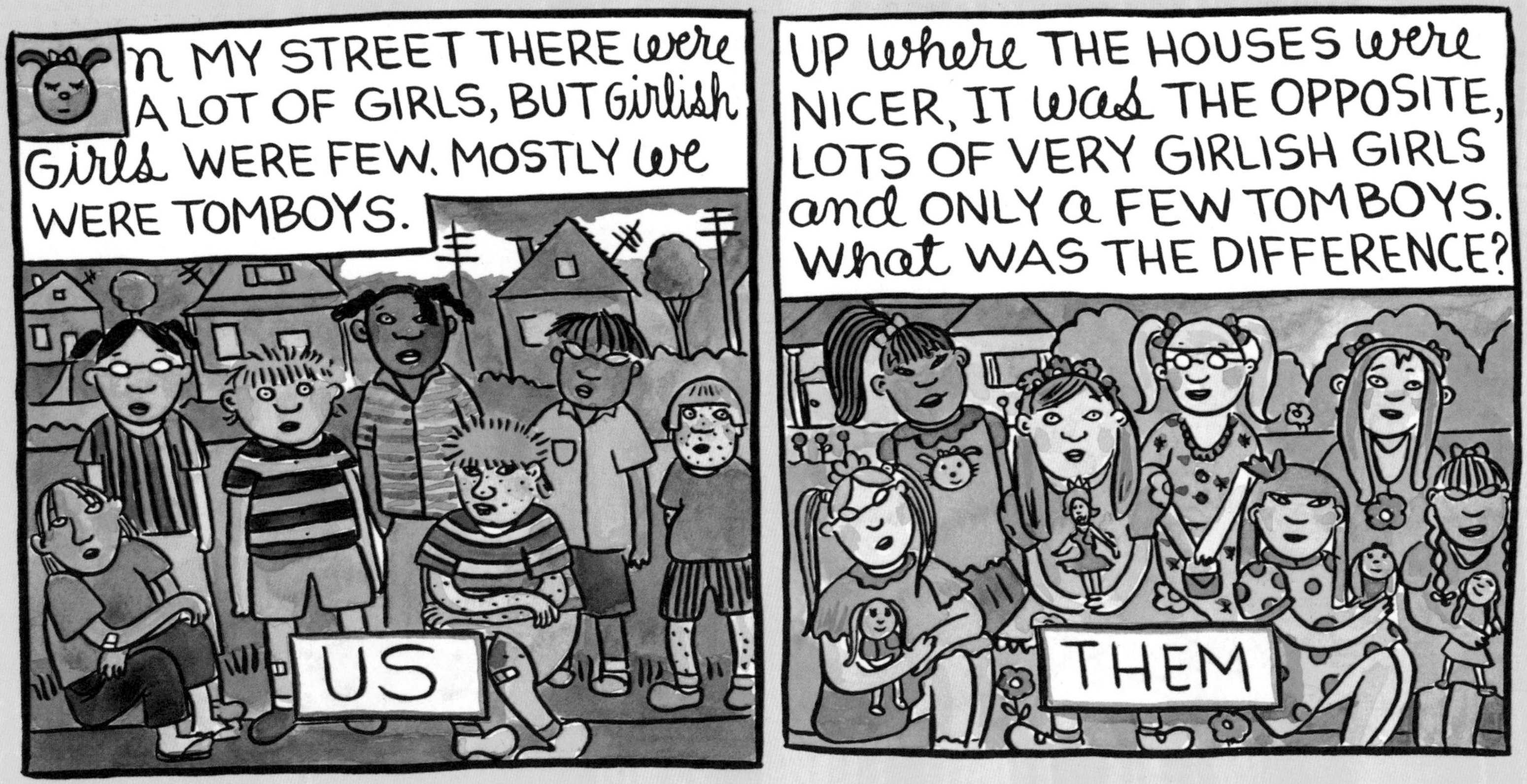
In MY STREET THERE were A LOT OF GIRLS, BUT Girlish Girls WERE FEW. MOSTLY we WERE TOMBOYS.
US
UP where THE HOUSES were NICER, IT was THE OPPOSITE, LOTS OF VERY GIRLISH GIRLS and ONLY a FEW TOMBOYS. What WAS THE DIFFERENCE?
THEM

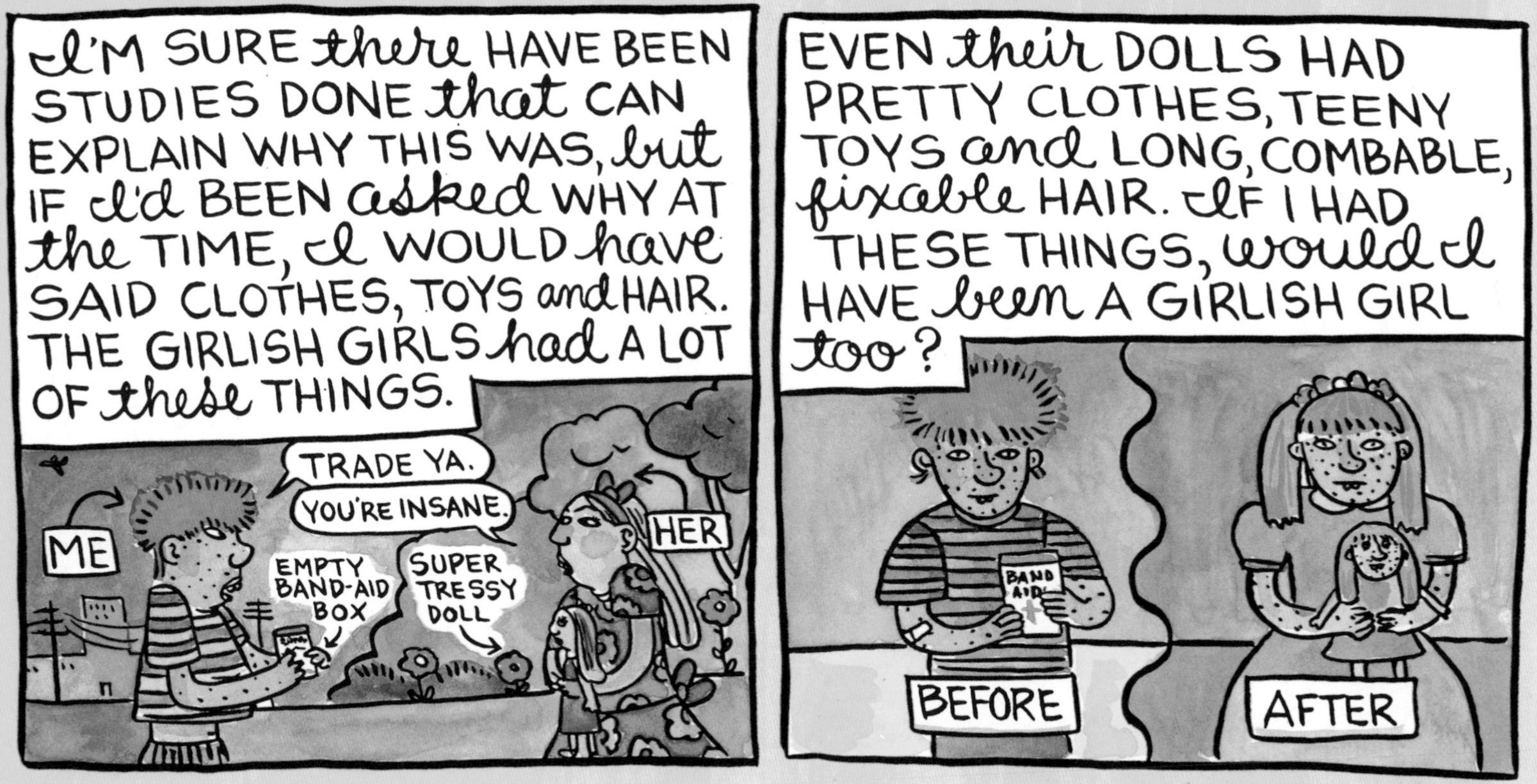
I'M SURE there HAVE BEEN STUDIES DONE that CAN EXPLAIN WHY THIS WAS, but IF I'd BEEN asked WHY AT the TIME, I WOULD have SAID CLOTHES, TOYS and HAIR. THE GIRLISH GIRLS had A LOT OF these THINGS.
TRADE YA.
YOU'RE INSANE.
ME
HER
EMPTY BAND-AID BOX
SUPER TRESSY DOLL
EVEN their DOLLS HAD PRETTY CLOTHES, TEENY TOYS and LONG, COMBABLE, fixable HAIR. IF I HAD THESE THINGS, would I HAVE been A GIRLISH GIRL too?
BAND AID
BEFORE
AFTER

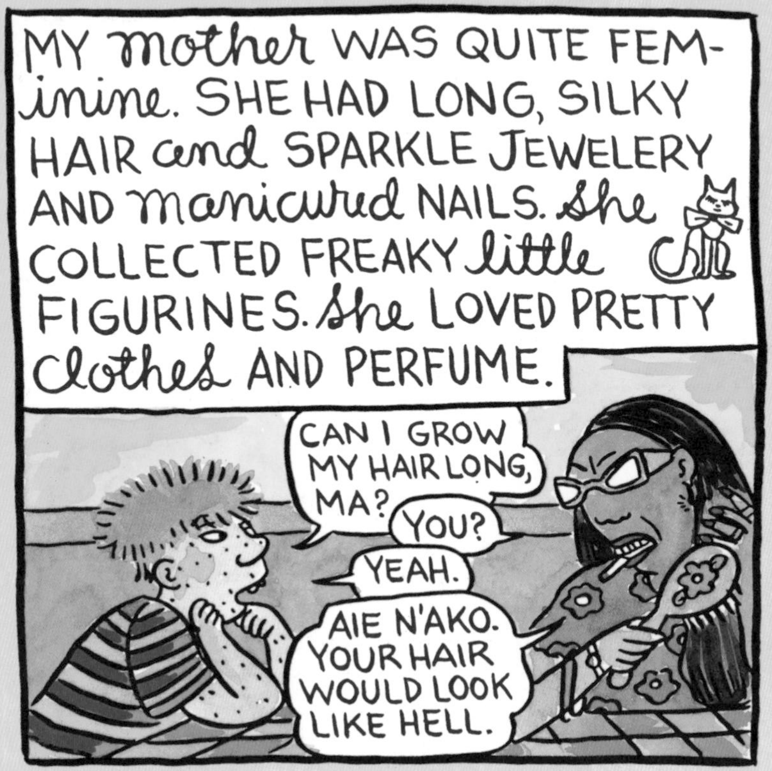
MY mother WAS QUITE FEMinine. SHE HAD LONG, SILKY HAIR and SPARKLE JEWELERY AND manicured NAILS. She COLLECTED FREAKY little FIGURINES. She LOVED PRETTY clothes AND PERFUME.
CAN I GROW MY HAIR LONG, MA?
YOU?
YEAH.
AIE N'AKO. YOUR HAIR WOULD LOOK LIKE HELL.

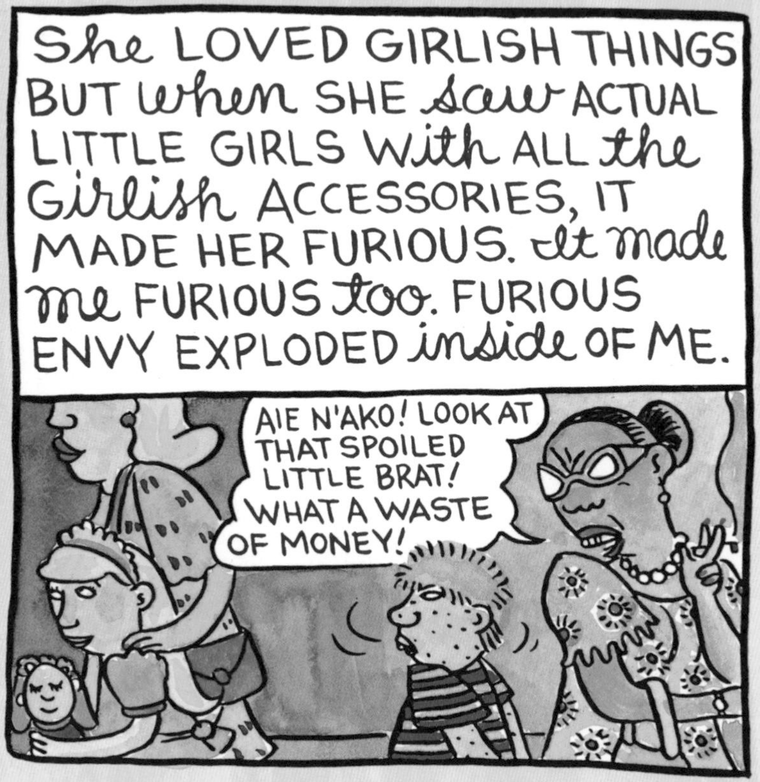
She LOVED GIRLISH THINGS BUT when SHE saw ACTUAL LITTLE GIRLS with ALL the Girlish ACCESSORIES, IT MADE HER FURIOUS. It made me FURIOUS too. FURIOUS ENVY EXPLODED inside OF ME.
AIE N'AKO! LOOK AT THAT SPOILED LITTLE BRAT! WHAT A WASTE OF MONEY!

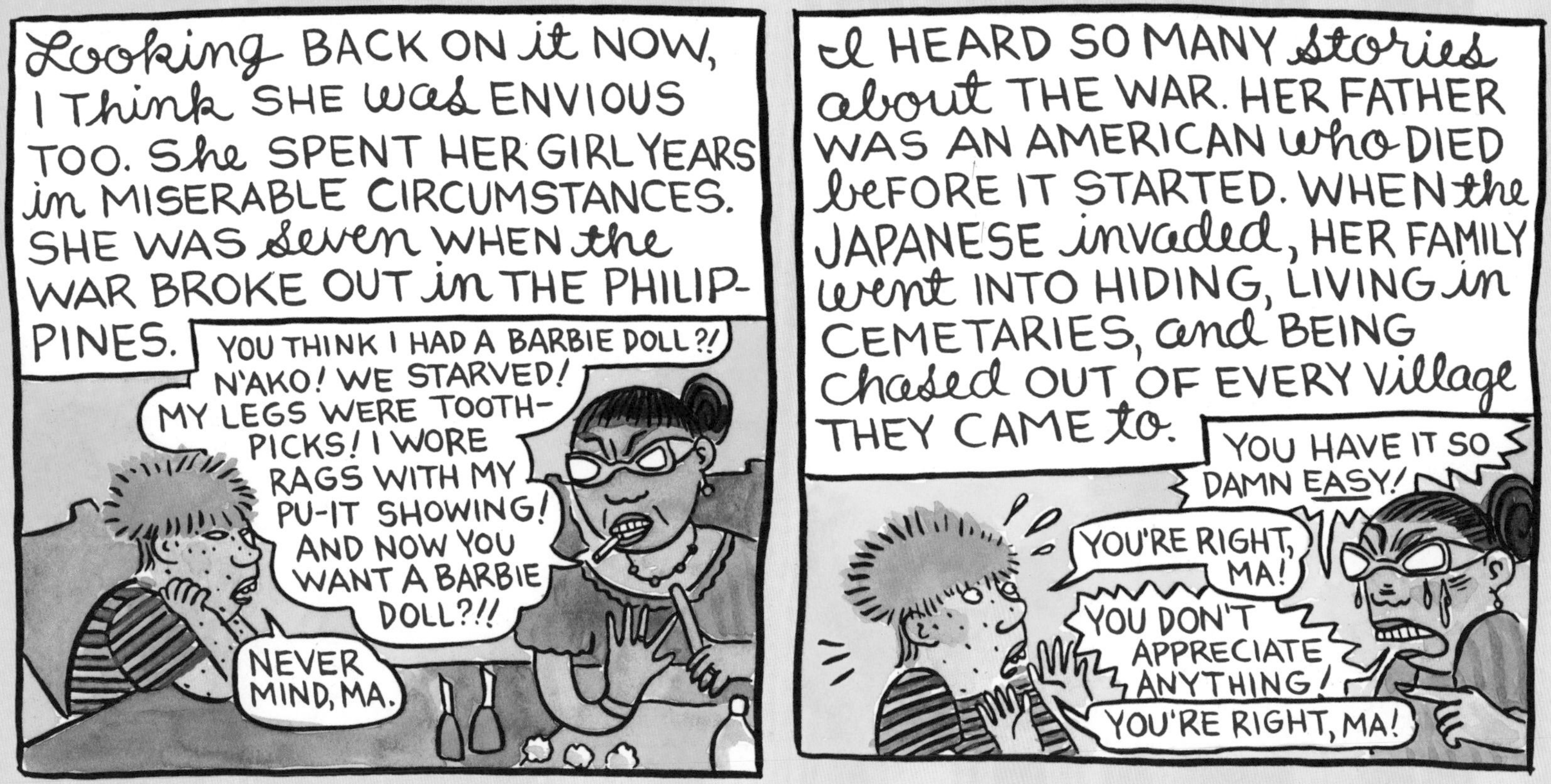
LOOKING BACK ON IT NOW, I THINK SHE WAS ENVIOUS TOO. SHE SPENT HER GIRL YEARS IN MISERABLE CIRCUMSTANCES. SHE WAS SEVEN WHEN THE WAR BROKE OUT IN THE PHILIPPINES.
YOU THINK I HAD A BARBIE DOLL?! N'AKO! WE STARVED! MY LEGS WERE TOOTHPICKS! I WORE RAGS WITH MY PU-IT SHOWING! AND NOW YOU WANT A BARBIE DOLL?!!
NEVER MIND, MA.
I HEARD SO MANY STORIES ABOUT THE WAR. HER FATHER WAS AN AMERICAN WHO DIED BEFORE IT STARTED. WHEN THE JAPANESE INVADED, HER FAMILY WENT INTO HIDING, LIVING IN CEMETARIES, AND BEING CHASED OUT OF EVERY VILLAGE THEY CAME TO.
YOU HAVE IT SO DAMN EASY!
YOU'RE RIGHT, MA!
YOU DON'T APPRECIATE ANYTHING!
YOU'RE RIGHT, MA!

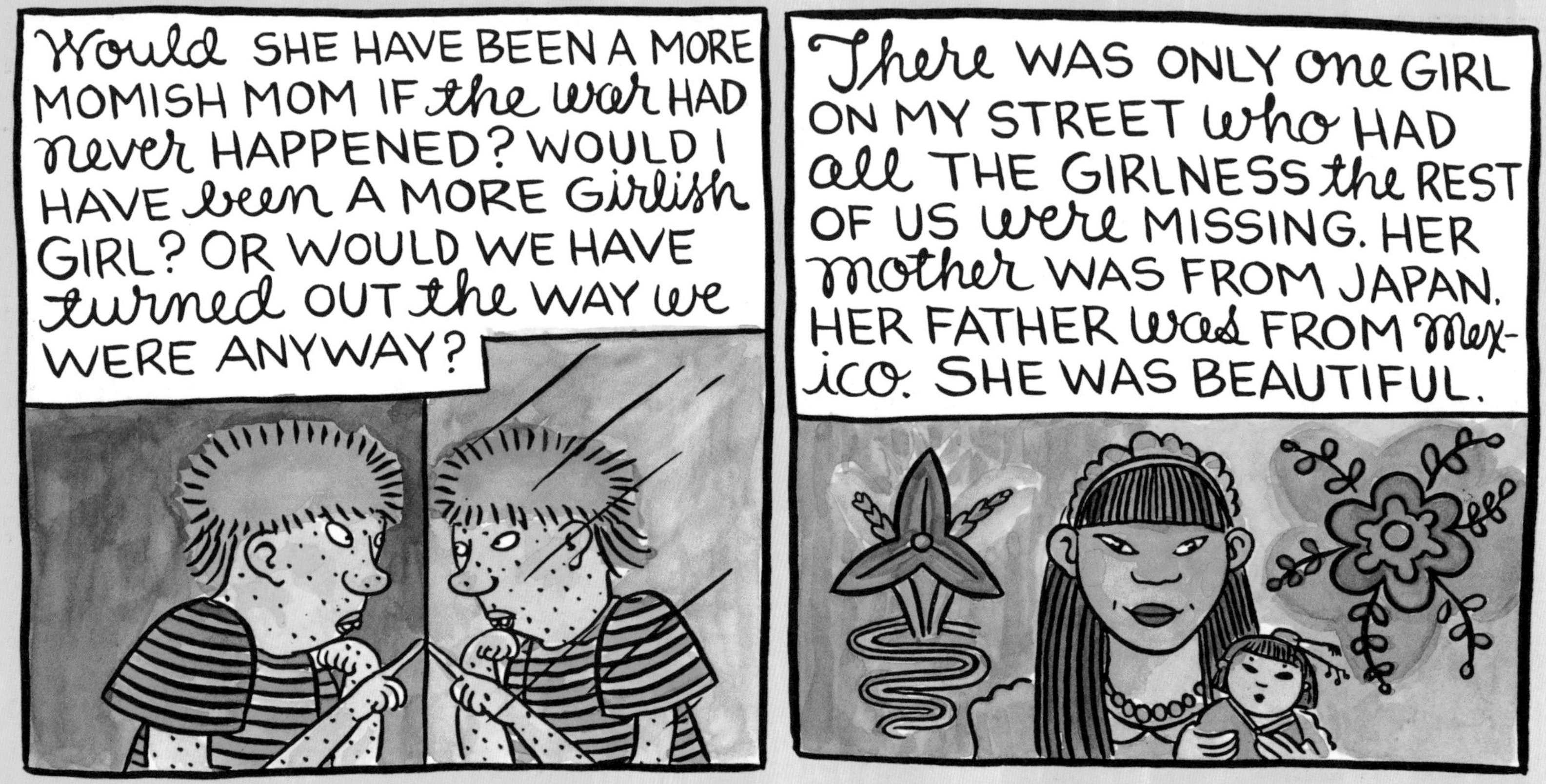
Would SHE HAVE BEEN A MORE MOMISH MOM IF the war HAD never HAPPENED? WOULD I HAVE been A MORE Girlish GIRL? OR WOULD WE HAVE turned OUT the WAY we WERE ANYWAY?
There WAS ONLY one GIRL ON MY STREET who HAD all THE GIRLNESS the REST OF US were MISSING. HER mother WAS FROM JAPAN. HER FATHER was FROM Mex-ico. SHE WAS BEAUTIFUL.

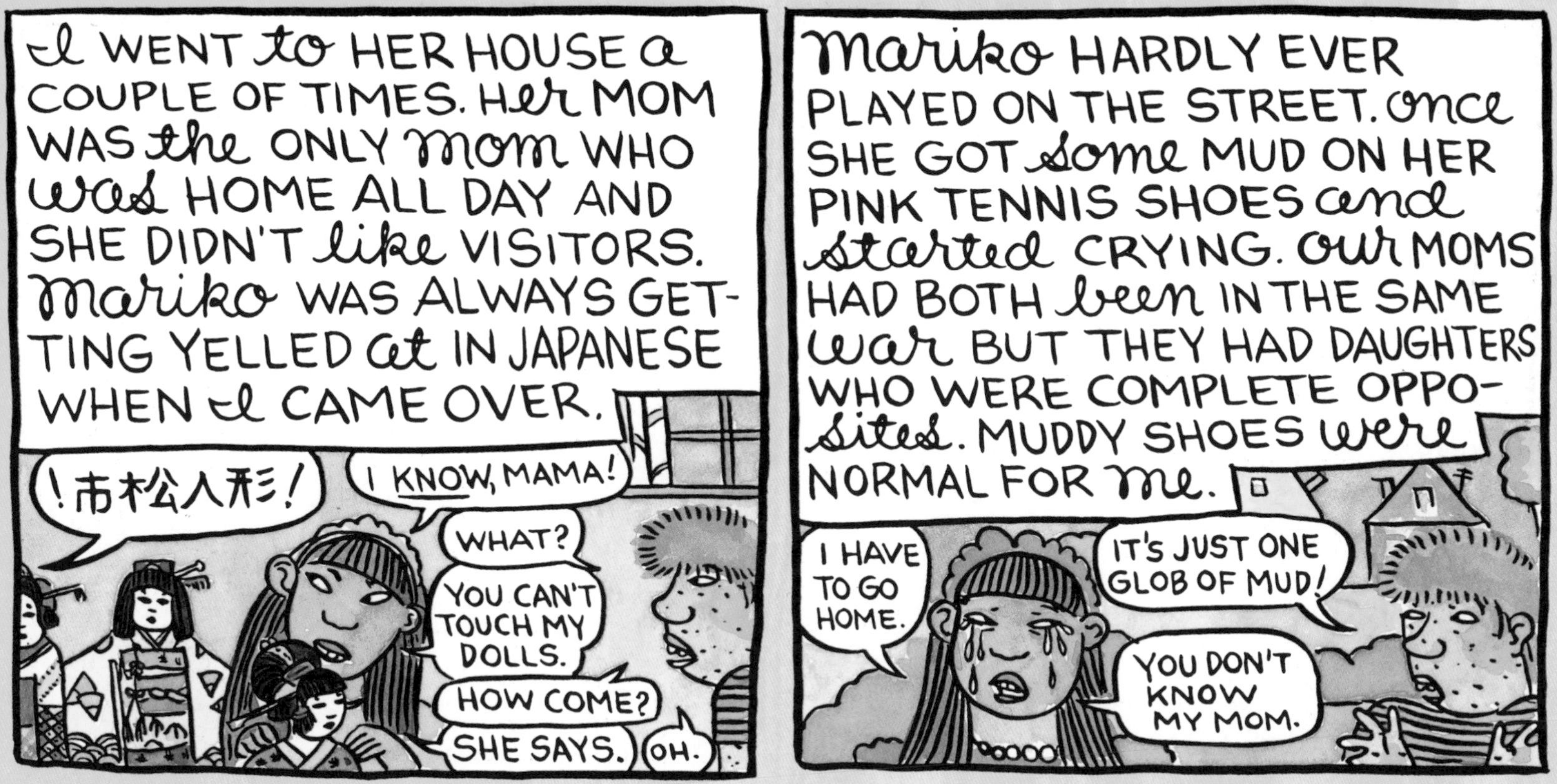
I WENT TO HER HOUSE A COUPLE OF TIMES. HER MOM WAS THE ONLY MOM WHO WAS HOME ALL DAY AND SHE DIDN'T LIKE VISITORS. MARIKO WAS ALWAYS GETTING YELLED AT IN JAPANESE WHEN I CAME OVER.
!市松人形!
I KNOW, MAMA!
WHAT?
YOU CAN'T TOUCH MY DOLLS.
HOW COME?
SHE SAYS.
OH.
MARIKO HARDLY EVER PLAYED ON THE STREET. ONCE SHE GOT SOME MUD ON HER PINK TENNIS SHOES AND STARTED CRYING. OUR MOMS HAD BOTH BEEN IN THE SAME WAR BUT THEY HAD DAUGHTERS WHO WERE COMPLETE OPPOSITES. MUDDY SHOES WERE NORMAL FOR ME.
I HAVE TO GO HOME.
IT'S JUST ONE GLOB OF MUD!
YOU DON'T KNOW MY MOM.

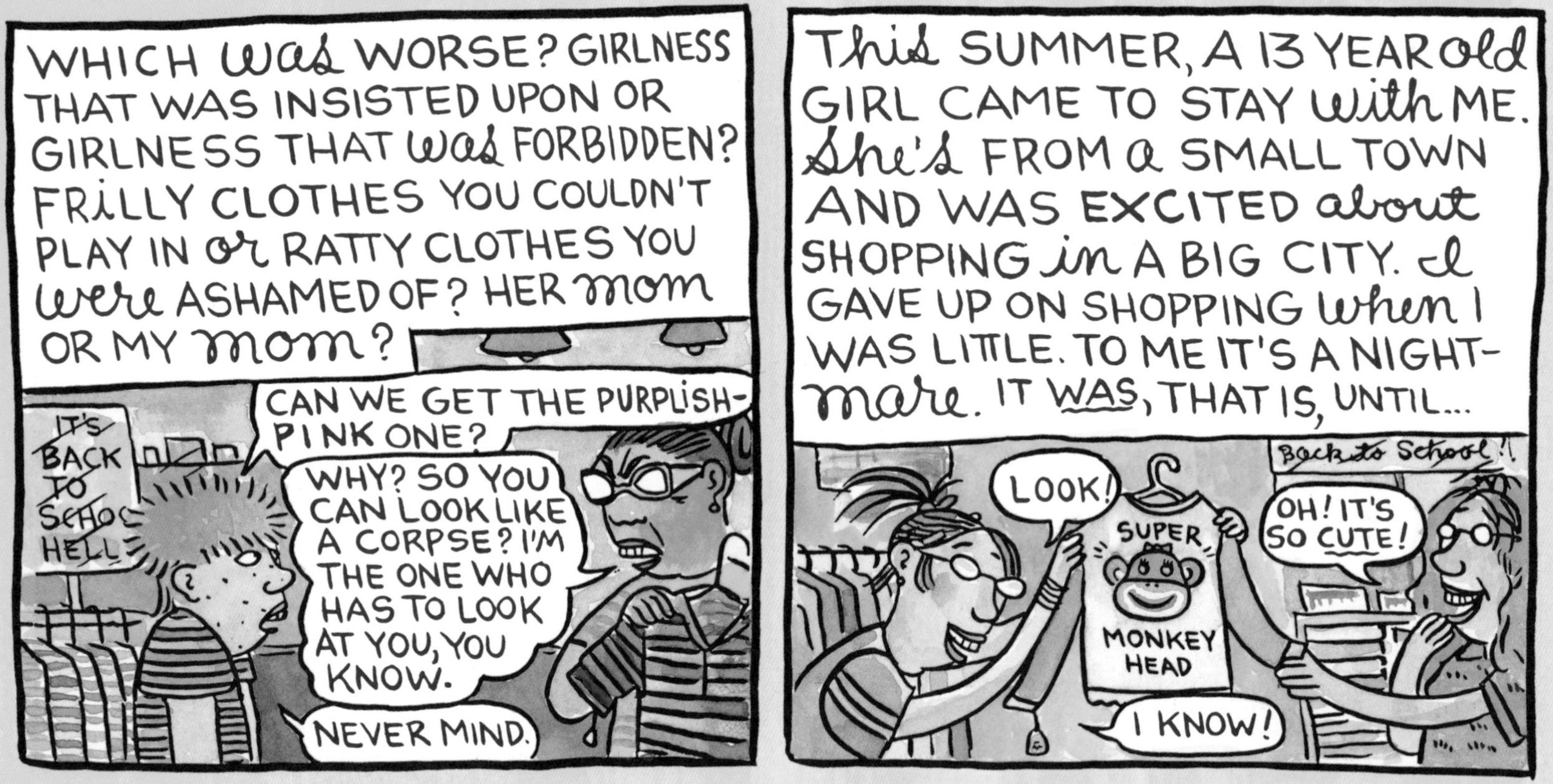
WHICH WAS WORSE? GIRLNESS THAT WAS INSISTED UPON OR GIRLNESS THAT WAS FORBIDDEN? FRILLY CLOTHES YOU COULDN'T PLAY IN OR RATTY CLOTHES YOU WERE ASHAMED OF? HER MOM OR MY MOM?
IT'S BACK TO SCHOOL HELL
CAN WE GET THE PURPLISH-PINK ONE?
WHY? SO YOU CAN LOOK LIKE A CORPSE? I'M THE ONE WHO HAS TO LOOK AT YOU, YOU KNOW.
NEVER MIND.
THIS SUMMER, A 13 YEAR OLD GIRL CAME TO STAY WITH ME. SHE'S FROM A SMALL TOWN AND WAS EXCITED ABOUT SHOPPING IN A BIG CITY. I GAVE UP ON SHOPPING WHEN I WAS LITTLE. TO ME IT'S A NIGHT-MARE. IT WAS, THAT IS, UNTIL...
Back to School!
LOOK!
SUPER MONKEY HEAD
OH! IT'S SO CUTE!
I KNOW!

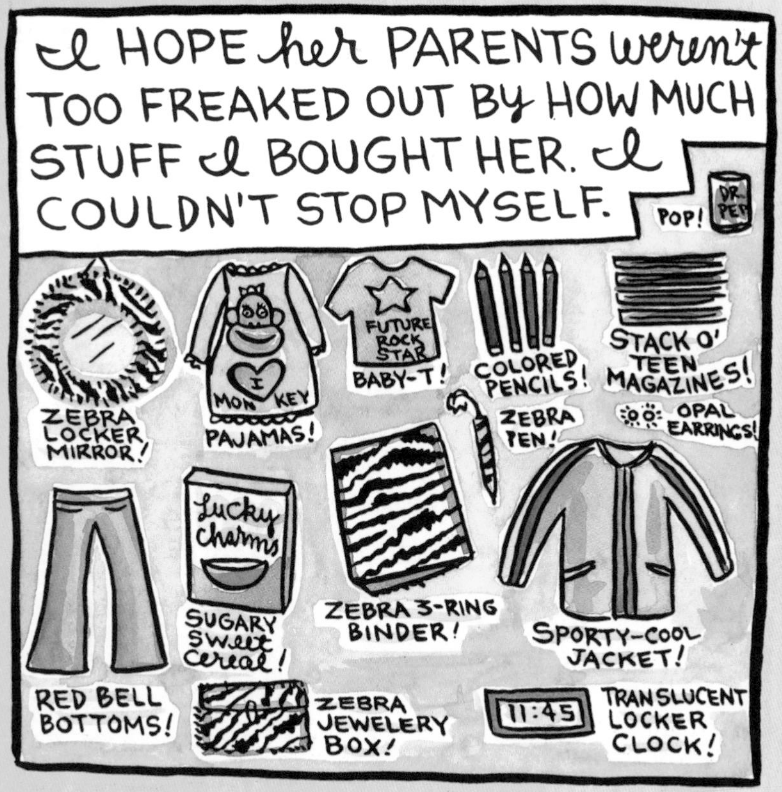
I HOPE her PARENTS weren't TOO FREAKED OUT BY HOW MUCH STUFF I BOUGHT HER. I COULDN'T STOP MYSELF.
POP!
DR. PEP
FUTURE ROCK STAR
BABY-T!
COLORED PENCILS!
STACK O' TEEN MAGAZINES!
I MON KEY
PAJAMAS!
ZEBRA LOCKER MIRROR!
ZEBRA PEN!
OPAL EARRINGS!
Lucky Charms
SUGARY Sweet cereal!
ZEBRA 3-RING BINDER!
SPORTY-COOL JACKET!
RED BELL BOTTOMS!
ZEBRA JEWELERY BOX!
11:45
TRANSLUCENT LOCKER CLOCK!

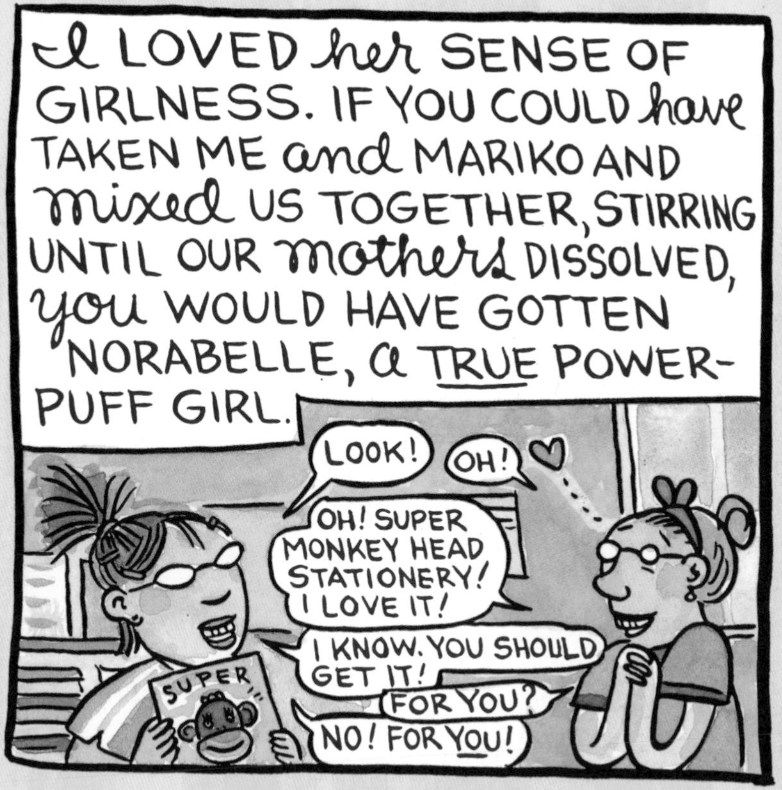
I LOVED her SENSE OF GIRLNESS. IF YOU COULD have TAKEN ME and MARIKO AND mixed US TOGETHER, STIRRING UNTIL OUR mothers DISSOLVED, you WOULD HAVE GOTTEN NORABELLE, a TRUE POWER-PUFF GIRL.
LOOK!
OH!
OH! SUPER MONKEY HEAD STATIONERY! I LOVE IT!
I KNOW. YOU SHOULD GET IT!
FOR YOU?
NO! FOR YOU!
SUPER

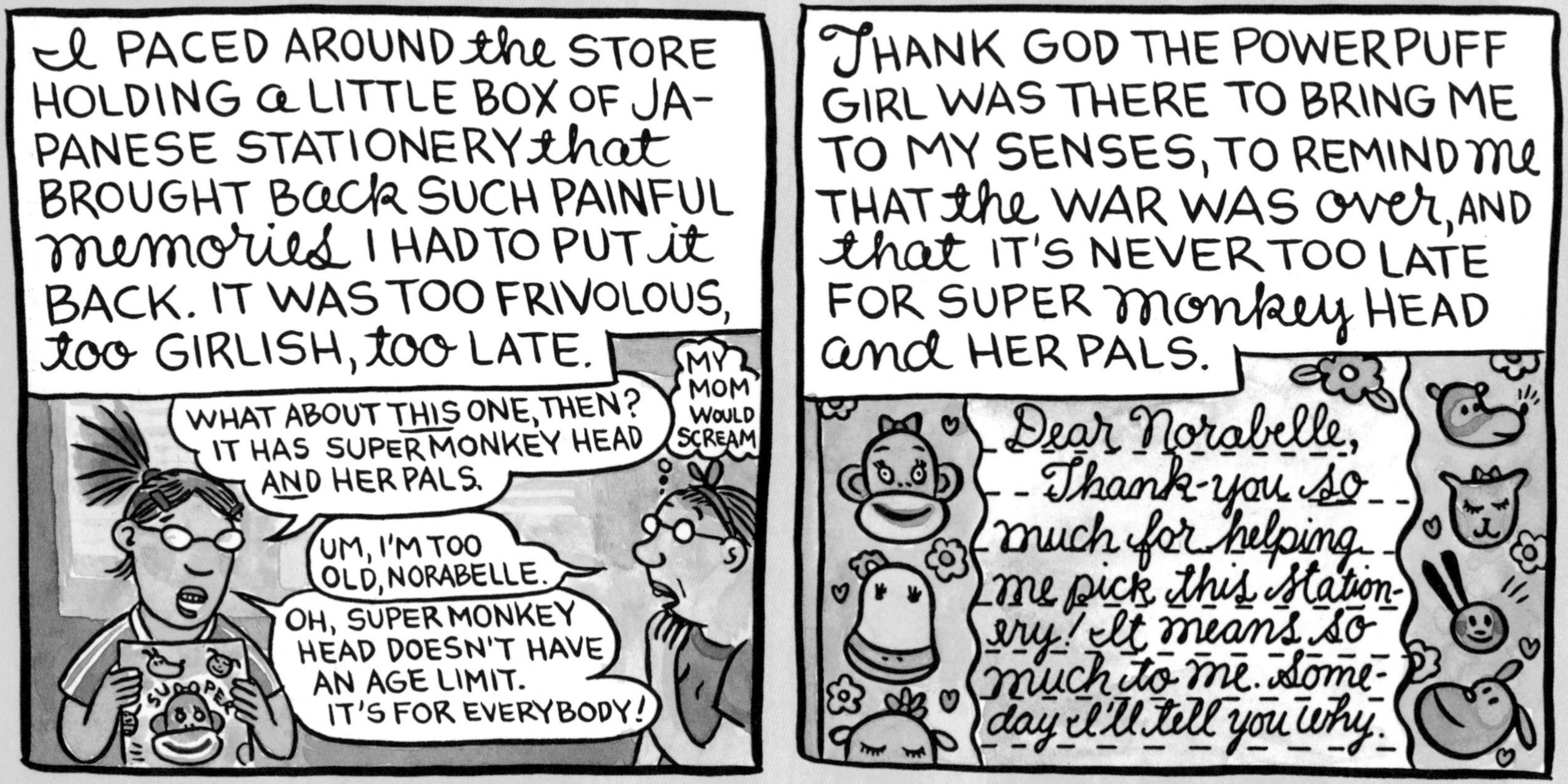
I PACED AROUND the STORE HOLDING a LITTLE BOX OF JAPANESE STATIONERY that BROUGHT Back SUCH PAINFUL memories I HAD TO PUT it BACK. IT WAS TOO FRIVOLOUS, too GIRLISH, too LATE.
WHAT ABOUT THIS ONE, THEN? IT HAS SUPER MONKEY HEAD AND HER PALS.
MY MOM WOULD SCREAM
UM, I'M TOO OLD, NORABELLE.
OH, SUPER MONKEY HEAD DOESN'T HAVE AN AGE LIMIT. IT'S FOR EVERYBODY!
SUPER
THANK GOD THE POWERPUFF GIRL WAS THERE TO BRING ME TO MY SENSES, TO REMIND me THAT the WAR WAS over, AND that IT'S NEVER TOO LATE FOR SUPER monkey HEAD and HER PALS.
Dear Norabelle,
Thank-you so much for helping me pick this Stationery! It means so much to me. Someday I'll tell you why.

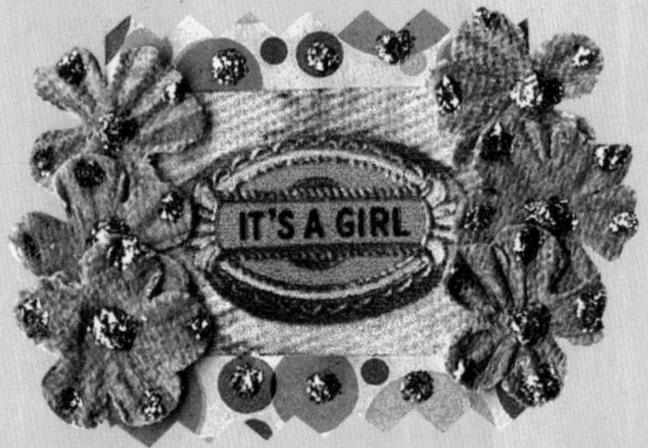
IT'S A GIRL

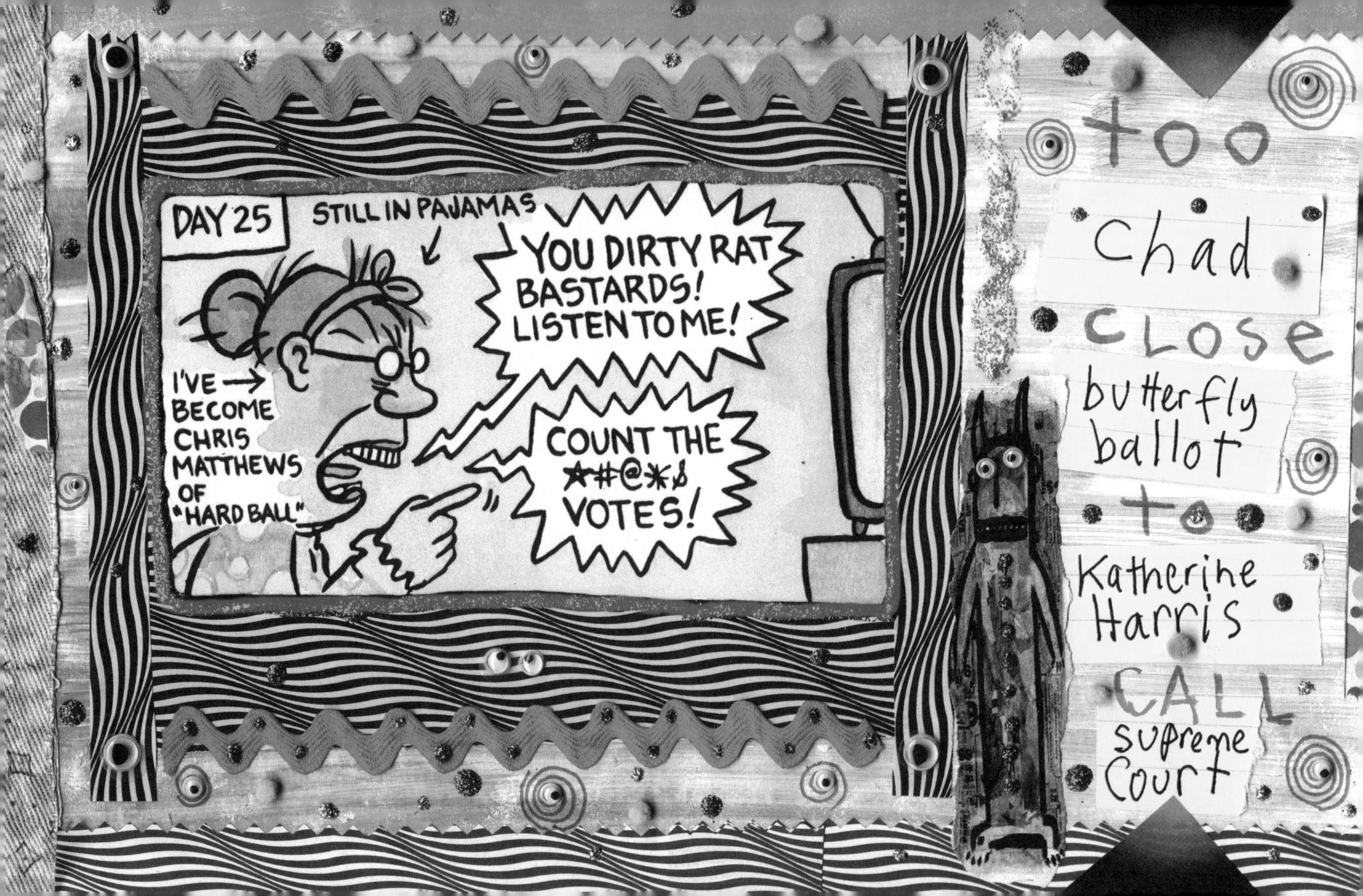

DAY 25
STILL IN PAJAMAS
YOU DIRTY RAT BASTARDS! LISTEN TO ME!
I'VE → BECOME CHRIS MATTHEWS OF "HARD BALL"
COUNT THE ★#@*$ VOTES!
too
chad
close
butterfly ballot
to
Katherine Harris
CALL
supreme Court

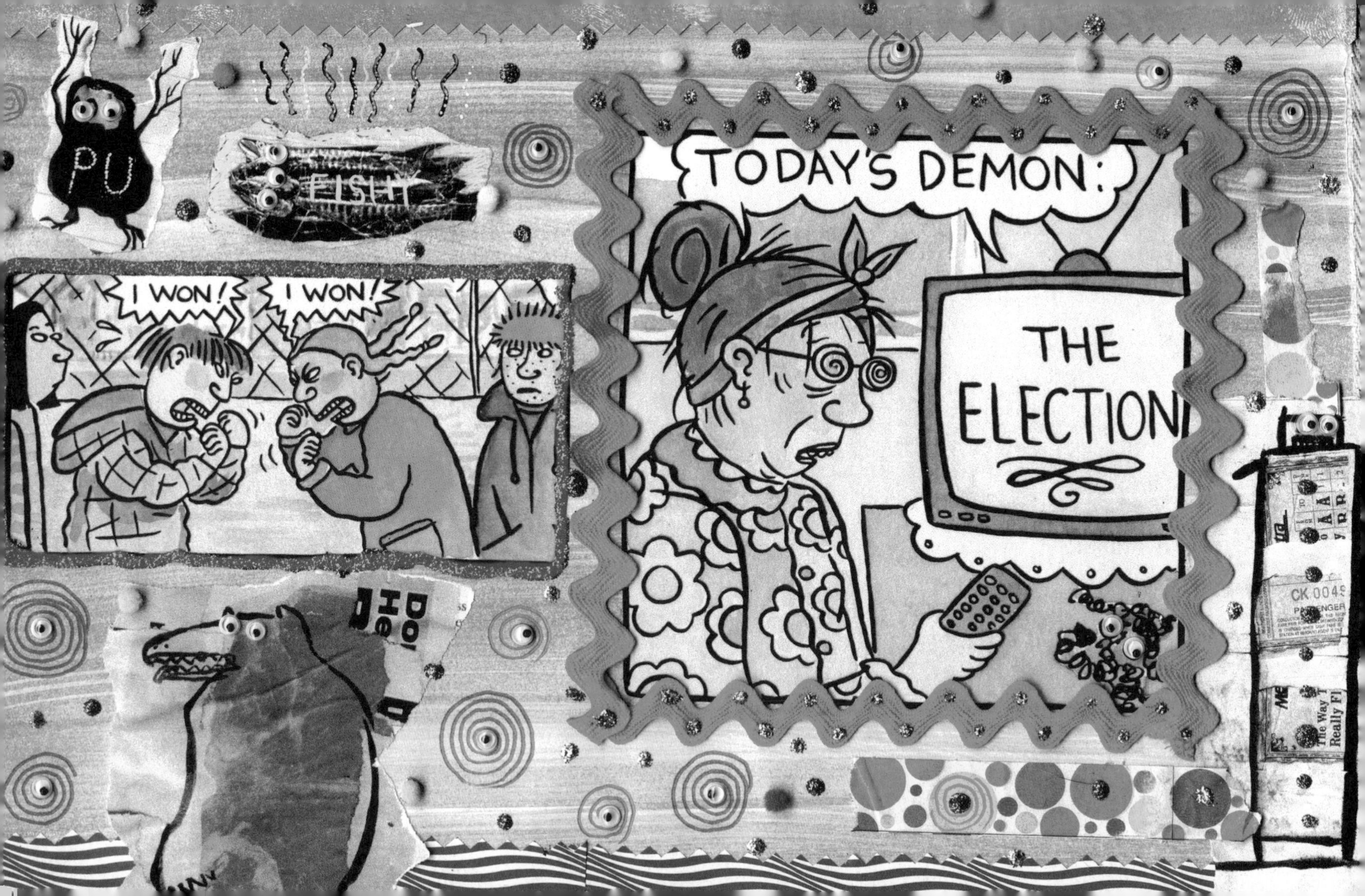
PU
FISHY
I WON!
I WON!
TODAY'S DEMON:
THE ELECTION

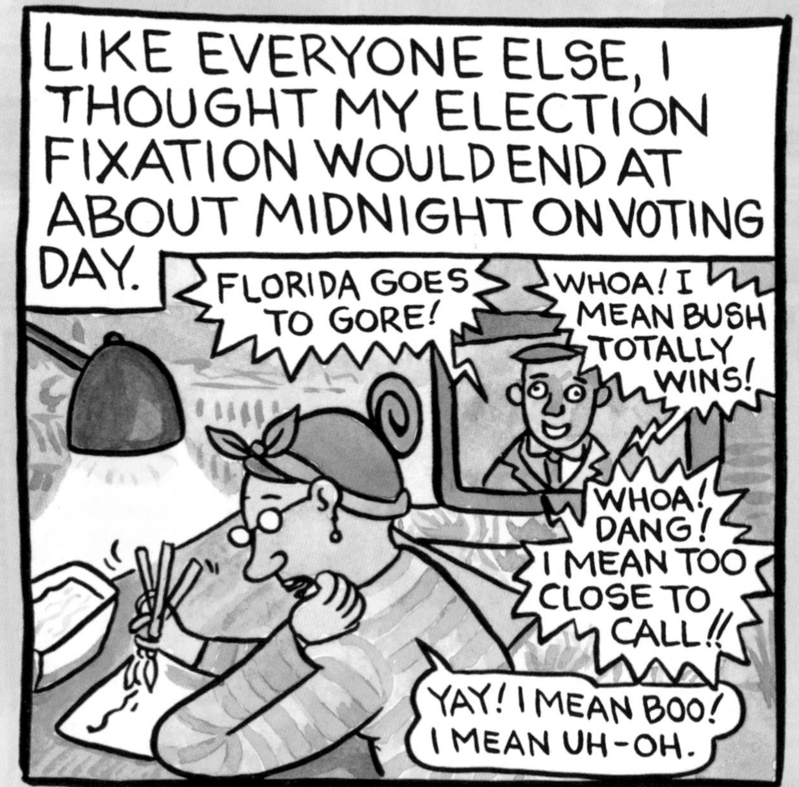
LIKE EVERYONE ELSE, I THOUGHT MY ELECTION FIXATION WOULD END AT ABOUT MIDNIGHT ON VOTING DAY.
FLORIDA GOES TO GORE!
WHOA! I MEAN BUSH TOTALLY WINS!
WHOA! DANG! I MEAN TOO CLOSE TO CALL!!
YAY! I MEAN BOO! I MEAN UH-OH.

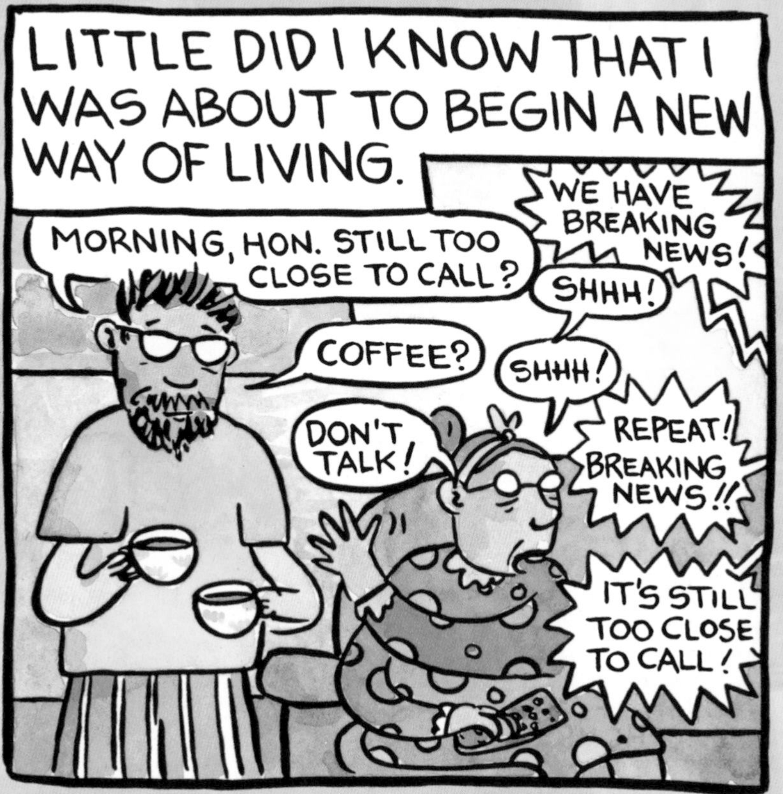
LITTLE DID I KNOW THAT I WAS ABOUT TO BEGIN A NEW WAY OF LIVING.
MORNING, HON. STILL TOO CLOSE TO CALL?
WE HAVE BREAKING NEWS!
SHHH!
COFFEE?
SHHH!
DON'T TALK!
REPEAT! BREAKING NEWS!!
IT'S STILL TOO CLOSE TO CALL!

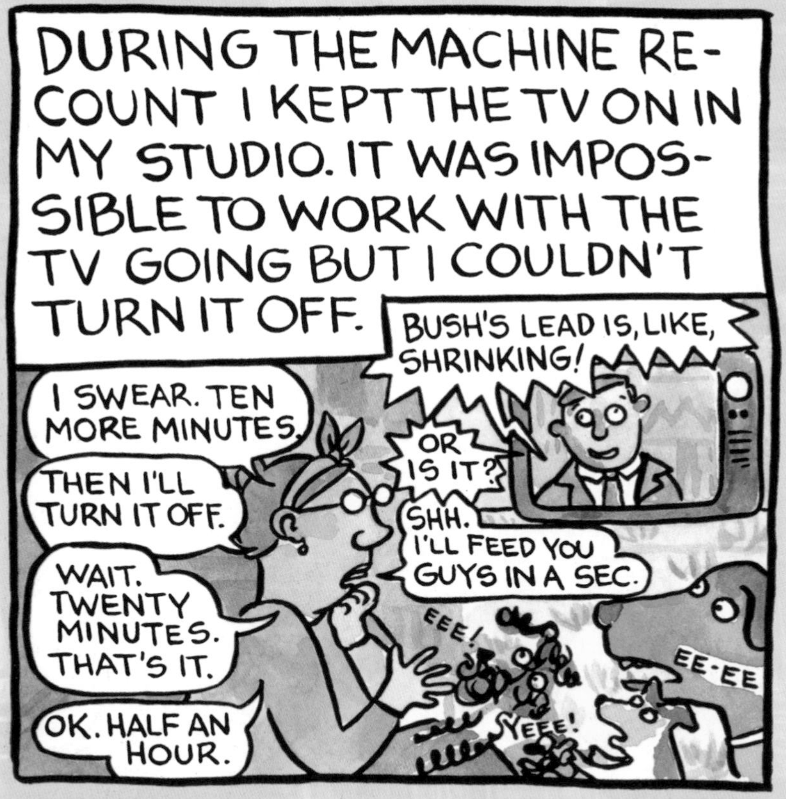
DURING THE MACHINE RECOUNT I KEPT THE TV ON IN MY STUDIO. IT WAS IMPOSSIBLE TO WORK WITH THE TV GOING BUT I COULDN'T TURN IT OFF.
BUSH'S LEAD IS, LIKE, SHRINKING!
I SWEAR. TEN MORE MINUTES.
OR IS IT?
THEN I'LL TURN IT OFF.
SHH. I'LL FEED YOU GUYS IN A SEC.
WAIT. TWENTY MINUTES. THAT'S IT.
EEE!
EE-EE
OK. HALF AN HOUR.
YEEE!

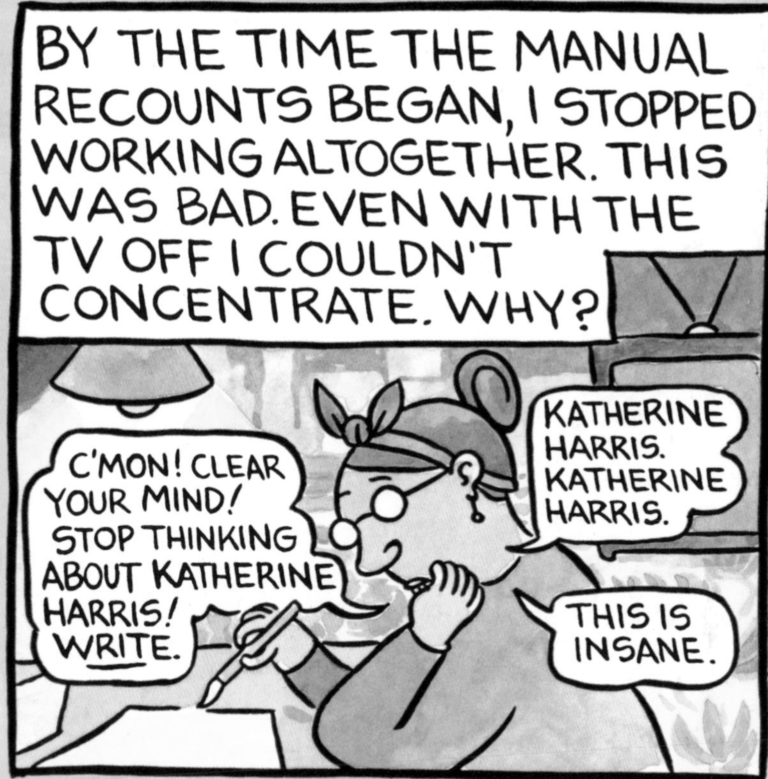
BY THE TIME THE MANUAL RECOUNTS BEGAN, I STOPPED WORKING ALTOGETHER. THIS WAS BAD. EVEN WITH THE TV OFF I COULDN'T CONCENTRATE. WHY?
KATHERINE HARRIS. KATHERINE HARRIS.
C'MON! CLEAR YOUR MIND! STOP THINKING ABOUT KATHERINE HARRIS! WRITE.
THIS IS INSANE.

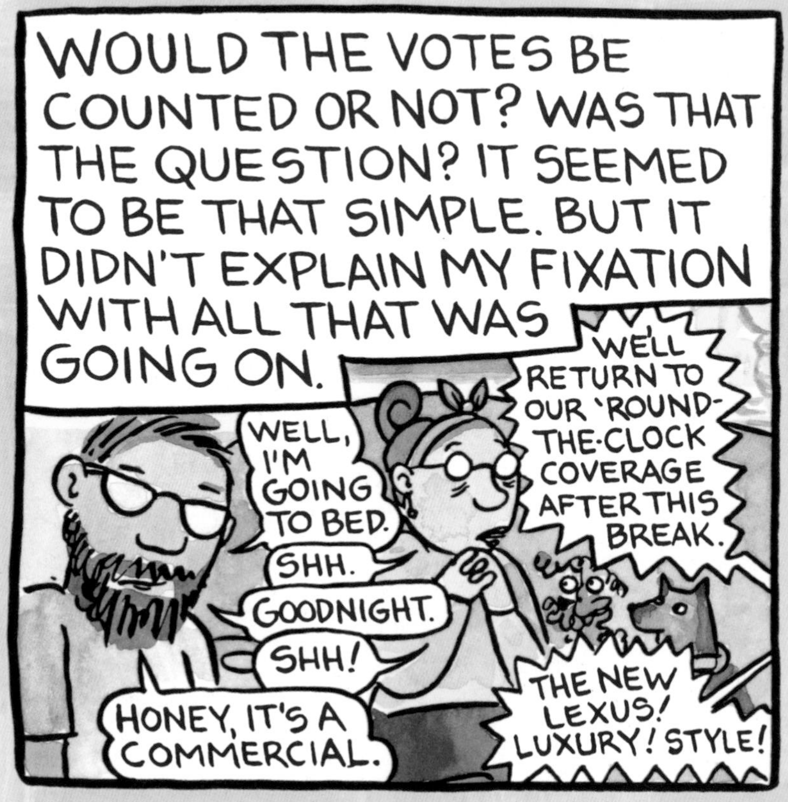
WOULD THE VOTES BE COUNTED OR NOT? WAS THAT THE QUESTION? IT SEEMED TO BE THAT SIMPLE. BUT IT DIDN'T EXPLAIN MY FIXATION WITH ALL THAT WAS GOING ON.
WE'LL RETURN TO OUR 'ROUND-THE-CLOCK COVERAGE AFTER THIS BREAK.
WELL, I'M GOING TO BED.
SHH.
GOODNIGHT.
SHH!
HONEY, IT'S A COMMERCIAL.
THE NEW LEXUS! LUXURY! STYLE!

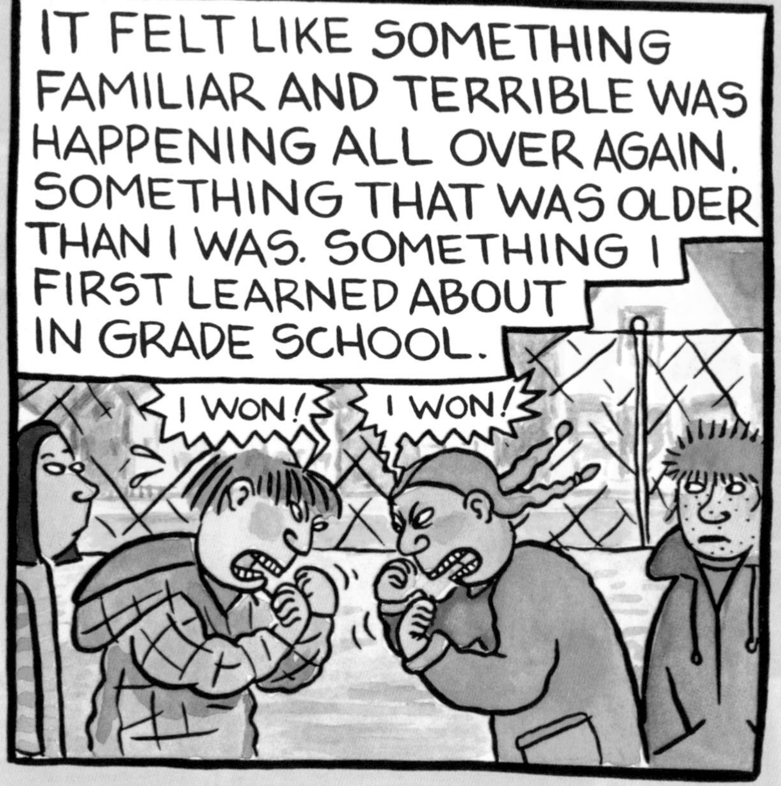
IT FELT LIKE SOMETHING FAMILIAR AND TERRIBLE WAS HAPPENING ALL OVER AGAIN. SOMETHING THAT WAS OLDER THAN I WAS. SOMETHING I FIRST LEARNED ABOUT IN GRADE SCHOOL.
I WON!
I WON!

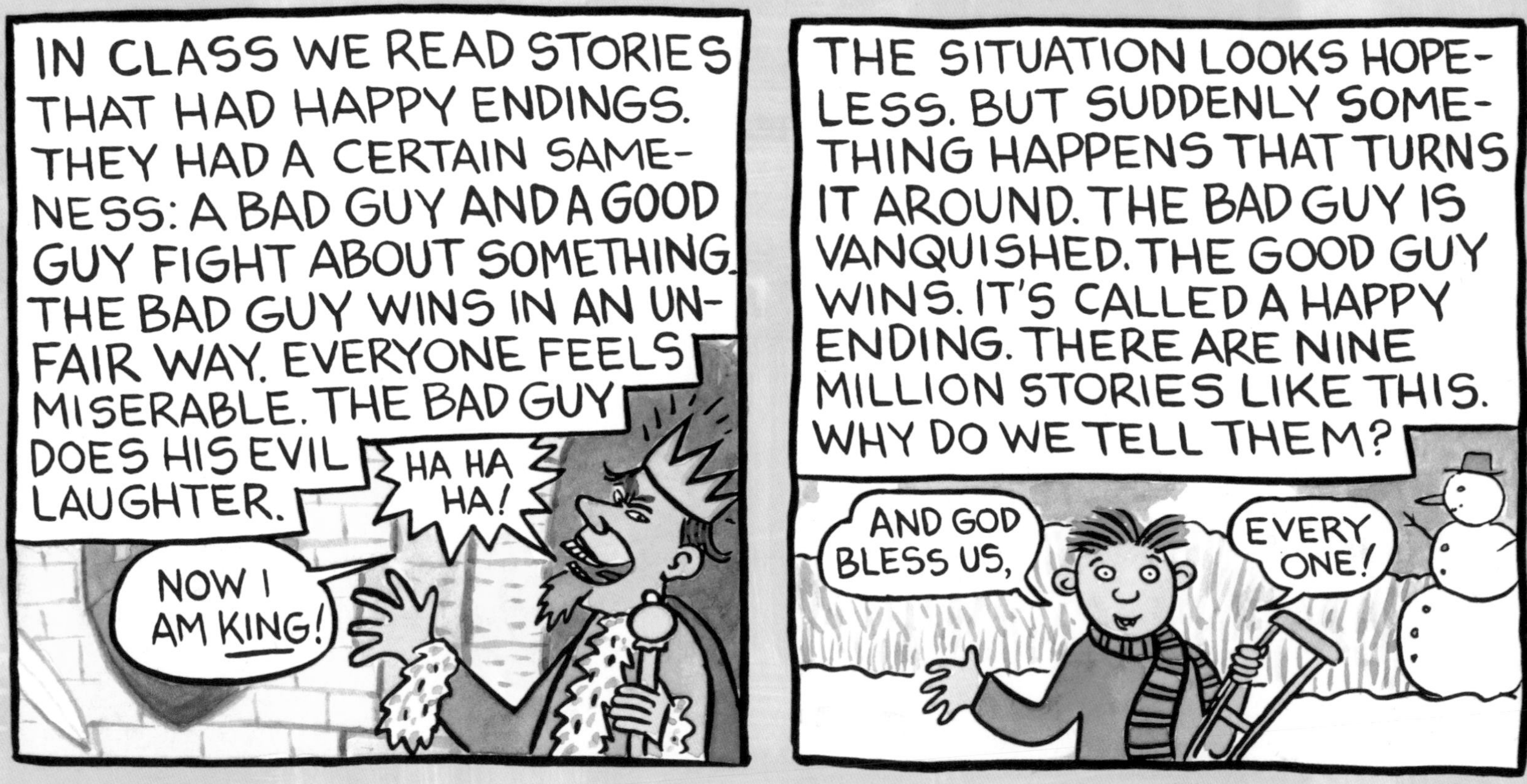
IN CLASS WE READ STORIES THAT HAD HAPPY ENDINGS. THEY HAD A CERTAIN SAMENESS: A BAD GUY AND A GOOD GUY FIGHT ABOUT SOMETHING. THE BAD GUY WINS IN AN UNFAIR WAY. EVERYONE FEELS MISERABLE. THE BAD GUY DOES HIS EVIL LAUGHTER.
HA HA HA!
NOW I AM KING!
THE SITUATION LOOKS HOPELESS. BUT SUDDENLY SOMETHING HAPPENS THAT TURNS IT AROUND. THE BAD GUY IS VANQUISHED. THE GOOD GUY WINS. IT'S CALLED A HAPPY ENDING. THERE ARE NINE MILLION STORIES LIKE THIS. WHY DO WE TELL THEM?
AND GOD BLESS US,
EVERY ONE!

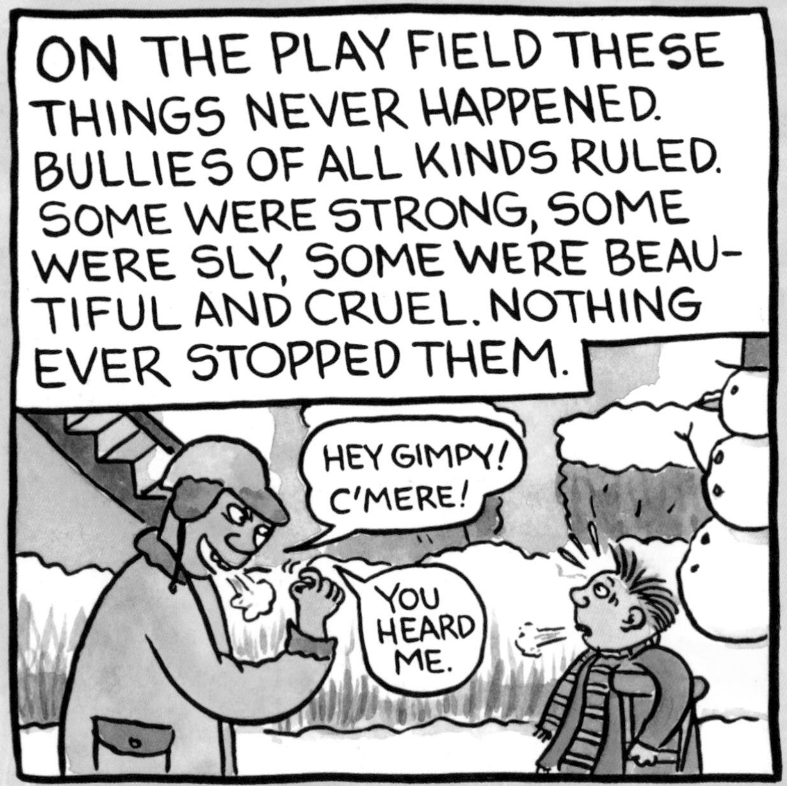
ON THE PLAY FIELD THESE THINGS NEVER HAPPENED. BULLIES OF ALL KINDS RULED. SOME WERE STRONG, SOME WERE SLY, SOME WERE BEAUTIFUL AND CRUEL. NOTHING EVER STOPPED THEM.
HEY GIMPY! C'MERE!
YOU HEARD ME.

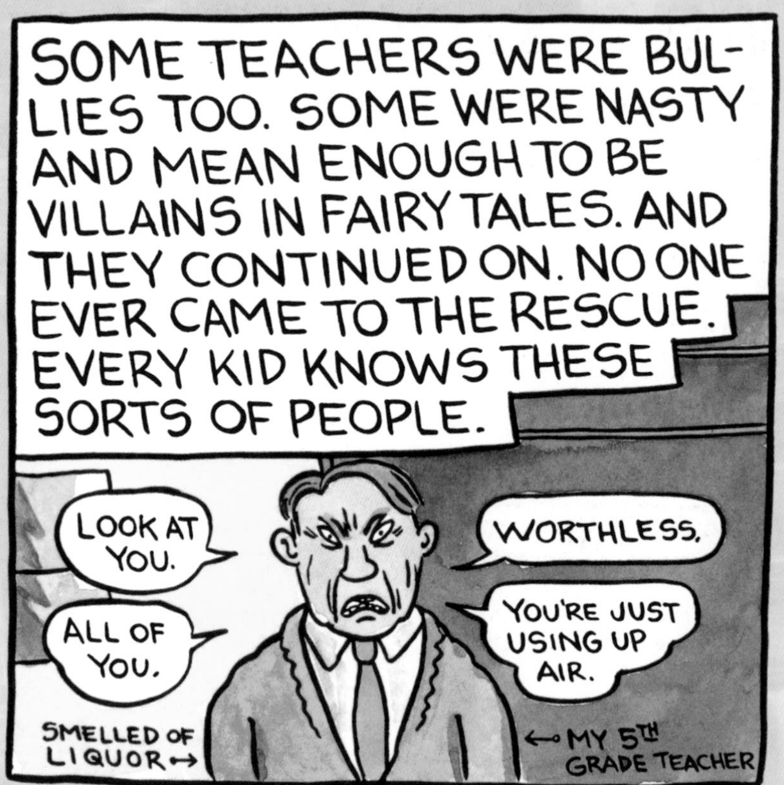
SOME TEACHERS WERE BULLIES TOO. SOME WERE NASTY AND MEAN ENOUGH TO BE VILLAINS IN FAIRY TALES. AND THEY CONTINUED ON. NO ONE EVER CAME TO THE RESCUE. EVERY KID KNOWS THESE SORTS OF PEOPLE.
LOOK AT YOU.
ALL OF YOU.
WORTHLESS.
YOU'RE JUST USING UP AIR.
SMELLED OF LIQUOR→
←MY 5TH GRADE TEACHER

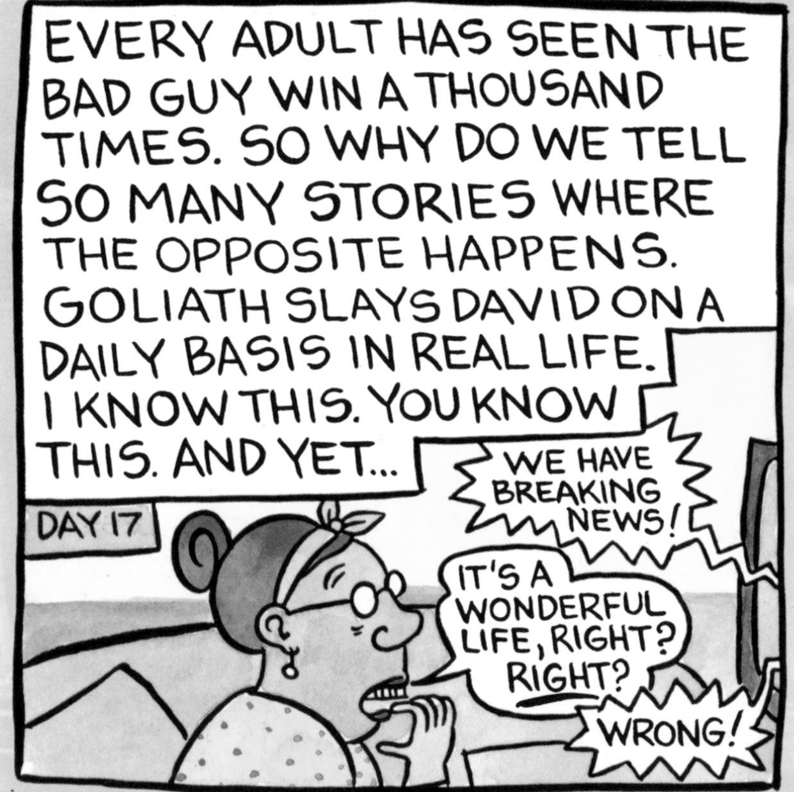
EVERY ADULT HAS SEEN THE BAD GUY WIN A THOUSAND TIMES. SO WHY DO WE TELL SO MANY STORIES WHERE THE OPPOSITE HAPPENS. GOLIATH SLAYS DAVID ON A DAILY BASIS IN REAL LIFE. I KNOW THIS. YOU KNOW THIS. AND YET...
DAY 17
WE HAVE BREAKING NEWS!
IT'S A WONDERFUL LIFE, RIGHT? RIGHT?
WRONG!

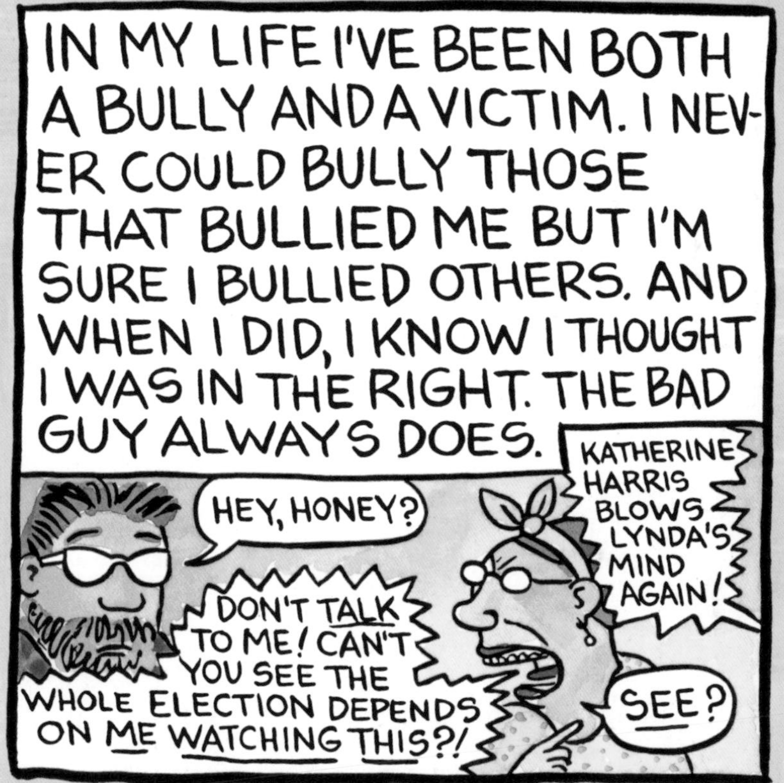
IN MY LIFE I'VE BEEN BOTH A BULLY AND A VICTIM. I NEVER COULD BULLY THOSE THAT BULLIED ME BUT I'M SURE I BULLIED OTHERS. AND WHEN I DID, I KNOW I THOUGHT I WAS IN THE RIGHT. THE BAD GUY ALWAYS DOES.
KATHERINE HARRIS BLOWS LYNDA'S MIND AGAIN!
HEY, HONEY?
DON'T TALK TO ME! CAN'T YOU SEE THE WHOLE ELECTION DEPENDS ON ME WATCHING THIS?!
SEE?

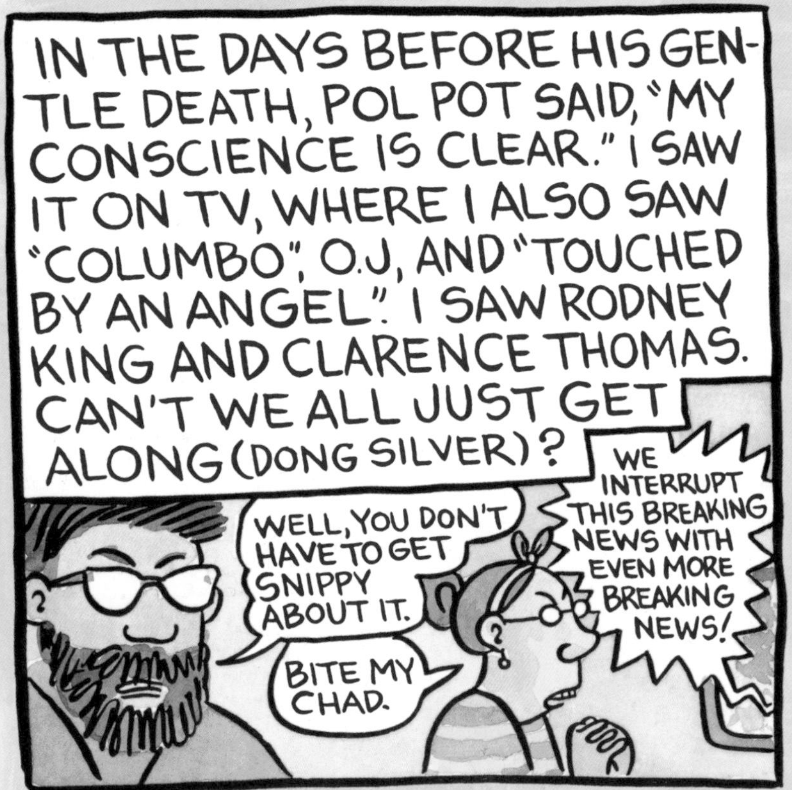
IN THE DAYS BEFORE HIS GENTLE DEATH, POL POT SAID, "MY CONSCIENCE IS CLEAR." I SAW IT ON TV, WHERE I ALSO SAW "COLUMBO", O.J, AND "TOUCHED BY AN ANGEL". I SAW RODNEY KING AND CLARENCE THOMAS. CAN'T WE ALL JUST GET ALONG (DONG SILVER)?
WE INTERRUPT THIS BREAKING NEWS WITH EVEN MORE BREAKING NEWS!
WELL, YOU DON'T HAVE TO GET SNIPPY ABOUT IT.
BITE MY CHAD.

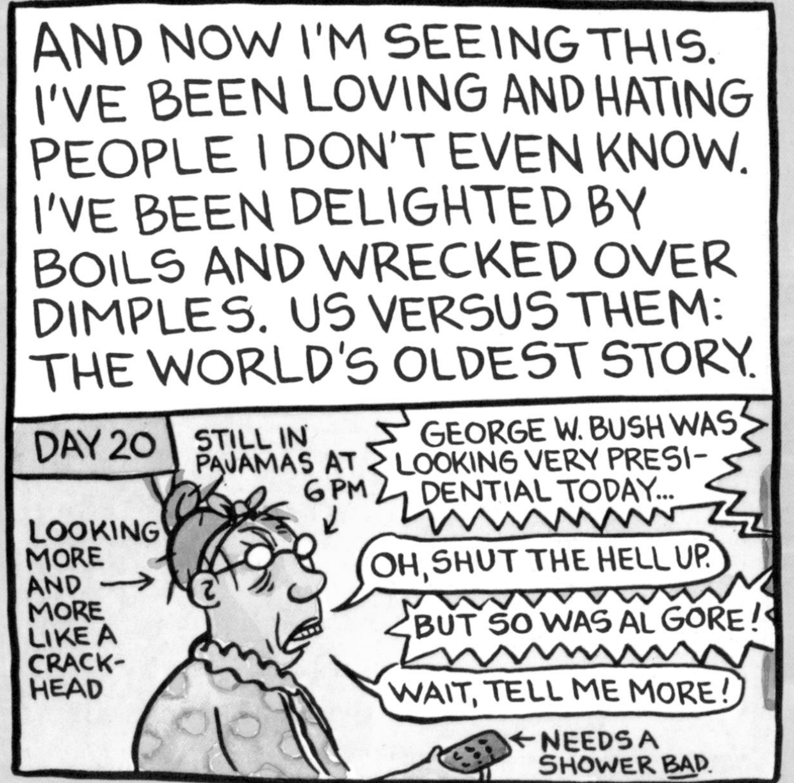
AND NOW I'M SEEING THIS. I'VE BEEN LOVING AND HATING PEOPLE I DON'T EVEN KNOW. I'VE BEEN DELIGHTED BY BOILS AND WRECKED OVER DIMPLES. US VERSUS THEM: THE WORLD'S OLDEST STORY.
DAY 20
STILL IN PAJAMAS AT 6 PM
LOOKING MORE AND MORE LIKE A CRACK-HEAD
GEORGE W. BUSH WAS LOOKING VERY PRESIDENTIAL TODAY...
OH, SHUT THE HELL UP.
BUT SO WAS AL GORE!
WAIT, TELL ME MORE!
NEEDS A SHOWER BAD.

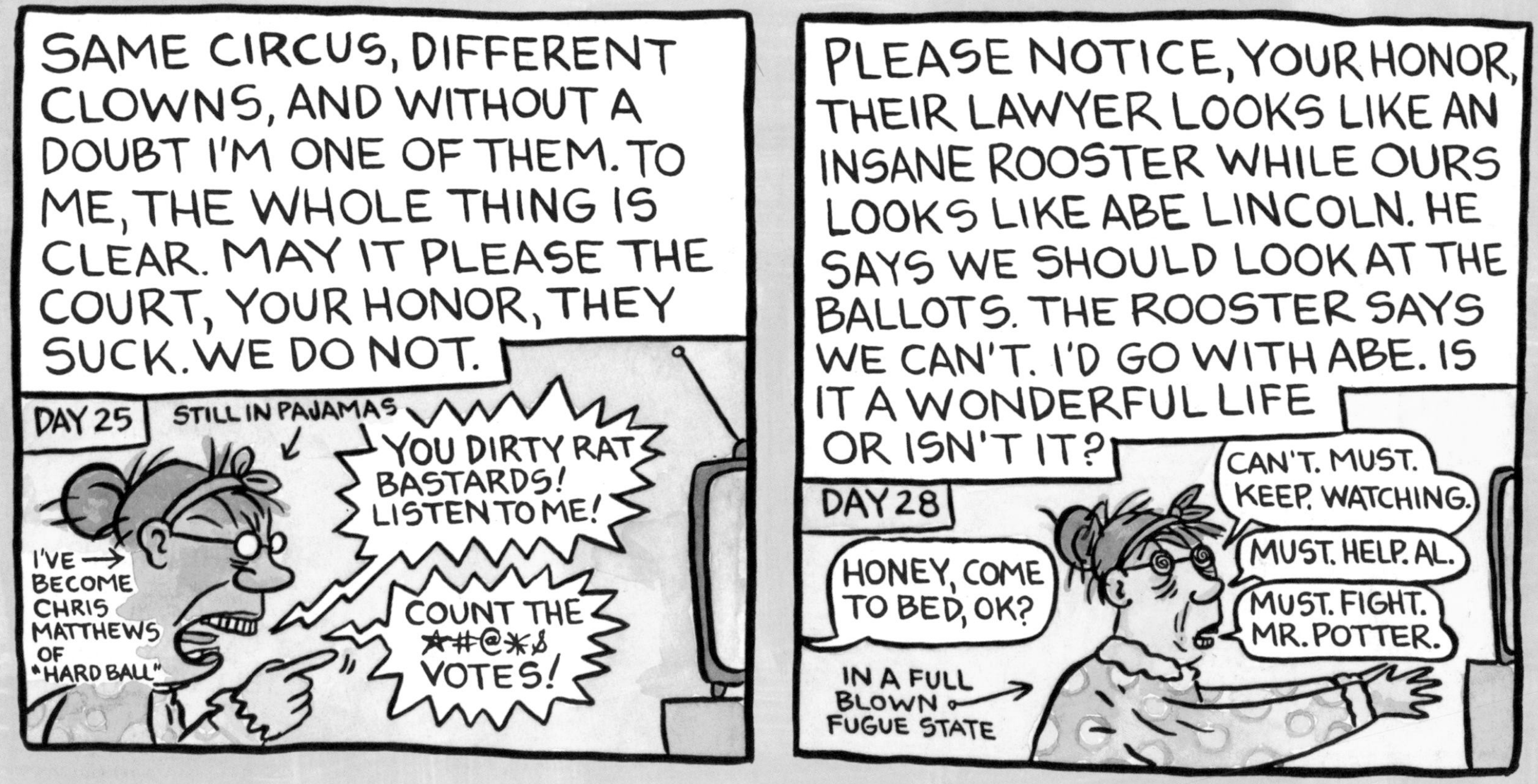

SAME CIRCUS, DIFFERENT CLOWNS, AND WITHOUT A DOUBT I'M ONE OF THEM. TO ME, THE WHOLE THING IS CLEAR. MAY IT PLEASE THE COURT, YOUR HONOR, THEY SUCK. WE DO NOT.
DAY 25
STILL IN PAJAMAS
YOU DIRTY RAT BASTARDS! LISTEN TO ME!
I'VE BECOME CHRIS MATTHEWS OF "HARD BALL"
COUNT THE *#@*$ VOTES!
PLEASE NOTICE, YOUR HONOR, THEIR LAWYER LOOKS LIKE AN INSANE ROOSTER WHILE OURS LOOKS LIKE ABE LINCOLN. HE SAYS WE SHOULD LOOK AT THE BALLOTS. THE ROOSTER SAYS WE CAN'T. I'D GO WITH ABE. IS IT A WONDERFUL LIFE OR ISN'T IT?
DAY 28
CAN'T. MUST. KEEP. WATCHING.
MUST. HELP. AL.
HONEY, COME TO BED, OK?
MUST. FIGHT. MR. POTTER.
IN A FULL BLOWN FUGUE STATE

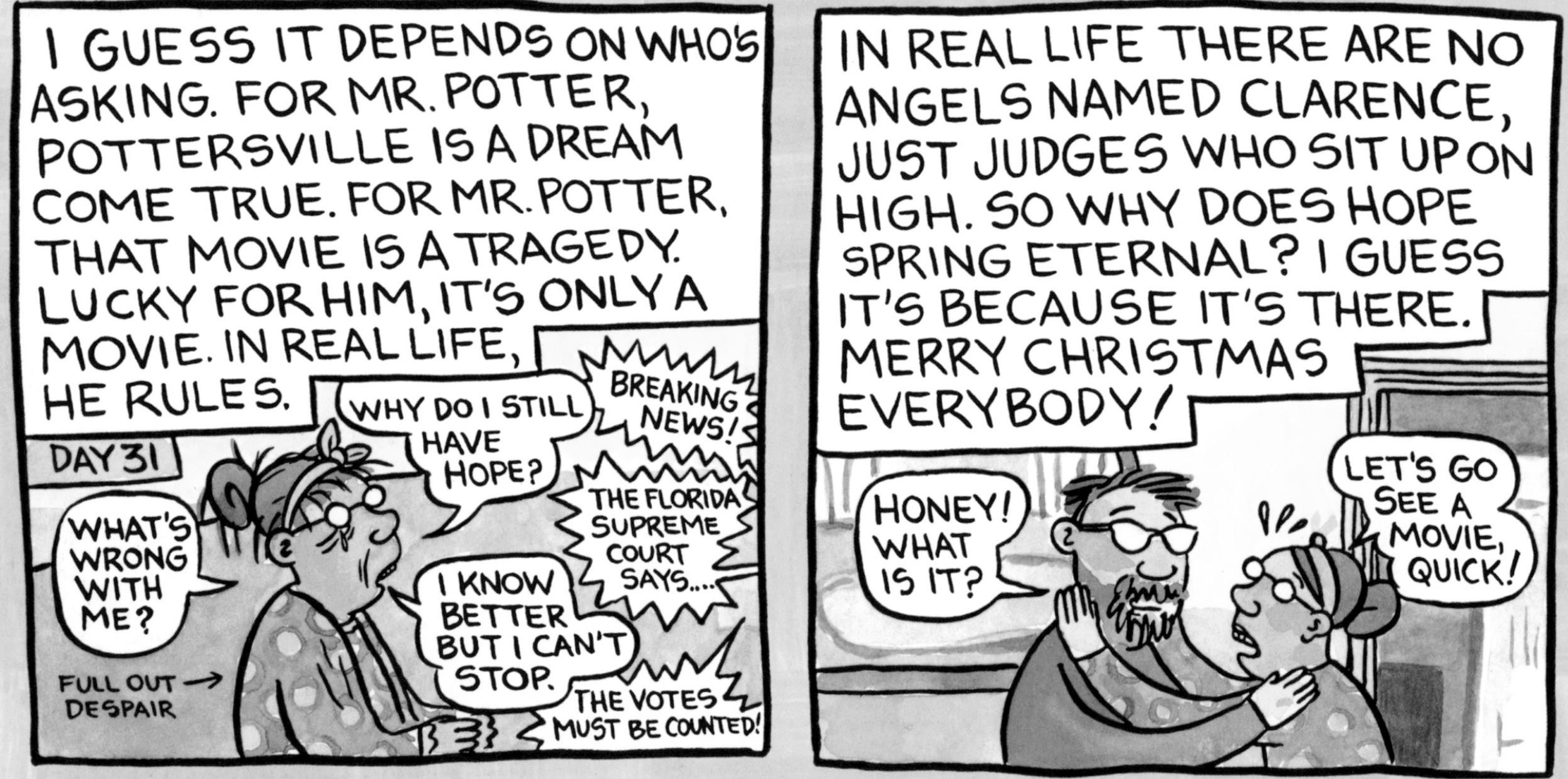
I GUESS IT DEPENDS ON WHO'S ASKING. FOR MR. POTTER, POTTERSVILLE IS A DREAM COME TRUE. FOR MR. POTTER, THAT MOVIE IS A TRAGEDY. LUCKY FOR HIM, IT'S ONLY A MOVIE. IN REAL LIFE, HE RULES.
DAY 31
WHAT'S WRONG WITH ME?
WHY DO I STILL HAVE HOPE?
I KNOW BETTER BUT I CAN'T STOP.
FULL OUT DESPAIR
BREAKING NEWS!
THE FLORIDA SUPREME COURT SAYS....
THE VOTES MUST BE COUNTED!
IN REAL LIFE THERE ARE NO ANGELS NAMED CLARENCE, JUST JUDGES WHO SIT UP ON HIGH. SO WHY DOES HOPE SPRING ETERNAL? I GUESS IT'S BECAUSE IT'S THERE. MERRY CHRISTMAS EVERYBODY!
HONEY! WHAT IS IT?
LET'S GO SEE A MOVIE, QUICK!

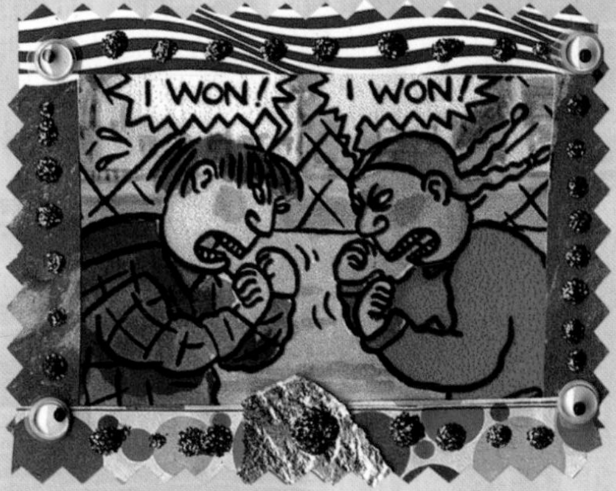
I WON!
I WON!

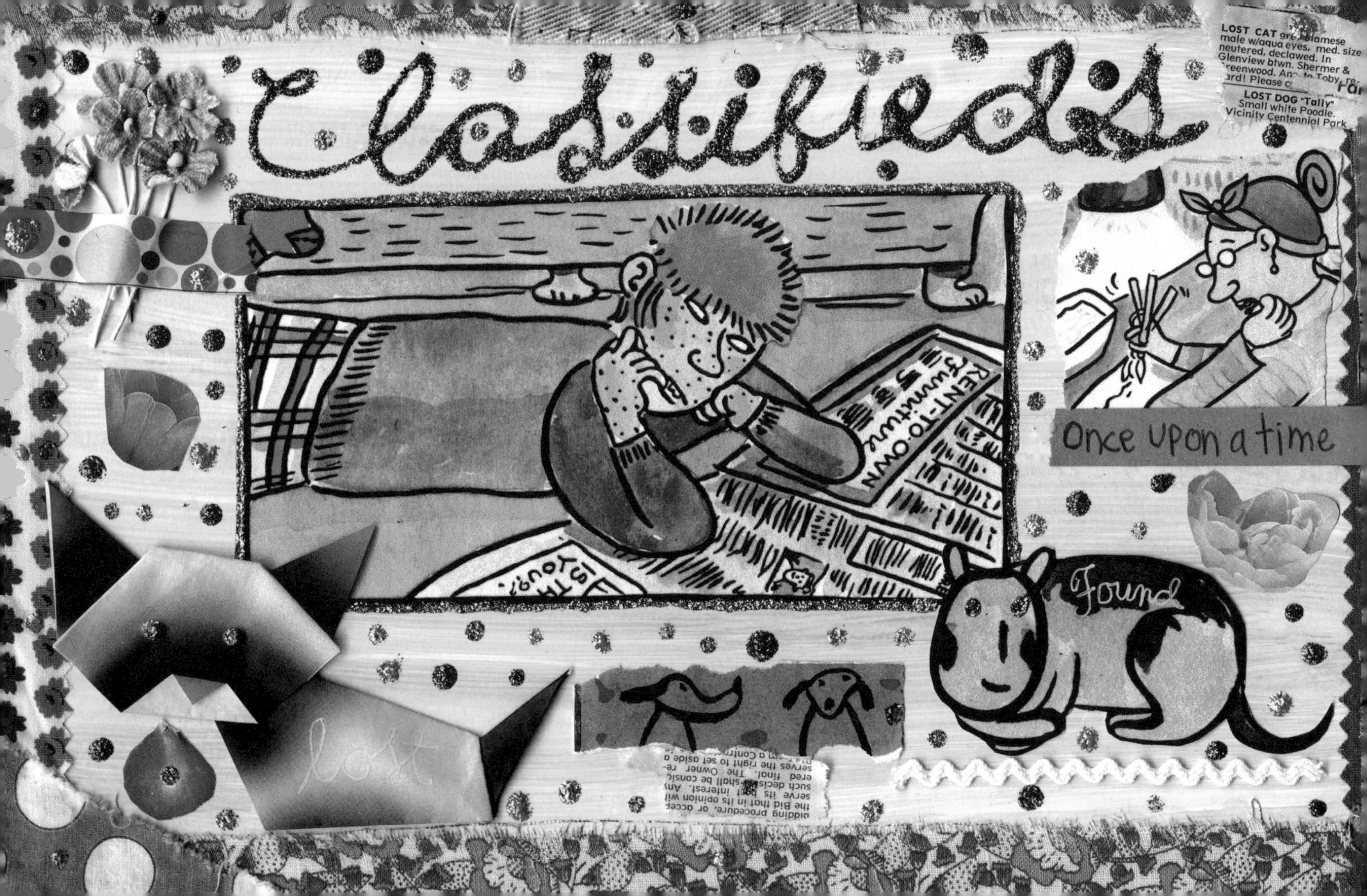
Classifieds
LOST CAT
male w/aqua eyes, med. size
neutered, declawed. In
Glenview btwn. Shermer &
LOST DOG "Tally"
Small white Poodle.
Vicinity Centennial Park
RENT-TO-OWN
Furniture
Once upon a time
Found
lost

too

SENSITIVE

Adoption	1005
Assumed Name	1008
Auction	1010
Bid Notices	1013
Divorce	1023
Foreclosures	1031
Foundation Notices	1034
Judicial Sales	1043
(with Legal Description)	
Liens	1046
Name Change	1053
Plan Commission	1060
Hearings	
Probate	1062
Public Notices	1066
Take Notices	1078
Zoning Hearings	1092
Legal Notice	1095
(Miscellaneous)	

TODAY'S DEMON:

CHERISH IS THE WORD I USE TO DIS-CRI-IBE...

LOST AND FOUND

CLASSIFIED

Birth Announcements	102
Car Pool & Rides	103
Disclaimer of Debts	104
Greetings	105
In Memoriam	106
Lost & Found	107
Personals	108
Announcements	109
Just A Friend	112
Single Scene	113

107- Lost & Found

FOUND Cat, short hair, striped, gray, black & white, young male, in N. Barrington

FOUND DOG Collie/Corgie mix, Fem, 2-3 yrs old. Tan.

FOUND : Key Chain, near

FREE Dirt/Clay Mix
NEED LOCATION FOR DUMPING LARGE AMOUNTS OF CLEAN FILL

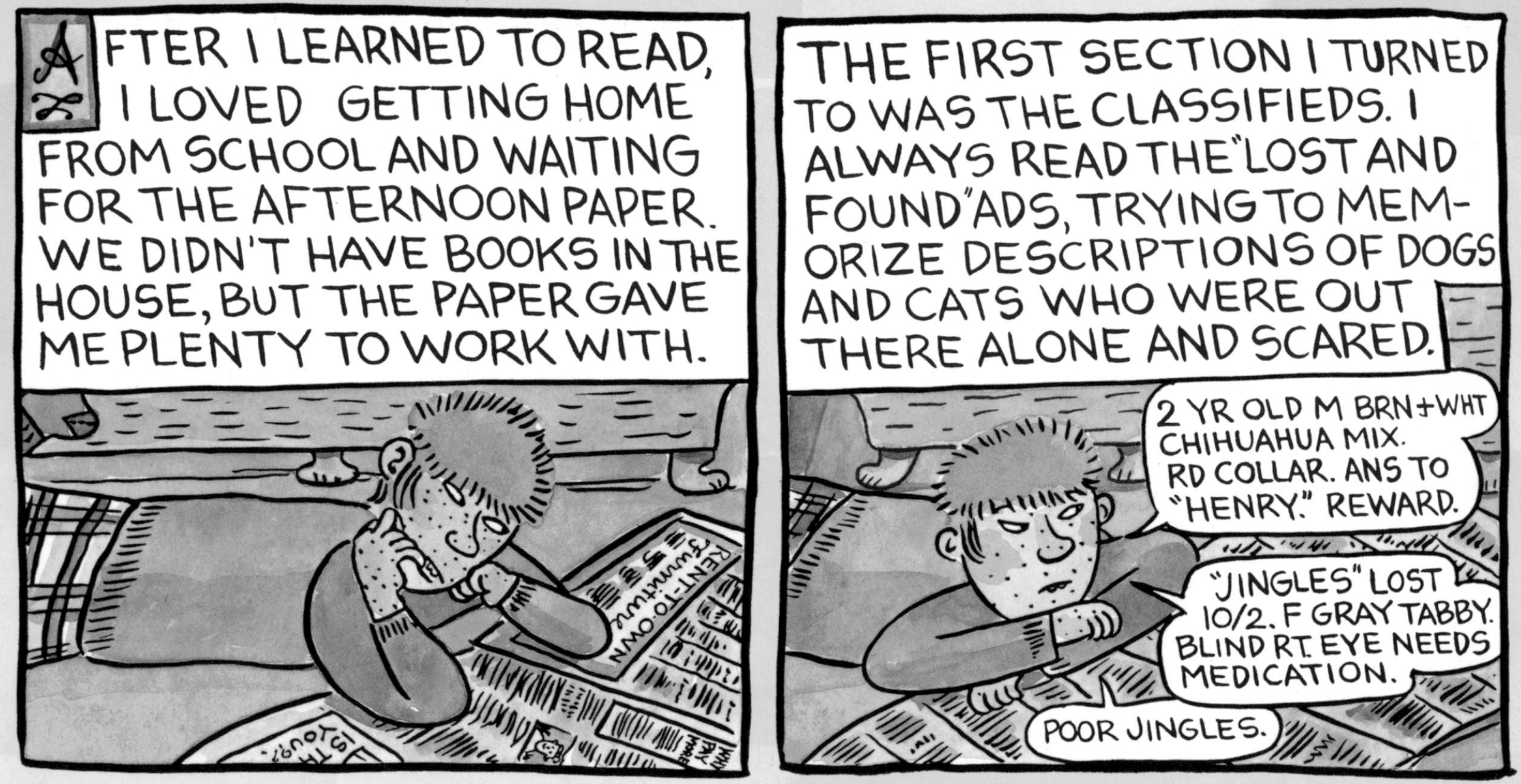
AFTER I LEARNED TO READ, I LOVED GETTING HOME FROM SCHOOL AND WAITING FOR THE AFTERNOON PAPER. WE DIDN'T HAVE BOOKS IN THE HOUSE, BUT THE PAPER GAVE ME PLENTY TO WORK WITH.
RENT-TO-OWN
furniture
THE FIRST SECTION I TURNED TO WAS THE CLASSIFIEDS. I ALWAYS READ THE "LOST AND FOUND" ADS, TRYING TO MEMORIZE DESCRIPTIONS OF DOGS AND CATS WHO WERE OUT THERE ALONE AND SCARED.
2 YR OLD M BRN+WHT CHIHUAHUA MIX. RD COLLAR. ANS TO "HENRY." REWARD.
"JINGLES" LOST 10/2. F GRAY TABBY. BLIND RT. EYE NEEDS MEDICATION.
POOR JINGLES.

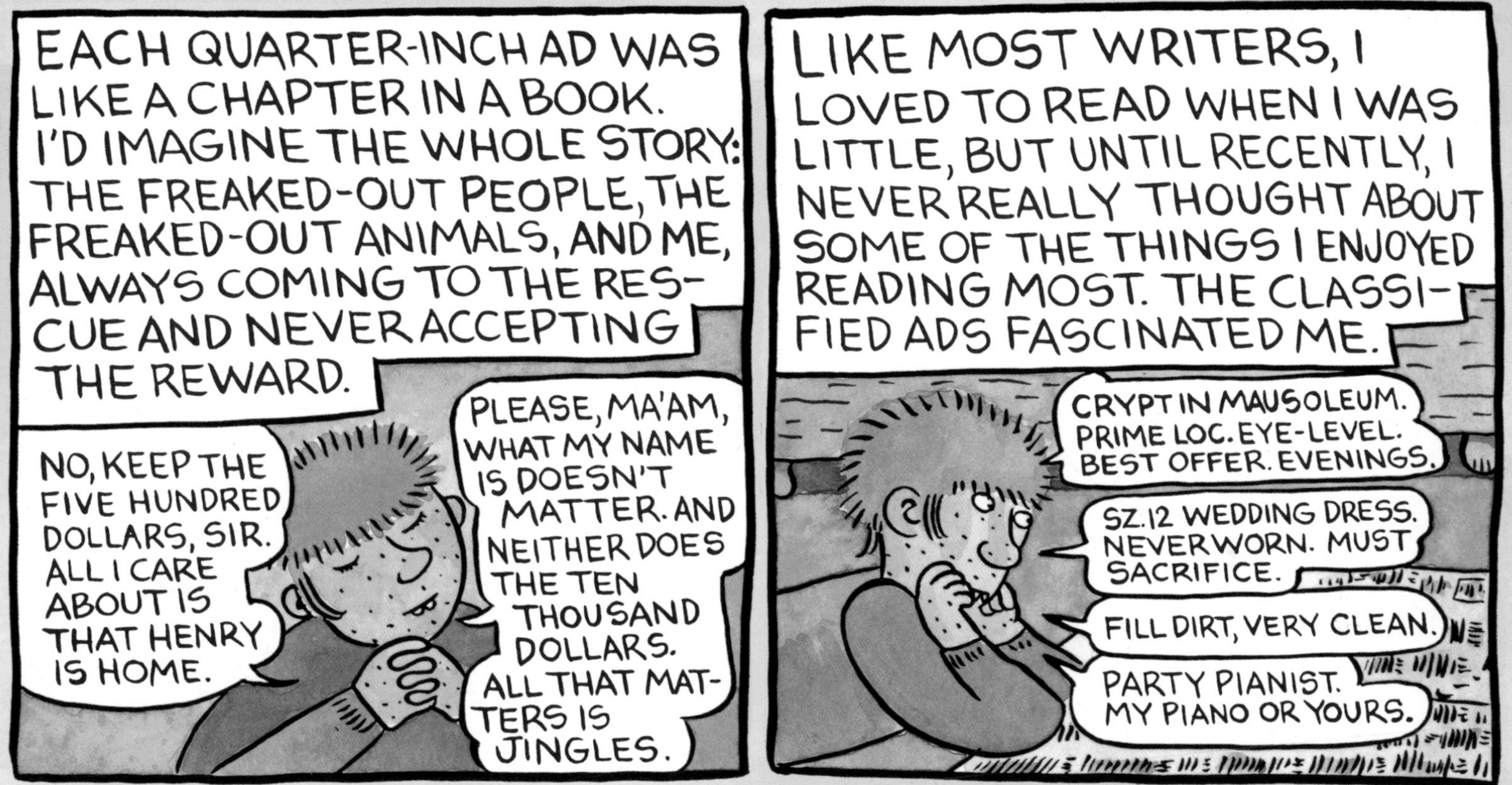
EACH QUARTER-INCH AD WAS LIKE A CHAPTER IN A BOOK. I'D IMAGINE THE WHOLE STORY: THE FREAKED-OUT PEOPLE, THE FREAKED-OUT ANIMALS, AND ME, ALWAYS COMING TO THE RESCUE AND NEVER ACCEPTING THE REWARD.
NO, KEEP THE FIVE HUNDRED DOLLARS, SIR. ALL I CARE ABOUT IS THAT HENRY IS HOME.
PLEASE, MA'AM, WHAT MY NAME IS DOESN'T MATTER. AND NEITHER DOES THE TEN THOUSAND DOLLARS. ALL THAT MATTERS IS JINGLES.
LIKE MOST WRITERS, I LOVED TO READ WHEN I WAS LITTLE, BUT UNTIL RECENTLY, I NEVER REALLY THOUGHT ABOUT SOME OF THE THINGS I ENJOYED READING MOST. THE CLASSIFIED ADS FASCINATED ME.
CRYPT IN MAUSOLEUM. PRIME LOC. EYE-LEVEL. BEST OFFER. EVENINGS.
SZ.12 WEDDING DRESS. NEVER WORN. MUST SACRIFICE.
FILL DIRT, VERY CLEAN.
PARTY PIANIST. MY PIANO OR YOURS.

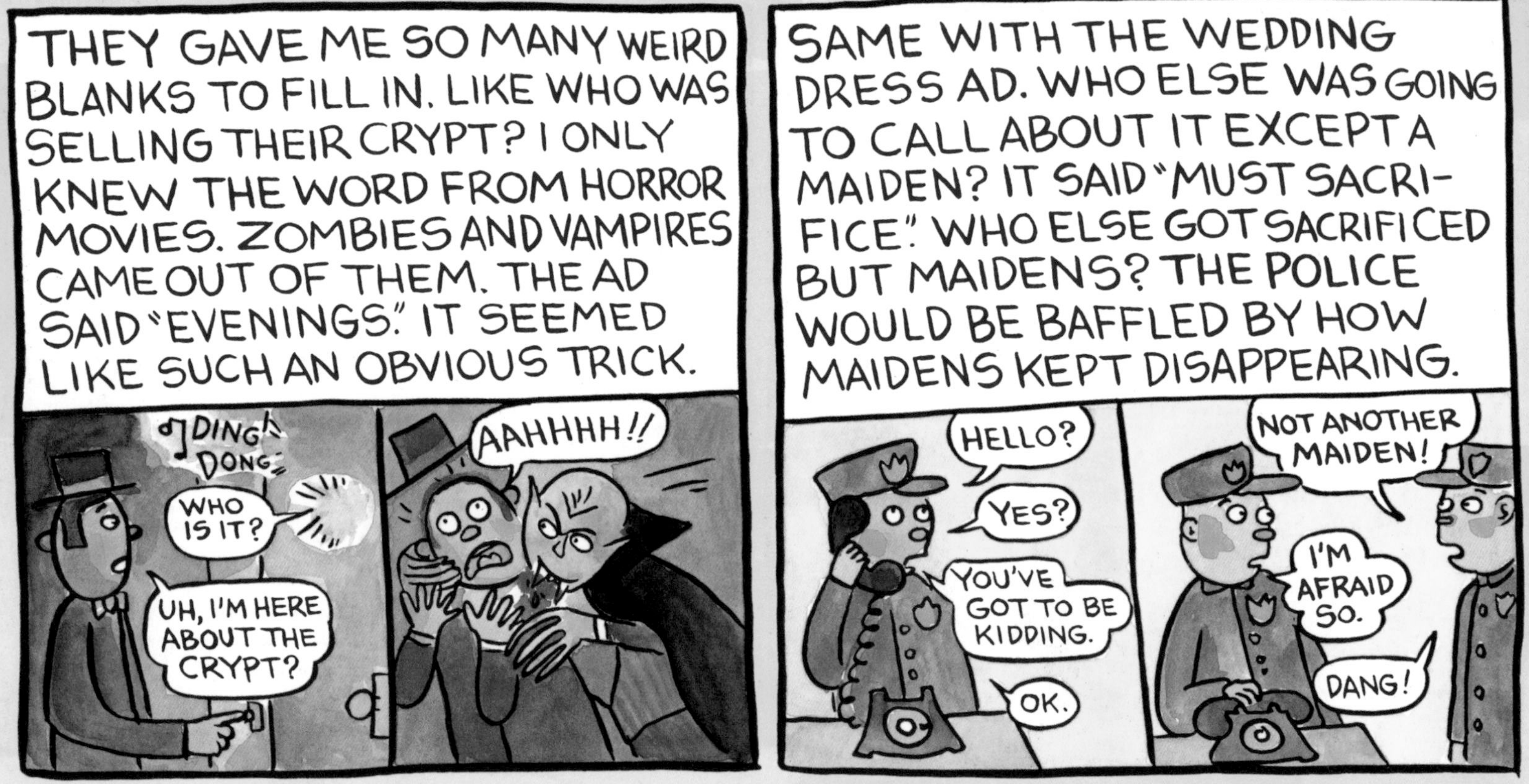
THEY GAVE ME SO MANY WEIRD BLANKS TO FILL IN. LIKE WHO WAS SELLING THEIR CRYPT? I ONLY KNEW THE WORD FROM HORROR MOVIES. ZOMBIES AND VAMPIRES CAME OUT OF THEM. THE AD SAID "EVENINGS." IT SEEMED LIKE SUCH AN OBVIOUS TRICK.
DING DONG
WHO IS IT?
UH, I'M HERE ABOUT THE CRYPT?
AAHHHH!!
SAME WITH THE WEDDING DRESS AD. WHO ELSE WAS GOING TO CALL ABOUT IT EXCEPT A MAIDEN? IT SAID "MUST SACRIFICE." WHO ELSE GOT SACRIFICED BUT MAIDENS? THE POLICE WOULD BE BAFFLED BY HOW MAIDENS KEPT DISAPPEARING.
HELLO?
YES?
YOU'VE GOT TO BE KIDDING.
OK.
NOT ANOTHER MAIDEN!
I'M AFRAID SO.
DANG!

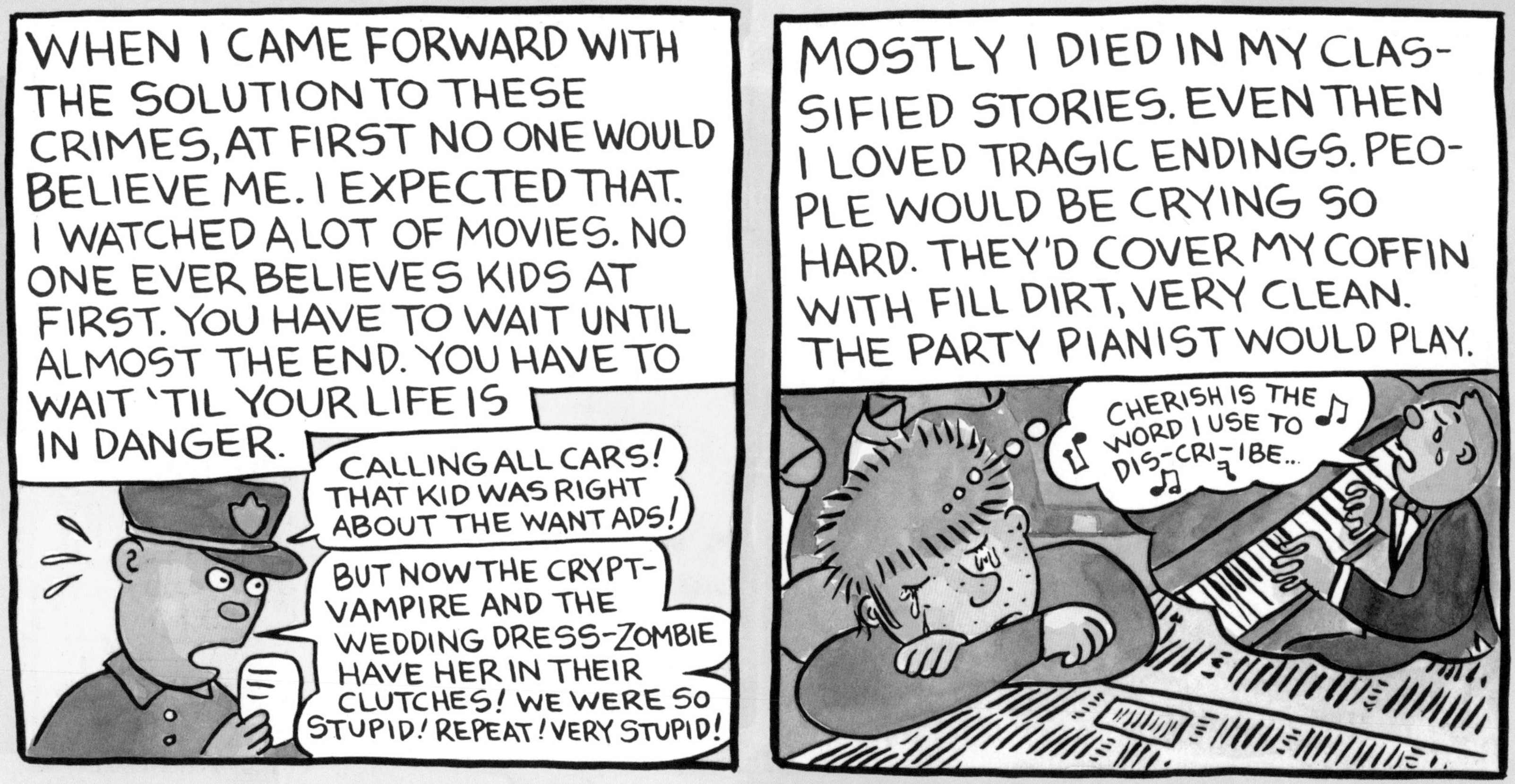
WHEN I CAME FORWARD WITH THE SOLUTION TO THESE CRIMES, AT FIRST NO ONE WOULD BELIEVE ME. I EXPECTED THAT. I WATCHED A LOT OF MOVIES. NO ONE EVER BELIEVES KIDS AT FIRST. YOU HAVE TO WAIT UNTIL ALMOST THE END. YOU HAVE TO WAIT 'TIL YOUR LIFE IS IN DANGER.
CALLING ALL CARS! THAT KID WAS RIGHT ABOUT THE WANT ADS!
BUT NOW THE CRYPT-VAMPIRE AND THE WEDDING DRESS-ZOMBIE HAVE HER IN THEIR CLUTCHES! WE WERE SO STUPID! REPEAT! VERY STUPID!
MOSTLY I DIED IN MY CLASSIFIED STORIES. EVEN THEN I LOVED TRAGIC ENDINGS. PEOPLE WOULD BE CRYING SO HARD. THEY'D COVER MY COFFIN WITH FILL DIRT, VERY CLEAN. THE PARTY PIANIST WOULD PLAY.
CHERISH IS THE WORD I USE TO DIS-CRI-IBE...

WHEN I READ ABOUT WRITER'S LIVES, THERE ARE USUALLY STORIES ABOUT WRITING FROM THE TIME THEY WERE LITTLE. I NEVER WROTE ANYTHING UNTIL I WAS A TEENAGER, AND THEN IT WAS ONLY A DIARY THAT SAID THE SAME THING OVER AND OVER.

I thought Bill liked me but turns out he doesn't. I'm so depressed about Bill. He didn't call me. I can't stop thinking about Bill.

WRITERS TALK ABOUT ALL THE BOOKS THEY LOVED WHEN THEY WERE CHILDREN. CLASSIC STORIES I NEVER READ, BUT I LIED ABOUT BECAUSE I WAS SCARED IT WAS PROOF I WASN'T REALLY A WRITER.

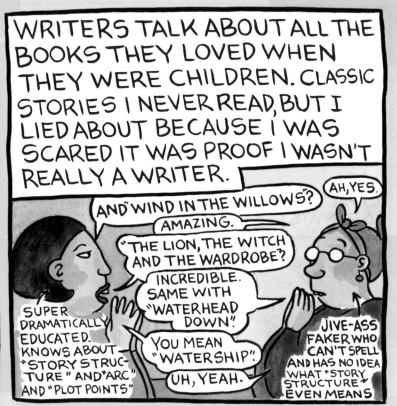

AND WIND IN THE WILLOWS?

AMAZING.

"THE LION, THE WITCH AND THE WARDROBE?"

INCREDIBLE. SAME WITH "WATERHEAD DOWN".

YOU MEAN "WATERSHIP".

UH, YEAH.

AH, YES.

SUPER DRAMATICALLY EDUCATED. KNOWS ABOUT "STORY STRUCTURE" AND "ARC" AND "PLOT POINTS"

JIVE-ASS FAKER WHO CAN'T SPELL AND HAS NO IDEA WHAT "STORY STRUCTURE" EVEN MEANS

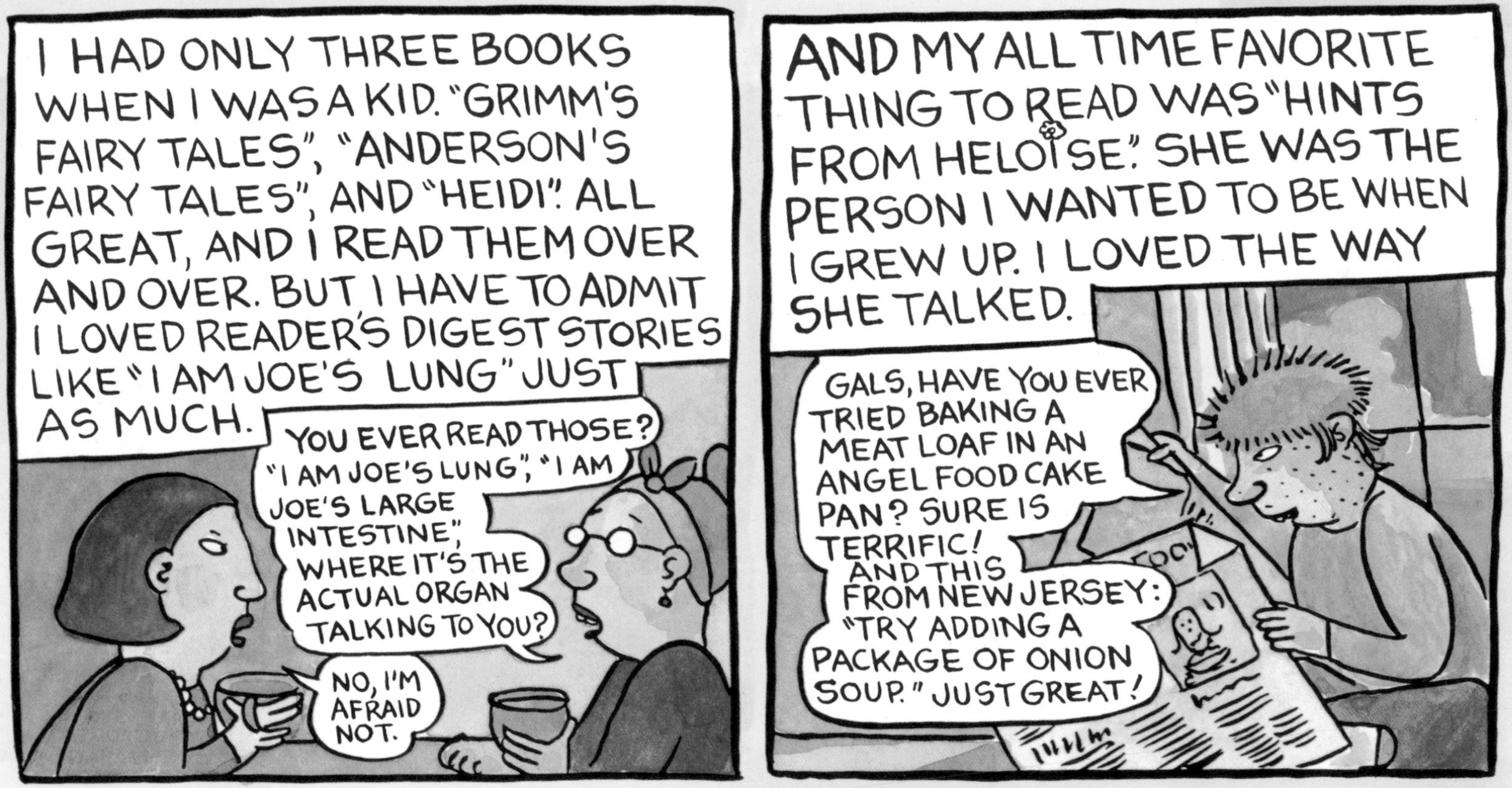
I HAD ONLY THREE BOOKS WHEN I WAS A KID. "GRIMM'S FAIRY TALES", "ANDERSON'S FAIRY TALES", AND "HEIDI". ALL GREAT, AND I READ THEM OVER AND OVER. BUT I HAVE TO ADMIT I LOVED READER'S DIGEST STORIES LIKE "I AM JOE'S LUNG" JUST AS MUCH.
YOU EVER READ THOSE? "I AM JOE'S LUNG", "I AM JOE'S LARGE INTESTINE", WHERE IT'S THE ACTUAL ORGAN TALKING TO YOU?
NO, I'M AFRAID NOT.
AND MY ALL TIME FAVORITE THING TO READ WAS "HINTS FROM HELOISE." SHE WAS THE PERSON I WANTED TO BE WHEN I GREW UP. I LOVED THE WAY SHE TALKED.
GALS, HAVE YOU EVER TRIED BAKING A MEAT LOAF IN AN ANGEL FOOD CAKE PAN? SURE IS TERRIFIC!
AND THIS FROM NEW JERSEY: "TRY ADDING A PACKAGE OF ONION SOUP." JUST GREAT!

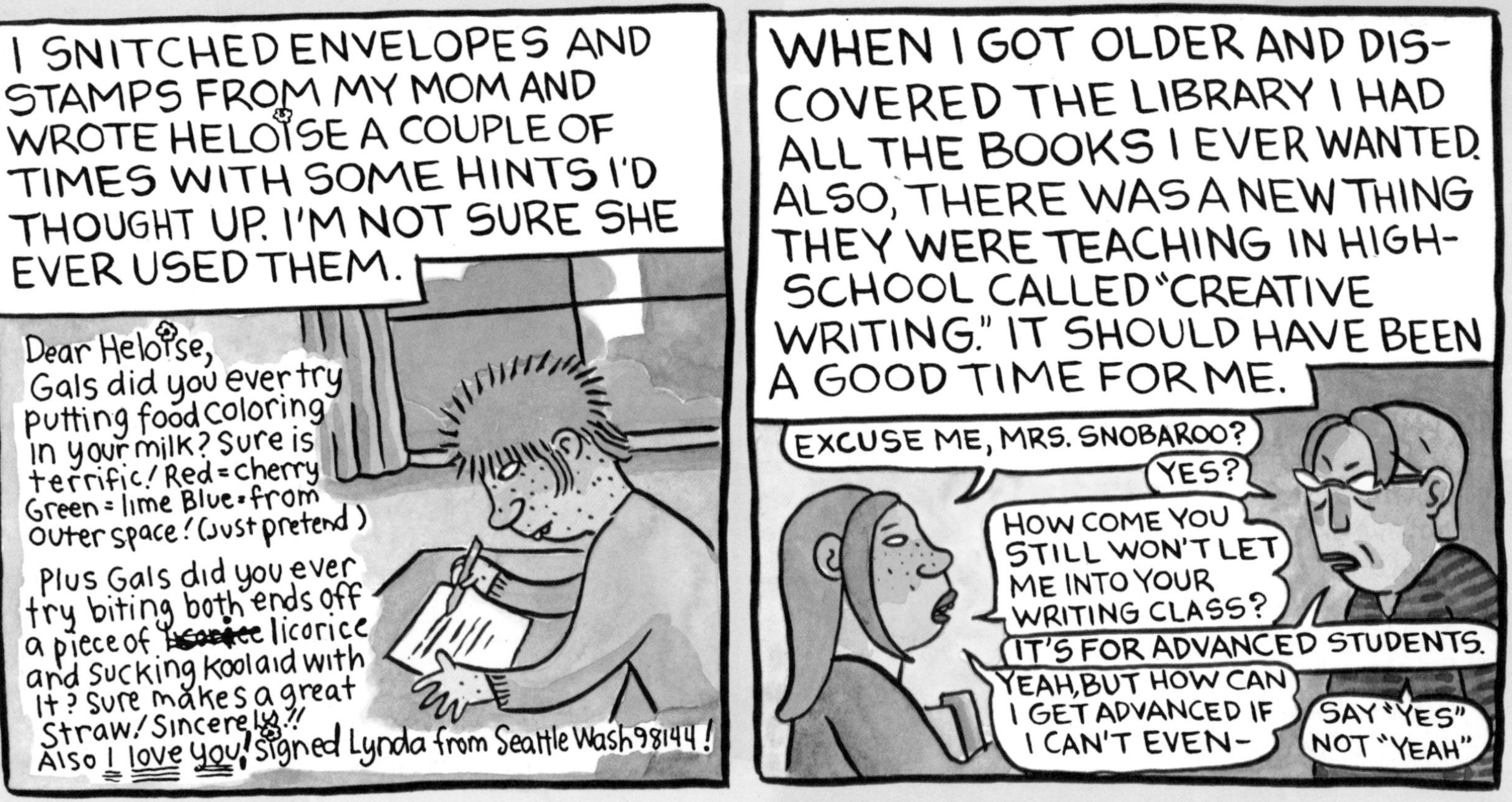
I SNITCHED ENVELOPES AND STAMPS FROM MY MOM AND WROTE HELOISE A COUPLE OF TIMES WITH SOME HINTS I'D THOUGHT UP. I'M NOT SURE SHE EVER USED THEM.
Dear Heloise,
Gals did you ever try putting food coloring in your milk? Sure is terrific! Red = cherry Green = lime Blue = from outer space! (Just pretend)
Plus Gals did you ever try biting both ends off a piece of licorice and sucking Koolaid with it? Sure makes a great straw! Sincerely!!! Also I love you! Signed Lynda from Seattle Wash 98144!
WHEN I GOT OLDER AND DISCOVERED THE LIBRARY I HAD ALL THE BOOKS I EVER WANTED. ALSO, THERE WAS A NEW THING THEY WERE TEACHING IN HIGH-SCHOOL CALLED "CREATIVE WRITING." IT SHOULD HAVE BEEN A GOOD TIME FOR ME.
EXCUSE ME, MRS. SNOBAROO?
YES?
HOW COME YOU STILL WON'T LET ME INTO YOUR WRITING CLASS?
IT'S FOR ADVANCED STUDENTS.
YEAH, BUT HOW CAN I GET ADVANCED IF I CAN'T EVEN-
SAY "YES" NOT "YEAH"

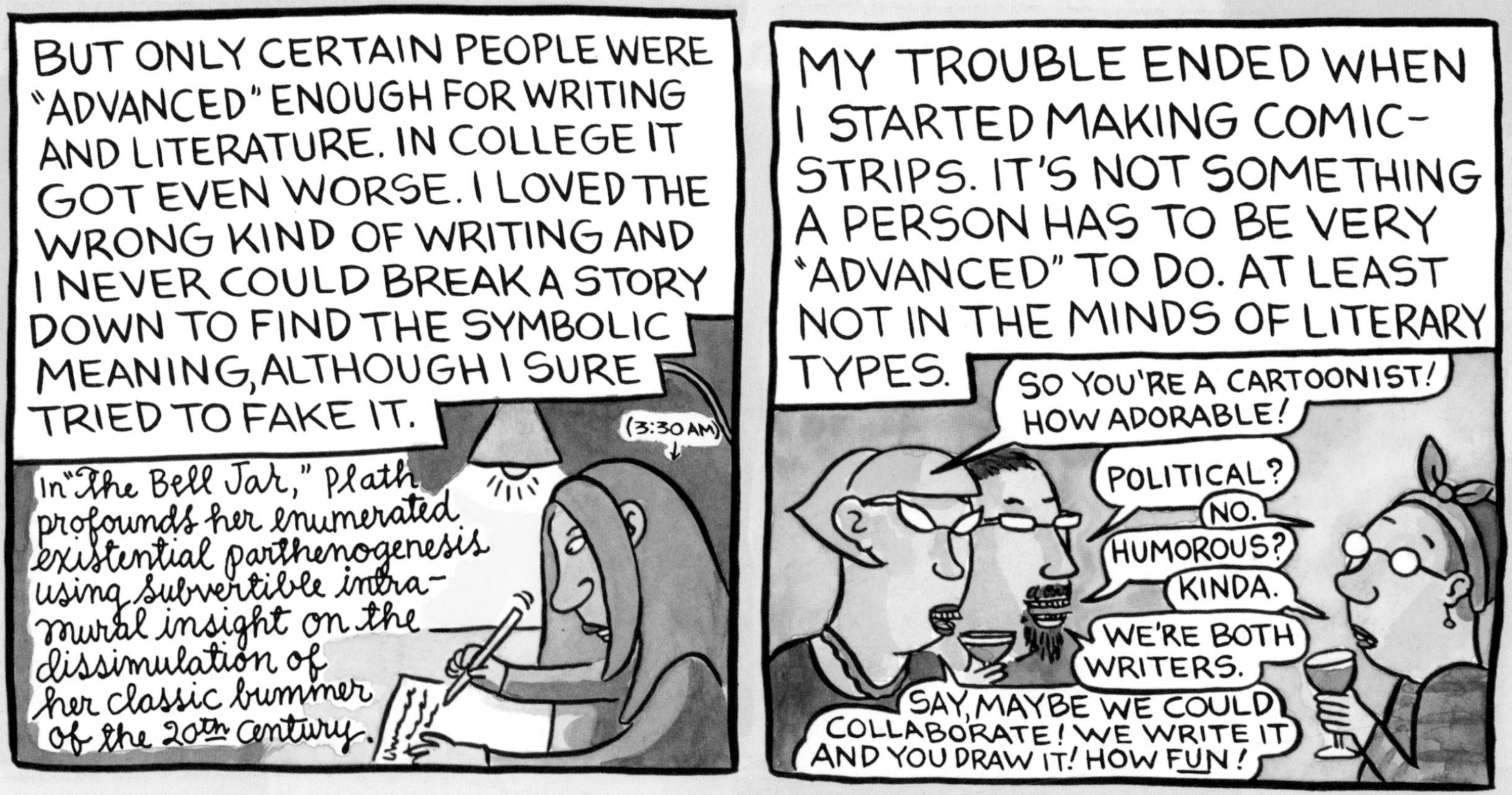
BUT ONLY CERTAIN PEOPLE WERE "ADVANCED" ENOUGH FOR WRITING AND LITERATURE. IN COLLEGE IT GOT EVEN WORSE. I LOVED THE WRONG KIND OF WRITING AND I NEVER COULD BREAK A STORY DOWN TO FIND THE SYMBOLIC MEANING, ALTHOUGH I SURE TRIED TO FAKE IT.
(3:30 AM)
In "The Bell Jar," Plath profounds her enumerated existential parthenogenesis using subvertible intra-mural insight on the dissimulation of her classic bummer of the 20th century.
MY TROUBLE ENDED WHEN I STARTED MAKING COMIC-STRIPS. IT'S NOT SOMETHING A PERSON HAS TO BE VERY "ADVANCED" TO DO. AT LEAST NOT IN THE MINDS OF LITERARY TYPES.
SO YOU'RE A CARTOONIST! HOW ADORABLE!
POLITICAL?
NO.
HUMOROUS?
KINDA.
WE'RE BOTH WRITERS.
SAY, MAYBE WE COULD COLLABORATE! WE WRITE IT AND YOU DRAW IT! HOW FUN!

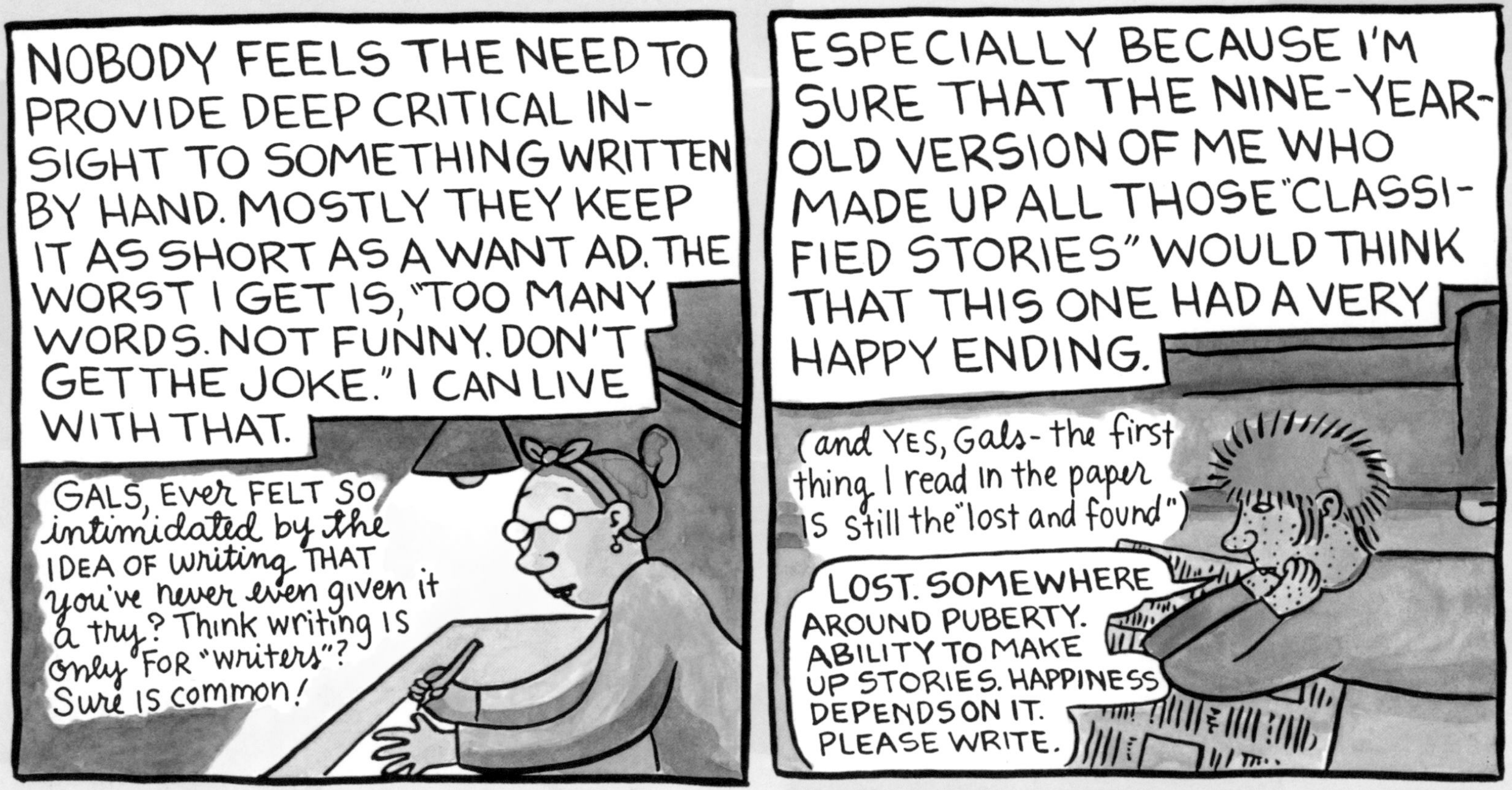

NOBODY FEELS THE NEED TO PROVIDE DEEP CRITICAL IN-SIGHT TO SOMETHING WRITTEN BY HAND. MOSTLY THEY KEEP IT AS SHORT AS A WANT AD. THE WORST I GET IS, "TOO MANY WORDS. NOT FUNNY. DON'T GET THE JOKE." I CAN LIVE WITH THAT.
GALS, EVER FELT SO intimidated by the IDEA OF writing THAT you've never even given it a try? Think writing IS only FOR "writers"? Sure IS common!
ESPECIALLY BECAUSE I'M SURE THAT THE NINE-YEAR-OLD VERSION OF ME WHO MADE UP ALL THOSE "CLASSI-FIED STORIES" WOULD THINK THAT THIS ONE HAD A VERY HAPPY ENDING.
(and YES, Gals- the first thing I read in the paper IS still the "lost and found")
LOST. SOMEWHERE AROUND PUBERTY. ABILITY TO MAKE UP STORIES. HAPPINESS DEPENDS ON IT. PLEASE WRITE.

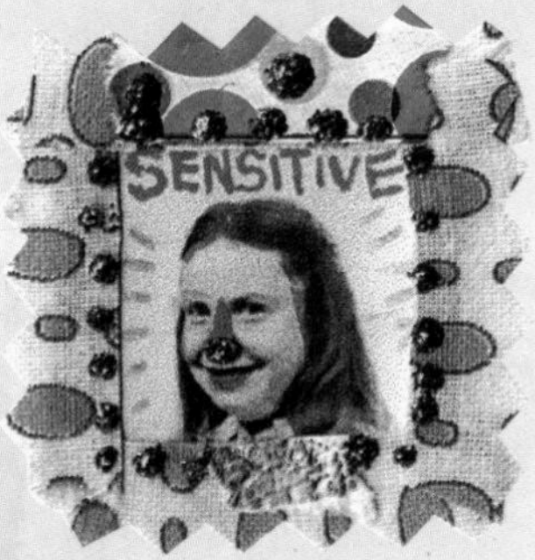
SENSITIVE

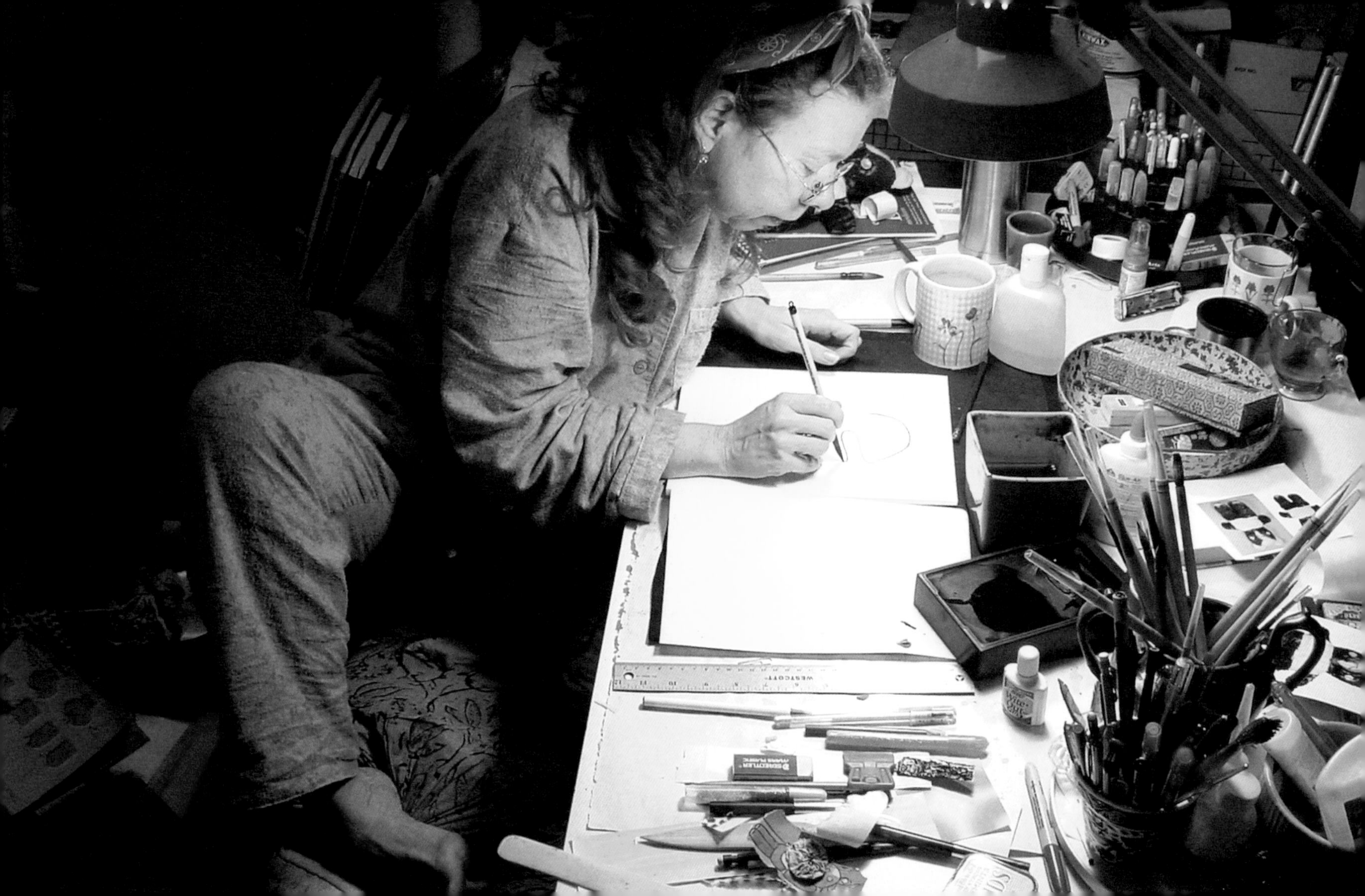
WESTCOTT

PAINT YOUR DEMON

Come On!
Don't you
want to
try it ??

JUST
TURN THE
PAGE →

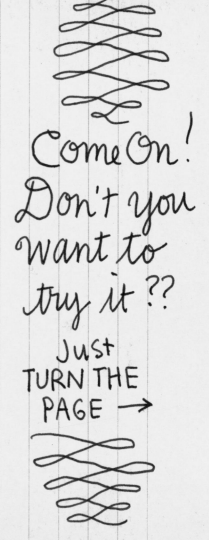

you will need AN INKSTONE ↵   AN INKSTICK ↵

water
area →

Grinding
area
↓

(This one
is hand-
carved)
→

make sure to get a NATURAL
stone — the man-made ones
aren't as good — at least 3 X 4 inches.
you can get a good, simple one for under $20.⁰⁰

made of soot compressed into
a hard stick — PERMANENT!!
ARCHIVAL!! Really fantastic!!
Comes in many shapes and
SIZES, plain and fancy,
a medium QUALITY inkstick
will work just fine.

A BRUSH ↓

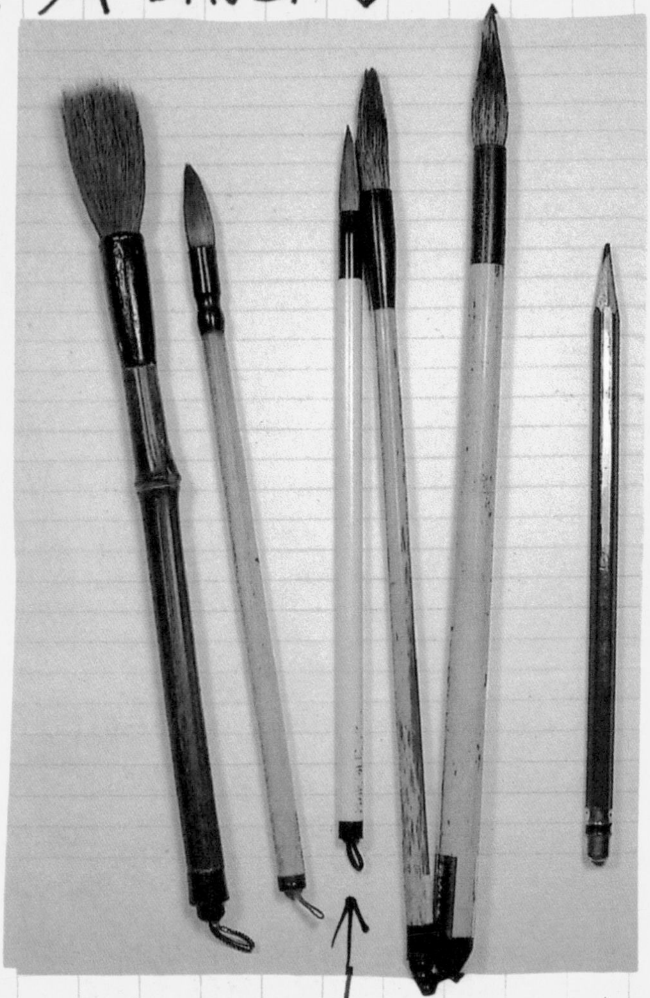

The demons came out of This one

asian style BRUSHES come in a LOT of sizes and HAIRSTYLES. The one I used for this book had a BRUSH HAIR LENGTH of 1 inch and a base diameter of 1/4 inch. The hair was pretty FIRM. For other kinds of paintings I use larger ones. A GOOD BRUSH is IMPORTANT!! But a good asian brush isn't insanely expensive! Keep them clean! Hang them to DRY!

I GET ALL OF MY SUPPLIES AT ACORNPLANET.COM.

YOU CAN E-MAIL THEM, ASK FOR A BEGINNERS SET-UP, AND THEY'LL Get you started!

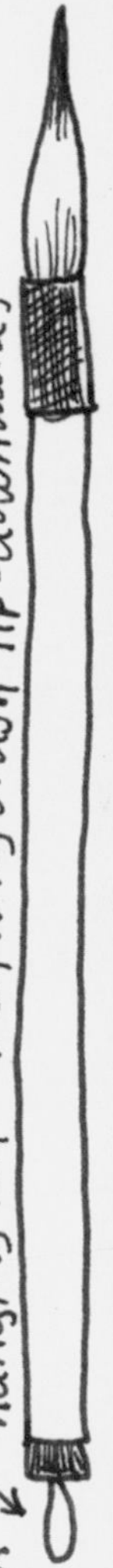
hanging loop - they hang brush-tip-downwards

JUST ADD water! ↳

and ADD INK! ↳

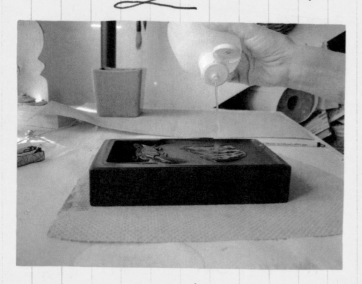

pour about a teaspoon onto the Grinding area. A plastic SQUIRT Bottle is perfect for this

although it's called GRINDING you actually USE very little pressure! Just move the INKStick in a light Circle Keeping the bottom of the INKStick Flat against the stone. Keep on going until It looks oily. Just mess around until you get It the way you LIKE IT!! It can take 5 or 10 minutes.

now HOLD your BRUSH ↙

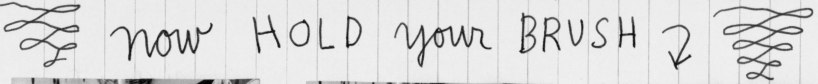

Wet your Brush in water and run it across a paper-towel to get Rid of excess water, Then Dip the TIP into the Ink, hold the BRUSH Straight up and down and slowly pull a line across the paper. There are MUCH BETTER instructions in books on Asian-style brushwork at your library!! But mostly you can learn alot by messing Around. I write the ALPHABET every day with a Brush.

Paint Your Demon!

MAKE FRESH INK EACH TIME YOU PAINT + Keep your inkstone clean!!

I like to PAINT on LEGAL paper or on the CLASSIFIED SECTION of the newspaper OR Even pages from OLD BOOKS! I will try ANY PAPER, typing paper, wrapping paper even PAPER BAGS!

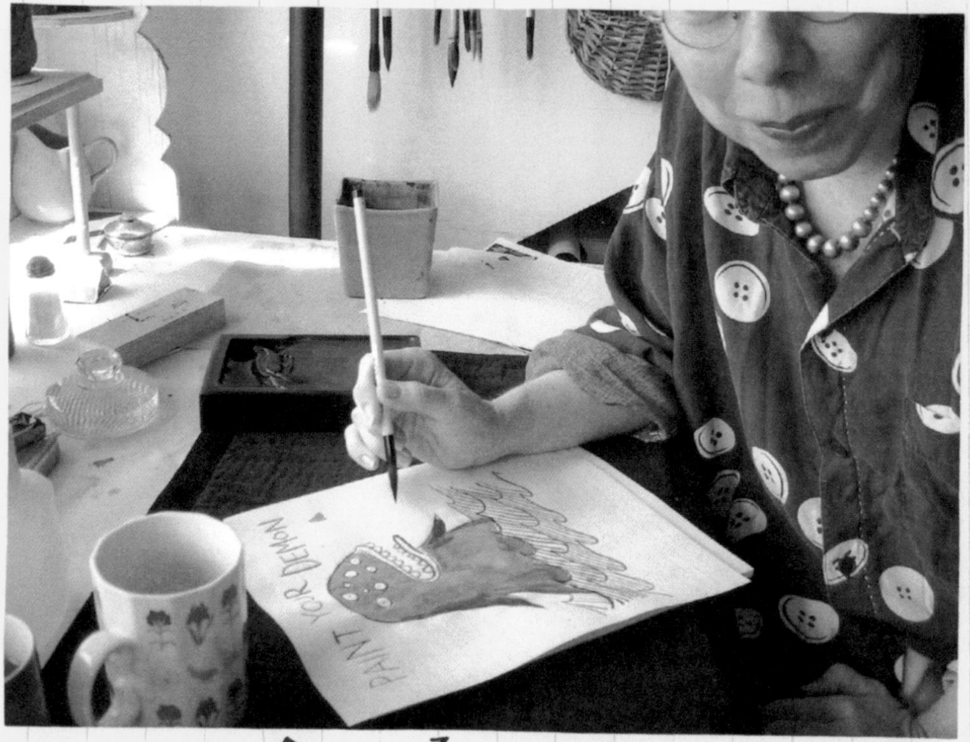

PAINT YOUR DEMON

Discovering The paintbrush, inkstone, ink-stick and resulting Demons has Been the most important thing to happen to me in years. TRY IT! You will dig it!

I made a cloth pad for under my paper It's an old black T-Shirt Quilted onto two layers of Flannel. IT absorbs excess water.

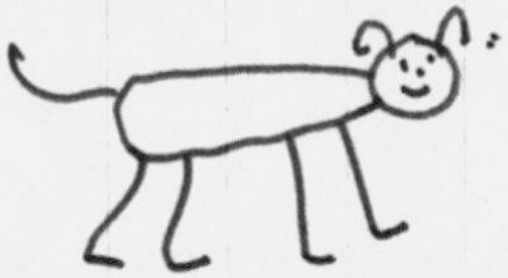

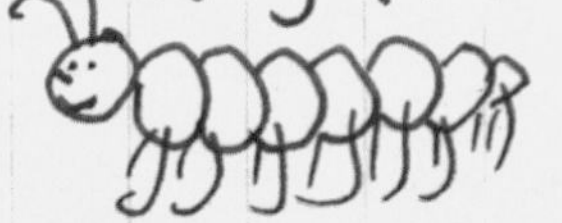